THE M & E HANDBOOK SERIES

General Principles of English Law

P. W. D. Redmond LLM

Barrister, Formerly Senior Lecturer in Law at the City of London College

revised by

J. P. Price MA B Phil

Barrister

and

I. N. Stevens LLB

Department of Law, The University College at Buckingham

FIFTH EDITION

MACDONALD AND EVANS

Macdonald & Evans Ltd.
Estover, Plymouth PL6 7PZ

First published 1964
Reprinted 1964
Second edition 1966
Reprinted 1966, 1967, 1969
Third edition 1970
Reprinted 1971, 1972, 1973
Fourth edition 1974
Reprinted 1975 (twice), 1976, 1977
Fifth edition 1979

© Macdonald & Evans Ltd. 1979

ISBN 0 7121 0725 8

Printed in Great Britain by
Richard Clay (The Chaucer Press), Ltd.,
Bungay, Suffolk

Preface to the Fourth Edition

The latest edition of this book has been necessitated by the continuing spate of new legislation and cases. For example, the Courts Act 1971, has necessitated a wholesale revision and rewriting of the sections of the book dealing with the judicial system. Less radical revisions have been necessitated by the Animals Act 1971, the Tribunals and Inquiries Act 1971, the Industrial Relations Act 1971, the Defective Premises Act 1972, the Legal Advice and Assistance Act 1972 and the European Communities Act 1972.

In addition a number of new cases have demanded inclusion, such as *Saunders* v. *Anglia Building Society* (1971) and *Lewis* v. *Averay* (1971), to name but two. I have also utilised the opportunity to improve (I hope) and amend various passages of the book, and am grateful to the publishers for their co-operative— and patient—attitude.

September, 1973

P. W. D. R.

Preface to the Fifth Edition

It has now been some years since the fourth edition of Mr. Redmond's *General Principles of English Law* appeared. In the meantime, many changes in the law, several of them major, have occurred.

Whilst the rewriting of several complete sections of the book has been necessitated by recent developments and in particular, by recent legislation, including the Criminal Law Act 1977, the Torts (Interference with Goods) Act 1977, and the Theft Act 1978, every effort has been made to retain the general scheme and concise approach of previous editions. This task has not been made easy by the accumulation of case-law, which has frequently extended or added to the law, permitting little excision of older material.

The overall purpose of the book remains much the same; it is hoped that it will be found useful by "A" Level and university students as well as those studying for professional examinations, including those students for whom law forms only part of their course.

Our thanks are due to the publishers and editor for their co-operation and assistance.

June, 1979
                                        J. P. P.
                                        I. N. S.

Contents

Table of Cases

(Where the facts are noted the page number is in italics.)

PART ONE

THE ENGLISH LEGAL SYSTEM

CHAPTER I

Nature and History of English Law

NATURE OF LAW

1. The meaning of "law". A law, in the widest sense, means a rule to which actions conform or should conform. Law therefore suggests a real or desired conformity. One can thus speak loosely of the laws of science, economics, logic, psychology, etc., as well as of the laws of nations.

2. Law in the strict sense. This book is concerned with law in the strict sense of the word, that is, rules of conduct imposed by a state upon its members and enforced by its courts. Such rules of conduct constitute the law of the land (or "municipal law"), the object of which is to enforce certain standards of behaviour among citizens in the interests of peace and good order.

3. Law and morality. Apart from the laws laid down by the state and enforced by the courts, there are also certain customary rules of behaviour called rules of morality. These are not enforced by the courts and depend for their effect solely on the force of public opinion, though many rules of morality may well be given the status of rules of law, by statutes etc., and thereby become enforceable in the courts. The crucial difference between rules of law and rules of morality therefore lies in the method of enforcement of each.

4. Public and private law.

(*a*) Public law is that part of the law which governs the relations of citizens with the state, and of one state with another (public international law). Public law thus includes criminal law, constitutional law and international law.

(*b*) Private or civil law is that part of the law of a country which governs the relations of citizens among themselves. It therefore includes the law of property, the law of persons, the law of contract and the law of torts (civil wrongs).

This book is concerned mainly with private law, and also with criminal law and constitutional law.

5. English and Roman law. In most parts of Europe, and in many other parts of the world, two main systems of law are now in force.

(*a*) *Modern Roman law*, derived from the ancient laws of the Roman Empire, as modernised and applied in France, Spain, Italy, most other European countries, South Africa, South America, certain parts of Canada (e.g. Quebec) and the United States (e.g. Louisiana).

(*b*) *English common law*. This is a native product of Britain which has absorbed only a few rules of Roman law and today is applied in most parts of the Commonwealth and of the United States.

6. Common law and equity. English law consists of two main and complementary components.

(*a*) *Common law*, comprising ancient customs, judicial precedents and enacted laws, and so called because it was made common to the whole of England and Wales after the Norman Conquest (1066). Prior to this time there was no common system of law for the whole country.

(*b*) *Equity*, comprising principles laid down in the Court of Chancery before 1873 and intended to supplement the common law by providing new rights and new remedies, and by softening the common law where this was too rigid and inflexible (*see* XXIII, 1).

7. Substantive law and procedure. A distinction is drawn by lawyers between:

(*a*) the rules of law themselves; and

(*b*) the procedural rules by which the law is enforced in the courts.

Substantive law means law in the strict sense. Procedural or adjectival law governs the machinery by which substantive law is applied, i.e. the rules of evidence and procedure in civil and criminal courts.

EXAMPLE: If a man kills another it is a question of substantive law as to whether the appropriate charge is murder (intentional killing) or manslaughter (unintentional, or mitigated killing). Once he has been charged with either of these crimes, the rules of procedure will then govern: (1) the method by which his guilt should be proved; (2) the evidence which should be admissible at his trial; and (3) the manner in which such evidence should be presented in court.

8. Law and fact. Lawyers always distinguish between the law involved in a case and the facts which the court has to consider in reaching its decision.

Thus, if a man is charged with murder it is a question of law as to what is the precise meaning of murder and whether the accused's conduct amounts to murder in the eyes of the law. But it will be the business of the prosecutor to put before the court such facts as show:

(*a*) that a murder has been committed; and
(*b*) that the accused was the person who committed the murder.

Wherever a case is tried by a judge and a jury, the judge decides on points of law and the jury decides on matters of fact. The jury will then decide the case, in terms of the law contained in the judge's direction.

HISTORY OF COMMON LAW

9. Anglo-Saxon law (pre-1066). Before the Norman Conquest England was only loosely united under the Crown. The central government was weak and inefficient, the local areas largely governed themselves and had their own systems of courts and local laws based on ancestral customs.

10. The Norman Conquest (1066). William I conquered England after winning the Battle of Hastings, which he regarded as a "trial by battle" which decided the issue of the disputed ownership of England. In accordance with mediaeval ideas he claimed to become the owner of every inch of English soil. Relying on this claim, he:

(*a*) established the feudal system of land tenure, under which all persons who possessed land did so merely as tenants or subtenants of the king; and
(*b*) established a strong central government and a national judicial system.

11. The feudal system. During the Middle Ages land was the principal form of wealth, and government in all parts of Western Europe was largely based on this fact. By introducing a highly efficient form of feudal land tenure, the Normans were able to establish an efficient central government and a common law, i.e. law common to all parts of England, and later, Wales.

The feudal system of land tenure involved the following points:

(*a*) All land belonged absolutely to the Crown.

(*b*) All persons holding land did so merely as tenants ("feudatories") of the Crown.

(*c*) Tenants paid for their occupation of land by rendering services to the Crown and its government, e.g. by providing and equipping soldiers (though from about 1166, money payments known as "scutage" were made instead).

(*d*) Sub-tenants rendered similar feudal services to their immediate landlords ("mesne" lords), e.g. tilling the landlord's fields.

(*e*) Feudatories holding land directly from the king were called tenants in chief ("tenants *in capite*") and comprised most of the lords and barons, who constituted the King's Grand Council (Curia Regis) which was the precursor both of the King's courts and of Parliament.

(*f*) Between tenants in chief and the lowest class of sub-tenants were several intervening ranks of sub-tenants, all owing feudal duties to their immediate mesne landlord.

(*g*) The lowest class were called villeins or serfs:

(*i*) they were tied to the land on which they lived and worked;

(*iii*) they could be sold with the land (though not apart from it);

(*iii*) they could not marry without their lord's consent; and

(*iv*) they rendered menial services to their lord such as tilling fields, keeping cattle, providing produce for the lord's kitchen.

12. Development of common law. The feudal system of land tenure enabled the Norman kings to establish efficient administration, despite bad roads and communications. Under Henry I (1100–35) and Henry II (1154–89) a definite attempt was made to establish a common legal system for the whole country. Royal judges were sent regularly to all parts of the country to settle disputes (mainly relating to possession of land) in the king's name. Gradually these itinerant judges (justices in eyre) extended their jurisdiction to criminal matters after the Assizes of Clarendon (1166) and Northampton (1176) so laying the foundations of a common law of property and of crime.

13. The writ system. To begin an action in a royal court a plaintiff had to obtain a writ, i.e. a written command issued by the Lord Chancellor in the king's name, ordering the defendant to appear in court and show cause why the plaintiff should not be given the relief he claimed.

If there was no appropriate writ to cover the type of claim the plaintiff was making there could be no remedy. The rule was: no writ, no remedy (*ubi remedium, ibi jus*).

At first there was no limit to the varieties of writ which the royal Chancery would issue, but in an attempt to stop royal courts competing with their own profitable feudal courts, the barons forced Henry III (1216–72) to forbid the issue of further new varieties of writ. This enactment, the Provisions of Oxford 1258, thus had the effect of restricting the growth of common law by tying it to the writs and remedies available before 1258.

14. The statute In Consimili Casu, 1285. In order to nullify the most harmful restrictions imposed by the Provisions of Oxford, 1258, Edward I (1272–1307) enacted the Statute of Westminster II 1285, which provided that new writs could be issued to cover new types of claim, if the new claims were analogous to those recognised before 1258. In other words, new writs could be issued by the Chancery provided they were "in like case" (*in consimili casu*) to those which could have been issued before the Provisions of Oxford.

This statute *In Consimili Casu* is of great importance because:

(*a*) it made possible the further development of common law; and

(*b*) it made future development extremely conservative and technical, since no revolutionary extensions could be made and new claims were remedied only if they were analogous to those recognised before 1258.

15. Later development of common law. After 1285 the common law developed steadily along conservative lines. As the government became stronger the royal courts increased in importance and prestige, and gradually took away all business from the barons' feudal or seignorial courts.

Consisting originally of criminal law and the law of property, the common law was expanded during the later Middle Ages to include a law of contract and a law of torts (civil wrongs not amounting to crimes). Because of the need to base all extensions of common law on writs existing before 1258, both contract and tort had to be developed with great subtlety, mainly from the ancient writ of trespass (*see* XIII, 2).

16. Mediaeval courts. There were four main types of court in the Middle Ages:

(*a*) *communal courts*, applying local customary law, e.g. shire or county courts, and hundred or parish courts. These declined in importance as common law spread;

(*b*) *seignorial courts*, held by feudal landlords for their tenants, e.g. baronial courts and manorial courts. These also decayed as the common law expanded. Fines levied by these courts went largely into the landlords' pockets. The landlords therefore bitterly resisted the competition and expansion of common law; their concern to maintain their interests is apparent in Magna Carta (particularly chapter 17, which fixed the location of some of the courts at Westminster);

(*c*) *ecclesiastical courts*, dealing with the discipline of the clergy, matrimonial and testamentary matters. These courts diminished in importance after the Reformation (*circa* 1535) and matrimonial and testamentary jurisdiction was taken from them and given to the High Court in 1857;

(*d*) *royal courts*, including courts of common law and equity (*see* 17).

17. Common law courts. The Curia Regis (King's Grand Council) originally had judicial as well as governmental functions, but during the Middle Ages the judicial powers were gradually deputed to various subsidiary courts.

(*a*) *Courts of Assize* (e.g. Assizes of Clarendon and Northampton). These dealt mainly with criminal matters, from the reign of Henry II (1154–89) onwards. They toured the country and the itinerant judges derived their authority from various royal commissions, i.e. oyer and terminer ("to hear and determine" more serious criminal questions), general gaol delivery (a commission to clear the prisons of persons awaiting trial), and Trailbaston (a commission to deal with abuses of justice).

(*b*) *The Court of King's Bench.* This separated from the Curia Regis in the thirteenth century. It had wide criminal jurisdiction, mainly appellate, and dealt also with civil actions in which the Crown was involved. This particularly meant jurisdiction in actions of trespass. This civil jurisdiction was gradually extended to cover all kinds of civil action.

(c) *The Court of Common Pleas.* This separated from the Curia Regis in the thirteenth century and dealt with all civil actions between subjects, and particularly with actions relating to land— in other words, matters which did not touch the king's own rights, or peace.

(d) *The Court of Exchequer.* This was the first branch of the Curia Regis to establish itself as a separate court. It dealt mainly with revenue matters, but also had a restricted civil jurisdiction.

(e) *The Court of Exchequer Chamber.* There have been several successive courts of this name set up to deal with appeals "in error" from the other common law courts. The last court of this name was abolished in the nineteenth century, when the present appellate system was established (*see* III, 2, 3, 10).

18. The Judicature Acts 1873–75. In the nineteenth century Parliament made extensive reforms in the judicial system and the administration of the law, culminating in the passing of the Judicature Acts. These ended many anachronisms in common law and fused its administration with that of its sister system, equity (*see* 37).

19. Modern common law. Common law is still the basis of modern English law and is constantly developing by means of the doctrine of precedent (*see* II, 19–22).

Common law is said to be "unwritten law" because no complete codification has ever been made, so that today it may be necessary for a lawyer to consult many statutes, judgments and books of authority to ascertain the principles of common law applicable to a particular case.

The modern law of property, contracts, torts and crimes is all based on ancient common law, though legislation has, now of course, added considerably to most of these.

HISTORY OF EQUITY

20. Origins of equity. From the thirteenth century all appeals against decisions of the royal judges were made direct to the king, who was regarded as the "fountain of justice", and was therefore head of the judicial system. Later, pressure of business forced the

kings to pass these appeals to the principal royal official, the Lord
Chancellor.

The Lord Chancellor was both

(a) the king's chief secretary; and

(b) his chaplain or "keeper of the king's conscience".

As a priest, he tended to decide cases on the basis of morality or
natural justice (i.e. equity) rather than in accordance with narrow
and technical rules of law. Equity, in its earliest or most primitive
sense, means "fairness" or natural justice.

21. Development of equity. Because it refused to be bound by
technicalities, and was not restricted by the writ system, the
Chancellor's court eventually became extremely popular. Vice-
Chancellors were appointed to deal with litigation, and a permanent Court of Chancery was established in London, which
dealt with

(a) matters where the common law provided no remedy; and

(b) matters where, although a remedy was available at common
law, it was either insufficient, or not forthcoming in the particular
case.

This led the Court of Chancery to offer remedies of its own to
supplement the common law, such as specific performance and
the injunction, and also to recognise rights which were unrecog-
nised by the common law, e.g. the rights of beneficiaries of uses
(trusts).

The restrictions imposed on the expansion of common law by
the Provisions of Oxford 1258 and the Statute of Westminster II
1285 caused Equity to increase in importance, and the Court of
Chancery and common law courts began to come into conflict.

22. Competition with common law. The great popularity of equity
led to harmful competition with the common law courts. The
dispute became increasingly bitter during the later sixteenth
century, with chancery and common law judges sometimes issuing
contradictory verdicts.

To terminate the dispute, which reached its peak in the *Earl of
Oxford's Case* (1615), James I (1603–25) forced Lord Chancellor
Ellesmere and the head of the common law system, Lord Chief
Justice Coke, to present the matter to the Attorney-General, Sir
Francis Bacon, to arbitrate. On Bacon's recommendation, James I
then ordered that in cases of conflict with common law, equity
should prevail.

The king's ruling was never completely accepted by the common law courts, and some competition continued until the administration of equity and common law was fused by the Judicature Acts 1873–75.

23. Advantages and defects of equity.

(*a*) Equity had the following advantages:

(*i*) it was less formal and technical than the common law;

(*ii*) its expansion was not restricted by the Provisions of Oxford since it did not depend on writs;

(*iii*) it would enforce entirely new claims, which the common law did not recognise, e.g. trusts (*see* XXIII, 8).

(*b*) The chief disadvantage of equity was its flexibility. Since decisions were not based on rigid rules, they might vary from Chancellor to Chancellor, depending upon the views of each. Thus although its flexibility was originally an advantage, as equity grew in importance it became a defect.

By the seventeenth century the fluctuations and uncertainty of equity had become a major reproach and John Selden, an eminent jurist, summed up the position by saying that "Equity varies with the length of the Chancellor's foot".

24. Formalisation of equity.
In order to achieve uniformity and stifle criticism, Lord Nottingham (Lord Chancellor 1673–82), sometimes called the "father of modern equity", attempted to reduce the vague rules of equity to a formal system. This work was carried on by his successors, notably Lord Hardwicke (Lord Chancellor 1736–56), and by the nineteenth century equity had become a system as rigid and formal as the common law itself.

As a result of the process of formalisation, the word equity had by the nineteenth century acquired two distinct meanings:

(*a*) natural justice, or fair play (the original meaning);

(*b*) the system of rules administered by the Court of Chancery before 1873, when the Judicature Act of that year amalgamated the administration of equity and common law.

25. Importance of equity.
The great importance of equity is that it introduced many new ideas into English law, mainly in the form of:

(*a*) new rights, such as trusts and the equity of redemption (*see* XXII, 11);

(*b*) new remedies, such as injunctions and specific performance (*see* XXIII, **6, 7**).

Equity is therefore a valuable supplement to the common law. But lawyers have always maintained that equity is not a completely separate system of law, but is intended merely to fill in gaps in the legal system. "Equity is a gloss on the common law": Frederic W. Maitland (1850–1906).

26. The Judicature Acts 1873–75. As part of a general process of reform of the law in the nineteenth century, the Judicature Acts were passed to abolish all existing courts and substitute a unified court structure, consisting eventually of the House of Lords and the Supreme Court of Judicature (*see* III). The Judicature Acts laid down that:

(*a*) equity and common law should in future be administered side by side in all courts;

(*b*) where there is any conflict between a rule of equity and a rule of common law, the rule of equity shall prevail: Supreme Court of Judicature Act 1873, s. 25 (now re-enacted in the Supreme Court of Judicature (Consolidation) Act 1925, s. 44).

(*See* XXIII, **1–7** for a more detailed analysis of modern equity.)

SUBSIDIARY SYSTEMS OF LAW

27. Multiplicity of systems. In addition to common law and equity there were in mediaeval England other parallel and competing systems. The most important of these were ecclesiastical or canon law, the law merchant (mercantile law), and later, the conciliar courts.

28. Ecclesiastical law. Before the Reformation in the sixteenth century the laws of the Roman Catholic Church were applied in England by ecclesiastical courts, claiming sole jurisdiction in certain spiritual and moral matters.

The Reformation severed the English Church's link with Rome and made the king the head of the Church of England. In legal matters the effect of this was to bring the ecclesiastical courts increasingly under the control of the state, and gradually much of their jurisdiction was handed over to the common law courts.

29. Ecclesiastical courts. These had jurisdiction primarily over the following matters.

(a) Discipline of the clergy. Bishops' consistory courts and Archbishops' provincial courts still have jurisdiction to punish clergy of the Church of England for moral offences, but criminal matters are dealt with by the ordinary common law courts. (There are today two provincial courts, the Court of Arches in the archdiocese of Canterbury, and the Chancery Court of York in the archdiocese of York.)

(b) Matrimonial causes, e.g. divorce, nullity, and legitimacy. This jurisdiction was transferred to a new civil court for divorce by the Matrimonial Causes Act 1857.

(c) Testamentary matters, i.e. the administration of the estates of deceased persons and the proving of wills. This jurisdiction was transferred to a new Court of Probate by the Court of Probate Act 1857.

30. The law merchant. Much of the commerce of the Middle Ages was conducted by travelling merchants who moved from fair to fair throughout the country. It was their custom to set up temporary informal courts at each fair or market to settle trading disputes.

The law administered by these informal courts was customary and international in character. It consisted of:

(a) international trade usages, based largely on the Roman *jus gentium* (that part of Roman law developed to meet the needs of merchants throughout the Roman Empire);

(b) maritime law, based largely on the ancient Rhodian Sea Laws of the Greeks; and

(c) police regulations for the conduct of the fair or market.

31. Courts merchant. Courts which administered the law merchant were as follows:

(a) informal courts ("pie powder" courts). These were the commonest merchants' courts, being set up informally at each fair or market to administer rough and ready justice. Professional lawyers were contemptuous of such courts, complaining that the merchant-judges came on to the bench with travel-stained and dusty feet. Consequently they called such courts *pieds poudres*, or "dusty feet" courts; the two French words were commonly mispronounced by the English as "pie powder";

(b) formal courts established by the Crown for the settlement of important commercial disputes. The most important of these were the courts of staple, set up in major trading centres to

encourage foreigners to trade in England by giving them favour-
able and understanding tribunals.

The High Court of Admiralty, established by Edward III
(1327–77), was another formal court charged with the task of
punishing pirates and settling international disputes connected
with shipping and sea-trading.

32. Decline of Courts Merchant. These courts gradually declined
in importance and their jurisdiction was taken over by the
common law courts. Reasons for the decline were:

(*a*) increased efficiency and centralisation of the common law
courts;

(*b*) statutory limitations imposed from 1477 onwards upon the
jurisdiction of the courts merchant.

33. Absorption by common law. By the middle of the eighteenth
century, the common law courts had taken over nearly all the jurisdiction of the pie powder and staple courts. Lord Mansfield, Lord
Chief Justice, established the principle that recognised mercantile
customs should be enforced at common law, thus obviating the
need for separate courts merchant.

The High Court of Admiralty survived as a separate court until
the nineteenth century when it was merged into the High Court
by the Judicature Acts 1873–75. Its work is now carried on in the
Admiralty Court of the Queen's Bench Division of the High
Court.

34. Conciliar Courts. Whilst the royal courts (common law and
equity) all sprang from the Curia Regis after the twelfth century,
the king nevertheless continued to exercise a "residuary" jurisdiction (as well as law-making capacity) through his Council
(Curia Regis). These notions have persisted in the form, for
example, of Orders in Council (*see* II, **15**). and in the jurisdiction
of the Privy Council.

Under the Tudors and early Stuart monarchs, particularly, the
Council was used as an instrument of law enforcement, and indeed creation.

The main organs of the Council thus involved were:

(*a*) *the Court of Star Chamber*. Established by an Act of 1487
to "punish divers misdemeanours". The work of the Star Chamber judges resulted in a large number of criminal offences being
introduced; these included conspiracy, attempts, forgery and

perjury. All of these have been assimulated into the common law, though not always in the form of misdemeanours;

(b) *the Court of Requests*. Developed by the Lord Chancellor, Wolsey, during the sixteenth century, it started life much earlier as a court of the Council, which heard petitions from the poor;

(c) *Local councils*. These were set up to maintain order, particularly in the borders between England and Wales and Scotland.

The conciliar courts were similar to the Court of Chancery in that they did not rely on common law writs and procedure. Under James I (1603–25) and Charles I (1625–49) they were used oppressively; the Long Parliament accordingly abolished the Star Chamber and local councils in 1641, and the Court of Requests lapsed at about the same time.

THE JUDICATURE ACTS

35. Need for reform. By the nineteenth century, the British legal system had become archaic, and too unwieldy to meet the requirements of modern society. Particularly, the continued separation of law and equity was a handicap. Under the influence of several thinkers, notably Jeremy Bentham (1748–1832), Parliament launched a programme of reform.

36. Preliminary reforms. One of the principal defects of the existing system was that a plaintiff seeking several simultaneous remedies might have to bring expensive proceedings in several courts to obtain them. In an action for breach of contract, for instance, he might have to bring a common law action for damages plus a further action in equity to obtain an order for specific performance, commanding the defendant to perform his bargain.

To prevent this need for multiple actions, legislation was passed to make both common law and equitable remedies available in all the principal courts:

(a) the Common Law Procedure Acts 1852–54, gave common law courts power to award certain equitable remedies in addition to or as alternatives to the ordinary remedy of damages, e.g. injunctions and discovery of documents. Also a defendant was to be allowed to raise certain discretionary defences previously available only in the Court of Chancery;

(b) the Chancery Amendment Act (Lord Cairns' Act) 1858, gave the Court of Chancery a discretion to award the common law remedy of damages as an alternative to the normal equitable remedies of injunction, specific performance, etc. (for equitable remedies generally, *see* XXIII, 5–7).

37. The Judicature Act 1873. This completely reorganised the judicial system by establishing a unified Supreme Court in place of the multiplicity of common law and equity courts existing previously (*see* III, 1–17).

The objects of the Act were:

(*a*) to fuse the administration of common law and equity, which therefore are now applicable side by side in all courts today;

(*b*) to simplify procedure;

(*c*) to establish a unified Supreme Court of Judicature consisting of a Court of Appeal and a High Court (*see* III, 10–17).

(*d*) It was thought expedient to abolish the judicial powers of the House of Lords also, since its members were not, of course, judges; in 1876, however, the House was reconstituted, with special Lords of Appeal in Ordinary (law-lords), sitting together as the highest court of appeal: Appellate Jurisdiction Act 1876.

38. Effect of the Judicature Acts.

(*a*) The Supreme Court of Judicature was established, consisting of a Court of Appeal (in place of the old Court of Exchequer Chamber) and a High Court, divided into three divisions —the Queen's Bench Division, the Chancery Division and the combined Probate, Divorce and Admiralty Division.

(*b*) The old common law courts of Queen's Bench, Common Pleas and Exchequer were merged into the Queen's Bench Division of the High Court.

(*c*) The Court of Probate, the court for divorce, and the High Court of Admiralty were merged in the Probate, Divorce and Admiralty Division of the High Court.

(*d*) The Chancery Court of Equity became the Chancery Division of the High Court.

(*e*) The House of Lords was established as the supreme appellate tribunal for Great Britain (though it remained outside the Supreme Court).

(*f*) Later, a Court of Criminal Appeal was established, leaving the Court of Appeal to deal with appeals in civil cases: Criminal Appeal Act 1907. In 1966, however, the Court of Criminal Appeal was abolished, and replaced by a Division of the Court of Appeal specifically established to hear criminal appeals: Criminal Appeal Act 1966.

39. Recent reforms. Further rationalisation of the judicial system has taken place in recent years. Thus:

(a) the old Court of Criminal Appeal was abolished in 1966. Now there is one general Court of Appeal which has (i) a civil division, and (ii) a criminal division;

(b) the Probate, Divorce and Admiralty Division was reorganised in 1971 and renamed the Family Division: Administration of Justice Act 1970 (see III, 17);

(c) assizes and quarter sessions were abolished in 1971 and replaced by the Crown Court: Courts Act 1971.

PROGRESS TEST 1

1. Distinguish between: (a) law and morality, and between (b) public and private law.   (3, 4).

2. How did the feudal system influence the development of English law? Explain the significance of the Provisions of Oxford 1258 and the statute *In Consimili Casu* 1285.   (10–15).

3. Describe: (a) the types of court existing in the Middle Ages and (b) the common law courts which developed from the Curia Regis.   (16–17)

4. Why is common law said to be unwritten?   (19)

5. What is equity and how did it originate? What is meant by the statement that equity is "a gloss on the common law"? (20–25)

6. Assess the advantages and defects of equity and explain how the system gradually became formalised.   (23, 24)

7. What is the importance of equity in the development of English law?   (22, 25, 26)

8. Explain what is meant by: (a) ecclesiastical law; (b) the law merchant and (c) the conciliar courts, and outline their respective jurisdictions.   (28–34)

9. What courts existed in England before the passing of the Judicature Acts 1873–75, and how did these Acts change the judicial system?   (17, 36, 37, 38)

10. What were the objects of the Judicature Acts 1873–75? (37)

11. Summarise the most recent statutory reforms of the judicial system.   (39)

CHAPTER II

Sources of English Law

PRINCIPAL SOURCES

1. General. The principal sources of English law are statute-law (legislation), case-law and custom.

Whilst these are the principal sources other sources do in fact exist:

(*a*) For instance, it is normal, in the absence of one of the above, or to elucidate a difficult point, to resort to the writings of the more important text-writers.

(*b*) Since 1972, certain laws made by the institutions of the European Communities may be applicable in the United Kingdom as a consequence of the European Communities Act 1972, ss. 2 and 3. Such laws may take the form of regulations and directives from the European Commission and Council of Ministers, and decisions of the European Court of Justice, which our courts are "bound to take notice of". Indeed, it has even been suggested that, so long as the U.K. is a member of the Community then European law should take precedence over an English statute: *per* Lord Denning, M.R., in *Coomes* v. *Shields* (1978). That view is not universally shared, however, for it contradicts the accepted doctrine of Parliamentary Sovereignty (*see* **8**).

CUSTOM

2. Customary origin of law. Most legal systems have their origins in ancient customs of a nation or tribe, e.g. Roman law. English common law was originally based on oral customs of the Anglo-Saxons, which the Norman judges welded into a formal system of law in the mediaeval royal courts.

Custom is therefore the oldest source of English law. Most of the more important national or general customs were absorbed into the common law very early, and by the fourteenth century custom had ceased to be the mainspring of common law development and had been replaced by judicial precedent.

3. Kinds of custom.

(a) *General custom.* This means a custom recognised and obeyed throughout the country even before it was enforced by the courts. General custom is the foundation of common law. All major general customs have been absorbed into the law already. It is unlikely that new ones could arise to create new law today.

(b) *Local custom.* This means a rule or tradition regularly obeyed by the inhabitants of a particular locality, e.g. a customary right of way used by the inhabitants of a village across neighbouring land. Such customs may be recognised and enforced by the courts and so become part of common law, though applicable only within a particular district. Local customs do still sometimes create new law, though rarely (*see* **4, 5**).

4. Validity of local customs.

In order to gain recognition and enforcement by the courts, a local or particular custom must be:

(a) reasonable;

(b) not contrary to any statute or any fundamental principle of law;

(c) observed as of right, i.e. *nec vi, nec clam, nec precario* (not by force, nor secretly, nor subject to permission);

(d) exercised from "time immemorial", i.e. since 1189 (*see* **5**);

(e) definite in nature and scope;

(f) exercised continuously and without interruption;

(g) recognised as binding by those who are affected by it.

5. Time immemorial.

In order to gain recognition from the courts a custom must, in theory, have been in force from "time immemorial", i.e. from the end of Henry II's reign in 1189. But in practice it is generally sufficient to show that the custom has existed as long as any living person can remember, i.e. "beyond living memory". If this is proved the court will presume that the custom has been in force since 1189.

The presumption can be rebutted by showing that for some reason it was impossible for the custom to have existed in 1189 or subsequently, e.g. where a right of way is claimed across land known to have been under water some time since the reign of Henry II.

6. Conventional usages.

In addition to general and local customs as sources of law, particular trades or groups of people may have their own professional customs or usages which may be recognised and enforced by the courts, provided they are of sufficiently long standing, definite, and recognised as obligatory by the persons to whom they apply.

Thus the Bills of Exchange Act 1882, is largely based on the customs previously existing among bankers regarding cheques and other bills of exchange.

LEGISLATION

7. Meaning of legislation. Legislation means enacted law, that is law laid down by a body constituted for the purpose, e.g. the British Parliament. Enacted laws of this kind are called statutes.

Legislation may be direct or indirect. Direct legislation means laws enacted by the legislature itself, e.g. Acts of Parliament. Indirect or delegated legislation means rules or laws laid down by a body or person to whom the legislature has delegated power to make such rules, e.g. regulations laid down by a Minister under power given him by an Act of Parliament.

8. Sovereignty of Parliament. In Britain today Parliament is the supreme legislative body. Therefore:

(a) Parliament can enact any law it chooses; and

(b) its enactments are absolutely binding on the courts and all citizens.

By virtue of this supremacy, or sovereignty, Parliament can delegate legislative power to subordinates, and the delegated or subordinate legislation laid down by such persons is also binding on the courts.

If, however, a person or body to whom legislative power has been delegated exceeds the scope of its powers, laws laid down in excess of power (*ultra vires*) are void and can be so pronounced by the courts. This *ultra vires* doctrine enables the courts to assert some control over delegated legislation. The same doctrine can also be invoked to prevent a company or corporation exceeding its legal powers.

9. Early legislation. Before the fifteenth century legislation was not an important source of law. Statutes were enacted by the king and Grand Council, a body consisting of the chief men of the realm, e.g. the barons and the aldermen of the City of London who together forced King John to pass the Magna Carta 1215, which stated the constitutional rights of English people.

In this early period statutes were comparatively infrequent and dealt mainly with matters of national importance, e.g. the Provisions of Oxford 1258, and the Statute of Westminster II 1285 (*see* I, 13, 14).

10. The rise of Parliament. During the thirteenth and fourteenth centuries the Grand Council was divided into two bodies, the Lords and Commons, and began to be called Parliament (from "parley", to discuss). For some time the king continued to legislate independently of Parliament, but the Civil War in the middle of the seventeenth century established the principle that in future all statutes had to have the consent of Parliament. From this time on therefore statute law consists of Acts of Parliament.

Parliament consists of three essential components: the Sovereign, the House of Lords and the House of Commons. Proposals for legislation must be put before both Houses in the form of bills. If approved by both Houses a bill is then placed before the Sovereign and does not become an Act of Parliament until it receives the royal assent (which, by convention, cannot be refused). Since 1911 (Parliament Act 1911 as amended in 1949) it has been possible for the Commons to send "public" bills up for royal assent even if the Lords oppose them; the Lords are permitted to veto a bill for two consecutive parliamentary sessions only.

It is also a convention of the constitution that matters of national importance should be initiated in the House of Commons, and financial bills must be so initiated: Parliament Act 1911.

11. Importance of legislation since 1832. The Reform Act 1832 made the House of Commons a genuinely democratic body representing the population as a whole, and thereby increased its importance as the means of expressing the national will. From this date onwards legislation becomes increasingly important as a source of law.

12. Nineteenth-century legislation. The Emperor Napoleon had reformed and codified French law by the Code Napoléon (1805), and Britain, profiting by the French example, increasingly used legislation as an agency for the reform of English law.

During the nineteenth century Acts of Parliament:

(a) reorganised the judicial system, e.g. by the Judicature Acts (*see* I, **37, 38**);

(b) reformed judicial procedure, e.g. by abolishing archaic procedures which had fallen into disuse since the Middle Ages, such as trial by battle;

(c) codified confused sections of the common law, *see* e.g. the Sale of Goods Act 1893, and the Bills of Exchange Act 1882 (dealing with mercantile law) and the Offences against the Person Act 1861 (dealing with parts of the criminal law).

13. Twentieth-century reforms. In this century legislation has been used increasing for the reform of the law; for example:

(a) the property legislation of 1922-25 reformed the law of property (*see* **XIX, 15–18**);

(b) the Crown Proceedings Act 1947, made the Crown liable for the first time for torts committed by its servants;

(c) the British Nationality Act 1948 defined British nationality and the position of Commonwealth citizens;

(d) the Legal Aid and Advice Act 1949 made provision for financial assistance for parties in civil and criminal cases;

(e) the Statute Law Revision Acts 1948, etc., repealed archaic statutes which had fallen into disuse;

(f) the Lord Chancellor's Law Revision Committee was established in 1932 to advise regularly on reform of the law. The reports of this Committee resulted in many reforming Acts of Parliament, e.g. the Law Reform (Frustrated Contracts) Act 1943, the Law Reform (Contributory Negligence) Act 1945; the Law Reform (Enforcement of Contracts) Act 1954;

(g) the Law Commission was established in 1965 to promote law reform: *see* the Law Commissions Act 1965. Members of the Commissions are salaried, appointed by the Lord Chancellor from among holders of high judicial office, experienced barristers and solicitors, and university teachers. The commissioners' duty is to review all of English law with a view to systematic reform and codification, elimination of anomalies and obsolete laws, etc. The commissioners' recommendations resulted in the Criminal Law Act 1967 and the commission has proposed the codification of the law of contract;

(h) the Administration of Justice Act 1970, re-allocated work between various branches of the High Court;

(i) the Courts Act 1971, re-structured the court system by abolishing the assizes and quarter sessions and substituting a

Crown Court staffed by High Court judges, circuit judges, recorders (part-time judges) and justices of the peace.

14. Delegated or subordinate legislation. By virtue of its sovereign position Parliament can delegate some of its legislative powers (by "parent" or "enabling" legislation), usually to Ministers of the Crown, local councils, etc. For example, the Minister of Housing and Local Government possesses delegated power to order the compulsory purchase of land in Britain under the Housing Act 1957.

Delegated or subordinate legislation has become increasingly important in recent years as a source of new law, for the following reasons.

(*a*) *Lack of Parliamentary time*. Parliament has insufficient time to debate in detail all the day-to-day measures needed for efficient government.

(*b*) *Technicality*. Parliament does not always have the specialised knowledge necessary to debate all matters in full.

(*c*) *Urgency*. Parliamentary procedure is necessarily too slow to cope with sudden emergencies, and these cases may in any event arise while Parliament is not in session.

(*d*) *Elasticity*. An Act of Parliament can be overruled only by another Act of Parliament, while a ministerial rule or regulation can be rescinded by the minister who issued it, if it proves impracticable or becomes outdated.

15. Types of delegated legislation.

(*a*) *Orders in Council*. These are orders made by the Queen and Privy Council either under statutory authority or by virtue of the residual powers of the Crown (called the royal prerogative). They do not usually require to be confirmed by Parliament.

(*b*) *Statutory instruments*. These must be put before Parliament for approval, the procedure being laid down by the parent Act, e.g.

(*i*) Negative procedure: the regulation comes into force at once and will remain in force unless annulled by resolution of either House of Parliament within 40 days.

(*ii*) Affirmative procedure: the regulation must be laid before Parliament for 40 days and will not come into force unless approved during the period.

(*c*) *Bye-laws of local authorities*. These rules of law restricted in operation to the area for which the local authority is responsible, e.g. bye-laws of the city of Liverpool. They generally require Ministerial confirmation: Local Government Act 1972, S 236.

16. Criticism of delegated legislation. The increase of delegated legislation has been severely criticised on the ground that it gives to non-elected persons a legislative power which should rightly be restricted to the nation's elected representatives (Lord Hewart, *The New Despotism*).

A further criticism is that Parliament exercises too little control over the issue of delegated legislation. The following controls, however, do exist:

(*a*) Parliament retains power to rescind any delegated power;

(*b*) the courts can declare an exercise of delegated power *ultra vires* and void (but this judicial safeguard can be expressly excluded by the Act delegating the power);

(*c*) public inquiries are sometimes required to be held before a piece of delegated legislation becomes effective, so as to give the public an opportunity to object. But the findings of such inquiries can sometimes legally be ignored by the body to whom power is delegated;

(*d*) a select Committee of the House of Commons (the "Scrutiny Committee") was set up in 1944 to examine ministerial rules and orders and report to Parliament any such measure which seems unreasonable, excessive or unduly expensive.

17. Control of delegated legislation. While delegating minor legislative functions to subordinate bodies, Parliament retains over-all control by:

(*a*) reserving authority to debate (and if necessary to veto) requests for delegated legislative power;

(*b*) appraising delegated legislation by requiring it (where appropriate) to be put before Parliament for review (after which either House may resolve on annulment within forty days).

(*c*) the Scrutiny Committee of the House of Commons scrutinising all statutory instruments and deciding whether any should be brought to the attention of the House for appraisal. Some statutory instruments require actual confirmation by Parliament before becoming effective.

(*d*) the courts, though subordinate to Parliament and unable to question the legality of the delegation of power by Parliament nevertheless act as watchdogs to ensure the delegated authority is properly exercised. The courts scrutinise not the granting, but the use of delegated legislative power and can declare *ultra vires* and void any such exercise if it offends against the following presumptions.

It is presumed that the enabling Act does not give power (unless expressly stated otherwise):

(*i*) to make unreasonable or uncertain rules; nor

(*ii*) to allow sub-delegation; nor

(*iii*) to levy taxes; nor

(*iv*) to infringe basic constitutional rights, such as freedom of speech, personal liberty.

18. Administrative law. In some countries, e.g. France, there is a separate branch of law dealing with the power of ministers and government departments, and the control of such powers. This is called administrative law (French *"droit administratif"*).

In Britain there is no clearly separate administrative law as yet, although many jurists believe that it is necessary and is beginning to develop spontaneously. Generally, however, control of the executive (government) is left entirely to the ancient common law, and in particular to the doctrine of *ultra vires*. Also, since 1967, the Parliamentary Commissioner for Administration has been empowered to investigate complaints arising out of maladministration in a government department, even when this is done within the power allowed it.

Administrative tribunals exist to enforce delegated legislation and to examine its application and misuse. These tribunals have been criticised as being arbitrary and tending to diminish the right of citizens to appeal to the courts. These criticisms led to the passing of the Tribunals and Inquiries Act 1958, which aimed at bringing administrative tribunals under more effective control and securing properly qualified chairmen by giving the Lord Chancellor supervisory powers over the membership of tribunals (*see* III, 42–45).

CASE LAW

19. The doctrine of precedent. The most outstanding characteristic of English law is that it is largely "judge-made". That is, the bulk of common law and equity has not been enacted by Parliament, but has been developed through the centuries by the judges applying established or customary rules of law to new situations and cases as they arise. The principle behind the doctrine of precedent is that in each case the judges apply existing principles of law; that is, they follow the example or precedent of earlier decisions.

20. Declaratory and original precedents. When a judge applies to a case an existing rule of law, without extending it, his decision is a declaratory precedent.

But where the case to be decided is one without precedent, i.e unlike any previous case, the judge must decide it according to general principles of law. By so doing he lays down an original precedent which later judges will follow if they encounter a similar case.

By means of original precedents the common law and equity are being constantly developed and expanded by the judges.

21. Geldart's criticisms of the doctrine. Professor Geldart described the advantages of the system of precedent as:

(*a*) certainty;

(*b*) flexibility and aptitude for growth;

(*c*) greater detail than is possible in a purely enacted system of law;

(*d*) practicality.

He also listed the disadvantages as:

(*a*) *rigidity*, since the discretion of every judge is restricted by the rule that he must follow the decisions of his predecessors;

(*b*) *over-subtlety*, which sometimes results from the need in a particular case to find a logical excuse for not following an existing precedent where it would cause hardship to do so;

(*c*) *bulk and complexity*. Much of English law is contained in multitudinous reports of cases dating back to the Middle Ages. These reports have to be consulted by lawyers to ascertain what rules of law are applicable to new cases.

NOTE: This has led to much agitation for the complete codification of English law along continental lines, but no general codification has yet been made, though individual Acts of Parliament have codified particular sections of the law, e.g. the Law of Property Acts 1922–5, the Sales of Goods Act 1893 and the Bills of Exchange Act 1882.

22. History of the doctrine. The doctrine began to develop in the royal courts after the reign of Henry II (1154–89), and in the equity courts rather later. But it did not become firmly established until the eighteenth century, though it had been widely adhered to before then. It did not take its modern form, however, until a hierarchy of courts was established by the Judicature Acts 1873–75. It had its origin in the desire of the mediaeval judges to create a system of law common to the whole country, and the consequent need to secure uniformity in their decisions.

23. The hierarchy of precedent: stare decisis. Some courts have greater authority than others, and this affects the importance of the precedents laid down by each. The most powerful court in Britain is the House of Lords, then comes the Court of Appeal, and then the High Court.

The general rule governing the standing of judicial decisions (known as the doctrine of "stare decisis") is that a decision made by a higher court must be followed by a lower court (i.e. "binds" that lower court). Thus:

(*a*) *The House of Lords* (H.L.) binds all lower courts. Until 1966, the H.L. was bound by its own previous decisions and ever since that time, the House has determined that they should only stray from previous decisions where there is good reason to do so, such as a "material change in circumstances": *Fitzleet Estates* v. *Cherry* (1977). This might take the form of a marked change in social conditions. When the H.L. decides on a point of Scots law, its decision is not binding on English courts, unless the point of law involved is equally relevant in England; as in *Donoghue* v. *Stephenson* (1932).

(*b*) *The Court of Appeal* (C.A.) is bound by the H.L.; it also binds itself (since 1944) subject to the following exceptions *Young* v. *Bristol Aeroplanes* (1944):

(*i*) the C.A. may choose either of two previous decisions which conflict with one another;

(*ii*) the C.A. must follow a H.L. decision, where that conflicts with its own previous decision;

(*iii*) the C.A. may decline to follow a previous C.A. decision if that was made *per incuriam* (i.e. where a statute, or other binding rule of law was not considered by the court in reaching that previous decision, thus making it unsound).

Unlike the H.L. the C.A. cannot revoke its decision to bind itself; certainly not since the H.L. decision in *Davis* v. *Johnson* (1978), where the H.L. confirmed that the C.A. was bound by its own previous decisions.

(c) *Divisional courts* of the High Court are bound by their own decisions and by decisions of the H.L. and C.A.

(d) *The High Court* is bound by the H.L. and C.A., as well as by decisions of its own divisional courts. High Court decisions bind inferior courts such as county courts. High Court judges are not bound by decisions of their predecessors or colleagues, but will rarely depart from them if:

    (i) the decision is of long standing; or

    (ii) they were laid down by judges of high repute.

(e) *The Crown Court, county courts, magistrates' courts,* etc., are bound by decisions of all superior courts, but do not themselves lay down binding precedents.

24. Ratio decidendi: obiter dicta. When a judge delivers his judgment he will normally begin by giving a résumé of the facts of the case, and then go on to give his decision and the reason for his decision (*ratio decidendi*). It is the *ratio decidendi* of a judgment which creates a precedent for the future. If there are several reasons, or *rationes*, for the one judgment these may create several precedents. "A case is only authority for what it actually decides": *per* Lord Halsbury, L.C. *Quinn* v. *Leathem* (1901).

Any general comments on law made "by the way" (*obiter dicta*) in the course of a judgment are disregarded in considering what part of the judgment constitutes the precedent.

25. Over-ruling and distinguishing precedents. If it would lead to injustice in the particular case before him a judge may refuse to apply an earlier precedent. If the precedent is one laid down by an inferior court he may overrule it. But if it was laid down by a superior court (so that in theory he should follow it) he will have to evade the precedent by distinguishing between the case he is deciding and the one in which the precedent was laid down.

When one of the parties to a case appeals to a higher court against the decision of the lower, the appeal court may reverse the decision of the lower court or confirm it.

26. Interpretation of statute law. Since Parliament is the sovereign legislative body, the courts cannot challenge the validity of an Act of Parliament. But they can influence the effect of an Act by the way in which they interpret it when called upon to apply it in a case. The interpretation of statutes is increasingly important as the bulk of legislation increases, and a large body of case-law has developed as the courts lay down precedents in their interpretation of Acts of Parliament.

27. Rules governing interpretation of statutes. There are three differing approaches to the problem of interpretation: in applying one of these, the courts will have recourse to various principles and rules. The three differing approaches, which will generally suit different circumstances, are known as:

(*a*) the Literal Rule (*see* 28);
(*b*) the Golden Rule (*see* 29);
(*c*) the Mischief Rule (*see* 30).

28. The literal rule. Where the words of a statute are clear and unambiguous, "you must follow them, even though they lead to an absurdity. The court has nothing to do with the question whether the legislature has committed an absurdity": *per* Lord Esher. Thus, if the words are clear, no "interpretation" as such can take place.

29. The golden rule. Where the words of a statute are not clear, then the court must apply this, or the mischief rule, to ascertain the intention of Parliament. The golden rule was expressed by Blackburn J. in *River Wear Commissioners* v. *Adams* (1877) as involving that "we take the whole statute together, and construe it altogether, giving the words their ordinary meaning" unless to do so would result in "some inconsistency, absurdity, inconvenience or repugnance". The natural meaning is therefore preferred, but this rule enables the courts to depart from this occasionally.

30. The mischief rule. This rule applies where a statute purports to remedy a particular "mischief", which, hitherto, had gone without remedy. It may be used, therefore, to expedite the intention of Parliament in providing such a remedy.

31. General rules and principles of interpretation: Whenever the courts are concerned to give their interpretation to a statute, they observe the following principles; this is, of course, unnecessary where the literal rule can be followed.

(*a*) The courts must always and only attempt to ascertain, and give effect to the intention of Parliament.

(*b*) The courts may not look into the "background" of a statute (*travaux préparatoires*) to assist them; they cannot, therefore, refer to Paliamentary debates, though in order to establish the mischief the statute seeks to remedy, they may look at such things as reports of commissions, like the Law Commission: *Black Clawson* v. *Papierwerke* (1975).

(*c*) Penal statutes should be interpreted favourably to persons accused of crimes so as not to conflict with their common-law rights.

(*d*) A major constitutional change, or a major change in the common law, can be effected only by clear and positive words; in the absence of such words, the courts will presume that no such change is intended.

(*e*) Words should be added or subtracted no more than is absolutely necessary.

(*f*) Ambiguities as to particular words may be resolved by the following rules of contruction:

(*i*) *Ejusdem generis:* where a number of words, all of similar meaning, are followed by one of doubtful meaning, then that word should be interpreted as having a similar meaning to the others.

EXAMPLE: "No tradesman, artificer, workman, labourer *or other person whatsoever.*" HELD: in *Gregory* v. *Fearn* (1953) that an estate agent was not included, as being different from "workmen, labourers, etc." (Sunday Observance Act 1677).

(*ii*) *Expressio unius est exclusio alterius:* the mention of one word in itself rules out a contrary meaning. EXAMPLE: It is an offence to have an unlicensed *motor*-vehicle; clearly, any vehicle which is propelled other than by a motor is not included.

32. Influence of jurists. The writings of famous lawyers may influence the development of case-law and so constitute an indirect source of law. Generally the writings of jurists long dead have more authority than those of living writers, though today the tendency of the courts is to permit citation of long-approved opinions of living jurists on difficult points of law, e.g. Cheshire *Private International Law.*

The influence of jurists was greater before law reporting became highly developed in the nineteenth century (*see* 33). Several famous books have had considerable influence in the development of the common law, e.g.:

(*a*) Bracton *De Legibus et Consuetudinibus Angliae* (Concerning the Laws and Customs of the English), thirteenth century;

(*b*) Lord Chief Justice Coke *Institutes and Commentaries*, and his Reports, seventeenth century;

(*c*) Blackstone *Commentaries*, 1765.

33. Development of law reporting. The efficient working of the doctrine of precedent depends largely on the existence of accurate reports of cases and decisions. To meet this need the Incorporated Council of Law Reporting was established (1865). The Council publishes detailed reports of cases heard in the superior courts, the reports being made by specially trained barristers and sometimes revised by the judges. In addition, several private firms publish similar series of reports, e.g. the All England Law Reports.

The earliest existing reports were informal notes made by students from the time of Edward I (1272–1307) to Henry VIII (1509–47) and published in a famous unofficial series of Year Books. These reports are written mainly in Anglo-French and are haphazard and inaccurate. Although interesting historically, they are not now much cited in the courts as containing precedents.

From the sixteenth century onwards the Year Books were superseded by series of reports of varying accuracy published by private reporters, e.g. Lord Chief Justice Coke's Reports (1572–1616) and Sir George Burrow's Reports (1756–72). Reports of this kind are from time to time consulted by present-day lawyers and may be cited in court in support of legal arguments.

PROGRESS TEST 2

1. State briefly what you consider to be the chief sources of English law. (1, 7, 19)

2. "Custom is the mother of substantive law." Discuss this statement. How far can custom be regarded as a living source of law today? (1–6)

3. Explain what is meant by the "sovereignty of Parliament". How does this doctrine accord with the increase of delegated legislation? (7, 8, 11, 14)

4. Summarise some of the chief reforms of the law by legislation during the nineteenth and twentieth centuries, and explain what machinery exists for reform today. (12, 13)

5. Explain what is meant by subordinate or delegated legislation, and state what advantages or disadvantages you consider this type of legislation possesses. (14–16)

6. "The doctrine of precedent is the corner-stone of English law." Discuss this statement and explain what is meant by the doctrine of precedent. (19–25)

7. How far is it true to say that English law is "judge-made"? (19–31)

8. What is the importance of *stare decisis* in the doctrine of precedent? Explain what is meant by: (*a*) *ratio decidendi*, (*b*) *obiter dicta*. (23, 24)

9. Summarise the rules which govern the interpretation of statutes. (27–31)

10. In what ways have eminent jurists influenced the development of English law? (32)

CHAPTER III

The Judicial System

INTRODUCTION

1. General. The judicial system today is organised in the form of a pyramid, with the House of Lords at the apex, the Supreme Court of Judicature below it (consisting of the Court of Appeal, the High Court and the Crown Court), and then the inferior civil and criminal courts (the county courts and magistrates' courts).

The present organisation of the judicial system is based partly on the Judicature Act 1873, and later statutes, and has been greatly reformed by the Administration of Justice Act 1970, and the Courfs Act 1971. This rationalised the structure overall (as dealt with below) and also abolished various obsolete courts, e.g. the assize courts, quarter sessions, the Bristol Tolzey and "pie powder" court, the Liverpool Court of Passage, some of which were survivals from the Middle Ages. In addition the old County Palatine Courts of Lancaster and Durham have been merged with the Chancery Division of the High Court.

THE HOUSE OF LORDS

2. Before 1873. In the Middle Ages the House of Lords had supreme appellate jurisdiction with respect to decisions of the Court of King's Bench, and also some jurisdiction in civil and criminal matters as a court of first instance, as follows:

(*a*) Civil cases: after the seventeenth century the only civil cases decided by the House of Lords at first instance were disputes about peerages and about the privileges of the House. (This jurisdiction survives today, but is rarely invoked.)

(*b*) Criminal cases: Magna Carta 1215 provided that every free man was entitled to trial by his equals or "peers". Thus, a member of the House of Lords charged with a serious criminal offence was entitled to be tried by the Lords, and by no other court; this privilege was abolished by the Criminal Justice Act 1948.

3. Appellate Jurisdiction Act 1876. This made the House of Lords Appeals Committee the supreme civil appeal court, and in 1907 it was also made the supreme criminal appeal court by the Criminal Appeal Act 1907.

Jurisdiction today covers:

(a) Civil appeals: to hear appeals from the Scottish Court of Session, the Supreme Court of Northern Ireland, and the English Court of Appeal (Civil Division). Appeal lies to the House of Lords with leave of the Court of Appeal or of the House of Lords itself.

(b) Criminal appeals: to hear appeals from the Criminal Division of the Court of Appeal, submitted to the Lords with leave of the C.A. or the House of Lords itself at the instance of defendant or prosecutor on a point of law of general public importance: Administration of Justice Act 1960. (Before 1960 appeal lay only with the certificate of the Attorney-General.)

4. Composition of the court. As one of the three divisions of Parliament, the House consists of hereditary peers, certain bishops of the Church of England and the archbishops, life peers and peeresses, and eleven Lords of Appeal in Ordinary (the "law lords").

When sitting as a court, however, only the law lords are entitled to participate in the Appeals Committee, together with the Lord Chancellor, the Lord Chief Justice, the Master of the Rolls, and any other peer who holds or has held high judicial office, e.g. a former Lord Chancellor. A quorum is any three of these. (Law lords are appointed from among barristers of at least fifteen years' standing, and judges of the Supreme Court of at least two years' standing.)

5. Effect of decisions. Decisions of the House of Lords Appeals Committee are absolutely binding on all other courts in the United Kingdom (except the Judicial Committee of the Privy Council) (see II, 23).

A decision of the House of Lords can be overruled only by:

(a) an Act of Parliament; or

(b) a subsequent decision of the House of Lords itself.

6. Administration of Justice Act 1969. This Act provides a new right of appeal direct from the High Court to the House of Lords where:

(*a*) the parties agree, and the trial judge grants a certificate; and

(*b*) the trial judge certifies that the case involves a point of law of general public importance which:

  (*i*) relates to the construction of an enactment; or

  (*ii*) is one in respect of which the judge is bound by a precedent laid down by the H.L. or C.A.

THE JUDICIAL COMMITTEE OF THE PRIVY COUNCIL

7. The Privy Council. This is a survival of the royal Council (Curia Regis) of the Middle Ages. Until the seventeenth century it wielded most of the governmental powers now possessed by the Cabinet. Today its duties are largely formal and advisory. It is composed mainly of cabinet ministers and ex-ministers and the law lords, and is led by a member of the Cabinet called the Lord President of the Council.

The Privy Council is also a minor source of delegated legislation in the form of Orders in Council. In addition, it issues royal proclamations by virtue of the Crown's residual prerogative powers, e.g. appointing a Council of Regency to act for the Queen when she is overseas.

8. The Judicial Committee. This consists of the Lord President of the Council (who rarely in fact participates), the Lord Chancellor, and a number of Privy Councillors who hold or have held high judicial office, e.g. the law lords. (A quorum is three.) The Judicial Committee is the supreme court of appeal:

(*a*) for Colonies, and certain Commonwealth nations which have chosen to preserve this link with London;

(*b*) for the English ecclesiastical courts of the Church of England;

(*c*) for appeals from medical tribunals; and

(*d*) for appeals from the Admiralty Court of the Q.B.D. on "prize" matters (captured vessels).

9. Effect of decisions. A decision of the Judicial Committee is binding on all courts in the territory from which the particular appeal was remitted.

Its decisions are not binding:

(*a*) upon territories other than the one from which the appeal came; nor

(*b*) upon British courts.

But its decisions always have great persuasive influence in every Commonwealth country, especially in Britain (since its members are largely the same judges as constitute the House of Lords Appeals Committee: *De Lasala* v. *De Lasala* 1979).

THE COURT OF APPEAL

10. The Court of Appeal (C.A.). This court ranks next below the House of Lords in the domestic structure (the J.C.P.C. being mainly concerned with Commonwealth matters).

The C.A. now has two divisions:

    (*a*) the Civil Division, which hears civil appeals from:

        (*i*) all divisions of the High Court; and

        (*ii*) the county courts;

    (*b*) the Criminal Division, which hears appeals from the Crown Court (*see* **19**).

11. The Civil Division. The Court is staffed by the Master of the Rolls (M.R.) and seventeen Lords Justices of Appeal (L.JJ.). In addition the Lord Chancellor (and former Lord Chancellors), the Lord Chief Justice, the President of the Family Division and the law lords are *ex officio* members of the court, and the Lord Chancellor has power to co-opt High Court judges from time to time. A quorum is any three of these or, in important cases, a "full court" may consist of five; a full court is nevertheless bound by previous C.A. decisions, even if those decisions were reached by only three judges: *Davis* v. *Johnson* (1978) (*see* II, **23**).

Lords Justices are appointed from among High Court judges or eminent barristers of at least fifteen years' standing. The jurisdiction of the civil division is as follows:

    (*a*) Appeals from the High Court (and county courts) on matters of law and of fact. Evidence on appeal usually consists of a transcript of that evidence, though fresh evidence may be admitted where deemed appropriate. The Court may allow or disallow an appeal in whole or in part.

    (*b*) Appeals from miscellaneous courts, e.g. the Court of Protection (dealing with mental patients), the Restrictive Practices Court and certain tribunals (such as the Lands Tribunal).

12. The Criminal Division.

    (*a*) *Composition.* The Court is composed of the Lord Chief Justice (L.C.J.) and Lords Justices of Appeal, but the L.C.J. (in consultation with the Master of the Rolls) may from time to time require judges of the Queen's Bench Division of the High Court to join the court. Decision is by majority vote.

(b) *Grounds for appeal to C.A.* Appeal lies:

(i) on any ground involving a point of law;

(ii) by leave of the C.A. or (rarely) of the trial judge on any ground; or

(iii) against sentence, with leave of the C.A. only.

(c) *Powers of the C.A.* The court may:

(i) dismiss the appeal; or

(ii) allow it or quash the conviction; or

(iii) order a new trial where there is new evidence: Criminal Justice Act 1968. The court can increase the severity of a sentence.

(d) *Appeal to the H.L.* is only allowed where:

(i) the C.A. certifies that a point of law of general importance is involved; and

(ii) either the C.A. or the H.L. grant leave to appeal. Either the accused or the prosecution may appeal.

(e) *Decisions by the C.A.* bind all lower courts, and the court will usually abide by its own earlier decisions, unless this would impair civil liberty generally: *R.* v. *Gould* (1968). A full court of the criminal division can overrule its own previous decisions.

THE HIGH COURT

13. Composition of the High Court. It consists of three divisions:

(a) the Queen's Bench Division;

(b) the Chancery Division; and

(c) the Family Division.

The court is staffed by a maximum of seventy puisne judges (pronounced "puny"), appointed from among barristers of at least ten years' standing: Administration of Justice Act 1968. In addition the Lord Chancellor may co-opt, when necessary, circuit judges or recorders from time to time: Courts Act 1971.

14. The Queen's Bench Division. The Q.B.D. consists of the Lord Chief Justice and about forty puisne judges.

Its jurisdiction is as follows:

(a) *Original jurisdiction.* The Q.B.D. is the largest and busiest division of the High Court, with the widest jurisdiction, exercised by several departments:

(i) the "ordinary court", which deals with all classes of

litigation not assigned expressly to other divisions, e.g. actions in tort and contract;

(*ii*) the Admiralty court, which deals with shipping matters such as salvage and "prize" disputes (relating to seizure of vessels): Administration of Justice Act 1970;

(*iii*) the Commercial Court, which deals with certain specialised commercial disputes assigned to it by the Administration of Justice Act 1970, s. 3(1).

(*b*) *Appellate jurisdiction.* A "divisional court" of the Q.B.D. (consisting of two or three Q.B.D. judges) hears appeals from inferior courts on matters not catered for by the C.A. (*see* 28). In addition a single Q.B.D. judge may hear appeals from certain administrative tribunals: *see* 45.

(*c*) *Supervisory jurisdiction* by means of prerogative orders (*see* 15).

15. Prerogative orders of the Q.B.D. These are used to ensure control over inferior courts and administrative tribunals and other public bodies exercising judicial or quasi-judicial powers, by way of Judicial Review. This must be specifically applied for: R.S.C. Ord. 53.

(*a*) *Mandamus.* This is a discretionary order commanding performance of a positive duty rather than a mere discretionary power, e.g. where a tribunal has improperly refused to accept jurisdiction over a case which it is under a legal duty to hear. Mandamus is not available against the Crown, but it may issue to compel a minister to carry out a statutory duty.

(*b*) *Prohibition.* This is an order forbidding an inferior court or tribunal or official from exceeding its jurisdiction. Prohibition is available against the Crown.

(*c*) *Certiorari.* This is an order commanding an inferior court or tribunal to bring before the High Court a matter decided or pending in the inferior court or tribunal, so that the High Court may satisfy itself:

(*i*) that no excess of jurisdiction occurs;
(*ii*) that natural justice has not been denied; or
(*iii*) that there is no error on the face of the record.

(*d*) The Q.B.D. may also issue the writ of habeas corpus, to secure a prisoner's presence before the court (*see* IV, 47).

(*e*) *An award of damages* may be made to an applicant for judicial review as well as or instead of the prerogative orders (R.S.C., Ord. 53, r. 7).

16. The Chancery Division. This consists of the Lord Chancellor (who rarely participates) and nine puisne judges. (A vice-chancellor has now been appointed to control the day-to-day working of the Division, as deputy for the over-worked Lord Chancellor: Administration of Justice Act 1970, s. 5).

Its jurisdiction is principally over the following matters:

(*a*) the administration of estates of deceased persons, and contentious probate matters: Administration of Justice Act 1970, s. 1(4);

(*b*) partnerships;

(*c*) mortgages;

(*d*) trusts;

(*e*) rectification and cancellation of written instruments;

(*f*) specific performance of contracts relating to land;

(*g*) bankruptcy;

(*h*) most company matters;

(*i*) revenue matters.

The Chancery Division also has appellate jurisdiction as

(*a*) a Divisional Court to hear appeals from county courts on bankruptcy and certain other matters; and

(*b*) a single Chancery judge hearing appeals from the Commissioners of Inland Revenue on certain tax matters.

The Chancery Division therefore includes a jurisdiction in those matters which, until its abolition in 1873, were exclusively dealt with in the old Court of Chancery, but unlike that court, does not administer, exclusively, the "system" of equity. Wherever necessary, the rules of the common law are used.

17. The Family Division. This consists of the President and sixteen puisne judges whose jurisdiction covers:

(*a*) non-contentious or formal probate matters;

(*b*) matrimonial causes, i.e. divorce, nullity, separation, etc;

(*c*) adoption, legitimacy and guardianship of minors.

Appellate jurisdiction covers appeals from:

(*a*) county courts and magistrates' courts under the Guardianship of Minors Acts 1971 and 1973;

(*b*) the Crown Court and magistrates' courts in affiliation cases; and

(*c*) juvenile courts in adoption cases.

The full list of the matters dealt with is contained in the Administration of Justice Act 1970, Sched. 1.

18. The former assize courts. Until they were abolished by the Courts Act 1971, the assizes exercised High Court jurisdiction in criminal and certain civil matters. England and Wales were divided into seven circuits, each of which was toured by two or more judges of the Queen's Bench Division and Probate Divorce and Admiralty Division three or four times a year. The assizes had equal status in civil and criminal matters with the High Court.

19. The Crown Court. The Courts Act 1971 abolished the old quarter sessional and assize courts, which formerly dealt with indictable offences, and transferred this jurisdiction to the new Crown Court. This consists of a jury and a judge appointed from among High Court judges, circuit judges and recorders (who are barristers or solicitors of at least ten years' standing, acting as part-time judges). Offences dealt with by the Crown Court are divided into four classes.

(a) *Class one offences* require to be tried by a High Court judge, i.e. any offence carrying the death penalty, misprision of treason, murder, certain offences under the Official Secrets Act 1911, or any attempt, incitement or conspiracy to commit any of the above.

(b) *Class two offences* are triable by a High Court judge also, but can be released for adjudication by an inferior judge, e.g. manslaughter, infanticide, child destruction, abortion, rape, incest, sedition, piracy, or any attempt, incitement or conspiracy to commit any of the above.

(c) *Class three offences* can be tried on indictment by a High Court judge, circuit judge or recorder, and include those offences not listed in classes one, two or four.

(d) *Class four offences* are normally tried by a circuit judge or recorder, though they may be tried on indictment by a High Court judge. They include wounding, robbery, offences relating to forgery, and incitement or conspiracy to commit any of these, as well as all offences triable either way (*see* XXV, 8).

NOTE: By the Powers of Criminal Courts Act 1973, s. 22, where a sentence of six months or less is imposed by any court it must be suspended for a period between one and two years, i.e. the prisoner is released but warned that if he is convicted of another offence during the operational period he may be sentenced for that offence and imprisoned for the earlier offence in respect of which the suspended sentence was awarded.

INFERIOR CIVIL COURTS

20. The county courts. These have existed since the Middle Ages, but fell into decay until they were modernised and revived by the County Courts Act 1846, which simplified their procedure and stipulated that county courts must in future be presided over by a judge who should be a barrister of at least seven years' standing, appointed by the Lord Chancellor.

As a result of the reorganisation effected by the Courts Act 1971, county court judges have been replaced by circuit judges, each of whom may serve several county courts and may (where necessary) move from one circuit to another. Circuit judges also sit in the Crown Court (*see* **19**). Also C.A. or High Court judges (and recorders) may act as circuit judges when directed by the Lord Chancellor: Courts Act 1971, s. 20.

There are now over 300 county courts in England and Wales, each court being served by a circuit judge (or a deputy).

Each judge is assisted by a registrar, appointed by the Lord Chancellor from solicitors of at least seven years' standing. The registrar has, himself, limited judicial authority (where not more that £200 is involved) as well as substantial administrative functions.

21. Jurisdiction of the county courts.

(*a*) Actions founded on contract or tort, where not more than £2,000 is involved: County Courts Act 1959, s. 39 (as amended from time to time). The limit may be raised if both parties agree, otherwise cases above the limit may go to the Q.B.D.

(*b*) Equity matters up to £15,000, e.g. trusts, mortgages.

(*c*) Actions for recovery of land and questions as to title to land, where the net rateable value of the land does not exceed £1,000.

(*d*) Probate matters where the value of the estate is less than £15,000

(*e*) Bankruptcies (in most courts outside the Metropolitan area).

(*f*) Winding up companies with a paid-up capital of less than £120,000

(*g*) Supervision of the adoption and guardianship of minors.

(*h*) Some county courts have Admiralty jurisdiction, i.e. those situated in large ports.

(*i*) Some county court judges have authority to act as special commissioners of divorce hearing undefended divorce petitions (for matrimonial causes *see* 22).

(*j*) Additional matters remitted by the High Court, and matters arising under various statutes, e.g. the Race Relations Act 1976, the Mental Health Act 1959 (*see* IV, 28).

22. Divorce county courts. Under the Matrimonial Causes Act 1967, a county court designated by the Lord Chancellor as a "divorce county court" has jurisdiction in undefended divorce actions. All divorces are now started in the county courts; defended actions are transferred to the Family Division, and even undefended actions may be so transferred: Matrimonial Causes Act 1967, s. 1.

Divorce county courts also have jurisdiction in ancillary matters, such as variation and enforcement of maintenance agreements, and protection of children.

23. Appeals from county courts. In matters of ordinary jurisdiction appeal lies to the C.A. on points of law or the admission or rejection of evidence. Bankruptcy appeals go to a Divisional Court of the Chancery Division.

24. Magistrates' and juvenile courts. Although mainly concerned with criminal matters (*see* **25**), these courts also exercise some civil jurisdiction.

(*a*) Magistrates' courts deal with:

(*i*) matrimonial (or "domestic") proceedings concerning separation, maintenance and custody of children;

(*ii*) guardianship of minors;

(*iii*) affiliation cases;

(*iv*) enforcement of debts in certain cases; and

(*v*) licensing matters.

(*b*) juvenile courts deal with adoption and care of minors under seventeen, under the Children and Young Persons Act 1969. (Jurisdiction also extends to criminal offences, excluding homicide.)

INFERIOR CRIMINAL COURTS

25. Summary and indictable offences. In criminal law less serious offences are dealt with summarily (at once) by the magistrates in the magistrates' courts (known formerly as "petty sessions"). Where the offence is too serious to be tried summarily in this way, the magistrates commit the offender to the Crown Court for trial by a judge and jury; it is then the duty of the magistrates to draw up an indictment stating the charge against the offender and to submit this to the higher court at the trial.

Because of the procedural differences in the method of treatment, less serious offences are called summary offences and more serious ones are called indictable offences. (As to the meaning of "arrestable offences" *see* XXV, 7.)

26. Magistrates' courts. These are presided over

(*a*) by two or more unpaid lay magistrates ("justices of the peace"), appointed by the Lord Chancellor and assisted by a legally qualified clerk of the court, or

(*b*) by one stipendiary magistrate appointed by the Lord Chancellor from among solicitors and barristers of at least seven years' standing.

Magisterial jurisdiction is of two kinds.

(*a*) *Initiatory*, e.g. taking depositions in indictable offences and deciding whether there is a prima facie case to justify committing the accused upon indictment to the Crown Court (*see* 25).

(*b*) *Summary*, i.e. deciding upon sentences for petty offences where, in most cases, the maximum penalty is £1,000 fine or six months imprisonment.

There is also a limited civil jurisdiction over matrimonial and domestic disputes, e.g. awarding maintenance to a deserted wife under an order for judicial separation, or adjudicating in bastardy proceedings. (*see* 24).

27. Juvenile courts. These are separate courts presided over by three specially qualified lay magistrates to deal with juvenile offenders, i.e. persons under seventeen. The public are excluded from proceedings, and the court has summary jurisdiction over all offences by juveniles, except homicide.

28. Appeals from magistrates' courts.

(*a*) To the Crown Court. In criminal cases against conviction and/or sentence. The local Crown Court will hear the appeal without a jury.

(*b*) To the Divisional Court of the Q.B.D. This is done by way of case stated on a point of law arising out of domestic or criminal proceedings.

29. Coroners' courts. These are presided over by a specially qualified coroner, (sometimes a barrister or solicitor and/or doctor), assisted by a jury. The functions of the court are to inquire into the causes of any death where these were not immediately apparent, or where the death was violent and unnatural.

The court also holds inquests into the ownership of treasure trove, i.e. coins, bullion or jewels found buried in any land where the owner of such valuables cannot be ascertained, or where the ownership is disputed.

30. Justices of the peace. Unpaid magistrates have been a feature of the English legal system since the Middle Ages. Originally they had wide administrative powers as well as judicial functions, e.g. regulating wages and administering the poor law. In the nineteenth century most of these administrative duties were taken from them and conferred on local authorities. The J.P.s' duties are now largely confined to acting as magistrates in the courts described above.

Justices of either sex are appointed by the Crown on the advice of the Lord Chancellor. There are now about 18,000 J.P.s in Britain.

THE JUDICIARY

31. The Lord Chancellor (L.C.). He is appointed by the Crown on the advice of the Prime Minister, and is a government minister, speaker of the House of Lords, and head of the Judiciary.

As head of the judicial system, the L.C. is President of the Court of Appeal and of the Chancery Division of the High Court, as well as chairman of the House of Lords appeals Committee. He is responsible for the appointment of J.P.s and advises the Crown on the appointment of High Court judges.

32. The Lord Chief Justice (L.C.J.). He is appointed by the Crown on the advice of the Prime Minister. He is the head of the Court of Appeal (Criminal Division) and of the Q.B.D. He is a member of the House of Lords.

33. The Master of the Rolls (M.R.). He is appointed by the Crown on the advice of the Prime Minister. He is the Lord Chancellor's deputy, acting as head of the C.A. He controls the admission of solicitors to the Rolls of the Supreme Court (such admission being necessary before any solicitor can practise).

34. The Lords of Appeal in Ordinary. The Law Lords are appointed by the Crown on the advice of the Prime Minister from among barristers of at least fifteen years' standing, or from among the existing ranks of judges of at least two years' standing. They are life peers and members of the House of Lords and the Judicial Committee of the Privy Council.

35. The President of the Family Division. The President of the Family Division is appointed by the Crown on the advice of the Prime Minister and is head of the Family Division and a member of the Court of Appeal.

36. The Lords Justices of Appeal (L.J., plural L.JJ.). They are appointed by the Crown on the advice of the Prime Minister and are judges of the Court of Appeal.

37. Puisne judges of the High Court (J., plural JJ.). They are appointed by the Crown on the advice of the Lord Chancellor, from among barristers of at least ten years' standing, and are assigned to a division of the High Court.

38. Circuit judges. They are appointed by the Crown on the advice of the Lord Chancellor, from among barristers of at least seven years' standing or recorders of three years' standing.

39. Length of appointment. All judges are appointed *quamdiu se bene gesserint* ("for so long as they are of good behaviour"): Bill of Rights 1689. They can be removed from office only for misconduct, by the Crown, upon the advice of both Houses of Parliament in a joint address. Since the Courts Act 1971 judges of the High Court and circuit judges retire at 70 (though the L.C. may extend this period to 75 in exceptional cases). Circuit judges may be removed from office by the Lord Chancellor for misconduct or incompetence.

40. Judicial immunity. Judges of the High Court and all other superior courts are immune from liability in civil proceedings for anything said or done by them in court. Judges of inferior courts, e.g. magistrates and circuit judges, have judicial immunity only so long as they were acting within their jurisdiction.

SPECIAL COURTS

41. Nature of special courts. In addition to the ordinary law courts, there are now a number of administrative tribunals and domestic tribunals which exercise judicial or quasi-judicial powers.

42. Administrative tribunals. These assist in the administration of Acts of Parliament and delegated legislation, and in determining disputes arising out of the operation of such legislation. There are now about 2,000 such tribunals.

EXAMPLES:

(a) *National Insurance Tribunals.* Disputes about family allowances and national insurance are heard by a local insurance officer, from whom appeal lies to a Local Appeal Tribunal (consisting of a lawyer and two laymen), and from the Tribunal further appeal lies to the National Insurance Commissioner.

(b) *National Health Service Tribunals.* A dissatisfied patient can apply to the service committee of his area family practitioner committee, which is a tribunal established under the National Health Service Reorganisation Act 1973. From this decision appeal lies to the National Health Service Tribunal, and finally to the minister.

(c) *Industrial Tribunals.* Set up to deal with disputes arising under the Contracts of Employment Act 1963, and Redundancy Payments Act 1965, their jurisdiction has increased considerably since the Race Relations Act, 1976 and the Sex Discrimination Act 1975 (*see* IV, **28**) as well as the Employment Protection (Consolidation) Act 1978.

(d) *The Lands Tribunal* deals with:

(i) disputes over the valuation of land compulsorily purchased by local authorities; and

(ii) appeals against assessments of the rateable value of property.

The Tribunal has a President, who must be a barrister of at least seven years' standing, or a person who has held high judicial office; other members must be barristers or solicitors of equal standing, or persons with special experience in valuation of land. Appeal lies to the C.A. on points of law.

(e) *Special Commissioners of Income Tax* hear appeals against income-tax assessments.

(f) *Rent Tribunals* assess rents for certain statutorily controlled tenancies.

43. Advantages of administrative tribunals. These were established mainly to save the ordinary courts from unnecessary additional work, to save cost to the citizen, and to provide specialised arbitrators for disputes of a technical nature.

The advantages are:

(a) expert knowledge is available where needed;

(b) quickness and cheapness of their proceedings;

(c) informality;

(d) wide discretion enables the tribunals to avoid rigid adherence to technicalities.

44. Disadvantages of administrative tribunals. They have been much criticised on the same grounds as the delegated legislation they have been set up to administer (*see* II, **15**).

Their disadvantages include:

(a) unpredictability, arising from the flexibility which is one of their advantages;

(b) Secrecy; the public is occasionally excluded from their hearings;

(c) reasons are not always given for their decisions;

(d) there is no representation by professional lawyers in some cases;

(e) appeal facilities are inadequate in some cases;

(f) bias is feared in cases where the members of the tribunal are on the staff of a ministry which may be a party to the dispute before the tribunal (although in fact there is very little evidence of bias in the vast majority of such cases).

45. The Tribunals and Inquiries Act 1971. Because of severe criticism, the Franks Committee was set up to investigate the operation of administrative tribunals, and the publication of the committee's report in 1957 led to the passing of an Act to reform some of the more obvious defects.

The Tribunals and Inquiries Act 1958 made the following provisions:

(a) A Council on Tribunals was established, with members to be nominated by the Lord Chancellor. Its function is to examine the personnel and workings of tribunals covered by the Act, and such other matters relating to the tribunals as the Lord Chancellor may refer to it from time to time.

(b) Appeal from tribunals to the High Court on points of law was established and cannot be ousted (save by a later Act of Parliament). The High Court can also exercise jurisdiction of a supervisory nature by means of prerogative orders (see 15).

(c) Tribunals must give reasons for decisions.

(d) Members of tribunals covered by the Act can be dismissed only with the approval of the Lord Chancellor, thus giving members greater freedom from fear of dismissal.

(e) Chairmen of some tribunals must be appointed by the Minister from a panel of suitably qualified persons appointed by the Lord Chancellor.

(f) By a 1966 Act members of the Council on Tribunals are empowered to attend local authority inquiries as observers.

The 1958 Act and later amendments have now been incorporated into the Tribunals and Inquiries Act 1971.

46. Judicial control of tribunals. By means of prerogative orders the Q.B.D. exercises a general supervisory jurisdiction over tribunals. The court's prime concern is to see that the principles of natural justice have been observed.

These principles of natural justice are vague, but can roughly be stated as follows, insofar as they relate to administrative bodies in general, and tribunals in particular.

(a) No man should be a judge in his own case, as he may be biased in his own favour. This rule covers cases where a minister appoints judges for a tribunal to decide a dispute between himself and a citizen, and the courts view such appointments with caution.

(b) *Audi alterem partem* (hear both sides), i.e. both sides must be given a fair chance to state their views, orally or in writing (depending on the requirements of the particular tribunal).

(c) There must be full investigation of facts.

(d) The tribunal should wherever possible give reasons for its decisions. This is now made compulsory in many cases by the Tribunals and Inquiries Act 1971.

NOTE: Of these principles, only the first two are usually stated to be "rules of natural justice" of general application.

47. The ultra vires doctrine. A further ground for interference by the courts is that the tribunal has acted beyond its powers (*ultra vires*).

This doctrine also covers the following situations:

(*a*) excess of authority by any government department or minister;

(*b*) excess of delegated powers by any local authority or other public body;

(*c*) a limited company or other corporation exceeding the powers granted to it.

Wherever an act is *ultra vires*, it is void and the court may so declare.

48. The Restrictive Practices Court. This was established for the purpose of suppressing such restrictive practices as agreements between suppliers of goods for the maintenance of prices: Restrictive Trade Practices Act 1956, and Resale Prices Act 1964. These Acts have now been consolidated into the Restrictive Trade Practices Acts 1976 and 1977.

The court consists of three High Court judges, one judge of the Scottish Court of Session, one judge of the Supreme Court of Northern Ireland, and not more than ten other persons appointed by the Crown on the advice of the Lord Chancellor by reason of their special knowledge. A hearing is presided over by one judge and two of the lay members. The court has the same status as a division of the High Court, and appeal lies to the Court of Appeal.

The chief permanent official of the court is the Registrar of Restrictive Trading Agreements, with whom all such agreements as fall within the scope of the Act must be registered for scrutiny by the court. If not so registered, all such agreements are void. Once registered, they will be examined by the court and pronounced void unless they appear to be in the public interest.

49. Other special courts. These include ecclesiastical courts, e.g the Consistory and Provincial Courts of the Church of England (*see* I, **29**), and courts martial, which enforces discipline in the armed services by applying a special body of military law.

Courts martial consist of military officers advised on points of law by a barrister employed by the office of the Judge Advocate General. Appeal lies to the Courts Martial Appeal Court, which

consists of the L.C.J. and any two puisne judges. Further appeal
lies to the House of Lords.

50. Domestic Tribunals. These maintain discipline among members of particular trades or professions. Some such tribunals are
set up by agreements among the members of an association (e.g.
trade union tribunals), and others are established by law (e.g. the
Solicitors Disciplinary Tribunal (solicitors), and the Disciplinary
Committee of the General Medical Council).

The Solicitors Disciplinary Tribunal consists of nine solicitors
specially appointed by the Master of the Rolls to deal with
complaints of unprofessional conduct by solicitors. It may order
a solicitor to be "struck off" the Rolls, or suspended from
practice for a time, or may impose fines. Proceedings are private,
and appeal lies to the Divisional Court of the Q.B.D., and thereafter to the C.A. and the House of Lords: Solicitors' Act 1974.

The Disciplinary Committee of the General Medical Council
consists of doctors (sometimes advised by a legally qualified
"assessor"), and can order a doctor to be barred from practice
for infamous conduct in his profession. Appeal lies to the J.C.P.C.
(A similar disciplinary committee exists for dentists: Medical
Act 1957; the Dentists Act 1957.)

Disciplinary tribunals of trades unions are not set up under legal
authority, but derive their authority solely from agreement of the
members of the Union. Their jurisdiction is fixed by the Union,
and usually includes power to expel a member from the Union or
impose fines. In *Bonsor* v. *Musicians' Union* (1955) it was established by the House of Lords that if a member is wrongfully
expelled he may obtain damages against his Union in compensation for any loss sustained as a result of the expulsion.

THE LEGAL PROFESSION

51. Membership of the profession. Judges, barristers and solicitors
constitute the three main branches of the profession. Judges are
usually selected from among the higher ranks of barristers, and
cannot practise as barristers after their appointment to the
judicial bench.

52. Barristers. In the Middle Ages several Inns of Court were
established for the training of barristers, i.e. lawyers who conduct
and argue cases in court. In 1852 a Council of Legal Education
was set up to regulate standards of professional education, and

this body is today responsible for conducting barristers' qualifying examinations.

Students begin their training by registering in one of the four remaining Inns of Court, i.e. Gray's Inn, Lincoln's Inn, Middle Temple, Inner Temple, and thereafter by passing their Bar Final exams and then being "called to the Bar" of their own Inn of Court, by the senior members (or "Benchers") of the Inn.

53. Queen's Counsel (Q.C.). Since the end of the seventeenth century the practice has developed of appointing senior barristers as King's Counsel, so as to have a body of eminent barristers available to advise the Crown on law. Appointment as Q.C. (or "silk") is made by the Lord Chancellor upon the application of the aspirant, on the grounds of seniority and eminence in his profession.

Before 1920 Q.C.s could not appear in cases against the Crown without special leave, but this is no longer necessary. The advisory duties of the Q.C.s to the Crown are also largely non-existent today.

In court Q.C.s are usually assisted by a junior barrister, though recently it was decided that Q.C.s may appear alone. Judges are usually appointed from among Q.C.s.

54. Junior barristers. All barristers other than Q.C.s are called juniors. They are entitled to commence practice as soon as they have been called to the Bar of their Inn, subject to a year's pupillage (apprenticeship) which includes six months' prohibition from appearing in court for clients. They cannot be called until they have passed their Bar Final examinations and been registered as a student of the Inn for three years and attended for twelve terms (by the formal device of dining in the Inn three times in each of the four legal terms each year, with "double dining" available for university graduates with high academic qualifications).

55. Conditions of barristers' work.

(*a*) Barristers have exclusive right of audience in the House of Lords, C.A., the High Court and J.C.P.C., and share with solicitors a concurrent right of audience in all other courts.

(*b*) Barristers cannot sue for fees owing to them, and since the decision in *Rondel* v. *Worsley* (1967) H.L., they have enjoyed an immunity from liability to actions in negligence brought by their clients. It was recently decided, however, that this immunity should be strictly confined to work which "is intimately connected with the conduct of the case in court": *Saif Ali v. Sydney Mitchell* (1978) H.L.

(*c*) A barrister can only be briefed through the agency of solicitor or, for non-court business, a patent agent. Generally the solicitor is entitled to be present at any interview between the barrister and the client.

56. Solicitors. The ancient professions of attorneys, proctors and solicitors were unified and regulated by a succession of Solicitor's Acts 1839–1974. These Acts established solicitors as officers of the Supreme Court, and set up a Law Society which supervises their training and discipline.

Training is commenced by the student becoming articled to a practising solicitor for a period of three to five years (depending on whether the student has a law degree or has passed the Common Professional Examination at the commencement of his articles). The articled clerk must also pass the Law Society Final Examination, after which he must be admitted to the Rolls of the Supreme Court before he can receive his licence to practise.

57. Position of solicitors.

(*a*) Unlike barristers, they are officers of the court.

(*b*) Unlike barristers, they have no right of audience in superior courts, but can act as advocates (like barristers) in the inferior courts, i.e. county and magistrates' courts and also in the Crown Courts in some matters.

(*c*) They can sue for their fees, and are liable for actions for professional negligence by their clients.

(*d*) Solicitors are primarily concerned with office work, e.g. drafting documents and advising generally; barristers are primarily concerned with advocacy in cases in court. But in practice many solicitors specialise in advocacy in cases in the inferior courts, and some barristers specialise in paper work, drafting documents, etc.

58. Discipline of the profession. Discipline of solicitors is in the hands of the Solicitors Disciplinary Tribunal (*see* 50).

Discipline of barristers is in the hands of the Senate of the four Inns of Court, which is appointed from among judges and senior barristers. (The Bar is less regulated by statute than the solicitorial side of the profession, e.g. Bencher's tribunals have no statutory constitution.)

The Lord Chancellor now has power to set up a tribunal to hear complaints against barristers or solicitors, and, if necessary, to bar a barrister or solicitor from acting for any legally aided client either temporarily or permanently: Criminal Justice Act 1967, s. 82. The Legal Aid in Criminal Cases (Complaints Tribunal) Rules 1968, have been issued in accordance with these provisions.

59. Institute of Legal Executives. The Institute was established in 1963 to give professional status to solicitors' clerks who are not themselves admitted solicitors, but who bear responsibility in advising clients for their solicitor employers. Admission to the Institute is by examination, leading first to Associateship, and secondly (at post-graduate level) to Fellowship. Fellows of the Institute have been granted certain (restricted) rights of audience in open court in county courts under the County Courts Act 1959, s. 89A.

LEGAL AID

60. Legal advice and assistance. Preliminary legal advice and assistance can be obtained by persons with low incomes under the Legal Aid Act 1974. This scheme is known as the "Green Form Scheme".

61. Legal aid in civil cases. Assistance is available under the Legal Aid Act 1974, s. 6, to enable a party to bring civil proceedings in court. The system is administered by the Law Society, through local Legal Aid Committees consisting of solicitors and barristers supervised by the Lord Chancellor. Eligibility for legal aid depends on the applicant's disposable income and capital, and funds are provided by the Treasury through the Legal Aid Fund. Generally an applicant is required to make some contribution towards the costs himself, depending on what the Committee thinks he can afford.

Legal aid will not be granted unless the Committee thinks the applicant has a reasonable case in law.

62. Legal aid in criminal cases. Legal aid is available now for all criminal proceedings, from Petty Sessions to the House of Lords. As in civil proceedings, the applicant may be called on to provide some of the costs himself: Legal Aid Act 1974.

NOTE: Dock Briefs. By an ancient tradition a prisoner in the dock can choose any barrister robed and present in the Crown

Court to defend him. The barrister so chosen is bound to accept the brief at a nominal fee.

ARBITRATION

63. Arbitration. Commercial agreements now frequently contain an "arbitration clause", under which in the event of any dispute arising between the parties to the contract (rather than go to the expense of suing each other in court) the dispute is to be referred to one or more arbitrators for informal settlement under the Arbitration Act 1950.

Arbitrators may be appointed from any suitable persons selected by the disputants at the time (or nominated in advance in the contract) or by a particular statute authorising arbitration as the appropriate way of settling particular types of dispute.

The advantages of arbitration as a way of settling disputes are:

(a) cheapness (by comparison with litigation in the courts);
(b) informality;
(c) speed and accessibility.

Any person can be an arbitrator, if acceptable to the disputants, but in practice arbitrators are usually selected from among lawyers or other professional men (who are chosen for their specialised knowledge in the field of the dispute), and are frequently members of the Institute of Arbitrators (a body composed of professional arbitrators). Ordinary judges may act as arbitrators, e.g. under the Administration of Justice Act 1970, s. 4, a judge of the Commercial Court of the Q.B.D. may act as arbitrator.

Where the matter for arbitration is not one arising out of a commercial agreement which involves the Arbitration Act 1950, then a circuit judge may act: Administration of Justice Act 1973, s. 7.

64. Conduct of arbitrations. Reference to arbitration under the Arbitration Act 1950, may be made either by a court order, by a particular statute or by agreement of the disputants. A court will not usually entertain proceedings in connection with any matter covered by an "arbitration agreement" unless (a) the dispute is outside the scope of the agreement, or (b) there are grounds to believe that arbitration would operate unfairly: Arbitration Act 1950, s. 24.

III. THE JUDICIAL SYSTEM

The Arbitration Act 1950 implies the following clauses into arbitration agreements, unless expressly excluded.

(*a*) Reference is to a single arbitrator, unless otherwise stated. (If reference is to two arbitrators, they must appoint an umpire to decide between them by a casting vote.)

(*b*) Examination on oath. Parties to arbitration must be prepared to submit to examination on oath and must produce necessary documents, etc. as in judicial proceedings. Witnesses may also have to submit to examination on oath.

(*c*) The arbitrator's award is final and binding. The courts will not set it aside unless bias or fraud can be proved, or some other exceptional cause.

(*d*) Arbitrators can order specific performance, except in relation to contracts concerning land.

(*e*) The parties may alter the arbitration agreement by mutual consent, but the arbitrator cannot do so on his own.

(*f*) Time for making the award may be fixed by the agreement; otherwise a reasonable time is implied.

(*g*) Death or bankruptcy of any party to an arbitration does not affect the validity of the agreement or the arbitrator's authority.

(*h*) An arbitration agreement may be revoked by the court if
    (*i*) the arbitrator shows bias; or
    (*ii*) there is any question of fraud in the dispute.

65. The European Court of Justice. The accession of the United Kingdom to the European Economic Community on 1st January 1973 has necessitated consideration of the European Court in the context of the English legal system.

Two separate issues are involved.

(*a*) The Treaty. Since this was a purely executive act, our courts are not bound by the Treaty provisions as such; "we take no notice of treaties until they are embodied in laws enacted by Parliament": *per* Lord Denning, M.R., in *Blackburn* v. *A.-G.* (1971).

(*b*) The European Communities Act 1972. The passing of this statute involved that "all rights, powers, liabilities, obligations and restrictions . . . under the Treaties, and all remedies and procedures under the Treaties . . . are to be given legal effect in the United Kingdom".

By virtue of this statute:

(*i*) Certain provisions become part of, and even prevail over, English Law: *Coomes* v. *Shields* (1978).

(*ii*) Matters relating to the meaning or effect of the Treaties, or of any other community instrument must be referred to the European Court, or, if not, decided in accordance with the principles laid down in that court: s. 3(1).

Thus, in matters with a "European element", the decisions of the European Court of Justice should be followed by United Kingdom courts; in any case, European law is enforced by the English courts.

The European Court will not, however, hear an action which is not referred to it by a national court; though under Article 177 E.E.C. Treaty, a court "against whose decisions there is no judicial remedy" *must* refer questions such as those given above to the European Court. Since this is a "procedure provided under the Treaty", then it is within the scope of the E.E.C. Act: s. 2(1).

66. Constitution of the European Court. The Court has nine judges and four Advocates-General.

(*a*) Judges. These are appointed every six years. In practice, one judge tends to come from each of the member states. All judges in the Court are eligible for the highest judicial office in their respective countries, (though they need not have actually sat as judges in domestic courts or are jurisconsults (legal advisers)).

(*b*) Advocates-General. These are similarly qualified to judges; their job, however, differs in that they give opinions, which are meant to state the issue and viewpoint of the point of European law involved in a case.

67. The European Convention on Human Rights 1950. Under this international convention a Commission and Court of Human Rights was established. These are not to be confused with the institutions of the E.E.C., and are quite separate.

The work of the Commission and of the Court depends upon the acceptance, on the part of states, of their jurisdiction. The United Kingdom has recognised their jurisdiction, and therefore an individual who alleges a breach of the terms of the convention (which safeguards human rights) on the part of the British Government or its agents can apply to the Commission to bring his case before the Court, whose rulings will be accepted in Britain.

PROGRESS TEST 3

1. State the composition and jurisdiction of the following courts:

(a) House of Lords;

(b) Court of Appeal;

(c) Judicial Committee of the Privy Council;

(d) Chancery Division of the High Court. **(3, 4, 8, 11, 12, 16)**

2. Explain briefly the original and appellate jurisdiction of the Queen's Bench Division of the High Court. **(14, 15)**

3. Explain the binding effect of decisions of:

(a) the House of Lords;

(b) the Court of Appeal;

(c) the judicial Committee of the Privy Council; **(5, 9, 11, 12)**

4. Outline the jurisdiction of the Family Division of the High Court. **(17)**

5. Summarise the jurisdiction of the county courts, and explain what is meant by a divorce county court. **(21, 22)**

6. Distinguish between summary and indictable offences and explain the functions of the magistrates' courts. **(25, 26)**

7. Distinguish between the Crown Court and magistrates' courts, explaining briefly the jurisdiction of each. **(19, 26)**

8. What is meant by a suspended sentence and in what circumstances must it be awarded? **(19)**

9. State what you know about the following:

(a) Lord Chancellor;

(b) Lord Chief Justice;

(c) Master of the Rolls;

(d) Law lords. **(31–34)**

10. What is meant by saying that judges are appointed *quamdiu se bene gesserint*? **(39, 40)**

11. What is meant by "an administrative tribunal"? Give examples. **(42)**

12. What are the advantages and disadvantages of administrative tribunals? **(43, 44)**

13. What were the main provisions of the Tribunals and Inquiries Act 1971? **(45)**

14. What do you understand to constitute the main principles of natural justice? **(46)**

15. Explain briefly the *ultra vires* doctrine. **(47)**

16. Explain the composition and functions of the Restrictive Practices Court. **(48)**

17. What is meant by a domestic tribunal? Give examples. **(50)**

18. Summarise the differences between barristers, solicitors and legal executives. **(51–59)**

19. Explain what is meant by arbitration and state how arbitrations are conducted. **(63, 64)**

20. Outline the jurisdiction and constitution of the European Court of Justice. **(65, 66)**

CHAPTER IV

The Law of Persons

LEGAL PERSONALITY

1. Meaning of legal personality. A person in law means any entity which is accepted by the law as having certain defined rights and obligations. Such persons may be natural (human beings) or artificial (corporations).

2. Corporations. A corporation is an artificial person composed of one or several natural persons. The corporations is recognised by the law as having a separate personality from its human members: *Salomon* v. *Salomon & Co. Ltd.* (1897) H.L.

3. Kinds of corporation. A corporation sole is one which consists of one human member only at any one time, or of the successive holders of certain offices, e.g. Bishops, the Crown, the Public Trustee.

Corporations aggregate consist of many members simultaneously, e.g. limited companies. Corporations aggregate are of three kinds, classified according to the method of their creation:

(*a*) chartered or common law corporations (*see* **4**);
(*b*) statutory corporations (*see* **5**);
(*c*) registered corporations (companies) (*see* **6**).

4. Chartered corporations. These are incorporated by the grant of a Royal Charter, creating the corporation and setting out its objects etc., e.g. the Chartered Institute of Secretaries, the Hudson's Bay Company.

This kind of corporation was the earliest known to the law but is increasingly rare because cheaper and easier methods of incorporation now exist.

The *ultra vires* doctrine (*see* **10**) does not apply to chartered corporations. But if such a corporation exceeds the powers granted in its charter this may be grounds for withdrawal of the charter. Procedure in such cases is for the Attorney-General to issue a writ of *scire facias* ("to know why you are doing . . .")

demanding to know why the corporation has acted in the way complained of. Failing a satisfactory answer, the charter may be withdrawn by the Crown: *Baroness Wenlock* v. *River Dee Corpn.* (1887).

5. Statutory corporations. These are incorporated by special Act of Parliament, a method largely used during the nineteenth century for the incorporation of railway companies but now increasingly rare. This method of incorporation today is used to set up public utilities and controlling bodies for the nationalised industries, e.g. the British Transport Commission and the various Gas and Electricity Boards.

(The *ultra vires* doctrine does apply to statutory corporations.)

6. Registered companies. These are incorporated merely by registration in the manner laid down by the Companies Acts 1948–76 (or one of the earlier similar Acts).

Registration is effected by depositing certain documents at the office of the Registrar of Companies (Department of Trade) in Cardiff, e.g.

(*a*) the memorandum of association, which sets out the capital and object of the company;

(*b*) the articles of association, which set out the rules governing the relations of the members among themselves and of the company to the members;

(*c*) various declarations by persons concerned in the promotion or direction of the proposed company to the effect that the statutory requirements have been complied with.

The vast majority of companies incorporated today are registered companies, and of these most are limited by shares (*see* 7(*a*)). There are now over 900,000 companies registered under the Companies Acts.

(The *ultra vires* doctrine does apply to registered companies.)

7. Kinds of registered companies.

(*a*) Limited companies, i.e. companies in which the liability of members to pay the debts of the company is limited:

(*i*) to the amount unpaid on their shares, if any (companies limited by shares); or

(*ii*) to the amount guaranteed by the members as their contribution towards the company's debts, and payable if the company is wound up (companies limited by guarantee).

Guarantee companies are comparatively rare, and where they exist they frequently also have a share capital.

(b) Unlimited companies, i.e. companies in which the liability of the members to pay the debts of the company is unlimited. These companies are rare nowadays, and are formed mainly in cases where the company is intended to be non-trading, non-profit-making, e.g. companies formed for furtherance of artistic or educational purposes.

8. Public and private companies. Registered companies may also be divided into two classes according to the number of their members.

(a) *Public companies:* those having a minimum of seven members and whose shares are freely transferable, e.g. on the Stock Exchange. This category comprises all the big industrial concerns whose shares are quoted on the Stock Exchange.

(b) *Private companies:* those having a minimum of two members and not more than fifty (not counting members who are past employees), and whose shares are not freely transferable. Private companies are required to restrict the transfer of their shares so that they cannot be made available to the general public. The articles of association of such companies therefore contain provisions for the sale of members' shares, usually through the directors; shares in private companies cannot be sold on the Stock Exchange.

9. Consequences of incorporation.

(a) The corporation or company can be sued in its own name, and can sometimes be prosecuted for criminal offences, e.g. tax evasion. Similarly, it can sue in its own name.

(b) Once incorporated, the company forms a legal personality, separate and distinct from the personalities of its members, whom it can therefore sue and who can sometimes sue it, and with whom it can make contracts, etc.: *Salomon* v. *Salomon & Co. Ltd.* (1897).

(c) The corporation can, within the limits of its powers, trade like an ordinary individual.

(d) The corporation can make contracts in its own name, through human agents.

Formerly such contracts had to be under seal, sealed by the company, but this rule has been abolished by (*i*) the Companies Act 1948, s. 32, which enables registered companies to make contracts in any form; and

    (*ii*) the Corporate Bodies Contracts Act 1960, which makes the same provision for other corporations.

    (*e*) The corporation can own and dispose of property like an ordinary individual. Formerly the Mortmain and Charitable Uses Acts imposed restrictions on a corporation's power to own land, but most of these restrictions have now been abolished.

10. The ultra vires doctrine. When a statutory or registered company exceeds the powers given it by its statute of incorporation (or memorandum of association, in the case of a registered company) any contract made in pursuance of such excess is void and cannot be ratified: *Ashbury Carriage Co.* v. *Riche* (1875) H.L.

    Thus, if a registered company not having power to borrow money enters into a contract for loan such contract is void. This means that the lender cannot legally recover money lent to the company. The European Communities Act 1972, s. 9(1), provides that where a person has dealt with a company in good faith, any transaction approved by the company's directors shall be presumed to be *intra vires* and therefore enforceable.

    If a registered company's directors exceed the powers delegated by the company to them in the articles of association any transaction thus entered into by them is voidable at the company's option. If in addition their act exceeds the powers of the company as implied by the memorandum of association it is void and cannot in any circumstances be ratified by the company: *Ashbury Carriage Co.* v. *Riche* (1875).

    The memorandum and articles of association, being registered at the office of the Registrar of Companies, are classed as "public documents", i.e. every person dealing with the company is presumed by the law to know their contents. Thus, no one can complain that he was deceived into entering into an *ultra vires* contract with a company because he did not know what its powers were: *Royal British Bank* v. *Turquand* (1855).

UNINCORPORATED ASSOCIATIONS

11. Unincorporated associations. These differ from corporate bodies in that they do not have a legal personality distinct from the members of the association. They include trades unions and most societies and clubs.

12. Legal position. The law generally disregards the association and treats it as simply a group of persons, who are thus individually responsible for the association's actions: *Brown* v. *Lewis* (1896).

Exceptions.

(*a*) Where a large number of persons have the same common interest in one case in court, the court or they may depute one or some of their numbers to sue or be sued on behalf of all of them: Rules of the Supreme Court (1965), Order 15, r. 12.

(*b*) Since the Law of Property Act 1925 forbids more than four people to own land together, such associations must nominate four of their number to hold land as trustees on behalf of the association. The trustees are then the legal owners of the land and can sue or be sued on behalf of the association.

(*c*) The association may by express or implied contract delegate powers to a committee to govern the association as a whole and, for instance, to hold a domestic disciplinary tribunal, e.g. the Stewards of the Jockey Club.

13. Trade unions. These were unlawful until legalised by the Trade Union Act 1871, and permitted to register an association name. They can sue or be sued in their registered name, if any: Trade Union Union and Labour Relations Act 1974 s. 2(1) (*c*).

The Trade Union and Labour Relations Act 1974, however, provided that, in general, no action in tort will lie against a trade union. A union may be sued in negligence, nuisance or breach of duty causing personal injury provided that these do not result from acts done "in contemplation or furtherance of a trade dispute": ss. 13 and 14.

14. Partnerships. A partnership is "the relationship which subsists between persons carrying on a business in common with a view of profit": Partnership Act 1890, s. 1. A firm, or partnership, has no separate legal personality distinct from its members.

Rules governing partnerships are laid down by the Partnership Act 1890.

EXAMPLES:

(1) Partners are agents for the firm in furthering the partnership business. The firm is therefore legally liable upon contracts made or torts committed by a partner on its behalf.

(2) For convenience, partners may sue or be sued in the firm's name.

(3) If a person who is not a partner allows outsiders to think he is a partner in a firm, he may be liable to such outsiders as though he were really a partner.

(4) If a firm trades under a name other than that of the part ners who compose it (e.g. Smith & Jones trading as "Smones & Co.") that name must be registered together with the names of the partners: Registration of Business Names Act 1916.

(5) A firm is dissolved:

(*i*) by the expiry of any agreed period;

(*ii*) by the completion of the particular undertaking for which it was formed;

(*iii*) by death or bankruptcy of any partner;

(*iv*) by mutual agreement; or

(*v*) by order of the court.

(6) Partners are jointly liable on the firm's contracts, and jointly and severally liable for the firm's torts.

(7) Rights of the partners are governed by the partnership articles (if any), or if there are no articles, then by the Partnership Act 1890. Under the Act partners are entitled to:

(*i*) share management;

(*ii*) invest equally and share profits equally; and

(*iii*) to settle disputes by majority vote.

Unless the articles expressly so provide, a partner is not entitled to receive remuneration for work done on behalf of the firm.

(8) A partner's liability may be limited to an agreed sum, if the other partners agree. A firm containing one or more partners whose liability for the firm's debts is limited in this way is a Limited Partnership, and must be registered as such under the Limited Partnership Act 1907. Such a partnership must have at least one "general" partner, i.e. one whose liability is unlimited. Limited partners cannot participate in the management of the firm without losing their limitation of liability.

(9) A partnership cannot generally have more than twenty members, or ten in the case of a banking partnership: Companies Act 1948, s. 434. (Firms of solicitors, accountants, auctioneers, estate agents, and members of the Stock Exchange, however, are now exempted from this limitation: Companies Act 1967, s. 120 and Board of Trade Regulations 1968.)

NATIONALITY AND DOMICILE

15. Status. The status of a person means his or her rank in society. In the Middle Ages there were many different ranks, from slave and serf up to peers of the realm; the duties and privileges of each rank were carefully defined. The tendency of the law has been towards the abolition of different grades of status. Now all adults have virtually equal status; but minors are still subject to certain incapacities intended for their protection.

Married women were formerly subject to similar incapacities to minors, on the supposition that they were incapable of protecting themselves, but these incapacities have been gradually abolished: Married Women's Property Act 1882; Law Reform (Married Women and Tortfeasors) Act 1935.

Recent legislation has ensured that all women, married or single, may enjoy the same rights as men with regard to employment, etc.: Equal Pay Act 1970; Sex Discrimination Act 1975.

16. Nationality. This implies allegiance to a particular state. With the exception of some persons, who have become stateless because of some political upheaval in their own country, every person must owe allegiance to some state. The state to which the allegiance is owed is under a reciprocal duty to protect the subject, though a person who is temporarily in the U.K., but who is not a national, owes what is known as "local" allegiance, and is therefore owed protection: *Johnstone* v. *Pedlar* (1921).

17. Domicile. This means the place where a person permanently resides, e.g. resides with *animus manendi* (intention of remaining), even for a short while. Thus, a French national who with *animus manendi* resides in Britain, may retain his French nationality while acquiring a British domicile. Note that length of residence is unimportant; it is the intention that matters. Thus, every person, even stateless persons, must have a domicil.

8. Kinds of domicile.

(*a*) Domicile of origin, acquired at birth by a child. A legitimate child inherits his father's domicile, and an illegitimate child his mother's. The law presumes that a person retains his domicile of origin all his life, until the contrary is proved.

(*b*) Domicile of choice, acquired where an adult voluntarily relinquishes his domicile of origin by taking up residence in some other country with *animus manendi*.

(c) Domicile of dependence is acquired by a child whose parents change their domicile by their own choice. Here the child's domicile changes with that of the parents.

Substantial changes in the modern law on this subject were made by the Domicile and Matrimonial Proceedings Act 1973.

19. Importance of domicile. It is important to discover a person's domicile in order to ascertain what system of law will govern certain matters. His *lex domicilii* (law of the domicile) governs:

(a) the jurisdiction of the courts in matters of divorce and the validity of his marriage;

(b) the legitimation of bastards;

(c) the validity of wills of movable property.

20. British Nationality Act 1948. This defines what is meant by British subject, and lays down how British nationality can be acquired.

British subjects are of two kinds:

(a) citizens of the United Kingdom and Colonies; and

(b) Commonwealth citizens (such as Canadians).

British nationality extends only to the former.

21. Acquisition of British nationality. Citizenship of the United Kingdom and Colonies can be acquired in the following ways.

(a) *By birth* within the United Kingdom or Colonies, irrespective of the nationality of the parents.

(b) *By descent.* The child of a father who was a United Kingdom citizen himself automatically acquires British nationality by descent, wherever born.

(c) *By registration.* A citizen of one of the self-governing nations of the Commonwealth may, if of full age and capacity, apply to the Secretary of State or a Colonial Governor for registration as a British citizen if he has satisfied certain requirements as to residence or is in the service of the Crown.

(d) *By naturalisation.* Aliens and British-protected persons may apply for a certificate of naturalisation as a British citizen to the Secretary of State or a Colonial Governor, on condition that they take the oath of allegiance to the Crown and are of satisfactory character.

(e) *By incorporation of territory.* The Sovereign may by Order in Council direct that all nationals of a newly acquired territory shall be British subjects.

2. Duties of British subjects.

(a) To serve the state when required, e.g. as a juryman.

(b) To assist the police in maintaining order and quelling disturbances. Refusal to do so is a punishable offence: *R. v. Brown* (1841).

(c) To pay rates and taxes.

(d) To register births and deaths of members of his family.

(e) To see that children of the family attend school.

(f) To obey the general laws of the kingdom.

3. British nationality may be lost. This occurs in the following cases.

(a) *Declaration of renunciation.* Such a declaration must be registered with the Secretary of State in order to be effective.

(b) *Deprivation of citizenship* by the Home Secretary in the case of citizens naturalised within the past five years, on the grounds of treasonous or seriously criminal conduct. (Where obtained by any process other than naturalisation, citizenship cannot be withdrawn in this way.)

4. Commonwealth Immigrants Acts. The social problems occasioned by unrestricted immigration from the Commonwealth led to the enactment of laws designed to limit immigration. Under the Acts of 1962 and 1968, the power to refuse admission to any Commonwealth citizen, except for those born in the U.K. or holding U.K. passports, was given to immigration officers.

Immigration officers were also given the power to impose conditions upon entry. The 1962 Act gave powers of deportation of Commonwealth citizens to the Home Secretary, and the 1968 Act made it an offence to land in Britain otherwise than in accordance with immigration regulations.

Immigration could not, however, be refused if the immigrant could show that:

(a) one of his parents or grandparents was born, naturalised, or adopted in the United Kingdom (or, or course, if he himself was); or

(b) he is self-supporting; or

(c) he is going into employment approved by the Department of Employment.

The Commonwealth Immigration Acts 1962 and 1968 were repealed by the Immigration Act 1971. This Act is a comprehensive one and also replaces the Aliens Restriction Act 1914; it deals with the regulation of entry and stay in the United Kingdom of aliens as well as Commonwealth citizens. S. 2 of the Immigration Act refers to the "right of abode"; everyone having that right is free to live in, work in, and come and go freely from the U.K. People who do not have that right are subject to control.

Basically, those Commonwealth citizens who had a right of unrestricted entry under the 1962 and 1968 Acts will now have a right of abode; those who had no such right will not. People who have such a right are now known as "patrials".

25. E.E.C. Nationals. It is necessary to consider nationals of E.E.C. countries as a special category; Article 48 of the E.E.C. Treaty gives rise to the right of workers to migrate freely from one member state to another, and such workers, as well as their families, may only be refused entry, or deported from a state, on grounds of the public interest. Public interest was held to have justified the refusal to admit a Dutch member of the Church of Scientology in *Van Duyn* v. *Home Office* (1975).

26. Married Women. Formerly, a woman on marriage automatically acquired the nationality of her husband, and lost her own, if different. Thus, a British woman marrying an alien lost her British nationality. Since the British Nationality Act 1948, the position is that a British woman who marries an alien retains her British nationality unless she expressly renounces it.

An alien woman who marries a British subject, on the other hand, retains her own nationality. She may, however, acquire British citizenship by registration. A female Commonwealth citizen who is married to any one of those categories of Commonwealth citizens who have unrestricted right of entry (i.e. right of abode) also has such a right of abode.

27. Aliens. Foreign nationals (non-patrials) must get leave to enter and may be subject to restrictions as to employment etc. A non-patrial is liable to deportation if:

(a) he does not observe such conditions as may be placed upon his entry or stay;

(b) the Home Secretary deems it to be in the public good;

(c) he is convicted of a criminal offence; or

(d) a member of his family is deported: Immigration Act 1971, s. 3.

Whilst in the country, however, an alien can enjoy the same rights as British subjects by virtue of "local" allegiance (*see* **16**), though this does not apply to enemy aliens: *Ex p. Kuechenmeister* (1947).

28. Race relations and discrimination. The Race Relations Act 1976, the Equal Pay Act 1970 and Sex Discrimination Act 1975, saw the establishment of two Commissions, one for racial equality and the other for equal opportunities, whose function it is to enforce the Acts and promote equality of opportunity. The purpose of the Acts is to prevent discrimination on racial or sexual grounds, and to ensure equal opportunities for all, irrespective of colour or sex, in such matters as employment and remuneration, as well as the obtaining of services, housing, education. The Sex Discrimination and Race Relations Acts are broadly similar; defining the remedies available in cases involving discrimination. Claims relating to employment should be made to an industrial tribunal, and those relating to education, housing and comparable matters to the county court (*see* III, **21**).

The Race Relations Act 1976 also makes it an offence to "stir up racial hatred" (*see* XXIX, **7**).

MARRIAGE

29. Husband and wife. Marriage is "the voluntary union for life of one man and one woman to the exclusion of all others": *per* Lord Penzance in *Hyde* v. *Hyde* (1866). Marriage in Britain is monogamous, but polygamous unions contracted overseas by foreign nationals may be recognised as valid by the British courts.

30. Capacity to marry. A party domiciled in England or Wales must have capacity according to English law, which requires the following.

(*a*) Neither party must be under 16.

(*b*) Neither party must be already married (unless the earlier marriage has been legally dissolved).

(*c*) Neither party must have been certified insane at the time of the marriage.

(*d*) One party must be male, and the other female. The sex of a party is "fixed at birth"; thus a man who undergoes a "sex-change" operation cannot marry a man: *Corbett* v. *Corbett* (1970).

(*e*) Neither party must be within the "prohibited degrees", i.e. related so closely that the law forbids them to inter-marry, e.g. brothers and sisters. The Marriage (Enabling) Act 1960 slightly reduced the prohibited categories, e.g. by providing that a widower may now marry his deceased wife's sister, aunt or niece, and a divorced man may make a similar marriage during the lifetime of the ex-wife.

31. Marriage by the Church of England. A marriage can be solemnised by the Church of England only where:

(*a*) a special licence has been issued by the Archbishop of Canterbury, or other authorised person: Ecclesiastical Licences Act 1533; or

(*b*) a common licence has been issued by a bishop or his surrogate (deputy) for the marriages of persons residing within his diocese within three months of the issue of the licence: Marriage Act 1949; or

(*c*) a certificate has been issued by a superintendent registrar (*see* **32**(*b*)); or

(*d*) banns have been published (i.e. a public announcement made) on three successive Sundays preceding the marriage in a church authorised by the bishop for the purpose and for the celebration of marriages, in the parish in which one or both of the parties reside.

Church of England marriages must be solemnised in the presence of two or more witnesses in addition to the clergyman, between the hours of 8.0 a.m. and 6.0 p.m.: Marriage Act 1949.

32. Marriage by other means. The following marriages may be solemnised on the authority of a superintendent registrar's certificate.

(*a*) A marriage in a registered building, in such form and ceremony as the parties see fit to adopt.

(*b*) A marriage in the office of the superintendent registrar.

(*c*) A marriage according to the usages of the Society of Friends (Quakers).

(*d*) A marriage between two professing Jews according to the usages of the Jewish religion.

(*e*) A marriage according to the usages of the Church of England (*see* **31**).

In each case the marriage must take place in the registrar's office or in a building approved by him. The registrar's certificate of authority to marry remains valid for three months. Two witnesses must be present at the ceremony, and the marriage must be celebrated by a person licensed for the purpose or by the registrar, and the doors of the building must remain open throughout so as to allow public access: Marriage Act 1949.

33. Legal consequences of marriage. These are chiefly as follows.

(*a*) The parties should co-habit unless separated by agreement or by a decree of judicial separation from a court.

(*b*) The husband must normally support the wife financially, in a style fitted to his income. (She loses this right if she deserts her husband or commits adultery.) At common law a wife was under no obligation to support her husband, but since the National Assistance Act 1948, and later social enactments, the wife may in certain circumstances be bound to assist the husband financially.

(*c*) Disputes as to property between spouses may be settled by the High Court or county court: Married Women's Property Act 1882, s. 17. (Under the Matrimonial Homes Act 1967, the court may give a spouse a right of occupation of the matrimonial home, even if it belongs legally to the other spouse.)

(*d*) One spouse can now be prosecuted for stealing from the other: Theft Act 1968.

(*e*) Spouses can now sue each other in contract and tort, though the court may stay any such tort action where it appears desirable: Law Reform (Husband and Wife) Act 1962.

34. Nullity. A marriage is null and void (i.e. regarded by the courts as never having taken place) where:

(*a*) one of the parties is already married;

(*b*) the parties are not respectively male and female (*see* **30**);

(*c*) the requirements of the Marriage Acts 1949–1970, have not been complied with. These requirements relate to:

(*i*) capacity (*see* **30**); and

(*ii*) formalities as to solemnisation (*see* **31, 32**).

These provisions are contained in the Matrimonial Causes Act 1973, s. 11.

35. Voidable marriages. Whilst such marriages as were dealt with in **34** are absolutely void, voidable marriages remain valid until declared void by the court. The Matrimonial Causes Act 1973,

s. 13, provides, however, that a decree of nullity in the case of a voidable marriage must *not* be granted if:

(*a*) the court is satisfied that the petitioner, knowing he (or she) could have avoided the marriage, conducted himself (or herself) in a way suggesting that he or she would not do so; and

(*b*) to grant the decree would be unjust.

The Matrimonial Causes Act 1973, s. 12, provides the following grounds for avoiding a marriage:

(*a*) non-consummation (whether due to refusal or incapacity);

(*b*) lack of consent;

(*c*) insanity such as to negative consent;

(*d*) where one party suffers from a communicable venereal disease; or

(*e*) where the respondent was pregnant by some person other than the petitioner.

NOTE: The grounds on which a marriage may be void or voidable (*see* 34 and 35) refer to marriages celebrated since the Nullity of Marriage Act 1971 was passed. The grounds set out in the Matrimonial Causes Act 1973 are the same as those originally contained in the Act of 1971.

36. Divorce under the Matrimonial Causes Act 1973. This Act re-enacted the provisions in the Divorce Reform Act 1969, thus affirming that "irretrievable breakdown of marriage" is the sole ground for divorce. What constitutes breakdown will clearly depend on the circumstances of each case, and for the prevention of rash divorces the Act makes provision for a reconciliation procedure which must be followed before any divorce can be granted.

To establish "irretrievable breakdown" one party must establish one or more of the following.

(*a*) that the respondent has committed adultery and the petitioner finds it intolerable to live with the respondent.

(*b*) that the respondent has behaved in such a way that the petitioner cannot reasonably be expected to live with the respondent.

(*c*) that the respondent has deserted the petitioner for a continuous period at at least two years immediately preceding presentation of the petition.

(*d*) that the parties have lived apart for a continuous period of at least two years immediately preceding presentation of the petition and the parties agree to divorce.

(e) that the parties have lived apart for a continuous period of at least five years immediately preceding presentation of the petition (whether they agree to divorce or not).

37. Magistrates' jurisdiction. Magistrates' courts have summary jurisdiction in domestic proceedings where a wife applies for maintenance from a deserting husband, or an order for judicial separation on the grounds of persistent cruelty or adultery.

The magistrates may also order husband and wife to live apart, and award custody of the children to either party, with provision of maintenance.

The magistrates' jurisdiction will closely resemble that of the High Court and divorce county courts when the Domestic Proceedings and Magistrates' Courts Act 1978 comes into operation.

INFANTS OR MINORS

38. Minority. A minor is a person under the age of eighteen: Family Law Reform Act (F.L.R.A.) 1969, s. 1(1).

A minor (or "infant") becomes an adult at the "commencement of the relevant anniversary of the date of his birth", i.e. the first moment of his or her eighteenth birthday: F.L.R.A. 1969, s. 9.

NOTE: (1) Formerly: (a) minority was called "infancy"; (b) infancy ended at 21 years of age; (c) the moment of termination of infancy was the first moment of the day preceding the twenty-first birthday. (2) Note particularly that the lowering of the age of majority extends (in the absence of contrary intention): (a) to any rule of law in any statute enacted before or after the coming into force of the F.L.R.A.; and (b) any deed, will or other instrument made on or after that date: F.L.R.A. 1969, s. 1(2). (3) Students are advised to regard the terms "infant" and "minor" as interchangeable, as it may take some time for the new terminology to gain universal support (cf. capacity in contract, tort, etc.).

39. Legitimation. An illegitimate child, i.e. one born out of wedlock, can now be legitimated by the subsequent marriage of its parents (legitimation *per subsequens matrimonium*): Legitimacy Act 1976. A child born of an adulterous association can now be legitimated in this way: Legitimacy Act 1976. The common law presumption that only legitimate children could inherit on the intestacy of their parents has been abolished: Family Law Reform Act 1969.

40. Adoption of minors. Adoption may be effected only by a single person, male or female, or by a married couple, provided that the adoptor is:

(a) at least twenty-five years of age; or

(b) a relative of the child and over twenty-one years of age; or

(c) the father or mother of the child irrespective of age: Adoption Acts 1958–68.

Adoption is effected by court order. Before granting the order the court must be satisfied that:

(a) every person whose consent is necessary has in fact consented, i.e. parents or guardians;

(b) the infant has consented if he or she is of sufficient age to do so;

(c) no bribe has been made to any person in connection with the proposed adoption, but only such payments as are authorised by the court;

(d) the child has been in the probationary care of the adoptor for at least three months prior to the application;

(e) if the child is under school-leaving age, that three months notice has been given to the local education authority. (Adoption of a female child by a single male will be allowed only in exceptional circumstances.)

The Children Act 1975 introduced certain changes. These did not, however, come into force until re-enacted in the Adoption Act 1976. The objects of the Act are:

(a) to provide a comprehensive adoption service; and

(b) to stamp out "third-party" adoptions, i.e. the arrangement of an adoption by a private person.

41. Guardians. Every minor should have some adult to safeguard its interests. In the absence of parents, the court will appoint a guardian.

Guardians may be appointed by

(a) the parents by will; or

(b) the High Court, county court, or magistrates where there is no one else to make appointment, otherwise by the High Court only where the minor has been placed under the care of the court, i.e. made a ward of court by its parents.

By the Administration of Justice Act 1970, jurisdiction in wardship was transferred from the Chancery Division to the Family Division of the High Court, which is charged with guardianship of wards of court. Interference with a ward of court is contempt of court, punishable by imprisonment. The court may appoint any person guardian of the minor, e.g. parents, under the supervision of the court. Consent of the court must be obtained before the minor can marry, leave the country, etc.

Custody of a minor may be awarded by a court to either parent in divorce or other matrimonial proceedings: Guardianship of Minors Acts 1971 and 1973. In deciding which parent should have custody, the welfare of the child is paramount and mother and father are regarded equally.

42. Incapacity of minors. Minors are in a special position in law, since they are deemed incapable of exercising the full rights of citizenship, or of being made fully responsible under the law.

(*a*) *Crimes.* A child under the age of ten is absolutely presumed *doli incapax* (incapable of evil) and cannot be prosecuted for any criminal offence. Between the ages of ten and fourteen there is a rebuttable presumption that the child is *doli incapax*. but this can be rebutted by strong evidence that the child knew its conduct was criminal. Over the age of fourteen, a child is fully open to prosecution. But children receive special treatment, e.g. are dealt with by special juvenile courts and cannot be sent to a normal prison, but are punished by being committed to care and control if under fourteen, or borstal institution if between fourteen and seventeen (*see* XXVI, 3).

(*b*) *Ownership of property.* A minor can be the owner of any sort of moveable property, but cannot legally own land: Law of Property Act 1925, s. 19.

(*c*) *Litigation.* Minors cannot sue on their own behalf. A special guardian *ad litem* must be appointed to represent a minor defendant, and a "next friend" to sue on behalf of a minor plaintiff.

(*d*) *Contracts.* A minor is not generally bound by his contracts (*see* VI, 10).

(*e*) *Torts.* A minor is generally liable for torts (*see* XIV, 7).

(*f*) *Marriage.* A minor cannot marry before the age of sixteen, and if under the age of eighteen must have the consent of his or her parents.

THE CROWN

43. Constitutional monarchy. A monarchy is a state in which all governmental power legally resides in one person, inheriting that power by birth, e.g. in Britain, the Queen.

However, the British monarch is not an absolute ruler, but must rule in accordance with the conventions and laws which together compose the British constitution. Where the powers of a monarch are curtailed by a constitution in this way, a special form of limited or constitutional monarchy arises.

44. Unwritten constitution. The British constitution is said to be "unwritten" because it is not contained, like that, e.g. of the United States or France, in one document or connected series of documents. It is also said to be "flexible", because it is possible for it to be changed by the normal law-making process of legislation.

The British constitution derives from:

(*a*) statutes, including certain celebrated statutes such as Magna Carta 1215, and the Bill of Rights 1689, which are regarded with great esteem;

(*b*) rules of common law;

(*c*) customary rules, including those customs observed by Parliament itself; and

(*d*) constitutional conventions.

These are like customs in that they are not enforceable in the Courts (i.e. are not rules of law), but are of considerable importance in that they are observed, and therefore bind, not only Parliament but the Executive, and the Queen herself; e.g. the Queen may not refuse her assent to a Bill which has been passed in both Houses of Parliament.

45. Constitutional law. This is composed partly of statutes and conventions, and regulates the powers of the government and Parliament, and the relationship between government and citizens. Constitutional law is part of public law, and is outside the scope of this book.

46. Rights of citizens: the rule of law. The rights of citizens under the state are protected in Britain by a doctrine called "the rule of law".

Dicey, in his *Law of the Constitution* (1885), analysed the rule of law as depending on three propositions.

(*a*) The ordinary common law overrides and excludes the arbitrary exercise of governmental power.

(*b*) All classes of persons are equally subject to the law and the courts, including the government.

(*c*) The law of the constitution is not contained in any piece of legislation, but is derived from the rights of individuals, as declared by the courts.

47. Personal freedom. This is one of the basic rights of citizenship. A British subject can enforce his rights by means of the following remedies:

(*a*) *Self-defence:* provided that if force is used it is only such as is proportionate to the harm threatened, and is reasonably necessary to protect oneself or one's property from unlawful interference: Criminal Law Act 1967, s. 3.

(*b*) *Judicial protection:*

(*i*) A civil action for damages for assault, false imprisonment, or malicious prosecution.

(*ii*) Criminal proceedings for assault or false imprisonment.

(*iii*) A writ of habeas corpus, i.e. a Q.B.D. writ ordering a person who is detaining another to produce the prisoner in court and show why he should not be released. (A single judge can order release; there is no appeal against his decision to order release in criminal cases, though appeals are possible in civil cases: Administration of Justice Act 1960, s. 15.)

(*c*) *European Convention 1950.* The U.K. has undertaken, under this convention, to guarantee basic human rights. Enforcement of the convention is carried out by the Commission and the Court of Human Rights in Strasbourg (*see* III, 67).

48. Freedom of speech. This is the right to speak or write freely on any matter, subject to the following limitations.

(*a*) A civil action for libel or slander for the publication of any false and defamatory matter (*see* XVIII, 1, 2).

(*b*) Prosecution for criminal libel (*see* XXIX, 14).

(*c*) Prosecution for blasphemy, obscenity or sedition (*see* XXIX, 5, 15).

49. Freedom of assembly. The right to hold meetings freely is now extensively curtailed by the laws against riots, routs, and unlawful assemblies, and by the law of trespass and nuisance (*see* XV).

A *rout* is a disturbance of the peace by three or more persons.

An *unlawful assembly* is a combination of three of more persons meeting to execute a common purpose in such a way as to inspire ordinary reasonable citizens to fear a breach of the peace.

A *riot* is a tumultuous disturbance of the peace by three or more persons assembling with intent to assist each other by force in the execution of a common purpose, and actually executing or attempting to execute such purpose in a violent manner calculated to alarm one or more ordinary reasonable citizens.

Provided a meeting is held in a public place, i.e. without trespassing on the land of another, and is not so noisy as to cause a nuisance, nor constituting a rout, unlawful assembly, etc., it may be legal.

50. "The Queen can do no wrong." Although the government and its agents are basically subject to the same law as everybody else, the sovereign, being regarded as "the fountain of justice", cannot legally be made liable to the jurisdiction of the courts, which themselves exist only by virtue of their authority from the sovereign. (This is a necessary principle dictated by logic in any monarchy). The maxim "The Queen can do no wrong" is today limited in application to the sovereign personally, i.e. the Queen in her personal capacity cannot be sued in any British court. But the government, and other agents of the Crown, can now generally be freely sued: Crown Proceedings Act 1947 (*see* **51**).

51. Crown Proceedings Act 1947. This provides that the Crown can now be made liable like an ordinary person for:

(*a*) torts committed by its servants or agents;

(*b*) breaches of duties imposed on occupiers or owners of property;

(*c*) breaches of duties owed by an employer to his servants or employees;

(*d*) breaches of contracts. But note that the Crown is still not bound by contracts it makes with its own servants, and cannot be sued on such contracts; civil servants, however, now have a statutory right to resist unfair dismissal: Trade Union and Labour Relations Act 1974.

The effect of the Crown Proceedings Act 1947 is that a citizen can now sue a Government department or minister for wrongs committed by employees or government servants, but cannot sue the Queen personally (although the department or minister derives its authority theoretically from the Queen).

52. The Parliamentary Commissioner ("Ombudsman"). Under the Parliamentary Commissioner Act 1967, his function is to investigate complaints of governmental administrative oppression or unfairness. But he cannot commence investigations unless first asked to do so by a Member of Parliament on behalf of the complainant. His jurisdiction is seriously limited and does not extend to local-government matters, nor to central-government actions if correct procedure was followed by the department or ministry concerned (even though this may have produced harsh or unfair results).

The reform of local government, however, occasioned by the Local Government Act 1974, saw the creation of special commissions for local government, based on the model of the Ombudsman. The Parliamentary Commissioner is, in fact, an *ex officio* member of these commissions, though complaints relating to local government go not to him but to local commissioners for investigation.

PROGRESS TEST 4

1. What kinds of personality are recognised by English law? (1–3)

2. How can corporations be formed? How far are corporations subject to the *ultra vires* doctrine? (2–7, 10)

3. Distinguish:

(*a*) incorporated and unincorporated associations;

(*b*) public and private companies;

(*c*) a partnership and a limited company. (8, 9, 11, 12, 14)

4. Define and distinguish nationality, domicile and status. (15–17)

5. How can British nationality:

(*a*) be acquired; and

(*b*) be lost? (20, 21, 23)

6. Summarise the main provisions of the Commonwealth Immigration Acts and the Race Relations Act 1976. (24, 28)

7. When a woman marries a man of different nationality, what effect has the marriage on her nationality? (26)

8. Summarise the grounds on which a divorce may be obtained. (36)

9. What is a minor or infant? At what age did infancy cease before 1970? Summarise the chief incapacities of minors. (38, 42)

10. Why is the British constitution said to be unwritten? What are the basic rights of British citizens and how are these protected? (44–49)

11. Summarise and explain the main provisions of the Crown Proceedings Act 1947. (51)

PART TWO

THE LAW OF CONTRACT

CHAPTER V

Formalities and Consent

INTRODUCTION

1. A simple contract. A contract is a legally binding agreement, that is, an agreement imposing rights and obligations on the parties which will be enforced by the courts.

Y is a newsagent. Z goes into his shop and offers him 10p. Y accepts the money and gives Z his newspaper. We have here the elements of a contract:

(*a*) the *offer* (*see* **10–12**);

(*b*) the *acceptance* (*see* **13–17**); and

(*c*) the 10p, which is called the *consideration* (*see* VI, **1–5**).

It is a simple contract, imposing straightforward rights and obligations.

(*a*) Suppose Z only has a £5 note. Y has no change. Y says "You can owe it me," and hands over the newspaper. Z then has an obligation to pay 10p.

(*b*) Suppose Z opens the paper and finds that the printing has missed the inside pages. Z then has a right to return the incomplete paper and to be given a complete copy or, if Y has sold out, to be returned his 10p.

A right enjoyed by one party implies an obligation owed by the other. We can express the same thing either way round.

After he has bought his newspaper Z gets on the bus to work. This time he is accepting an implied offer by the bus company. Z must pay the fare to the conductor (as agent for the bus company (*see* XI, **1**)) in return for being taken to his destination. That is the consideration.

FORMALITIES

2. Formal requirements. As we have seen Z enters into a series of binding contracts as he walks down the street, buying a newspaper and mounting the bus, without any formalities. Z enters into these contracts orally, and they are therefore called parol contracts. Most contracts can be made in any way: orally, in writing, by telephone or telex.

A few contracts require a particular form, usually to provide better evidence of the terms and so to prevent disputes. Some contracts must be:

(a) under seal (*see* 3);
(b) in writing (*see* 4);
(c) evidenced by writing (*see* 5–7).

3. Contract under seal. A contract under seal is called a deed or a specialty contract. A document becomes a deed if it is:

(a) *signed*;
(b) *sealed*. Sealing is now usually effected by affixing a disc or wafer of red paper at the bottom of the deed;
(c) *delivered*. Delivery is largely a matter of intention, and a deed may be delivered (by constructive delivery) even though it remains in the possession of the maker. A deed by a corporation does not need to be delivered.

When a deed is signed, sealed and delivered it is executed. An *escrow* is a deed executed subject to a condition that it is not to become operative until a certain contingency is satisfied, for example the occurrence of a certain event or the expiry of a period of time.

Deeds are of two kinds.

(a) A *deed poll*, to which there is only one party, for example a deed of gift.
(b) An *indenture*, to which there are two or more parties.

A deed does not need to be supported by consideration, and can therefore be sued to make a gratuitous promise binding. A deed *must* be used:

(a) to confer or create a legal interest in land (*see* XIX, 22);
(b) to transfer a British ship or any share in a British ship.

If a deed is not used the contract is void.

A deed is subject to a longer period of limitation (*see* IX, 11) and makes certain additional defences available:

(a) *non est factum* (*see* VIII, 6);
(b) estoppel by deed (*see* IX, 5);
(c) merger (*see* IX, 6).

4. Contracts in writing. Some contracts are required to be in writing. The consequences if they are not in writing differ.

Contracts which are *void* if not in proper written form include:

(*a*) a bill of sale (*see* XXII, **15**); and

(*b*) a hire-purchase or other regulated consumer credit agreement (*see* XII, **22**) if not in the statutory written form (*see* XII, **24**).

On the other hand there are such contracts as a bill of exchange (*see* XII, **5**), which is defined by the Bills of Exchange Act 1882, s. 3(1), as an "unconditional order in writing". If it is not in writing it still takes effect as a simple contract.

5. Contracts evidenced by writing. Some contracts are required to be evidenced in writing. If there is not sufficient evidence, then the contract will not be enforced in the courts. Examples are:

(*a*) contracts of marine insurance;

(*b*) moneylenders' contracts;

(*c*) assignments of copyright;

(*d*) contracts of guarantee (*see* **6**);

(*e*) contracts for the sale or other disposition of land (*see* **7**).

The minimum of necessary written evidence suffices: any signed note or memorandum of the material terms of the contract on any scrap of paper. It must contain:

(*a*) the *signature of the party to be charged* or his agent. The party to be charged is the party against whom an action on the contract is brought. The note need not be signed by the plaintiff.

(*b*) all *material terms* of the contract:

(*i*) names of sufficient identification of the parties;

(*ii*) description of the subject matter;

(*iii*) price or other consideration;

(*iv*) all other material terms, e.g. covenants in a lease.

The memorandum can be made *at any time* after the contract is agreed, provided it is made before the contract is disputed in court. It may consist of several separate documents, provided there is sufficient evidence to connect them beyond reasonable doubt. A letter headed "Dear Sir" could be linked to the envelope which contained it, so providing the name and address of the recipient: *Long* v. *Millar* (1879).

6. Contracts of guarantee. There is an important distinction between a guarantee and an indemnity.

(*a*) A guarantee is a contract "to answer for the debt, default, or miscarriage of another": Statute of Frauds 1677, s. 4. The primary liability is on that other; the guarantee is a contract of secondary liability.

(*b*) An indemnity is itself the assumption of a primary liability.

"If two come to a shop and one buys, and the other, to gain him credit, promises the seller, 'If he does not pay you, I will', this is a collateral undertaking. But if he says, 'Let him have the goods, I will be your paymaster', or 'I will see you paid', this is an undertaking as for himself": *Birkmeyr* v. *Darnell* (1704) *per* Holt, C.J.

The first is a guarantee; the second an indemnity.

Being a primary obligation, an indemnity does not need to be evidenced in writing. A guarantee requires a written memorandum (*see* **5**) with two exceptions.

(*a*) The consideration need not be stated in the memorandum: Mercantile Law Amendment Act 1856.

(*b*) There is no need for a memorandum where the guarantee is part of a larger transaction, for example a guarantee given by a *del credere* agent (*see* XI, **2**).

7. Contracts for the sale of land. A contract for the sale or other disposition of land or of any interest in land must be supported by a memorandum in writing: Law of Property Act 1925, s. 40. If it is not, the contract is unenforceable in court but the parties retain other rights. Thus if a deposit has been paid the court will not assist the purchaser to recover it from the vendor: *Monickendam* v. *Leanse* (1923).

The only exception to this is the doctrine of *part performance*. If A has performed his part of the contract, and B then refuses to perform his, the court will intervene to save A from hardship by ordering B to perform his side of the contract.

The court has a discretion whether to apply the doctrine of part performance and will do so when four conditions are satisfied.

(*a*) The contract is one for which damages would be inadequate and of which specific performance can be ordered (*see* XXIII, **6**).

(*b*) The act of part performance is referable to the contract alleged. X orally promised a woman to leave her his house in his will if she gave up her own house and came to keep house and care for him until his death. She did so, but paid for her own board. When he died his will made no mention of the bargain. She sought to enforce the bargain and it was held that her actions had been sufficiently clear part performance of the oral contract: *Wakeham* v. *McKenzie* (1968). The categories of act which will be regarded as constituting part performance are not closed: *Steadman* v. *Steadman* (1974).

(*c*) The act of part performance is such that it would amount to fraud on the part of the defendant to take advantage of the absence of writing. A orally agreed to rent a flat from B, who at A's request made improvements to the flat. B's action was exclusively referable to the contract alleged and A will not be allowed to refuse to take the flat: *Rawlinson* v. *Ames* (1925).

(*d*) There is sufficient oral or other evidence of the material terms of the contract: *Parker* v. *Clark* (1960).

It is important not to confuse the doctrine of part performance with the remedy of specific performance (*see* XXIII, **6**).

INTENTION TO CREATE LEGAL RELATIONS

8. Intention to create legal relations. For an agreement to be enforceable as a binding contract it must have been the intention of the parties to create legal relations. There is no exhaustive list of situations in which there is no such intention, but they mainly fall into three categories:

(*a*) *Social and domestic arrangements.* "There are agreements between parties which do not result in contracts within the meaning of that term in our law. The ordinary example is where two parties agree to take a walk together, or where there is an offer and acceptance of hospitality. Nobody would suggest in ordinary circumstances that those agreements result in what we know as a contract, and one of the most usual forms of agreement which does not constitute a contract appears to me to be the arrangements which are made between husband and wife": *Balfour* v. *Balfour* (1919) *per* Atkin L.J. This presumption may be rebutted. A husband's agreement to pay money to his wife may be a contract if the parties are separated: *Merritt* v. *Merritt* (1970). An agreement between relatives to share a house may be a contract if one party has in consequence sold her own house: *Parker* v. *Clark* (1960).

(*b*) *Intention to create legal relations expressly denied.* The presumption that a contract is intended in a commercial agreement may be expressly rebutted:

(*i*) by a clause stating that the agreement "shall not be subject to legal jurisdiction in the law courts": *Rose & Frank* v. *Crompton Bros.* (1925);

(*ii*) by the words "subject to contract" on an agreement for the sale of land: *Tiverton Estates* v. *Wearwell* (1975).

(*c*) *Collective agreements.* A collective agreement between a trade union and an employer under the Trade Union and Labour Relations Act 1974, s. 18, is not legally enforceable unless:

(*i*) it is in writing; and

(*ii*) it states that the parties intend it to be binding.

The trivial nature of an agreement is not relevant to whether it is intended to be binding: *Esso* v. *Commissioners of Customs and Excise* (1976). However, the courts tend to find the presence of consideration (*see* VI, **1**) as an indication that a legal obligation is intended.

9. Consensus ad idem. The consent of the parties is necessary for a contract to be enforceable.

The classical nineteenth-century view was that there must be a *consensus ad idem*: the minds of the parties must meet and agree. In *Cundy* v. *Lindsay* (1878) Alfred Blenkarn ordered a consignment of handkerchiefs from P. Alfred signed himself "A. Blenkarn & Co. of 37 Wood Street". P knew the respectable firm "W. Blenkiron & Sons of 123 Wood Street." Believing Alfred to be this firm, they sent the handkerchiefs to him as "Messrs. Blenkiron & Co. of 37 Wood Street." Alfred did not pay for the handkerchiefs but sold them to D. The House of Lords, as Lord Cairns L. C. observed, had "to determine as between two parties, both of whom are perfectly innocent, upon which of the two the consequences of a fraud practised upon both must fall." Lord Cairns resolved the problem by applying the consensus test. Was it in P's mind to enter into a contract with Alfred? "Of him they knew nothing, and of him they never thought. With him they never intended to deal. Their minds never, even for an instant of time, rested upon him and as between him and them there was no consensus of mind which could lead to any agreement or any contract whatever."

This approach works admirably where a man sells something

to another man. One man makes an offer; the other accepts; consideration changes hands. But in modern life contracts may arise in many other ways.

(a) *By conduct*. A contract is concluded as soon as money is put into an automatic ticket machine. "The offer is made when the proprietor of the machine holds it out as being ready to receive money. The acceptance takes place when the customer puts his money into the slot": *Thornton* v. *Shoe Lane Parking* (1971) *per* Lord Denning, M.R. There is no consensus between the proprietor and the customer.

(b) *By operation of law*. Where there is a contract for the sale of goods (*see* XII, 9) in which no price has been agreed the buyer must pay a reasonable price: Sale of Goods Act 1893, s. 8(2). This is one of many cases where the law intervenes and takes a matter out of the hands of the parties.

(c) *By inference*. A famous example is *Clarke* v. *Dunraven* (1897). The yachts *Satanita* and *Valkyrie* were entered for a race, each owner undertaking to observe the yacht club rules. The yachts collided, and the question arose whether the owners had entered in to a contract with each other. The House of Lords decided that they had. "The effect of their entering for the race, and undertaking to be bound by these rules to the knowledge of each other, is sufficient, I think to create a contractual obligation to discharge that liability": *per* Lord Herschell. The knowledge, of course, was that all competitors had undertaken to the yacht club to observe the rules; it does not follow that one competitor knew of the existence or identity of the others.

As Lord Wilberforce said recently in *The Eurymedon* (1975): "The precise analysis of this complex of relations into the classical offer and acceptance, with identifiable consideration, seems to present difficulty, but this same difficulty exists in many situations of daily life, e.g. sales at auction; supermarket purchases; boarding an omnibus; purchasing a train ticket; tenders for the supply of goods; offers of reward; acceptance by post; warranties of authority by agents; manufacturer's guarantees; gratuitous bailments; bankers' commercial credits. These are all examples which show that English law, having committed itself to a rather technical and schematic doctrine of contract, in application takes a practical approach, often at the cost of forcing the facts to fit uneasily into the marked slots of offer, acceptance and consideration."

With this warning we will now consider the classical elements of a contract:

(a) offer (see 10–12);

(b) acceptance (see 13–17);

(c) termination of offer (see 18, 19);

(d) consideration (see VI, 1–5).

THE OFFER

10. Offeror and offeree. The offer, made by the offeror to the offeree, is the statement of a willingness to be bound on certain specified terms. The offer may be oral, written or implied from conduct.

Offers are of two kinds:

(a) A *specific* offer is made to a specific offeree. No one else can accept it. "If you propose to make a contract with A, then B cannot substitute himself for A without your consent and to your disadvantage, securing to himself all the benefit of the contract": *Boulton* v. *Jones* (1857) *per* Pollock C.B.

(b) A *general* offer can be accepted by anyone, and usually without prior notification of acceptance. In *Carlill* v. *Carbolic Smoke Ball Co.* (1893) D were advertising their patent medicine in a newspaper. If anyone used it as directed for two weeks and contracted influenza the advertisement provided that D would pay £100. £1000 was deposited in a bank "showing our sincerity in the matter". P bought a smoke ball, used it as directed for two months, and then contracted influenza. Bowen L.J. found that there was:

(i) "an offer made to all the world";

(ii) "to ripen into a contract with anybody who comes forward and performs the condition"; and that

(iii) "as notification of acceptance is required for the benefit of the person who makes the offer, the person who makes the offer may dispense with notice to himself it he thinks it desirable to do so."

11. Characteristics of the offer. A valid offer has certain characteristics.

(a) *Certainty*. A promise to pay an extra £5 or to buy another horse if a horse "proves lucky to me" is too vague to amount to an offer: *Guthing* v. *Lynn* (1831).

(b) *Communication.* An offer must be communicated to the offeree before it can be accepted.

Thus if a seaman helps to navigate a ship home without informing the owners in advance he cannot insist on payment, since the owners have not had notice of his offer, and therefore no opportunity to accept or reject it: *Taylor* v. *Laird* (1856). This has raised problems in the reward cases. Suppose there is an armed robbery and the insurance company offers a reward for information leading to the conviction of the robbers. Your suspicions are aroused by the diamonds you see through the window next door. You inform the police and your neighbour is ultimately convicted. Are you entitled to the reward if you did not know that it had been offered? This also raises difficulties with counter-offers (*see* 15).

12. Statements not amounting to an offer. A preliminary statement, on analysis, may turn out not to be an offer.

(a) *Invitation to treat.* A statement which is intended to elicit an offer from someone else is called an invitation to treat: *Gibson* v. *Manchester City Council* (1979). It has no legal force: the offer it elicits can be accepted or not without obligation. There are many examples of invitations to treat.

(i) An auctioneer's request for bids: *Payne* v. *Cave* (1789). The bid itself is the offer, which can be retracted at any time until the fall of the hammer signifies the auctioneer's acceptance: Sale of Goods Act 1893, s. 58(2).

(ii) The display of goods in a shop window with prices marked on them: *Fisher* v. *Bell* (1961).

(iii) The display of priced goods in a self-service store: *Pharmaceutical Society* v. *Boots* (1952).

(iv) A catalogue or price list advertising goods for sale: *Grainger* v. *Gough* (1896).

(b) *Statement of intention.* The announcement of a forthcoming auction: *Harris* v. *Nickerson* (1873).

(c) *Communication of information in the course of negotiations.* A statement of the price at which one is prepared to consider selling a piece of land: *Harvey* v. *Facey* (1893).

THE ACCEPTANCE

13. Manner and communication of the acceptance. Subject to the following qualifications acceptance may be made in any manner provided it is communicated to the offeror.

(a) *Prescribed manner of acceptance.* "It may be that an offeror, who by the terms of his offer insists upon acceptance in a particular manner, is entitled to insist that he is not bound unless acceptance is effected or communicated in that precise way, although it seems possible that, even so, if the other party communicates his acceptance in some other way, the offeror may by conduct or otherwise waive his right to insist upon the prescribed method of acceptance": *Manchester Diocesan Council for Education* v. *Commercial & General Investments Ltd.* (1970) *per* Buckley J.

(b) *Acceptance by positive conduct.* Acceptance must be active. An offer by letter containing the words "If I hear no more, I shall consider the horse is mine" is incapable on its own of constituting its own acceptance; there must be some positive act by the offeree: *Felthouse* v. *Bindley* (1862).

A recipient of unsolicited goods may treat them as a gift unless the sender takes possession of them within a limited period: Unsolicited Goods and Services Act 1971.

(c) *Waiver of communication.* An offeror may waive the need for communication of the acceptance: *Carlill* v. *Carbolic Smoke Ball Co.* (1893) (*see* **10**).

(d) *Contracts by post.* Here acceptance is complete as soon as it is posted, provided it is properly stamped and addressed: *Household Fire Insurance Co.* v. *Grant* (1879).

In such cases therefore it does not matter if the letter of acceptance is lost in the post and never reaches the offeror: the contract is complete as soon as the letter is posted.

There are three exceptions to this rule.

(i) "If, having regard to all the circumstances, including the nature of the subject-matter under consideration, the negotiating parties cannot have intended that there should be a binding agreement until the party accepting an offer or exercising an option had in fact communicated the acceptance or exercise to the other": *Holwell Securities* v. *Hughes* (1974) *per* Lawton L.J.

(ii) An offer by telex is not accepted until notice of the

acceptance is received by the offeror: *Entores* v. *Miles Far East Corporation* (1955).

(*iii*) Mere posting is not sufficient in contracts governed by the Uniform Laws of International Sales Act 1967.

14. Contents of the acceptance. The acceptance must be un-qualified and must correspond in every detail with the terms of the offer.

Sometimes an acceptance purports to be conditional. "It appears to be well settled by the authorities that if the documents or letters relied on as constituting a contract contemplate the execution of a further contract between the parties, it is a question of construction whether the execution of the further contract is a condition or term of the bargain or whether it is a mere expression of the desire of the parties as to the manner in which the trans-action already agreed to will in fact go through. In the former case there is no enforceable contract either because the condition is unfulfilled or because the law does not recognise a contract to enter into a contract. In the latter case there is a binding contract and the reference to the more formal document may be ignored": *Hatzfeldt-Wildenburg* v. *Alexander* (1912) *per* Parker J.

Two other problems may arise:

(*a*) where the acceptance introduces new terms (*see* **15**);
(*b*) where the terms are uncertain (*see* **16**).

15. Counter offers. An acceptance which imposes new terms is a counter offer which rejects the original offer and causes it to lapse. Thus, where a house is offered for sale at £1,000 and the offeree offers £950 the offer lapses: *Hyde* v. *Wrench* (1840).

A common and striking example of counter offers is the "battle of the forms" in which two firms exchange their standard forms (*see* VII, **10**). One firm makes an offer, enclosing its standard terms. The offeree firm accepts this offer, enclosing its own stand-ard terms. The firms then perform the contract. Later a problem arises. Whose standard terms apply? Technically the offeree firm, by changing the terms, made a counter offer which was accepted by performance. However, everything seems to depend on the circumstances of each case: *Butler* v. *Ex-Cell-O* (1979).

16. Certainty of terms. It is for the parties to make their inten-tions clear in their contract. The courts will not enforce a contract the terms of which are uncertain.

Where the terms of a contract are too vague, the contract will fail for uncertainty, e.g. sale of a van "on hire-purchase terms" is too vague, since there are several varieties of hire-purchase terms: *Scammell* v. *Ouston* (1941).

An agreement which is definite on the whole will be enforced, notwithstanding the addition of some meaningless or unnecessary words or phrases. The court in such a case will ignore the meaningless words and enforce the contract without them: *Nicolene Ltd.* v. *Simmonds* (1953).

An agreement which at first sight appears to be too vague will be enforced if:

(*a*) The parties themselves have provided machinery in the contract for resolving the uncertainty, e.g. where no price was fixed for the sale of petrol, but the agreement provided that all disputes should be referred to arbitration, it was held that the arbitrator could fix the price and so resolve the uncertainty: *Foley* v. *Classique Coaches Ltd.* (1934).

(*b*) The deficiency can be remedied by the court implying a term (*see* VII, 3) either:

   (*i*) from the course of dealing between the parties in the past;

   (*ii*) from trade usages; or

   (*iii*) where certain terms are implied by statute in similar contracts, e.g. the Sale of Goods Act 1893.

17. Tenders and standing offers. A tender is a form of offer for the supply of goods or services, usually made in response to a request for tenders from several possible suppliers.

Tenders take the following forms.

(*a*) *Single offer*, e.g. a tender to build a factory. Acceptance of such a tender constitutes a contract.

(*b*) *Standing offer*, e.g. a tender to supply goods as and when required. Here the tenderer must supply as and when agreed, whenever an order is made. But he cannot insist on any orders being made at all.

EXAMPLE: P tendered to supply goods up to a certain amount to the L.C.C. over a certain period. The L.C.C.'s orders did not come up to the amount expected and P sued for breach of contract. HELD: Each order made a separate contract and P was bound to fulfil the orders made, but there was no obligation to make any orders at all: *Percival Ltd.* v. *L.C.C.* (1918).

(c) *Sole supplier*. The person seeking the tender may agree to take all his requirements for certain goods from the tenderer. This agreement does not oblige him to make any orders at all, but if he does require goods within the category agreed he must take them from the tenderer: *Kier* v. *Whitehead Iron Co.* (1938).

TERMINATION OF OFFER

18. Lapse of offer. An offer lapses:

(a) if either offeror or offeree dies before acceptance: *Kennedy* v. *Thomassen* (1929).

But the death of the offeror may not invalidate subsequent acceptance provided:

(i) the offeree did not know of the death when he accepted; and

(ii) the personality of the offeror is not vital to the contract: *Bradbury* v. *Morgan* (1862).

(b) if it is not accepted within:

(i) the specified time (if any); or

(ii) a reasonable time, if none is specified.

What is a reasonable time depends on the facts. Five months has been held to be an unreasonable delay in accepting an offer to take shares in a company: *Ramsgate Victoria Hotel Co.* v. *Montefiore* (1866).

(c) if the offeree does not make a valid acceptance, e.g. makes a counter offer (*see* **15**) or conditional acceptance (*see* **14**).

(d) if the offer is subject to the fulfilment of a condition and that condition is not fulfilled, e.g. an offer to buy a car provided it is in working order: *Financings Ltd.* v. *Stimson* (1962).

An offer to keep an offer open for a specified time (an option) is not binding unless:

(i) made under seal, or

(ii) supported by valuable consideration like any other simple contract: *Routledge* v. *Grant* (1828).

19. Revocation. An offer may be revoked at any time before acceptance.

(a) Revocation must be communicated. Until the offeree actually received the revocation, he is entitled to accept: *Byrne* v. *Van Tienhoven* (1880).

(b) Indirect communication. If the offeree learns of the revocation he cannot later accept, even though he hears of it only indirectly, e.g. where a prospective purchaser of land learned through a reliable third party that the offeror had already agreed to sell the land to another offeree: *Dickinson* v. *Dodds* (1876).

In the case of a unilateral or general contract (*see* **10**(*b*)) it seems that "once the offeree has embarked on performance it is too late for the offeror to revoke his offer": *Daulia* v. *Four Millbank Nominees* (1978) *per* Goff L.J.

PROGRESS TEST 5

1. What contracts require to be made by deed, and which must be wholly written? **(3, 4)**

2. What contracts are unenforceable unless evidenced in writing? What is meant by "unenforceable" and "evidenced" in this context? **(5)**

3. What is a contract of guarantee and how does it differ from an indemnity contract? **(6)**

4. What must be contained in the note or memorandum of a contract covered by the Statute of Frauds, and when may such a note or memorandum be made? **(5, 6)**

5. Explain the doctrine of part performance, and give examples of its operation. **(7)**

6. When is a contract unenforceable for want of an intention to create legal relations? **(8)**

7. Distinguish between a general and specific offer. **(10)**

8. Distinguish an offer from:

(*a*) an invitation to treat;
(*b*) a statement of intention. **(12)**

9. Apply the rules of offer and acceptance to the following situations:

(*a*) bidding at an auction;
(*b*) putting a coin into a slot machine;
(*c*) display of goods in a shop window with the price marked;
(*d*) prices marked on goods in a catalogue. **(9, 12)**

10. In what circumstances does an offer lapse? **(18)**

11. How may an offer be revoked? **(19)**

12. What is a counter offer? What is the effect of the phrase "subject to contract" in a written agreement? **(8, 15)**

13. Comment on the statement that there cannot be a contract to make a contract. **(14)**

14. When, if ever, can communication of acceptance be dispensed with? **(13)**

15. What forms are commonly taken by tenders? **(17)**

16. A borrowed £1,000 from B for use in his business, and said that if business was good he would repay £12,000 in a month's time. He had a very profitable month, but refuses to honour his promise. Can B enforce it? **(11)**

17. A telephoned B offering to buy B's car for £500. B said he would consider the offer, and the next day telephoned A to accept the offer, but there was no reply. B therefore posted a letter of acceptance. Before receiving B's letter, A posted a letter revoking the offer. The letters crossed in the post. Is there a contract? **(11, 13)**

18. Under a heading "Articles for Sale" in a newspaper, A advertised as follows: "Nearly new Mini, good condition, £500" and his name and address. B saw the advertisement and sent a cheque for £500, saying in his letter, "If I don't hear to the contrary I shall assume the car is mine and will collect it tomorrow". Is there a contract? **(10, 13, 18)**

CHAPTER VI

Consideration, Privity and Capacity

CONSIDERATION

1. Meaning of valuable consideration. The courts will not enforce a simple contract unless it is supported by valuable consideration.

The classic definitions of consideration are in terms of benefit and detriment. "A valuable consideration may consist either in some right, interest, profit or benefit accruing to one party, or some forbearance, detriment, loss or responsibility given, suffered or undertaken by the other": *Currie* v. *Misa* (1875) *per* Lush J.

It is easier to think of the consideration as the price paid for the contract. It means the element of exchange in a bargain, and in order to satisfy the requirement of English law it must be valuable, i.e. something which is capable of being valued in terms of money or money's worth, however slight.

An interesting example is *Chappell* v. *Nestlé* (1960). As an advertising gimmick, D offered a record of the tune "Rockin' Shoes" to any member of the public who sent them 3 chocolate wrappers and 1s 6d (7½p). D threw the wrappers away. Under the Copyright Act 1956, s. 8, D was required to pay P, as copyright owner, a royalty of 6¼ per cent "of the ordinary retail selling price." Were the wrappers part of this selling price? By a bare majority the House of Lords decided that they were. The wrappers were part of the consideration. "It is said that when received the wrappers are of no value to Nestle's. This I would have thought irrelevant. A contracting party can stipulate for what consideration he chooses. A peppercorn does not cease to be good consideration if it is established that the promisee does not like pepper and will throw away the corn. As the whole object of selling the record was to increase the sales of chocolate, it seems to me wrong not to treat the stipulated evidence of such sales as part of the consideration": *per* Lord Somervell of Harrow.

Consideration is of two kinds.

(*a*) *Executed* consideration, i.e. where the act constituting the consideration is wholly performed.

(*b*) *Executory* consideration, i.e. where the consideration consist of a promise to do something in the future.

Thus, if X pays a shop-keeper now for goods which are to be delivered later, X is giving executed consideration and the shop-keeper is giving executory consideration, i.e. a promise to be executed in the future.

2. Adequacy of consideration. Consideration must be real. That is it must not be vague, indefinite or illusory, e.g. a son's vague promise to "stop being a nuisance" to his father: *White* v. *Bluett* (1853).

But although the consideration must be real, it need not be adequate, i.e. it is up to the parties to fix their own prices, and providing there is some definite valuable consideration the court will not set a contract aside merely because the price fixed is inadequate: *Haigh* v. *Brooks* (1839).

"The adequacy of the consideration is for the parties to consider at the time of making the agreement, not for the court when it is going to be enforced": *Bolton* v. *Madden* (1873) *per* Blackburn J.

But a ridiculously inadequate consideration may be prima facie evidence of misrepresentation or coercion (*see* VIII, 7–11, 13).

3. Characteristics of consideration.

(*a*) *Consideration must be legal* (*see* VIII: 14).

(*b*) *Consideration must move from the promisee.* There are two rules which are similar but which can be distinguished as they were by Lord Haldane in *Dunlop* v. *Selfridge* (1915):

(*i*) "Only a person who is a party to a contract can sue on it." This is the doctrine of privity (*see* 6).

(*ii*) "If a person with whom a contract not under seal has been made is to be able to enforce it consideration must have been given by him to the promisor or to some other person at the promisor's request." This is the rule that consideration must move from the promisee.

In many cases the two rules lead to the same result. *Dunlop* v. *Selfridge* (1915) is an example. D supplied goods to a wholesaler X. In return for supplied goods X promised not to resell the goods below the price fixed by D. X resold the goods to S on the same terms, but S retailed them below the fixed price. Certainly

X could have sued S for breach of contract. However, D sued S. There were two objections to this.

(*i*) There was no contract between D and S, and S were not privy to the contract between D and X.

(*ii*) S had promised not to resell the goods below the fixed price. But this promise was made to X. D had not given consideration and could not enforce S's promise.

(*c*) *Consideration must be something beyond the promisee's existing obligation to the promisor.*

That is, the promisee must have undertaken to do something, for the person whose promise he is seeking to enforce, beyond what he was already bound to do either:

(*i*) as part of his public duty as a citizen; or

(*ii*) as part of any private contractual duty owed to the promisor.

Thus, if a seaman deserts his ship—so breaking his contract—and is induced to return to his duty only by a promise of extra wages, he cannot sue for the additional sum, since he has only done what he had already contracted to do: *Stilk* v. *Myrick* (1809), which was considered and followed as recently as *North Ocean Shipping* v. *Hyundai* (1978) (*see* VIII, 12). A special version of this is the rule in *Foakes* v. *Beer* (1884) (*see* 4).

There is also the question of an existing obligation owed to a third party. The old authority on this was accepted by the Privy Council in *The Eurymedon* (1975) (*see* 6). Lord Wilberforce, delivering the majority opinion, said "An agreement to do an act which the promisor is under an existing obligation to a third party to do, may quite well amount to valid consideration and does so in the present case: the promisee obtains the benefit of a direct obligation which he can enforce".

(*d*) *Consideration must not be past.* That is, a promise made in return for some past service is unenforceable, e.g. where, having bought a horse, the purchaser promised to give the seller an extra sum if the horse proved satisfactory:

HELD—the promise was unenforceable since it related to a past sale already completed: *Roscorla* v. *Thomas* (1842).

EXCEPTIONS: Past consideration is sufficient in the following cases:

(*i*) To revive a statute-barred claim, a mere written acknowledgment is enough without any fresh consideration: Limitation Act 1939. (For limitation of claims generally, *see* IX, 11.)

(*ii*) A bill of exchange can be supported by an antecedent debt or other past liability: Bills of Exchange Act 1882, s. 27.

(*iii*) Where the past consideration was rendered in response to an earlier request: the Rule in *Lampleigh* v. *Braithwaite* (1615). Here the promisor's earlier request is held to imply a promise to pay a reasonable sum later, and the subsequent promise to pay merely fixes the sum to be paid: *Stewart* v. *Casey* (1892).

Thus, where A asked B to use his influence with the king to obtain for A a royal pardon for a crime, and B did as he was asked so that A in gratitude subsequently promised to pay him £100, it was HELD that B could enforce the promise: *Lampleigh* v. *Braithwaite* (1615).

4. The rule in Foakes v. Beer, The case of *Foakes* v. *Beer* (1884) concerned a judgment debt. B had obtained judgment against F for £2,000. The parties agreed that F should pay £500 at once and the balance in instalments and this was done. B then claimed interest, on the basis that the agreement to accept a bare £2,000 was unsupported by consideration. The House of Lords accepted this, relying on *Pinnel's Case* (1602) where Brian C.J. said that "payment of a lesser sum on the day in satisfaction of a greater cannot be any satisfaction for the whole".

Thus the rule in *Foakes* v. *Beer* is that payment of a smaller sum will not discharge liability to pay a larger. If A owes B £100 and B agrees to accept £50 in complete discharge of the debt, there is nothing to stop B later changing his mind and suing for the remaining £50.

5. Exceptions to the rule in Foakes v. Beer. Contractual rights can be abandoned or *waived*. A right which is waived without consideration can again be enforced on giving proper notice: *Banning* v. *Wright* (1972). In two cases the waiver is binding and operates as an exception to the rule in *Foakes* v. *Beer* (1884).

(*a*) *Accord and satisfaction.* This exception, like the rule, dates back to Brian C.J. in *Pinnel's Case* (1602), who went on to say: "But the gift of a horse, hawk or robe, etc, in satisfaction is good. For it shall be intended that a horse, hawk, or robe, etc. might be more beneficial to the plaintiff than the money in respect of some circumstance, or otherwise the plaintiff would not have accepted it in satisfaction."

The modern definition is by Scrutton L.J. in *British Russian Gazette* v. *Associated Newspapers* (1933): "Accord and satisfaction is the purchase of a release from an obligation, whether arising under contract or tort, by means of any valuable consideration, not being the actual performance of the obligation itself. The accord is the agreement by which the obligation is discharged. The satisfaction is the consideration which makes the agreement operative".

(b) *Promissory estoppel.* Estoppel is a rule of pleading and evidence, a device by which the court decides to estop someone from saying in court something which he would be entitled to say if the court did not prevent him. The only form of estoppel of real importance today is equitable estoppel.

Promissory estoppel is an estoppel which is raised by four circumstances.

(*i*) There is a pre-existing legal relationship between the parties.

(*ii*) The plaintiff deliberately waived his legal rights against the defendant.

(*iii*) The defendant gave no consideration for the waiver.

(*iv*) The defendant altered his position in reliance on the waiver, so that it would be inequitable to allow the plaintiff to capitalise on the lack of consideration.

This is illustrated by: the *High Trees Case* (*Central London Property Trust* v. *High Trees House*) (1947).

A let property to B at a rent of £2,500 p.a., but agreed to accept half this sum during the war years, and B relied on his promise, making no attempt to raise the full rent. If later A went back on his promise and sued for the full amount owing during the war years the court would exercise its equitable discretion and estop A from retracting his promise.

Two points should be noted.

(*i*) A promisor can withdraw his promise on giving reasonable notice provided the promisee is able to resume his position.

(*ii*) Promissory estoppel is "a shield and not a sword".

W divorced H, and before the divorce became absolute, H promised to pay £100 p.a. by way of maintenance. He failed to honour this agreement, and W sued him, relying on equitable estoppel to remedy the lack of consideration. HELD: The doctrine did not create a new cause of action, and consideration was still necessary. Equitable estoppel could be used only as a defence at the descretion of the court: *Combe* v. *Combe* (1951).

PRIVITY

6. The doctrine of privity. A contract is a private relationship between the parties who make it, and no other person can acquire rights or incur liabilities under it.

Compare this doctrine with the separate rule that "consideration must move from the promisee" (*see* 3(*b*)). The two rules together mean that a person seeking to sue upon a contract must satisfy the court:

(*a*) that he is a party to the contract; and

(*b*) that he has given consideration for the promise he seeks to enforce (or that the contract is under seal) (*see* **1**).

Contrast a legal duty with a contractual duty. A legal duty is one which, if not performed, can be sued upon by any person injured thereby: actions for tort are actions for breach of this kind of duty. A contractual duty is one which is owed only to the other party to the contract, and only that party can sue to enforce it.

The doctrine of privity has two aspects (*see* **7**).

(*a*) No one can acquire rights under a contract to which he is not a party.

(*b*) No one can incur liabilities under a contract to which he is not a party.

EXAMPLE: B sold his business to C on condition that C should pay (i) £6.50 per week to B for life, and (ii) £5 per week for life to Mrs. B after B's death. B died and C refused to pay Mrs. B, since she was not a party to the contract. HELD: (1) Mrs. B was not party to the contract and could not personally enforce it, but (2) as administratrix of her late husband's estate she could enforce the contract, on behalf of the estate: *Beswick* v. *Beswick* (1968).

In the area of mercantile law we will find two fundamental exceptions to the doctrine of privity.

(*a*) Assignment (*see* XII, **1**).

(*b*) Agency (*see* XI).

The position of agency and privity has been discussed in two major cases.

(*a*) *Scruttons* v. *Midlands Silicones* (1962). A shipping company P agreed to carry a drum of chemicals belonging to Q across the Atlantic. The bill of lading limited the liability of "the carrier" to $500. In London P employed stevedores R to unload the drum. R negligently dropped the drum causing damage in excess of $500. The House of Lords decided that R could not rely on the bill of lading. There was nothing to indicate that P was contracting on behalf of R or that the bill of lading was intended to benefit R.

(b) *The Eurymedon* (1975). In this case the Privy Council considered the application to very similar facts of a very different bill of lading. The exemption from liability was for the benefit of the carrier and of "all persons who are or might be his agents from time to time (including independent contractors)". The stevedores were independent contractors (*see* XIV, **17**) and a majority of the Privy Council held that "the exemption is designed to cover the whole carriage, from loading to discharge, by whomsoever it is performed". Lord Wilberforce analysed the transaction: "the bill of lading brought into existence a bargain initially unilateral, but capable of becoming mutual, between the shippers and the stevedore, made through the carrier as agent. This became a full contract when the stevedore performed services by discharging the goods. The performance of these services for the benefit of the shipper was the consideration for the agreement by the shipper that the stevedore should have the benefit of the exemptions and limitations contained in the bill of lading". Lord Simon of Glaisdale's dissenting opinion should also be read for its interesting analysis.

7. Acquisition of rights and liabilities.

(a) *Rights*. If A and B make a contract whereby B is to pay A to do something for X, X cannot sue A if he fails to do what he promised. X cannot sue even if:

(i) he has given consideration: *Price* v. *Easton* (1820);

(ii) he is closely related to the promisee: *Tweddle* v. *Atkinson* (1861).

Apart from assignment and agency (*see* **6**) there are exceptions to this rule.

(i) *Constructive trust*. Where B is regarded as a trustee for X, X may sue A (and join B as co-defendant) if the contract is broken.

This is a constructive trust (*see* XXIII, **20**). However, it has been said that "unless an intention to create a trust is clearly to be collected from the language used and the circumstances of the case, I think that the court ought not to be astute to discover indications of such an intention": *Re Schebsman* (1944) *per* Du Parcq L.J. A constructive trust is rarely found.

(*ii*) *Statutory exceptions.* There are limited statutory exceptions to the doctrine of privity in connection with price maintenance, insurance and covenants over land.

(*iii*) *Third party joined in proceedings.* In *Snelling* v. *J. A. Snelling Ltd.* (1972) X, Y and Z were brothers and were co-directors of a family company. They agreed that if any one of them resigned he would forfeit all money due to him from the company. X resigned and brought an action against the company for money due to him. Ormrod J. said that "in a case such as this where the promisees under the agreement and the party to be benefited by the agreement are all before the court and the promisees have succeeded against the plaintiff on their counter-claim, the right view is that the plaintiff's claim should be dismissed".

(*b*) *Liabilities.* A contract between A and B cannot impose liabilities on X. The two major exceptions to this are the following.

(*i*) Sale of Ships. If X buys a ship from B which has previously been chartered by A he may be bound by the charter party if he has notice of its terms: *Strathcona S.S.* Case (1926)

(*ii*) Restrictive covenants affecting land. These may run with the land, i.e. X may be bound by a covenant in favour of A attaching to land which X purchases from B (*see* XXI, **14**).

CAPACITY

8. Capacity. These are certain special rules relating to capacity to contract.

(*a*) *Aliens.* They have full capacity, save that they cannot own or hold shares in British ships.

Aliens resident in countries at war with Britain are classed as enemy aliens. They cannot sue in British courts during war-time, but can be sued, and if sued they can defend the action, appeal, and lodge counter claims in the normal way, either personally or through agents: *Porter* v. *Freudenberg* (1916).

(*b*) *Foreign sovereigns and diplomats.* They have diplomatic immunity and cannot be sued in British courts, unless they voluntarily submit to the jurisdiction.

(*c*) *Mentally disordered persons.* These are persons within the

Mental Health Act 1959, s. 4. A contract is valid unless the person can prove:

(*i*) that he was so insane as not to understand what the contract was about; and

(*ii*) that the other party was aware of this: *Imperial Loan Co.* v. *Stone* (1892).

Mentally disordered persons are subject to the Sale of Goods Act 1893 s. 2 (*see* 10).

(*d*) *Drunken persons*. These seem to be subject to the same rules as mentally disordered persons: *Gore* v. *Gibson* (1845). They are also subject to the Sale of Goods Act 1893 s. 2 (*see* 10).

(*e*) *Corporations* (*see* 9).

(*f*) *Minors* (*see* 10).

9. Corporations. These can make any contracts within the powers granted to them at the time of their incorporation or later.

The powers of a statutory company are generally stated in the Act of Parliament which created the company. Those of a registered company are implied in its memorandum of association, which states the object for which the company is formed; a registered company has such powers as are reasonably necessary to enable it to achieve its objects.

If a corporation acts beyond its powers (*ultra vires*) the contract is void. If a contract is *ultra vires* a corporation, it cannot be ratified in any circumstances, even if all the members unanimously vote to ratify it, or to change the objects clause of the memorandum of association to prevent such contracts being *ultra vires*: *Ashbury Carriage Co.* v. *Riche* (1875). (Such a change in the memorandum may be effective for future contracts, but cannot influence the validity of contracts already made.)

In a registered company the articles of association generally fix the limits of the directors' powers. If the directors exceed the powers granted to them by the articles, but what they do is still within the wider powers of the company as a whole, the company can ratify their *ultra vires* act if it so pleases.

10. Minors. An infant or minor attains his majority at the first instant of his eighteenth birthday.

Minors' contracts are roughly divisible into three classes: binding, voidable and void.

(*a*) *Contracts binding on minors.*

(*i*) Executed contracts for "necessaries", i.e. goods and

services necessary to maintain the minor in the style to which he is accustomed, having regard to his social position. A married minor may be liable for necessaries supplied to his wife and children and for funeral and legal expenses, etc.

GOODS: An infant must pay (1) a reasonable price for goods (2) suitable to the condition in life of the infant and (3) to his actual requirements at the time of (4) sale, and (5) delivery: Sale of Goods Act 1893, s. 2. Thus if an infant orders eleven fancy waistcoats he cannot be made to pay for them, since so many cannot be suitable to actual requirements, though one or two might be: *Nash* v. *Inman* (1908). (There is no liability for undelivered goods.)

(*ii*) Beneficial contracts of service, i.e. contracts of benefit to the minor in his education or training for a career, such as apprenticeships. Such contracts are binding even if they contain one or two burdensome terms, provided they are on the whole beneficial.

A contract signed by an infant boxer, which was intended to protect him from exploitation during his infancy, contained a clause by which he was to forfeit his pay for a fight if disqualified for fouling. HELD: This clause was burdensome but was binding since the contract as a whole was beneficial: *Doyle* v. *White City Stadium* (1935).

C contracted with a publisher to publish his autobiography, since his wife and child needed money. Later C tried to avoid the contract. HELD: It was binding, as beneficial in earning C a livelihood: *Chaplin* v. *Leslie Frewin (Publishers) Ltd.* (1966).

(*b*) *Contracts voidable by a minor.* Contracts requiring express repudiation are those involving a continuing interest in property of a permanent nature. Such a contract becomes binding when the infant is eighteen unless he expressly repudiates it before or within a reasonable time after reaching eighteen, e.g. leases, contracts to take shares in a company, partnerships, and some marriage settlements.

In a lease a minor must pay agreed rent until he disclaims the lease, and may be unable to disclaim unless he does so before or within a reasonable time after his eighteenth birthday: *Davies* v. *Benyon-Harris* (1931).

(*c*) *Contracts void against minors.* The following are absolutely void against a minor.

(*i*) Contracts for repayment of money lent or to be lent.

(*ii*) Contracts for goods supplied or to be supplied (other than necessaries).

(*iii*) All accounts stated, e.g. IOUs and other admissions of indebtedness: Infants Relief Act 1874, s. 1.

The Betting and Loans (Infants) Act 1892, makes void any promise made by a person after he comes of full age to pay a loan contracted during minority.

NOTE ALSO:

(*a*) A minor incurs no liability by signing a bill of exchange, such as a cheque, as drawer, endorser, or acceptor: Bills of Exchange Act 1882, s. 22.

(*b*) If a minor fraudulently obtains goods under a void contract he must return them, but he cannot be made to pay for them: *Leslie* v. *Sheill* (1914).

(*c*) A minor can only recover money or property he has transferred under a void contract if he has received no benefit under the contract: *Valentini* v. *Canali* (1889).

(*d*) If an adult guarantees a loan made to a minor, the guarantee is void as well as the contract of loan: *Coutts* v. *Browne-Lecky* (1947).

(*e*) If a minor borrows money to buy necessaries he must repay the loan, as the lender is placed in the position of the seller of the necessaries, i.e. is "subrogated" into the position of the seller.

PROGRESS TEST 6

1. What is meant by valuable consideration? **(1)**

2. What is meant by saying that consideration must move from the promisee? **(3)**

3. What is meant by saying that consideration must be real but need not be adequate? **(2)**

4. What is past consideration and when, if ever, will it suffice to support a simple contract? **(3)**

5. State the rule in *Foakes* v. *Beer* (1884) and mention any exceptions to it. **(4, 5)**

6. State the rules governing promissory estoppel, and explain why it is "a shield and not a sword". **(5)**

7. Explain the doctrine of privity of contract. **(6)**

8. Summarise the exceptions to the doctrine of privity of contract. **(7)**

9. When, if ever, will the contracts of an insane person be enforceable? (8)

10. What types of corporation are covered by the *ultra vires* doctrine, and what is the effect of an *ultra vires* contract? (9)

11. What is an infant? How, if at all, does an infant differ from a minor? What contracts are binding on infants? (10)

12. A minor is bound by executed contracts for necessaries. What is meant by necessaries here? Must the minor pay the full price asked? (10)

13. What contracts are (a) void, and (b) voidable against a minor. (10)

14. A orally promises to leave his house to B by will if B would go and live with him and look after him till he died. B did so, but after some years A ejected B and refused to honour his promise to make a will in B's favour. Consider. (5)

15. A orally promises to sell his house Blackacre to B for £5,000. B then gave A a cheque for £500, and on the back of the cheque wrote: "10 per cent deposit for freehold of Blackacre, vacant possession on completion." He asked A to sign the back of the cheque under the words he had written, which A did. A has now had a better offer for the house, wishes to return B's £500 and refuses to go ahead with the sale to B. Is there a binding contract? (1)

16. A asked B, a police constable, to keep an eye on A's house while he was on holiday promising him £5 if he did so. The house was on B's beat, and he agreed. When A returned he refused to give B the £5. Can B enforce the promise? (3)

17. A's car broke down when he was in a hurry to reach an important meeting. B was passing in his car and offered to help. A said: "Take me to the Savoy, and I shall be most grateful." B took him to the Savoy, and A then said: "As soon as I get home I'll send you a cheque for £100." He has not done so, and B wishes to know if he can enforce the promise. Advise B. (1, 3)

18. A owed B £1,000, which he was paying by yearly instalments of £100. A's mother was taken ill, and A asked B to forgo the final instalment, so that he could take his mother on holiday to Spain. B agreed. Later B changed his mind and sued A for the £100. Will he succeed? (5)

19. A, a minor, has just got engaged to X. He persuaded B, a jeweller, to let him have an engagement ring worth £100 for a deposit of £10. The engagement has now been broken, X has

not returned the ring to A, and A refuses to pay B the remaining £90. Advise B.

Would it make any difference to your answer if B had not yet delivered the ring? (10)

20. A, an adult, lent £100 to B, a minor, to buy necessary food and clothing, and B spent the money as agreed. B failed to repay the loan, and A wishes to know what action to take. Advise A.

What difference would it make to your answer if A were the minor, and B the adult? (10)

21. A, a minor, promised to marry B, an adult, and as a future home leased a flat for three years. Two months later A became eighteen. Just before his eighteenth birthday he broke off his engagement to B, but six months later he again promised to marry her, provided she paid the six months rent he owed on the flat. She did so, but A has again refused to marry her. There is a further three months rent owing on the flat. Advise B and also A's landlord. (10)

CHAPTER VII

The Terms of a Contract

GENERAL CONSIDERATIONS

1. The contents of a contract. There are three aspects of the contents of a contract which we need to consider.

(*a*) *What are the terms?* A contract is a bargain between the parties. The contents of the contract are therefore principally *express terms*: what the parties agreed orally or in writing (*see* **2**). In strictly limited circumstances the courts are prepared to *imply* terms (*see* **3**).

(*b*) *What is the status of those terms?* Obviously not all terms are of equal importance. If you buy a car and find that it does not have, as advertised, a radio, then the seller is in breach of a term. It is not a very important term, and you will be satisfied if the seller gives you money with which to buy a radio. If you buy a car and find there is no engine then a far more important term is in breach. It may be that money will not be enough: you will want to repudiate the contract altogether. The more important terms of a contract are called *conditions* (*see* **4**); less important terms are called *warranties* (*see* **4**). Where the importance of a term is not apparent until it is in breach, then the term is called *innominate* (*see* **6**).

(*c*) *When do those terms come into effect?* Sometimes a term operates to suspend or terminate the contract. The term is then called a *condition precedent* or a *condition subsequent* (*see* **7**).

2. Express terms. As we have already seen (*see* V, **2**) the terms of a contract may be:

(*a*) wholly oral;
(*b*) wholly in writing; or
(*c*) partly oral and partly in writing.

(*a*) *Terms wholly oral.* This presents a pure question of fact. What did the parties actually say?

(b) *Terms wholly in writing*. A contract which is wholly in writing is subject to the *parol evidence rule*. The rule is this: "if there be a contract which has been reduced into writing, verbal evidence is not allowed to be given of what passed between the parties, either before the written instrument was made, or during the time that it was in a state of preparation, so as to add to or subtract from, or in any manner to vary or qualify the written contract": *Goss* v. *Lord Nugent* (1833) *per* Lord Denman. The parol evidence rule applies only to the express terms of the contract. It does not apply, for example, to:

(*i*) the validity of the contract (whether there was a mistake, misrepresentation or absence of consideration);

(*ii*) implied terms (*see* 3);

(*iii*) construction of ambiguities (*see* 8);

(*iv*) rectification (*see* 9).

(c) *Terms partly oral and partly in writing*. Sometimes the actual agreement may be oral, for example an agreement to buy a ticket, but it may be subject to a set of written standard terms (*see* 10). In *Mendelssohn* v. *Normand* (1970), P left his car in D's garage. He was told by an attendant not to lock the car, so he gave the keys to the attendant, who agreed to lock the car when he had moved it. The attendant gave P a ticket. The ticket exempted D from liability for any loss or damage however caused. Later P found that his luggage was stolen. The Court of Appeal HELD: as Phillimore L. J. put it, that "if one has an express undertaking, as here, followed by printed clauses, the latter must fail in so far as they are repugnant to the express undertaking".

3. **Implied terms.** The general rule is that the parties are presumed to have expressed their intentions fully. "An unexpressed term can be implied if and only if the court finds that the parties must have intended that term to form part of their contract. It is not enough for the court to find that such a term would have been adopted by the parties as reasonable men if it had been suggested to them. It must have been a term that went without saying, a term necessary to give business efficacy to the contract, a term which although tacit, formed part of the contract which the parties made for themselves": *Trollope & Colls* v. *N. W. Metropolitan Regional Hospital Board* (1973) *per* Lord Pearson.

There are three situations in which the courts will imply terms into contracts.

(*a*) To give effect to the *clear intentions* of the parties.

(*b*) Where *custom or statute* requires it. Examples are found in the Sale of Goods Act 1893 (*see* XII, **11**).

(*c*) Where, in certain circumstances, it is necessary to give *business efficacy* to the contract: *The Moorcock* (1889).

Lord Denning, M. R., has recently suggested that a term should be implied where this would be reasonable as well as where it is necessary. However, the House of Lords has rejected this idea and restated the traditional position in *Liverpool City Council* v. *Irwin* (1976), a case which discussed the obligations of local authority landlords towards their tenants in high rise or multi-storey dwellings. The issue was whether there was an implied term that the council should maintain the stairs, lifts and other common parts of the tower block in question. The decision that they should was because stairs, lifts and lights were "essentials of the tenancy, without which life in the dwellings, as a tenant, is not possible". As Lord Wilberforce stated the test, "such obligation should be read into the contract as the nature of the contract implicitly requires, no more, no less; a test in other words of necessity".

4. Conditions and warranties. As we have seen (*see* 1(*b*)), the difference between a condition and a warranty is apparent on breach. The distinction is illustrated by two operatic cases reported in 1876.

(*a*) In *Poussard* v. *Spiers and Pond* (1876) a lady was engaged to perform in an opera from the first night. She fell ill and the producer was forced to employ a substitute. Although she recovered after ten days the uncertainty entitled the producer to repudiate the contract. "Failure on the plaintiff's part went to the root of the matter and discharged the defendants": *per* Blackburn J.

(*b*) In *Bettini* v. *Gye* (1876) a singer fell ill, but only missed part of the rehearsals and recovered in good time for the performance. This did not go to the root of the matter: it was only a breach of warranty giving rise to damages.

The breach of a condition gives the innocent party a choice.

(*a*) He can repudiate the contract. He is then free from his own future obligations and he can recover damages to compensate him for any obligations he has already performed. This is discharge by breach (*see* IX, **9**).

(*b*) He can affirm the contract and recover damages to compensate him for the breach.

The breach of a warranty only entitles the innocent party to damages: he does not have the choice of repudiation.

How do we know whether a term is a condition or a warranty? Use of the word condition is not decisive: *Schuler* v. *Wickman Machine Tool Sales* (1974). Nor is use of the word warranty: Sale of Goods Act 1893, s. 11(1) (*b*). Sometimes a statute tells us which terms are conditions and which warranties. The Sale of Goods Act 1893, ss. 10–15 sets out the conditions and warranties implied in a contract for the sale of goods (*see* XII, **11**), but this does not cover all the terms in a contract for the sale of goods, nor does it apply to other types of contract. The law was discussed by the Court of Appeal in *The Hansa Nord* (1976). Two approaches have been followed in recent cases. The courts have looked at;

(*a*) the status of the term at the time when the contract was made (*see* **5**); and

(*b*) the consequences of the breach (*see* **6**).

5. Conditions. The traditional approach of distinguishing the important terms as conditions at the time when the contract was made was used in *The Mihalis Angelos* (1970). This was a shipping case in which the Court of Appeal had to decide the status of the term "expected ready to load" in a charterparty. The shipowner undertook that he expected his ship to be ready to load by about a certain date. It was not ready, and the question was whether the charterer could repudiate the contract. The Court of Appeal decided that the term in question was a condition and the charterer could repudiate, even though he could not establish that the breach had produced serious consequences. Megaw L.J. gave several reasons for this approach.

(*a*) *Certainty*. There are obvious advantages in a predictable and uniform "legal categorisation of a particular, definable type of contractual clause in common use".

(*b*) *Justice*. "If a shipowner has chosen to assert contractually, but dishonestly or without reasonable grounds, that he expects his vessel to be ready to load on such and such a date, wherein does the grievance lie?"

(*c*) *Consistency* with decisions on similar clauses contained in analogous documents.

This approach is useful in unilateral contracts. A unilateral contract is one in which one party's obligation only arises if the other party does something. The newsagent is only obliged to give me a newspaper if I give him the money first. "The commonest contracts of this kind in English law are options for good consideration to buy or to sell or to grant or take a lease, competitions for prizes, and such contracts as that discussed in *Carlill* v. *Carbolic Smoke Ball Co.*" (*see* V, **10**): *United Dominions Trust* v. *Eagle* (1968) *per* Diplock L.J. Since there is no obligation to do anything in a unilateral contract, the courts will not look at the consequences of breach. The status of the obligations in a unilateral contract is defined at the time the contract is made.

6. Innominate terms. Many contracts are not unilateral. They are, to use Lord Diplock's term, synallagmatic. A synallagmatic contract is one in which "each party undertakes to the other to do or to refrain from doing something, and in the event of his failure to perform his undertaking, the law provides the other party with a remedy. The remedy of the other party may be limited to recovering monetary compensation for any loss which he has sustained as a result of the failure, without relieving him from his own obligation to do that which he himself has undertaken to do and has not yet done or to continue to refrain from doing that which he himself has undertaken to refrain from doing. Or it may, in addition, entitle him, if he so elects to be released from any further obligation to do or to refrain from doing anything": *United Dominions Trust* v. *Eagle* (1968) *per* Diplock L.J.

At the time when the contract is made it is not clear which the law will do. The terms of the contract are *innominate*: that is, their status is not known until the consequences of the breach are apparent. The breach will justify repudiation if the effect of it is to "deprive the party who has further undertakings still to perform of substantially the whole benefit which it was the intention of the parties as expressed in the contract that he should obtain as the consideration for performing those undertakings": *Hong Kong Fir Shipping Co.* v. *Kawasaki Kisen Kaisha* (1962) *per* Diplock L.J.

Some criticism of the stricter rules relative to the sale of goods (*see* **4**) has been expressed in *The Hansa Nord* (1976) and by the House of Lords in *Reardon-Smith Line* v. *Hansen-Tangen* (1976). In the latter case Lord Wilberforce, also speaking for other law lords, said that "The general law of contract has developed along much more rational lines (e.g. *Hong Kong Fir*) in attending to the nature and gravity of a breach or departure rather than in accepting rigid categories which do or do not automatically give a right to rescind, and if the choice were between extending cases under the Sale of Goods Act 1893 into other fields, or allowing more modern doctrine to infect those cases, my preference would be clear". The future of the innominate term approach seems assured.

7. Terms defining the operation of a contract. There are three special kinds of conditions.

(*a*) *Condition precedent*, a condition that the contract shall not bind one or both of the parties until such condition is fulfilled, e.g. "this contract not to be binding until the war ends."

(*b*) *Condition subsequent*, a condition under which the contract shall cease to be binding at the option of one party on the happening of a certain event, e.g. "this contract shall cease to be binding if war breaks out." This is called a *determinable contract* and is binding until the condition subsequent is satisfied; contrast a *voidable* contract (*see* VIII, 1).

(*c*) *Condition concurrent*, a condition under which performance by one party is made dependent on performance by the other at the same time, e.g. payment of price upon delivery of goods ordered.

8. Construction of terms. Every case or contract involves the construction of terms, and all we can do here is to summarise some of the rules.

(*a*) Language used must be construed as far as possible in such a way as to give effect to the *intentions* of the parties.

"When one speaks of the intention of the parties to the contract, one is speaking objectively—the parties cannot themselves give direct evidence of what their intention was—and what must be ascertained is what is to be taken as the intention which reasonable people would have had if placed in the situation of the parties": *Reardon–Smith Line* v. *Hansen Tangen* (1976) *per* Lord Wilberforce.

(*b*) Words must be presumed to have their *normal literal meaning*.

(*c*) Where there are *two possible meanings*, one legal and one illegal, the legal meaning is to be preferred so as to render the contract enforceable. (Illegal contracts are void.)

(*d*) The contract is to be construed most strongly against the party who drew it up (the *contra proferentem* rule).

(*e*) Contracts are to be construed according to their *proper law*, i.e. usually the law of the country where they were made. (*See* IX, 10).

(*f*) If the contract fails to express the undoubted intentions of the parties the court will *rectify* it so as to make it express such intentions (*see* 9).

9. Rectification. Rectification is an equitable remedy (*see* XXIII, 5). The courts will rectify the written instrument embodying the contract, not the contract itself. The remedy is available where:

(*a*) the mistake to be rectified lies only in the words used;

(*b*) there is a completed contract with all terms finally agreed;

(*c*) there is convincing proof, based on oral or written evidence, of a common continuing intention of the parties, and that the instrument fails to express that intention: *Joscelyne* v. *Nissen* (1970);

(*d*) the mistake is common to both parties: *Craddock Bros.* v. *Hunt* (1923).

STANDARD FORM CONTRACTS

10. Standard form contracts. "Standard form contracts are of two kinds. The first, of very ancient origin, are those which set out the terms on which mercantile transactions of common occurrence are to be carried out. Examples are bills of lading, charter-parties, policies of insurance, contracts of sale in the commodity markets. The standard clauses in these contracts have been settled over the years by negotiation by representatives of the commercial interests involved and have been widely adopted because experience has shown that they facilitate the conduct of trade." The other kind "is of comparatively modern origin. It is the result of the concentration of particular kinds of business in relatively few hands". These are the contracts which "have been dictated by that party whose bargaining power either exercised alone or in conjunction with others providing similar goods or services, enables him to say: If you want these goods or services at all, these are the only terms on which they are obtainable. Take it or leave it": *Schroeder Music Publishing* v. *Macaulay* (1974) *per* Lord Diplock.

(*a*) *Commercial contracts*. It is inevitable that large firms should contract on standard terms. Two engineering firms for example, will contract on their own standard terms or on terms provided by the Institute of Civil Engineers. They have no time to reconsider and renegotiate standard problems such as the details of delivery, when payment is to be made, or who is to bear (and therefore insure against) predictable risks. The legal problem here is that where the parties exchange standard terms it may be hard to see whose terms define their contractual obligations. This is a question of fact in each case: *Butler* v. *Ex-Cell-O* (1979).

(*b*) *Consumer contracts*. There is an increasing tendency for an offeror dealing with consumers to write out the contract entirely himself and to demand that the offeree accept all the terms of the offer without modification. The offeror may state all his terms in one document, or, as in the case of railway tickets, may simply incorporate by reference certain standard conditions contained in another document. These "offers with terms annexed" are subject to special rules. They include railway tickets, air and steamship tickets, any printed leases, and most contracts for the supply of gas and electricity.

EXCLUSION CLAUSES

11. Exclusion clauses. Standard form contracts invariably contain exclusion or exemption clauses. These may be clauses which:

(*a*) exclude liability for certain kinds of damage;

(*b*) Limit the amount of damages which can be recovered for breach of the contract (liquidated damages: *see* IX, **14**). In shipping cases this is called a demurrage clause;

(*c*) exclude certain risks in an insurance contract;

(*d*) provide for disputes to be submitted to arbitration. This is called a *Scott* v. *Avery* (1856) clause.

There are two issues to consider with an exclusion clause.

(*a*) Is the clause incorporated as a term of the contract? (*see* **12**).

(*b*) If incorporated, is the clause effective? (*see* **13**).

12. Incorporation of exclusion clauses.

(*a*) *Effect of signature*. "When a document containing contractual terms is signed, then, in the absence of fraud, or, I will add, misrepresentation, the party signing it is bound, and it is wholly immaterial whether he has read the document or not": *L'Estrange* v. *Graucob* (1934) *per* Scrutton L.J. Apart from fraud or misrepresentation (*Curtis* v. *Chemical Cleaning & Dyeing Co.* (1951)) the defence of *non est factum* may also be available (*see* VIII, **6**).

(*b*) *Ticket cases*. If the contract is unsigned the offeree is bound by all the terms in the document, or annexed to it, if:

(*i*) a reasonable man would assume the document to be contractual, e.g. not merely a receipt for money: *Chapelton* v. *Barry U.D.C.* (1940).

(*ii*) reasonable care was taken by the offeror to bring the terms to his attention, e.g. by a notice "for conditions see Company's rules and regulations" clearly displayed on the face of the ticket.

If the notice given is reasonable, it is immaterial whether the offeree actually reads the conditions: *Parker* v. *S.E. Railway* (1877). Or even whether the offeree is illiterate and unable to read them: *Thompson* v. *L.M.S. Railway* (1930).

(*iii*) notice of annexed conditions was contemporaneous with the making of the contract. Thus, a hotel guest makes his contract with the hotel when he signs the visitors' book, and is not bound by conditions contained in a notice he does not see until he reaches his room: *Olley* v. *Marlborough Court Hotel* (1949); *see also Thornton* v. *Shoe Lane Parking Ltd* (1971) (*see* V, 9).

(*c*) *Previous course of dealing.* Even if an exclusion term is not part of the signed terms of the contract, and has not been specifically brought to the offeree's attention, it may be effective if the parties have previously consistently relied on it: *Hardwick Game Farm* v. *Suffolk Agricultural Producers' Association* (1969). The courts are more inclined to apply this rule to a contract between commercial men.

13. Restrictions on exclusion clauses.

(*a*) *Strict construction.* Under the *contra proferentem* rule exclusion clauses are narrowly construed, against the person who inserted them. "In construing an exemption clause certain general rules may be applied: first the defendant is not exempted from liability for the negligence of his servants unless adequate words are used; secondly, the liability of the defendant apart from the exempting words must be ascertained; then the particular clause in question must be considered; and if the only liability of the party pleading the exemption is a liability for negligence, the clause will more readily operate to exempt him": *Rutter* v. *Palmer* (1922) *per* Scrutton L.J.

(*b*) *Fundamental breach.* A fundamental breach is one which goes to the root of the contract. "Where such a fundamental breach has been established, and the innocent party has elected to treat the breach as a repudiation, then the whole contract has ceased to exist, including the exclusion clause, and that clause cannot then be used to exclude an action for loss which will be suffered by the innocent party after it has ceased to exist": *Suisse Atlantique* (1966) *per* Lord Reid. A recent example is *Photo Production* v. *Securicor* (1978). D undertook to provide a guard for P's factory. One thing he was to guard against was fire. However, the guard deliberately lit a fire and the factory was burned down causing £615,000 loss. D tried to rely on two exclusion clauses. The Court of Appeal decided that he could not. All three members agreed that D had been guilty of a fundamental breach: "a breach repugnant to and destructive of the whole object and purpose of a contract" *per* Shaw L.J. "It cannot be said that the contractor is carrying out the contract at all because he is destroying the subject of the contract": *per* Waller L.J.

   (*c*) *Statute.* The Unfair Contract Terms Act 1977 renders invalid an exclusion clause relied on by a party in the course of business against a consumer except in so far as the clause is a fair and reasonable one in the circumstances.

PROGRESS TEST 7

   1. What is the parol evidence rule?   (2)
   2. In what circumstances will terms be implied into a contract? (3)
   3. Distinguish between conditions and warranties.   (4).
   4. How do the courts assess the consequences of the breach of a term?   (5, 6).
   5. Distinguish between a condition precedent and a condition subsequent   (7).
   6. Outline the rules governing the equitable remedy of rectification   (9).
   7. What is a standard form contract?   (10)
   8. When does an exclusion clause become incorporated in a contract?   (12)
   9. Outline the restrictions on exclusion clauses.   (13).

CHAPTER VIII

Invalidity

INTRODUCTION

1. Invalid contracts. Now that we have established the necessary elements of a valid contract, we must look at the factors which will render a contract invalid. These factors are:

(*a*) mistake (*see* 2–6);
(*b*) misrepresentation (*see* 7–11);
(*c*) duress (*see* 12);
(*d*) undue influence (*see* 13);
(*e*) illegality (*see* 14–17).

It is not possible to categorise very precisely the kinds of invalidity which these factors will cause. There are, however, four broad categories of invalidity.

(*a*) A *void* contract is generally one which is deemed never to have existed at all. If property is transferred under a contract which is later held to be void then the property can usually be recovered on a quasi-contract (*see* X).

(*b*) A *voidable* contract is one which exists but can be brought to an end by one party if he chooses.

(*c*) An *illegal* contract is one which contravenes a statute or rule of the common law.

(*d*) An *unenforceable* contract is one which, though perfectly valid in all other respects, lacks some technical requirement, e.g. some necessary written evidence. Such a contract will not be enforced by the courts unless and until the defect is rectified.

EXAMPLE: Contracts for the sale of land must be evidenced in writing and signed by the defendant before they can be the subject of an action in the courts. If not so written they are unenforceable by action: Law of Property Act 1925, s. 40.

But such contracts are not void, and if they have been performed and property has been transferred the court will not intervene to set them aside. Thus, if A orally agrees to buy B's house and pays a deposit to B, and later changes his mind and refuses to sign a written memorandum of the contract the contract will be unenforceable, but the court will not assist A to recover his deposit: *Leroux* v. *Brown* (1852).

MISTAKE

2. Operative mistake. In general, a mistake made by one or both parties in making the contract has no effect on the validity of the contract. In some cases, however, a mistake will operate to render the contract either void or voidable. This is called an operative mistake.

(*a*) *Mistake of law.* A mistake of law will only be operative in two cases.

(*i*) *Mistake of foreign law*, since the law of a foreign country must be proved in an English court as a fact.

(*ii*) *Mistake as to title.* A contract to lease land one already owns is apparently treated as a mistake of fact: *Cooper* v. *Phibbs* (1867).

(*b*) *Mistake of fact.* Most operative mistakes are mistakes of fact. They fall into three categories.

(*i*) *Common mistake*, where both parties make the same mistake (*see* 3).

(*ii*) *Mutual mistake*, where each party is making a different mistake and they are never *ad idem* (*see* 4).

(*iii*) *Unilateral mistake*, where one party is mistaken as the other party knows or ought to know (*see* 5, 6).

3. Common mistake. Common mistakes are of two kinds.

(*a*) *Mistake as to the existence of the subject-matter.* If there is no subject-matter, it follows there can be no contract. This is partly a matter of construction, partly a statutory provision: "Where there is a contract for the sale of specific goods, and the goods without the knowledge of the seller have perished at the time when the contract is made, the contract is void": Sale of Goods Act 1893 s. 6.

(*b*) *Fundamental mistake of fact.* Where the parties contract under a fundamental misapprehension as to a state of affairs, or facts forming the basis of the contract, the contract is void. The contract will therefore be void if the life of a dead man is insured (*Scott* v. *Coulson* (1903)) or unmarried parties make a separation agreement (*Galloway* v. *Galloway* (1914)).

The mistake must relate to the *fundamental nature* of the subject-matter, or its *identity*. Mere mistakes as to the *value or quality* of the subject-matter, even though common to both parties, apparently do not make the contract void. In *Bell* v. *Lever Bros.* (1932) L employed B as managing director of one of L's subsidiary companies at a salary of £8,000. After three years L decided to close down B's company, and paid B £30,000 as compensation for loss of office. Later L discovered that B, unknowingly, had committed irregularities which would have entitled L to dismiss him without compensation. L sued for recovery of the £30,000 on the grounds of common mistake. HELD: There had been common mistake, but merely as to the *value* or quality of what was bought (i.e. discharge from B's service contract). The mistake was not operative, and the contract could not be set aside.

Where there is a fundamental mistake which does not render the contract void at common law, equity may still give a remedy. Equitable remedies in connection with a contract which is not void include:

    (*i*) rectification (*see* XXIII, 5);

    (*ii*) specific performance (*see* XXIII, 6). The limitations of this remedy are shown by the case where A agreed to buy a house from B, both parties mistakenly believing it to be rent-controlled (which greatly reduced the value). When the truth was discovered A endeavoured to enforce the contract. HELD: This was a mistake as to value, not sufficient to render the contract void at law. But since specific performance is an equitable remedy and "he who comes into equity must come with clean hands", specific performance would be granted only on terms that a more realistic price should be paid: *Grist* v. *Bailey* (1967).

    (*iii*) rescission of the contract, where "the mistake was fundamental and the party seeking to set it aside was not himself at fault": *Solle* v. *Butcher* (1950) *per* Denning L.J.

4. Mutual mistake. Here the contract is void because the parties *misunderstand* each other as to the basis of the contract, i.e. each makes a *different* mistake. Thus there is no real concurrence of offer and acceptance; A is offering one thing, B accepting another.

The test applied by the courts is: what inference would a reasonable man draw from the parties' conduct?

EXAMPLES: (1) A and B contracted for the shipment of a cargo on the ship *Peerless* out of Bombay. Unknown to either party, there were two ships of the same name in Bombay at the time, each leaving on different dates. A meant *Peerless* No. 1, and B meant *Peerless* No. 2. HELD Contract void, since the date of departure was fundamental to the contract: *Raffles* v. *Wichelhaus* (1864).

(2) A an auctioneer was offering two for sale. B bid a high price, thinking that hemp was being sold. HELD: No contract. B offered for one thing, A accepted for another: *Scriven* v. *Hindley* (1913).

5. Unilateral mistake as to the identity of the person contracted with. A contract is voidable where:

(a) A contracts with B under the impression he is contracting with C;

(b) before or at the time of contracting B knew of this mistake;

(c) it was of fundamental importance to A that he should be contracting with C; and

(d) A took all reasonable steps to verify that he was contracting with C.

Where the parties contracted "face to face" the presumption is that there can be no mistake as to identity: *Phillips* v. *Brooks* (1919), and *Lewis* v. *Averay* (1971). But this presumption can be rebutted by clear evidence to the contrary: *Ingram* v. *Little* (1960). Contrast the following cases.

(1) A rogue, X, entered a jeweller's and offered to buy goods. His offer was accepted, and he then offered to pay by cheque. The jeweller accepted the cheque but said delivery would be delayed until the cheque was cleared. The rogue then said that he was a well-known person and asked to take some of the jewels immediately. Deceived as to his identity, the jeweller let him take some of the goods. X then took jewels and sold them to a pawnbroker, and the cheque proved worthless. HELD: the contract was made *before* the identity became important, therefore it was *not void* on the grounds of mistake: *Phillips* v. *Brooks* (1919). (The contract was in fact merely *voidable* on the grounds of misrepresentation.)

(2) L advertised his car for sale and B, a rogue, answered, describing himself as a well-known film star. L was impressed and accepted B's cheque after B had produced a film-studio admission card as proof of identity. B then took the car and sold it to A, a bona fide purchaser. When L discovered the fraud he sued A to recover the car. HELD: L intended to contract with the man he

met "face to face" and the contract was therefore *not* void for mistake, but merely *voidable* for misrepresentation: *Lewis* v. *Averay* (1971) C.A.

(3) A rogue, X, offered to buy a car from I and to pay by cheque. I refused the offer and the cheque, since she did not know X. X then convinced her that he was a well-known person, and being convinced, she accepted his cheque and let him take the car. He sold the car to L and the cheque proved worthless. HELD: The contract between X and I was *void* for mistake, since the mistake occurred during the negotiations, and I would not have accepted X's offer if she had not been convinced of his identity: *Ingram* v. *Little* (1960). Consequently, X never had any right to the car and could not lawfully sell it to L, so that in the action in court I was allowed to recover the car from L. (In *Phillips* v. *Brookes* the jeweller was not allowed to recover the jewels from B, the pawnbroker, who had bought them in good faith from X, since X had a *voidable* title to the jewels.)

6. Unilateral mistake as to the nature of the contract signed. Generally a person who signs a contract is bound by it, even if he has not read it: *L'Estrange* v. *Graucob* (1934) (*see* VII, 12).

The defence of *non est factum* operates to avoid this rule in a very limited number of cases. The extent of the defence was discussed by the House of Lords in *Saunders* v. *Anglia Building Society* (1970). P, a lady of 78, signed a document transferring her house to D. She did not read the document, and she signed it believing that she was giving her house to her nephew who would allow her to continue to live there. On the facts of the case P failed. To succeed, she would have needed to establish three things:

(*a*) the document was radically different in type from what she thought she was signing;

(*b*) she was not careless;

(*c*) she would not have signed had she known the true facts. "There must be a heavy burden of proof on the person who seeks to invoke this remedy": *per* Lord Reid.

MISREPRESENTATION

7. Misrepresentation. A person who has entered into a contract as a result of a misrepresentation may be entitled to rescind the contract or to be compensated by damages.

To amount to a misrepresentation the statement must have the following characteristics.

(*a*) *It must be made by a party to the contract or his agent.* A misrepresentation made otherwise than by a party to a contract may be actionable in tort (*see* XVI, **10–11**).

(*b*) *It must be a positive statement.* Except in the case of a contract *uberrimae fidei* (*see* **11**) there is no general duty of disclosure. A buyer has no remedy against a seller who sells pigs "with all faults" knowing that they had swine fever and knowing that the buyer was unaware of this. He did not positively represent the pigs as healthy: *Ward* v. *Hobbs* (1878).

(*c*) *It must be false,* whether negligent (*see* **8**) or fraudulent (*see* **9**).

(*d*) *It must state an existing fact.* In tort a negligent expression of opinion may be actionable (*see* XVI, **10–11**).

(*e*) *It must be material,* and not a mere advertising puff.

(*f*) *It must be relied upon.* A sold a broken gun to B, and patched the barrel with clay to conceal a crack. B did not examine the gun, and so was not misled by the patch. HELD: The Misrepresentation was not actionable, since it had no effect on B: *Horsfall* v. *Thomas* (1862).

(*g*) *It is not a term of the contract.* If a misrepresentation is made during negotiations and is later incorporated as a term in the contract, the remedies of the injured party will be basically those for *breach of contract.* The remedies available will then depend on whether the term incorporating the representation is a *condition* or a *warranty* (*see* VII, **4**). The contract can, however, still be rescinded for misrepresentation (*see* **8** (*a*)).

8. Misrepresentation Act 1967. The basis of the modern law is the Misrepresentation Act 1967. The Act has four main provisions.

(*a*) Section 1 permits rescission of the contract (*see* **10**) even though
  (*i*) the misrepresentation has become a term; or
  (*ii*) the contract has been performed.

(*b*) Section 2(1) permits damages to be recovered for loss suffered as a result of a misrepresentation made by a party to the contract unless the party making the misrepresentation proves that he had reasonable ground to believe and did believe up to the time that the contract was made that the facts represented were true. This is a negligent misrepresentation in the sense of innocent but careless. It differs from negligent misrepresentation in tort (*see* XVI, **10**) in two respects.

(*i*) In tort there must be a special relationship; under the Act the representation must be made by a party to the contract.

(*ii*) Under the Act negligence is presumed; the tort depends on the reliance.

(*c*) Section 2(2) permits the court to declare the contract subsisting and to award damages even though the plaintiff is seeking rescission.

(*d*) Section 3, as substituted by the Unfair Contract Terms Act 1977 (*see* VII, **13**), provides that a term excluding liability for misrepresentation has no effect except in so far as its reasonable, and that the party claiming the term is reasonable must prove it. This differs from negligent misrepresentation in tort (*see* XVI, **10–11**) where the parties can exclude liability by express agreement.

9. Fraudulent misrepresentation. A fraudulent misrepresentation is "An untrue statement made knowingly, or without belief in its truth, or recklessly, careless whether it be true or false": *per* Lord Herschel in *Derry* v. *Peek* (1889) H.L.

A person to whom a fraudulent misrepresentation is made has a choice of two remedies.

(*a*) To affirm the contract and claim damages for the tort of deceit or fraud. (*See* XVI, **10**).

(*b*) To repudiate the contract, or have it rescinded, with or without claiming damages for deceit.

10. Limits to the right of rescission. Although the misled party can generally get the contract rescinded (set aside), this right is lost in the following cases.

(*a*) *Affirmation.* Where the injured party has expressly or impliedly affirmed the contract after learning of the misrepresentation.

(*b*) *Restitution impossible.* Where the parties cannot be restored to their original position, i.e. *restitutio in integrum* (total restitution) is impossible.

(*c*) *Prejudice of third parties.* Where an innocent third party had obtained an interest in the subject matter of the contract in good faith and for value: *Phillips* v. *Brooks* (1919) (*see* **5**).

(*d*) *Undue delay.* Where in a case of innocent misrepresentation the plaintiff delays unreasonably in seeking rescission, the court may refuse him the discretionary equitable remedy of rescission. A bought a drawing from B, which B described as being "by Constable". Five years later A discovered the drawing was not by Constable, and was worth less than he had paid for it. He sued for rescission. HELD: He might have been entitled to damages for breach of warranty (which he had not sought), but he was not entitled to rescission because of his delay: *Leaf* v. *International Galleries* (1950).

11. Contracts uberrimae fidei, ("of the utmost good faith"). Although there is no general duty of disclosure, in some exceptional contracts the law imposes a special duty to act with the utmost good faith, i.e. to disclose all material information.

Failure so to disclose renders the contract *voidable* at the option of the other party.

EXAMPLES: (1) *Contracts of insurance*. The insured must disclose all facts which would influence the judgment of a prudent insurer, whether to decline the risk or to increase the premium.

(2) *Contract of family arrangement*, for the settlement of family property, etc. Each member of the family must disclose any portions he or she has already received without the knowledge of other members of the family.

(3) *Company prospectuses*. Directors or promoters must make full disclosure in any prospectus inviting the public to subscribe for shares in the company: Companies Act 1948, s. 43. (Failure to do so renders the contract voidable, and makes the director, etc. liable for damages.)

(4) *Contracts for sale of land*. The vendor must disclose any defects in title. The duty does not extend to other matters, e.g. the physical quantities of the land.

(5) *Guarantee and partnership contracts*. These contracts are not *uberrimae fidei* at their formation, but once made, they impose a duty on the parties to disclose all matters coming to their knowledge subsequently and likely to influence the judgment of other parties.

DURESS

12. Duress. It is well established that where a person enters into a contract by reason of actual or threatened violence, for example unlawful confinement or violence threatened to his wife, children or parents, then the contract is voidable for duress: *Cumming* v. *Ince* (1847).

The position is less clear where violence or restraint is threatened to the person's property. The traditional view is that this does not amount to duress, although money paid as a direct result of the restraint can be recovered: *Maskell* v. *Horner* (1915). In recent years this traditional view has been criticised and a wider doctrine of "economic duress" seems to be growing. In *North Ocean Shipping Co.* v. *Hyundai Construction Co.* (1978) Mocatta J. surveyed the English and the American cases and reached three conclusions. "First, I do not take the view that the recovery of money paid under duress other than to the person is necessarily limited to duress to goods falling within one of the categories hitherto established by the English cases. Secondly, from this it follows that the compulsion may take the form of 'economic duress' if the necessary facts are proved. A threat to break a contract may amount to such 'economic duress'. Thirdly, if there has been such a form of duress leading to a contract for consideration, I think that contract is a voidable one which can be avoided and the excess money paid under it recovered."

UNDUE INFLUENCE

13. Undue influence. Undue influence is an equitable doctrine under which a contract may be voidable if it derives from pressure or coercion short of duress. The test is whether free judgment has been exercised. "There are two well established classes of undue influence. The first is where the donee stands in such a fiduciary relation to the donor that a presumption of undue influence arises which prevails unless rebutted by the donee; and secondly, where undue influence is established independently of such a presumption": *Re Craig* (1971) *per* Ungoed-Thomas J.

(*a*) *Presumption of undue influence*. Ungoed-Thomas J. went on to say: "What has to be proved to raise the presumption of undue influence is first a gift so substantial (or doubtless otherwise of such a nature) that it cannot prima facie be reasonably accounted for on the ground of the ordinary motives on which ordinary men act; and secondly, a relationship between donor and donee in which the donor has such confidence and trust in the donee as to place the donee in a position to exercise undue influence over the donor in making such a gift."

(*i*) *The gift*. It is clear from *Re Brocklehurst* (1978) that the test is not objective. The court takes full account of the particular character and attitudes of the particular donor.

(*ii*) *The relationship*. The presumption arises in contracts between, for example, parent and child, trustee and beneficiary, solicitor and client, doctor and patient, priest and communicant, teacher and pupil.

(*b*) *Rebutting the presumption*. "It is necessary for the donee to prove that the gift was the result of the free exercise of independent will": *Inche Noriah* v. *Shaik Allie Bin Omar* (1929) *per* Lord Hailsham L.C. This can be shown by proving, for example, that

(*i*) full disclosure of all material facts was made;

(*ii*) the consideration was adequate;

(*iii*) the weaker party was in receipt of independent legal advice; or

(*iv*) the gift was spontaneous: *Re Brocklehurst* (1978).

(*c*) *Other cases of undue influence*. Even where it is not presumed, undue influence may still be alleged. In such cases the plaintiff must prove:

(*i*) that it existed; and

(*ii*) that it was exerted: *Hodgson* v. *Marks* (1971).

(*d*) *Right to relief lost*. Relief for undue influence is discretionary, and the claim for avoidance of the contract may be disallowed where:

(*i*) the plaintiff's conduct has been tricky or unfair; or

(*ii*) the plaintiff has delayed unreasonably in seeking relief: *Allcard* v. *Skinner* (1887).

VOID AND ILLEGAL CONTRACTS

14. Void and illegal contracts. The courts "have this paramount policy to consider—that you are not lightly to interfere with the freedom of contract": *per* Jessel M.R. in *Printing & Numerical Co.* v. *Sampson* (1875).

They will only declare a contract void or illegal where.

(*a*) a *statute* clearly prohibits the contract; or

(*b*) a well-established common law rule makes such a contract illegal on the grounds of public policy. This legal presumption in favour of validity is expressed in Latin as *ut res magis valeat quam pereat* ("it is better to preserve than to destroy").

15. Consequences of illegality. Void and illegal contracts have slightly different consequences.

(*a*) *Ex turpi causa non oritur actio* ("From an evil cause, no action arises"). Where a plantiff seeking the court's protection must rest his claim on his own immoral or illegal act his claim will fail.

Thus A rented a flat to R at £1,200 p.a. To avoid tax they agreed that the money should be paid as £450 for rent and £750 for "services". A sued R for unpaid sums for "services". HELD: the agreement was made by both parties to defraud the revenue authorities. A, the plaintiff, was equally guilty with R, therefore the contract would not be enforced, and he could not recover the money owing: *Alexander* v. *Rayson* (1936).

(*b*) *Severance.* If a contract is illegal it is all bad. If, however, it has valid aspects then the void aspects may be severed, either:

   (*i*) by removing any void provision altogether; or
   (*ii*) by restricting the scope of any void provisions.

(*c*) *Money paid* under a void contract can in some cases be recovered on a quasi-contract (*see* X, **5**), but a claim cannot be founded on illegality.

(*d*) *Negotiable securities,* such as cheques, exchanged by the parties are *void* as between them. But an innocent third party who takes such a security in the ordinary course of business and for value may be a holder in due course, in which case he will be legally entitled to enforce the security: Bills of Exchange Act 1882 (*see* Appendix).

16. Contracts void or illegal by statute.

(*a*) *Gaming and wagering contracts.* A wager is a promise to give or pay something on the ascertainment of an uncertain future event, e.g. a horse race. A bet is a wager upon the result of a game.

Such contracts are *void* under the Gaming and Wagering Acts 1845–1968. The position is complex, but the following basic rules apply.

   (*i*) Money earned as commission on bets and wagers is irrecoverable: Gaming Act 1892. An agent cannot therefore recover commission from his principal. But the principal can recover winnings from the agent: *De Mattos* v. *Benjamin* (1894).
   (*ii*) Negotiable instruments given for a bet are given for an illegal consideration and are void: Gaming Act 1835. (Though a

holder in due course may be protected under the Bills of Exchange Act 1882 (*see* XII, 7)).

(*iii*) Money lent to a loser to pay his bets is recoverable: *Re O'Shea* (1911), but not if the lender himself pays the winner, as he is then participating in the forbidden transaction: *Macdonald* v. *Green* (1951).

(*iv*) The winner of a wager cannot sue the loser for his winnings, even though the loser later makes a fresh promise to pay, supported by fresh consideration: *Hill* v. *William Hill Ltd.* (1949).

(*v*) Money paid to a stakeholder to retain pending the result of a wager can be recovered from him by the payer: *Burge* v. *Ashley & Smith Ltd.* (1900).

(*b*) *Contracts for trading or selling on a Sunday*. Except those made lawful in accordance with the Shops Act 1950, under which shops can be licensed to open on Sundays.

(*c*) *Registration of Business Names Act* 1916. Any person trading under a name other than his own must register his trade name. If he, or his firm, fails to do so, any contracts made are void (*see* IV, **14**).

(*d*) *Illegal contracts*. "Where statute has intervened to strike a transaction with illegality, the courts must give effect not only to the direct provisions of the statute but also to their necessary consequences": *Spector* v. *Ageda* (1971) *per* Megarry J. An example is the Trading with the Enemy Act 1939.

17. Contracts void or illegal at common law.

(*a*) *Contracts to oust the jursdiction of the courts.*

(*b*) *Contracts prejudicial to the status of marriage.* This includes:

(*i*) *Contracts affecting the freedom of marriage*, e.g. imposing a general restraint upon a person marrying, also marriage brokage contracts, i.e. contracts to arrange marriages for a reward: *Hermann* v. *Charlesworth* (1905).

(*ii*) *Contracts tending to interfere with the sanctity of marriage*, e.g. a promise by a married man to marry another woman as soon as his wife is dead: *Wilson* v. *Carnley* (1908).

Engagements to marry are no longer enforceable at law: Law Reform (Miscellaneous Provisions) Act 1970, s. 1.

(*c*) *Contracts to commit crimes or torts*, whether in Britain or in any friendly nation, e.g. a contract to smuggle goods into the United States of America: *Foster* v. *Driscoll* (1929).

(*d*) *Sexually immoral contracts*. If a carriage proprietor hires a carriage to a woman knowing that it will be used for the purpose of prostitution, the contract is illegal, and he cannot recover hiring charges: *Pearce* v. *Brooks* (1866).

(*e*) *Contracts involving trade with an enemy nation*, illegal at common law and also under the Trading with the Enemy Act 1939.

(*f*) *Contracts tending to impede the administration of justice*, e.g. a promise by an accused to indemnify a person who has stood bail for him: *Herman* v. *Jeuchner* (1885). A contract is also illegal if it tends to maintenance or champerty. Maintenance means giving financial or other assistance to a party in a lawsuit, where the maintainer has no satisfactory legal or moral interest in the case. Champerty means maintenance with a view of sharing the proceeds of the action. A common commercial interest is sufficient to negative maintenance: *Martell* v. *Consett Iron Co. Ltd.* (1955).

(*g*) *Contracts tending to corrupt public life*

(*i*) *Contracts for the sale of public offices*, e.g. a promise, for reward, to use influence to obtain a title or commission for the payer: *Parkinson* v. *College of Ambulance Ltd.* (1925).

(*ii*) *Contracts to obtain an unfair benefit from the government*, e.g. a promise to use influence to obtain exemptions from legal duty: *Montefiore* v. *Motor Components Ltd.* (1918).

(*h*) *Contracts to defraud the Revenue*: *Alexander* v. *Rayson* (1936) (*see* 15(*a*)).

CONTRACTS IN RESTRAINT OF TRADE

18. Restraint of trade. Any contract which restricts a person from freely exercising his trade or profession is a contract in restraint of trade. Such contracts are prima facie void, but may be enforced if:

(*a*) *they are reasonable as between the parties*, i.e. seek to protect a legitimate *proprietary interest*, such as trade secrets or business goodwill;

(*b*) *they are reasonable in the public interest*: *Nordenfelt* v. *Maxim-Nordenfelt Co.* (1894).

Whether a restraint is reasonable or not is a question of law.

The categories of restraint of trade are not closed, but the cases fall into three broad classes.

(*a*) Restraints upon employees (*see* 19).

(*b*) Restraints on the sale of a business (*see* 20).

(*c*) *Solus* agreements (*see* 21).

19. Restraints upon employees. An employer may force an employee to sign a covenant promising not to injure the employer's interests after the employment ceases, e.g. by seducing his former employer's clients.

Such restraints are viewed with distrust by the courts, and will be enforced only if they satisfy the following rules:

(*a*) *The restraint is void unless* the employee has some real *capacity to damage* his former employer's business, e.g. some knowledge of trade secrets which he might impart to competitors, or some real influence with his former employer's clients which he could use to seduce them into supporting some other firm.

Thus, the servant must generally be in some moderately confidential capacity, e.g. a solicitor's managing clerk; but not a door-to-door salesman with no real influence over customers: *Mason* v. *Provident Clothing Co.* (1913).

Similarly, a covenant aimed at merely restricting competition is void: *Eastham* v. *Newcastle Utd.* (1964). Thus a covenant by a tailor's assistant not to open a competing business within ten miles of his former employer's: *Attwood* v. *Lamont* (1920).

(*b*) *The restraint must be reasonable* having regard to:

    (*i*) the *type* of employment: *Mason* v. *Provident Clothing*.

    (*ii*) the *period* of restraint: *Kores Ltd.* v. *Kolok Ltd.* (1959).

    (*iii*) the *area* of the restraint, e.g. a solicitor's managing clerk covenanted not to open a competing business within seven miles of his former employer's. HELD: reasonable: *Fitch* v. *Dewes* (1921).

EXAMPLE: S, an estate agent, had two offices at X and Y. J was employed by S and signed a covenant promising not to open a competing business within five miles of either office within three years of leaving S. J was employed only at the X office. HELD: The restraint was too wide, since J never worked at Y office: *Scorer* v. *Seymour-Jones* (1966).

20. Restraints on the sale of a business. Restraints imposed by the purchaser of a business on the seller, preventing the latter from competing with the business sold *so as to damage the good-will* sold, are enforceable if reasonable.

Restraints of this kind are more readily enforced than those between employer and employee, since they lack the element of compulsion that may exist between the parties in a contract of employment.

EXAMPLES: (1) N, an inventor of guns, sold his *world-wide* business to M and promised not to manufacture guns anywhere in the world for twenty-five years. HELD: reasonable and binding: *Nordenfelt* v. *Maxim-Nordenfelt Co.* (1894).

(2) S sold his *localised* business to C (who had branches all over Britain) and promised not to open a competing business anywhere within ten miles of any of C's branches, HELD: void. The restraint was more than was necessary to protect the small local business purchased from S: *British Concrete Co.* v. *Schelff* (1921).

21. Solus agreements. The typical *solus* agreement is one between a garage proprietor and an oil company, under which the garage promises to sell only the petrol and oils provided by the oil company (usually in return for a loan of money). Such agreements are valid if reasonable, and void if not.

EXAMPLE: A solus agreement contained a clause by which the garage proprietor promised that if he decided to sell his garage within twenty-one years he would do so only to a buyer who would accept the same solus agreement. HELD: The restraint was unreasonable in the circumstances. *Esso Petroleum Co. Ltd.* v. *Harpers Garage (Stourport) Ltd.* (1968), H.L.

This also applies to mortgages (*see* XXII, 12). By similar reasoning an exclusive right to publish songs may, if unreasonable and based on the abuse of superior power, constitute a restraint of trade: *Schroeder Music Publishing Co.* v. *Macaulay* (1974).

COMPETITION LAW

22. Competition Law. Competition law falls into four categories.

(*a*) *Monopolies and mergers* are subject to the control of the Monopolies Commission.

(*b*) *Restrictive trading agreements* are controlled by the Restrictive Trade Practices Act 1976. All agreements by which producers, suppliers, or exporters of goods restrict the manufacture, supply, or distribution of goods by collective agreements between themselves, usually by fixing prices, are void unless they are registered with the Director-General of Fair Trading. Once registered, such agreements are submitted for consideration by the Restrictive Practices Court (consisting of one High Court judge and two lay members) which may pronounce the agreement void as contrary to the public interest, or valid.

All agreements between *two or more persons* carrying on business in the United Kingdom are registrable if they relate to:

(*i*) prices to be charged for goods, or processes of manufacture;

(*ii*) conditions of supply;

(*iii*) quantities and descriptions of goods;

(*iv*) processes of manufacture to be applied to goods;

(*v*) persons with whom the parties may deal.

(*c*) *Resale price maintenance* is governed by the Resale Prices Act 1976. Price maintenance agreements are prohibited unless the Restrictive Practices Court considers them to be in the public interest.

(*d*) Agreements affecting trade between member states of the European Community are governed by the E.E.C. Treaty.

PROGRESS TEST 8

1. When, if ever, will a mistake of law invalidate a contract? (2)

2. Distinguish between common, mutual, and unilateral mistake and summarise the categories of operative mistake. (2)

3. A sold 1,000 bicycles to B on the 1st February. Unknown to either party a fire destroyed the bicycles on 31st January. What is the effect of their contract and why? (3)

4. On 1st March A bought an annuity for his mother (B), paying C Co. Ltd. £5,000 for the annuity. Unknown to either party, B had died on 28th February preceding, and could never have received the annuity. Discuss. (3)

5. A sold to B for £10,000 a painting which both believed to be by Rubens. Four years later B has discovered the painting is by X, an unknown artist, and is worth only £100. What remedies has B? Would it make any difference to your answer if B discovered the mistake four months after the sale? (3)

6. What is meant by the defence *non est factum*? If A signs an agreement to sell his house, believing it to be merely a mortgage of the house, can he escape the contract? (6)

7. Explain the rules governing unilateral mistakes as to identity. (5)

8. What is a misrepresentation? (7)

9. When, if ever, are damages obtainable for innocent misrepresentation? (8)

10. What constitutes fraudulent misrepresentation? What are the remedies for fraudulent misrepresentation? (9)

11. The equitable remedy of rescission is not always available where misrepresentation is proved. Explain this statement. (10)

12. What is meant by *uberrima fides*? What contracts are *uberrimae fidei*? (11)

13. Define duress and undue influence and explain the distinction. When is undue influence presumed? (12, 13)

14. A joined an eccentric religious order, and B, the head of the order, persuaded A to give £5,000 to the order. Later A left the order and three years thereafter sued for the return of the £5,000 on the grounds of undue influence. Discuss. (13)

15. Explain the doctrine of severance. (15)

16. Define a wager and summarise the chief effects of a wagering contract. (16)

17. Define champerty and maintenance and explain their effect. (17)

18. What is a contract in restraint of trade, and what is the attitude of the courts to such contracts? (18)

19. In what circumstances will the courts enforce a contract in restraint of trade imposed by an employer on his employee? (19)

20. A owned three grocery shops in Liverpool, Manchester, and Bolton. He sold them to B Ltd., a large national retailing company, with 400 branches throughout the United Kingdom. At the time of sale A signed a covenant not to open a competing shop within one mile of any of B's businesses. Is the covenant enforceable? Would it make any difference to your answer if the covenant restricting A's opening of competing businesses was limited to Lancashire? (20)

21. A bought a garage with money lent to him by B Oil Co. Ltd. The loan agreement contained a clause to the effect that A would sell no petrol other than that supplied by B; if A sold the garage he would impose the same term on any purchaser. A does not wish to sell the garage, but he does wish to get petrol supplies from C Co. Ltd. He maintains that the restrictive clause is void. Advise B. (21)

22. Outline the extent of competition law (22).

CHAPTER IX

Discharge of Contracts

INTRODUCTION

1. Methods of discharge. Discharge brings the contract to an end. A contract may be discharged in any one of five ways:

   (a) by performance (*see* 2–4);
   (b) by agreement between the parties (*see* 5);
   (c) by operation of law (*see* 6);
   (d) by frustration (*see* 7, 8);
   (e) by breach (*see* 9).

DISCHARGE BY PERFORMANCE

2. Complete performance. Performance must be complete and exactly in accord with the terms of the contract.

There are three circumstances in which performance may be partial and yet render the party performing able to be paid.

   (a) *Instalments.* If performance is to be by instalments, payment can be recovered for instalments actually completed (unless the intention of the parties is to the contrary).

   (b) *Partial performance accepted.* If the promisee voluntarily accepts less than complete performance where he had genuine freedom of choice, the promisor is entitled to claim payment on quantum meruit (*see* X, 7). A contracted to erect a building for B. When the work was half done A abandoned the job. B had to complete the building himself, but A sued him for payment for work done on a quantum meruit. HELD: B need pay nothing, as he had not freely chosen to complete the building, but had no choice: *Sumpter* v. *Hedges* (1898).

   (c) *Substantial performance* of a contract for work or services, i.e. where performance is as complete as a reasonable man could expect. This is a question of fact; e.g. A decorated B's flat for £750, but because of faulty workmanship, B had to pay an extra £290 to complete the job. B refused to pay any money to A. HELD:

A was entitled to recover £750 less the £290 paid to make good his defective workmanship: *Hoenig* v. *Isaacs* (1952).

3. Manner of performance.

(*a*) *Tender*. It is sometimes sufficient if the promisor *attempts* to perform. If performance is rejected, the promisor is discharged from further liabilities, and may sue for breach of contract if he so wishes.

Tender of payment relieves the promisor from future liability to make further tenders, but does not discharge his liability to pay.

(*b*) *Time for performance or payment*. Failure to perform or pay on time may be a breach of warranty, but is rarely a breach of condition, i.e. is rarely "of the essence" of the contract.

(*i*) *Time of payment:* is not of the essence unless a contrary intention appears in the contract. (This rule is statutorily applied to contracts for the sale of goods: Sale of Goods Act 1893, s. 10.)

(*ii*) *Time of performance:* is not usually of the essence, but may be made so by agreement, and this is usually done in mercantile contracts.

EXAMPLE: O waived original delivery date, but stipulated a later date as final. HELD: this made the later date "of the essence," i.e. a *condition* of the contract: *Rickards* v. *Oppenheim* (1950).

(*c*) *Payment.*

(*i*) *Payment of a smaller sum* will not usually discharge liability to pay a greater (*see* VI, **4**).

(*ii*) *Payment to an agent* is usually a good discharge, if the agent is held out as having authority to receive money.

(*iii*) *Payment by a third party* is not a good discharge, unless he pays as agent for the debtor: *Smith* v. *Cox* (1940).

(*iv*) *Payment to one joint creditor* discharges liability to the others.

(*v*) *Payment by negotiable instrument* is conditional payment only, until the negotiable instrument is cashed, or as otherwise agreed.

(*vi*) *Payment by post* is ineffective if the letter is lost in the post, unless the creditor requested this method of payment. Contrast the rules relating to acceptance of offers by post (*see* V, **13**).

(*vii*) *Payment by cheque* is now prima facie evidence of

receipt, but a formal receipt can also be demanded: Cheques Act 1957, s. 3.

4. Appropriation of payments. Where there are several debts outstanding between the parties, it is sometimes important to ascertain what payment has discharged what debt. In the absence of express agreement to the contrary, the *following legal rules apply*:

(*a*) *The debtor can appropriate any payment* to any debt, no matter which is the longest outstanding.

(*b*) *If the debtor fails to appropriate* expressly, the *creditor* can appropriate in any way he chooses, e.g. applying the money to pay off a statute-barred debt: *Seymour* v. *Pickett* (1905).

(*c*) *The rule in Clayton's Case* (1816). If there is a *current account* between the parties, subject to constant incomings and outgoings, then if neither party appropriates expressly, the law *presumes* that the first payment in discharges the earliest outstanding debt.

DISCHARGE BY AGREEMENT

5. Types of agreement. The method of discharge depends on the state of the contract.

(*a*) *Executory contracts*, i.e. those wholly unperformed by either side, can be discharged by *simple waiver*. Consideration for the waiver lies in the exchange of promises not to sue to enforce the contract.

(*b*) *Executed contracts*, i.e. those wholly or partly performed by one party. Discharge of such contracts must be supported by consideration, or must be under seal.

There are three broad categories to consider.

(*a*) *Release*. This can be:
(*i*) under seal;
(*ii*) supported by consideration, in which case it amounts to accord and satisfaction (*see* VI, **5**).

(*b*) *Variation*. This can be:
(*i*) supported by consideration;
(*ii*) waiver, in which case it may constitute an estoppel (*see* VI, **5**);
(*iii*) rescission by mutual release. Variation (which may amount to partial discharge) can generally take *any form*, except

that contracts unenforceable unless evidenced in writing can only be varied in writing: *Morris* v. *Baron* (1918).

(Total rescission can always be made in any form, e.g. a specialty contract can be rescinded orally : *Berry* v. *Berry* (1929).)

(*c*) *Novation.* A contract can also be discharged by the parties making a fresh contract in substitution for the old. But this method is available only where the contract is not yet wholly performed on either side, i.e. is still partly executory on both sides.

A new contract substituted for an earlier in this way is called a *novation*.

DISCHARGE BY OPERATION OF LAW

6. Operation of law.

(*a*) *Estoppel by record.* A person is estopped from raising facts disposed of by a judgment in earlier litigation.

(*b*) *Set off and counterclaim.* If the defendant is owed money by the plaintiff he may set it off, as a defence to the plaintiff's claim on the contract, or counterclaim it.

(*c*) *Merger.* A contract is discharged if it is merged in a higher obligation, e.g. a deed swallows or merges into itself a simple contract on the same terms and between the same parties.

(*d*) *Unauthorised material alteration.* If one party makes a material alteration to a contract without the consent of the other, the contract is automatically discharged.

A material alteration is one which alters the effect of the contract, e.g. altering the crossing or the amount payable on a cheque.

(*e*) *Contracts for personal services.* These are automatically discharged by death in most cases. Other contracts enure for the benefit of the estate of the deceased.

(*f*) *Discharge in bankruptcy.* Where a bankrupt obtains his discharge or reaches a composition with his creditors (*see* XXIV, **26**) the order for discharge or composition automatically cancels liability on all existing debts as at that date (except such debts as are not allowable in bankruptcy (*see* XXIV, **27**)).

DISCHARGE BY FRUSTRATION

7. The doctrine of frustration. Where at the outset it is clearly impossible to perform a contract, such contract lacks an essential element for validity and is void, e.g. a contract to walk across the Atlantic.

But sometimes a contract, possible when made, subsequently becomes impossible to perform, e.g. a lawful contract involving trade between Britain and Russia became impossible when the Crimean War broke out between the two countries: *Avery* v. *Bowden* (1856).

"The doctrine of frustration operates as a rule which the court will apply in certain limited circumstances for the purpose of deciding that contractual obligations, ex facie binding, are no longer enforceable against the parties": *Davis Contractors Ltd.* v. *Fareham U.D.C.* (1956) *per* Lord Radcliffe.

The limited circumstances in which frustration occurs include:

(*a*) *Basis destroyed.* If the contract depends on the continued existence of some thing, and that thing is destroyed, e.g. hire of a theatre frustrated by the theatre being burned down: *Taylor* v. *Caldwell* (1863).

(*b*) *Non-occurrence of an event.* If the contract depends on the occurrence of an event which does not in fact happen: compare

(*i*) To watch the coronation procession of Edward VII, A hired a room from B. The procession was cancelled because of illness of the king. HELD: Contract frustrated: *Krell* v. *Henry* (1903).

(*ii*) A hired a boat from B to watch coronation review of the fleet by Edward VII. The fleet assembled, but the king was unable to be present through illness. HELD: Contract not frustrated, since A could have used the boat to see at least a major part of what he wanted: *Herne Bay Steamboat Co.* v. *Hutton* (1903).

(*c*) *Death or illness.* A contract for personal services may be frustrated by death or unduly prolonged illness of the employee: *Robinson* v. *Davison* (1871).

(*d*) *Government interference.* Where the Government prohibits performance for such a period that it would be unreasonable to expect performance after the prohibition ceases: *Metropolitan Water Board* v. *Dick, Kerr & Co. Ltd.* (1918).

(*e*) *Change in law.* Where a contract legal when made, subsequently becomes illegal through a change in the law: *Avery* v. *Bowden* (1856).

(*f*) *Method of performance impossible.* If a particular manner of performance is essential, and when the time comes for performance this particular method has become impossible.

Frustration only applies in exceptional cases. It will not, for example, apply in the following cases.

(a) *Express terms may cover the contingency* complained of. The court will refuse to treat the contract as frustrated where to do so would be contrary to such express terms: *British Movie-tonews Ltd.* v. *London etc. Cinemas Ltd.* (1951).

(b) *Self-induced frustration* cannot be pleaded, as it may amount to breach of contract.

(c) *Leases and sales of land are* probably *not subject to frustration: Paradine* v. *Jayne* (1647).

(d) The event is not vital to the contract. A contracted to build for B 78 houses in eight months for £92,000. It was impossible to meet the contract date, and rises in costs added £17,000 to A's bill. There was no clause in the contract to cover this eventuality. The time ultimately taken by A was 22 months. A claimed that the original contract was frustrated by impossibility, and sued for £109,000 on quantum meruit. HELD: Contract was not frustrated, and therefore A had no quantum meruit claim. He should have foreseen his troubles and written a clause into the contract to cover them: *Davis Contractors Ltd.* v. *Fareham U.D.C.* (1956).

8. Effects of frustration. The contract is discharged for the future, but is not void *ab initio*. Therefore it may be important to ascertain who should bear losses and who should pay for services already rendered.

(a) Before 1943. At common law the loss lay where it fell, i.e. *money payable before* frustration remained payable, and money *paid before* frustration could not be recovered, and money which did not become payable till after frustration ceased to be payable: *Chandler* v. *Webster* (1904). This harsh rule was later modified to allow distribution of loss where there had been total failure of consideration: *Fibrosa Case* (1943) H.L.

(b) The Law Reform (Frustrated Contracts) Act 1943, reformed the above position by providing:

(i) money paid before frustration is prima facie recoverable;

(ii) money payable before frustration prima facie ceases to be payable;

(iii) benefits received before frustration must be paid for, and a party who has undergone expenses is entitled to compensation: *B.P.* v. *Hunt* (No. 2) 1979.

NOTE: The Act can be excluded by express agreement, and in

any case it does not apply to charter parties, carriage of goods by sea, sales of specific goods, and insurance contracts.

DISCHARGE BY BREACH

9. Effect of breach. Breach occurs where one party

    (*a*) *repudiates* his obligation;

    (*b*) *disables* himself from performing his part of the contract;

    (*c*) *fails to perform* his part of the contract on the date agreed.

In (*a*) and (*b*) above the breach may, of course, occur before the date fixed for performance and is then called an *anticipatory breach*.

EXAMPLE: Where A hired B to act as a courier commencing employment 1st June, but wrote to B in May repudiating the agreement, it was HELD that B was entitled in May to sue for breach of contract, and need not wait until June: *Hochster* v. *De la Tour* (1853).

The effect depends largely on whether the breach is of a condition or of a warranty, using the traditional categories (*see* VII, 1).

    (*a*) *Breach of warranty:* the injured party can only sue for damages and must go on with the contract, i.e. the breach does not operate to discharge the contract.

    (*b*) *Breach of condition:* the injured party can choose whether

        (*i*) to treat the breach as a breach of ex post facto warranty (and sue for damages while going on with the contract), or

        (*ii*) to treat the breach of condition as automatically discharging the contract.

NOTE: *If he chooses alternative (ii)* he cannot also sue for damages for breach, since he has indicated a willingness to regard the contract as dead and has therefore waived his right of action for damages (but if he has incurred expense under the contract he can bring a quasi-contractual quantum meruit action for compensation).

If he chooses alternative (i) he keeps the contract alive, and should immediately commence action to enforce it, i.e. should sue for damages or specific performance. If he delays suing he takes the risk that some unforeseen event may occur to discharge the contract by frustration, thus depriving him of his right of action.

EXAMPLE: A hired B's ship to carry a cargo from Russia. Later B repudiated the contract, thus entitling A either to treat the contract as discharged or to sue for damages. A delayed a decision hoping B would change his mind before the performance date. War broke out between Russia and Britain before the performance date, frustrating the contract. HELD: A had lost his right to sue for damages by his delay: *Avery* v. *Bowden* (1856).

PROPER LAW

10. Proper law. The proper law of a contract is the law that governs it. Often the parties state in an express clause that the law of a particular country is to apply. In the absence of such a term the courts look at where the contract is made and where it is to be performed, in order to see with which country the contract has its closest and most real connection.

LIMITATION

11. Limitation. The Limitation Act 1939 lays down that actions for breach of contract must be commenced within a certain time of any breach, otherwise the right lapses and it cannot be enforced. The periods are:

(*a*) simple contracts: 6 years;
(*b*) contracts by deed: 12 years.

The limitation period is generally calculated from the moment the breach occurs, except where:

(*a*) the plaintiff was under a legal disability at the date of the breach, e.g. minority or mental incapacity, time begins to run from the date when the disability ceases or the plaintiff dies while still disabled.

(*b*) the action is based on fraud or mistake, time begins to run from the date when the fraud or mistake is discovered, and not from the date when the cause of action arose.

When a right of action has lapsed it may be revived by:

(*a*) *a written acknowledgment* constituting an express or implied admission of liability; or
(*b*) *a part payment* of a statute-barred debt.

A letter admitting a debt but refusing to pay in reliance on the

Limitation Act has been held to be a sufficient acknowledgment for this purpose: *Re Coliseum (Barrow) Ltd.* (1930). If the written acknowledgment is lost its contents can be proved by oral evidence: *Read* v. *Price* (1909).

Where there is an acknowledgment or part payment, it starts time running again, i.e. the plaintiff has a further six years (or twelve if a deed is involved) in which to commence the action. Acknowledgment of the existence of a debt is sufficient, even if it does not state the amount: *Dungate* v. *Dungate* (1965).

REMEDIES

12. Remedies. The basic common law remedy for breach of contract is damages (*see* 13, 14).

Where a quasi-contract has arisen the injured party can sue on a quantum meruit (*see* X, 7).

In appropriate circumstances an equitable remedy will be available.

(*a*) Specific performance (*see* XXIII, 6).

(*b*) Injunction (*see* XXIII, 7).

(*c*) Rescission (*see* XXIII, 5).

(*d*) Rectification (*see* XXIII, 5).

13. Damages recoverable. The plaintiff can recover financial *compensation for his actual loss, provided* it is not too remote.

Under the rule in *Hadley* v. *Baxendale* (1854) damage is not too remote if the following hold.

(*a*) It is the natural consequence of the breach, e.g. B unduly delayed delivery of a mill-shaft to A's mill, whereby the mill was out of action for a considerable time. A had not informed B that lack of the shaft would necessitate closing the mill. HELD: A could recover damages for the delay in delivery, but not for loss of profits occasioned by closure of the mill, since there was no way B could have foreseen that his delay would mean closure of the mill: *Hadley* v. *Baxendale*.

(*b*) Although not arising naturally from the breach, the damage is something which should have been foreseen by the defendant when making the contract.

EXAMPLES: (1) In *Hadley* v. *Baxendale* the mill-owner could have recovered damages for loss of profits if he had informed B that this was a likely result of delayed delivery.

Similarly, where A was to supply a boiler to B's laundry and delivery was delayed five months, it was HELD that: (i) B could recover damages for loss of ordinary profits occasioned by the delay (since A knew the laundry would lose profits by his delay); (ii) but not special profits lost under a very valuable contract of which A did not know and which he could not reasonably have foreseen: *Victoria Laundry* v. *Newman Industries* (1949).

(2) Contrary to former opinion, it has now been held that loss of resale value resulting from breach of contract (ship charter) can be recovered. Thus A commissioned B to carry goods by ship for delivery at port by a certain date, and A resold the goods in the port of delivery. B unduly delayed delivery, and the resale value of the goods dropped materially. HELD: A could recover damages: (i) for delay in delivery; and (ii) for loss of resale value: *Koufos* v. *Czarnikow Ltd.* (1967) H.L.

(3) Foreseeable loss may now include "disappointment, distress, upset and frustration caused by the breach" *Jarvis* v. *Swan Tours* (1973).

14. The measure of damages. Damages for breach of contract are intended to compensate the plaintiff, not to punish the defendant.

The injured party must minimise, or mitigate, the damage he sustains as far as he reasonably can; he cannot recover additional damages occasioned by his failure to mitigate.

Interest on any sum claimed is not allowed unless:

(a) the parties have previously so agreed; or

(b) the claim is on a bill of exchange or promissory note; or

(c) the court exercises its statutory discretion to award interest under the Law Reform (Miscellaneous Provisions) Act 1934.

Where the amount of compensation claimed is left to be assessed by the court, damages are called unliquidated.

But sometimes the parties agree in advance the amounts payable in the event of breach. Such an amount is called liquidated damages, and in any action for breach of the contract the court will award the pre-assessed sum unless it has been fixed in such a way as to break the rules against penalties.

Liquidated damages are a genuine pre-estimate of the measure of loss which a breach would occasion. A penalty, on the other hand, is a sum fixed at random to frighten a party into performing his contract: *Dunlop Pneumatic Tyre Co.* v. *New Garage Ltd.* (1915).

Consequently a sum is a penalty if:

(*a*) it is extravagant having regard to the maximum possible loss which could result from the breach; or

(*b*) if failure to pay a sum of money results in liability to pay a larger; or

(*c*) if a single sum is payable upon the occurrence of any of several events of differing importance: *Kemble* v. *Farren* (1829).

If a sum is a penalty, the court will not award it but will make its own assessment of damages. (The fact that the parties describe a sum as a penalty or a clause as a "penalty clause" is not decisive. The court will apply the above tests and if satisfied that the sum is in fact a genuine pre-estimate of loss, will treat it as liquidated damages and award it to the plaintiff.)

PROGRESS TEST 9

1. When, if ever, will partial performance suffice to discharge a contract? (2)

2. How far is it true to say that delay in performance is not vital in a contract? (3)

3. Summarise the rules governing the appropriation of payments? (4)

4. How may an executed contract be discharged by agreement? (5)

5. Explain briefly the effect to the Limitation Act 1939, on the discharge of contracts. (11)

6. A borrowed various sums of money from B in 1960. A then went to live in Australia and in 1970 returned on holiday to England, having in the meantime become a millionaire. B wrote reminding him of the loans in 1960. A wrote replying: "I do remember borrowing some money from you some time, but I can't remember when or how much, and I do not propose to bother with trivialities like this now. In any case the debt would be barred by the Limitation Acts." Advise B. (11)

7. What exceptions are there to the general rule that supervening impossibility of performance will not discharge a contract? (7)

8. Summarise the main provisions of the Law Reform (Frus-

trated Contracts) Act 1943. Are there any contracts not covered by the Act? **(8)**

9. Explain how a breach of contract may occur and state what is meant by an anticipatory breach of contract. **(9)**

10. What are the effects of breach of: (*a*) a condition; and (*b*) a warranty? **(9)**

11. What is the rule in *Hadley* v. *Baxendale*? Give examples of the rule in operation. **(13)**

12. When, if ever, may a plaintiff claim interest on a sum claimed against a defendant in an action for breach of contract? **(14)**

13. What is meant by saying that a plaintiff must mitigate his loss? **(14)**

14. Define: (*a*) a penalty; and (*b*) liquidated damages. **(14)**

CHAPTER X

Quasi-Contract

1. The doctrine of quasi-contract. The doctrine of quasi-contract is usually treated as an appendix to the law of contract and is sometimes (e.g. in *Sinclair* v. *Brougham* (1914) *per* Lord Sumner) said to be based on an implied contract. The better view is that it is a quite separate doctrine which applies in four well-defined cases.

(*a*) Money paid at the request of another (*see* 2).

(*b*) Money had and received to the use of another (*see* 3).

(*c*) Money voluntarily paid under a material mistake of fact (*see* 4).

(*d*) Money paid upon a total failure of consideration or under a contract which is void for illegality or frustration (*see* 5).

In each of these cases one party is unjustly enriched at the expense of another and the law allows that other to recover his money.

2. Money paid at the request of another. If A, at the express or implied request of B, pays to X a sum of money legally owed by B to X, the law implies a quasi-contract between A and B, whereby B must pay compensation to A for the money paid by A on his behalf, e.g. where A pays rent owed by B, to avoid seizure of his own goods which are on B's premises: *Edmunds* v. *Wallingford* (1885).

3. Money had and received to the use of another. If A wrongfully obtains money to which B is legally entitled B can sue A for recovery of the money in a quasi-contractual action for money had and received, e.g. where a servant receives money on behalf of his master and refuses to pass it on to the master.

EXAMPLE: where B used the authority of his army uniform to assist in smuggling activities it was held that the army as his employer was entitled to claim the profit he made by smuggling: *Reading* v. *Attorney-General* (1951).

In the case of torts such as conversion (*see* XV, **22**), trespass to goods (*see* XV, **20**) and to land (*see* XV, **10**), and deceit (*see* XVI, **10**), the person who has suffered loss may "waive the tort" and bring his action against the tortfeasor for money had and received.

4. Money paid voluntarily under a material mistake of fact. Where money is paid under a mistake of fact it is generally recoverable by the payer, e.g. where an employer overpays wages under a mistake as to the employee's entitlement: *Larner* v. *L.C.C.* (1949).

Money paid under mistake of law is generally irrecoverable, except in the following cases.

(*a*) Where the payee knew of or induced the payer's mistake.

(*b*) Where the money was paid to an officer of the court, e.g. a trustee in bankruptcy: *Ex parte James* (1874).

(*c*) Where money was paid under an unjustified threat of legal proceedings.

(*d*) Where the payee was under a fiduciary duty to the payer, e.g. where paid by a beneficiary to his trustee.

(*e*) Where the mistake of law is treated legally as one of fact, e.g.

(*i*) mistakes of foreign law;

(*ii*) mistakes as to private rights, such as ownership of property.

5. Void contract.

(*a*) *Total failure of consideration.* Where a valid contract has been made between A and B (supported by consideration) but subsequently B fails to render any of the promised consideration, there is said to be a total failure of consideration, and A can sue for recovery of any money he has paid.

Contrast the case where the consideration has only partly failed, e.g. where A pays money for goods to B, who later delivers some but not all of the goods. Here A can only sue for breach of the contract, recovering damages by way of compensation but not the complete sum that he has paid.

(*b*) *Money paid on an illegal contract.* Money paid or property transferred under an illegal contract may be recovered by the transferor, with the aid of the court, only in the following exceptional cases.

(*i*) Where the transferor repents of making the contract, before any part of the illegal purpose is carried out; or (*ii*) Where:

(1) eh is not in pari delicto (equally guilty) e.g. where he was innocently induced to make the contract by the fraud of the defendant; or

(2) the transferee was under a fiduciary duty to protect the plaintiff's interests, e.g. as his trustee or lawyer; or

(3) the contract is made illegal by a statute intended to protect a class of which the plaintiff is a member.

6. Accounts stated. Where there has been a series of transactions between A and B and they agree a balance, showing a sum payable by A to B, the agreed balance constitutes an "account stated".

If B now has occasion to sue A for the amount agreed he does not need to prove the details of the transactions between them, but can rely entirely on the account stated as an admission of indebtedness.

7. Quantum meruit. Where there is a breach of an essential condition in a contract, the injured party may either:

(*a*) seek to enforce the contract and sue for damages (of an ex post facto warranty) by way of compensation; or

(*b*) treat the contract as discharged, in which case he cannot sue for damages for its breach.

However, where he adopts course (*b*) above, and treats the contract as discharged, he is entitled to bring a quasi contractual action for compensation for work done or services rendered, etc. This is called a quantum meruit action (literally "how much is it worth?"), and it may be available even where there was no contract between the parties, but reasonable compensation is sought for work done.

EXAMPLE: L, a builder, did certain work for D on the understanding that D would give him a contract later for some major building work. D did not give L the expected contract, and L sued for:

(*i*) damages for breach of contract; or

(*ii*) quantum meruit relief.

HELD: There was no contract between L and D, and therefore L could not claim damages, but he was entitled to reasonable compensation on a quasi-contract: *William Lacey Ltd.* v. *Davis* (1957).

A claim on a quantum meruit can arise where:

(*a*) the defendant has abandoned or repudiated the contract, e.g. where after commissioning a writer to do a series of articles, a magazine closes down before the series is completely written; here the writer can sue on a quantum meruit for the articles actually done: *Planché* v. *Colburn* (1831).

Note that in *Planché* v. *Colburn* the writer could not sue for moneys due under the contract, since he had not completed his performance and so had not discharged his obligations;

(*b*) Under a void contract one party has done work and the defendant has received the benefit of it: *Craven-Ellis* v. *Canons Ltd.* (1936).

Here again the plaintiff could not have sued on the contract, since the contract is void;

(*c*) The parties have agreed to terminate a contract, and the plaintiff has performed a substantial part of his obligations. Here again the plaintiff can sue on quantum meruit, but not upon the contract, since he has agreed to its termination: *Dakin* v. *Lee* (1916);

(*d*) One party has obtained a benefit which he could not reasonably expect to get without paying for it, e.g. where a builder leaves the building materials on X's land and X uses the materials, the builder can sue on a quantum meruit: *Sumpter* v. *Hedges* (1898).

EXAMPLE: A contracted to pay B £30 for supervising building work at A's house. Later A commissioned additional work, which B supervised without mentioning a fee. B subsequently claimed an extra £105 for the additional supervision involved. HELD: B failed, since he could not claim on quantum meruit while the original contract subsisted. He should at the outset have secured a fresh contract: *Gilbert & Partners* v. *Knight* (1968).

PROGRESS TEST 10

1. What is a quasi-contract? When if ever can money paid by mistake be recovered?   (1, 4)

2. Explain what you understand by actions for: (*a*) money paid to the use of another; and (*b*) money had and received.   (2, 3)

3. What do you understand by the term account stated?   (6)

4. What is the meaning of quantum meruit? In what circumstances is such an action appropriate?   (7)

5. A employed B as architect to supervise the building of a house for £5,000, agreeing to pay him scale fees amounting to 10 per cent of this sum. When the house was half-built A changed his plans and spent a further £2000 on making the house larger. B supervised the additional work and now claims to be entitled to a further £200, being 10 per cent of the additional £2,000 spent. Advise A.   (7)

CHAPTER XI

Agency

INTRODUCTION

1. Definitions. An *agent* acts on behalf of another (the *principal*) in making contracts with a third party. Agency is the relationship between the agent, his principal and the third party.

There are two classes of agent, although the distinction is no longer one of great importance.

(*a*) A *special* agent is authorised to act on behalf of his principal for a purpose outside the normal course of the agent's business. In *Brady* v. *Todd* (1861) D's agent sold a horse to P, warranting that the horse was "quiet in harness". This was an unauthorised warranty, and it turned out to be false. Since D's agent was not in the business of selling horses, he was a special agent, and the warranty was therefore not binding on D.

(*b*) A *general* agent acts on behalf of his principal in the course of his business. In *Howard* v. *Sheward* (1866) D and his agent were both horse dealers. D's agent sold P one of D's horses, warranting that "the horse is sound". Again the warranty was unauthorised and false, but because the agent was a horse dealer himself he was a general agent and the warranty was binding on D. "It cannot be out of the scope of a horse-dealer's business to give a warranty, if a warranty may ordinarily form part of the transaction between buyer and seller": *per* Willes J.

There are many examples of general agents (*see* 3).

When an agent enters into a contract with a third party he may:

(*a*) *disclose* that he is acting for a principal and identify or *name* the principal (*see* 16);

(*b*) *disclose* that he is acting for a principal but leave the principal unidentified or *unnamed* (*see* 17);

(*c*) leave the existence of the principal *undisclosed* (*see* 17).

2. Characteristics of principal and agent. A man may always act through an agent unless he is required by statute to act in person: *Re Whitley Partners* (1886).

The use of an agent is not a way of avoiding incapacity (*see* VI, 8–10). The principal must always have capacity to make the contract, although this is not necessarily true of the agent. No consideration is required to support an agency, although in practice, of course, agents are always paid.

Agents' powers are very various:

(*a*) Many agents are *mercantile agents* within the definition in the Factors Act 1889, s. 1(1): one "having in the course of his business as such agent authority either to sell goods or to consign goods for the purpose of sale, or to buy goods, or to raise money on the security of goods".

(*b*) A *del credere* agent is an agent employed to sell goods and who promises to make sure that clients introduced by him to his principal will pay for the goods sold. (NOTE: This is not a contract of guarantee and therefore does not require to be evidenced in writing.)

(*c*) Some agents (e.g. stockbrokers) have power to make contracts for P but are under general fiduciary duties.

(*d*) Some agents (e.g. estate agents) have no power to make contracts for P: *Sorrell* v. *Finch* (1977).

3. Examples of agency.

(*a*) *Factors.* A factor is an agent employed to sell goods for a commission. A factor has *possession of the goods* (unlike a *broker*), and can therefore claim a *lien* over the goods for unpaid commission. He can also *pledge*, *insure* or *sell* the goods, even if he exceeds his actual authority by so doing, and receive payment: *Factors Act* 1889.

If a professional factor has possession of goods otherwise than for the purpose of sale he can nevertheless give a good title to an innocent purchaser of the goods, since the principal is estopped from denying that he was entrusted with sale: *Factors Act*, s. 2.

(*b*) *Brokers.* A broker is a mercantile agent employed to make commercial contracts between other parties for a commission usually called *brokerage*. (An agent employed to make non-commercial contract is therefore not a broker, e.g. a contract to hire a singer for a concert.)

Unlike factors, brokers *do not have possession* of goods for sale and cannot sell in their own name. They have no lien over goods and no power to pledge them.

A broker is primarily agent for the seller of goods, but on making a contract with a purchaser he becomes agent for the purchaser also.

(*c*) *Bankers.* The relationship between banker and customer is primarily that between debtor and creditor, but in addition the banker is employed to pay sums of money at the direction of the customer. A banker has a *general lien* over securities belonging to the customer and which have previously been deposited with him, and can retain such securities pending settlements of debts owed by the customer to the bank. He must not disclose the state of a customer's account, except under compulsion of law. (For further details concerning banks, banking students *see* Appendix.)

(*d*) *Auctioneers* are agents employed to sell goods by auction. An auctioneer is primarily agent for the seller, but when he accepts a bid from a purchaser he becomes agent for the purchaser also, e.g. he can sign a note or memorandum on behalf of the purchaser so as to satisfy the Law of Property Act 1925, s. 40 (*see* XX, 12).

He does not warrant the seller's right to sell property, but is liable to an action for damages by the purchaser if he fails to deliver property sold, and is liable to the seller if he delivers before receiving payment. He has *possession* of goods and a *lien* over them for his commission. He must sell only for cash (unless otherwise authorised), and at the best price available.

If the seller fixes a minimum or *reserve* price the auctioneer is liable in damages to the seller if he sells the property for less than the reserve price. But in such cases the buyer gets a good title to the goods, unless he knew of the auctioneer's breach of authority.

(*e*) *Estate agents.* These are agents employed to sell land or houses as agents for the seller. The scope of their authority varies, e.g. where an estate agent receives a deposit from a buyer to confirm purchase, it is a question of fact in each case whether he does so as

(*a*) agent for the seller; or

(*b*) merely as an independent stakeholder.

If the agent absconds or goes bankrupt, the purchaser will only be able to recover his deposit from the seller if he can show that the estate agent had authority to receive the deposit on the seller's behalf: *Burt* v. *Claude Cousins & Sons Ltd.* (1971).

CREATION

4. Express creation. "The relationship of principal and agent can only be established by the consent of the principal and agent. The consent must have been given by each of them, either expressly or by implication from their words and conduct": *Garnac Grain* v. *Faure & Fairclough* (1967) *per* Lord Pearson.

Where the agent is employed to execute a deed on behalf of his principal his appointment must also be by deed, and the agency is called a power of attorney.

Where the agent is appointed to sign a lease for more than three years on behalf of his principal his appointment must be in writing: Law of Property Act 1925, s. 54.

In most other cases the agent's appointment can be in any form.

5. Implied agency.

(*a*) Where they live together as one household, there is a presumption that a wife has authority to pledge her husband's credit for household expenses. The same presumption arises where a man lives with his mistress.

(*b*) An agent expressly appointed for one purpose may have implied authority to perform acts reasonably and ordinarily incidental to that purpose. An estate agent appointed to negotiate the sale of a house has implied authority to receive the deposit: *Burt* v. *Claude Cousins & Sons Ltd.* (1971).

(*c*) An agent appointed in a particular market has implied authority to do anything which is customary in that market. Authority is not implied if the custom is unreasonable and an agent is in general not allowed to perform unreasonable customary duties. In *North & South Trust Co.* v. *Berkeley* (1971) P employed A, who were Lloyd's brokers, to insure goods in transit. A placed the insurance with D, who were Lloyd's underwriters. On arrival the goods proved short and P claimed on the insurance. A arranged for assessors to investigate the claim and, in accordance with the market custom, sent their report only to D. The question was whether by following this custom A were acting in breach of their duty as agents of P. Donaldson J. accepted that they were. The custom was unreasonable: "Fully informed consent apart, an agent cannot lawfully place himself in a position in which he owes a duty to another which is inconsistent with his duty to his principal."

(*d*) In an emergency an agent may act beyond his authority. In *Great Northern Railway* v. *Swaffield* (1874) **P** were **D**'s agents to transport his horse. On arrival, **D** did not collect the horse, and **P** recovered the cost of its stabling and feed. This agency of necessity is rare and the courts are reluctant to extend it. It can only exist when three conditions are satisfied:

(*i*) there must be a pre-existing agency;
(*ii*) there must be actual and definite commercial necessity;
(*iii*) it must be impossible to communicate with the principal.

6. Agency by estoppel. Where A allows third parties to believe that B is acting as his agent he will be estopped from denying the agency if such third parties rely on it to their detriment.

This role applies even where no agency was ever intended by the principal. Similarly, a husband, partner, or master who allows a wife, co-partner, or servant to act as his agent cannot evade liability for the agent's contracts even after the agency is revoked, unless he has expressly notified third parties with whom the agent has habitually been dealing of the revocation of the agency: *Scarf* v. *Jardine* (1882).

7. Ratification. Ratification is where the principal adopts an unauthorised act of his agent as his own. If ratification is not possible the agent remains personally liable. Ratification is effective if the following conditions are fulfilled.

(*a*) The agent must have purported to act on behalf of his principal. "Civil obligations are not to be created by or founded upon undisclosed intentions": *Keightley Maxted* v. *Durant* (1901) *per* Lord MacNaghten.

(*b*) The principal must have been in existence at the time the contract was made. Under the European Communities Act 1972, s. 9(2), a contract made on behalf of a company which is not yet in existence takes effect as a contract with the person purporting to act for the company.

(*c*) The principal must have been competent to make the contract himself at the time when the contract was made. A principal who was an enemy alien when the contract was made cannot later ratify it: *Boston Deep Sea Co.* v. *Farnham* (1957).

(*d*) A purported contract which is void cannot be ratified. An *ultra vires* act performed by the director of a company cannot be ratified by the shareholders: *Ashbury Railway Carriage Co.* v. *Riche* (1875).

(*e*) The principal must have had full knowledge of the facts: *Marsh* v. *Joseph* (1897).

(*f*) The principal must ratify within a reasonable time, and cannot ratify if the contract can no longer be made. A contract of fire insurance cannot be ratified after a fire: *Grover* v. *Matthews* (1910).

Ratification operates to put all parties in the position they would have been if the agent's act had been authorised from the beginning. This was established in *Bolton* v. *Lambert* (1889). A contracted to buy a house from D on behalf of P. The contract was not authorised, and D repudiated it. P later ratified the contract, and it was held that this was effective in spite of D's repudiation.

TERMINATION

8. By act of the parties. Since agency is founded on consent (*see* 4) the agent's authority can be terminated by:

(*a*) express revocation by the principal; or

(*b*) express renunciation by the agent

unless steps have been taken to make the agency irrevocable (*see* 9).

There are two situations to consider.

(*a*) *Where the principal and agent are subject to a binding contract.* In the absence of an express term, agency founded on a contract can be terminated on reasonable notice. In *Martin–Baker Aircraft* v. *Canadian Flight* (1955) McNair J. assessed reasonable notice at twelve months and this has been followed in subsequent cases.

(*b*) *Where there is no contract.* An agency agreement may not impose immediate contractural obligations. An estate agent, for example, may be paid only on sale. If the agency is terminated before he negotiates a sale he has no claim. It was established in *Luxor* v. *Cooper* (1941) that there was no implied term that the principal could not sell elsewhere. "If B is under no obligation to do the work, why should A be under an implied obligation not to prevent him from doing it?" *per* Lord Romer.

9. Irrevocable authority. Revocation is not possible where:

(*a*) the authority is "coupled with an interest", i.e. where the agent was appointed in order to enable him to secure some benefit already owed to him by the principal: *Smart* v. *Saunders* (1848).

(*b*) a power of attorney is expressed to be irrevocable and is given to secure:

(*i*) a proprietary interest of the donee of the power; or

(*ii*) the performance of an obligation owed to the donee. Whilst these conditions remain unaltered, the power remains irrevocable by the donor (except with the consent of the donee), even on the death or the incapacity or bankruptcy of the donor: Powers of Attorney Act 1971, s. 4(1);

(*c*) where revocation would involve personal loss to the agent, the principal may be estopped from revoking without the consent of the agent: *Seymour* v. *Bridge* (1885);

(*d*) the principal cannot revoke so as to damage the interests of innocent third parties, e.g. by breaking contracts the agent has already made with them.

10. By operation of law. Like any other contract an agency agreement will come to an end:

(*a*) in the event of supervening illegality (*see* VIII, **14–17**) or frustration (*see* IX, **7, 8**);

(*b*) at the expiration of the term (if any) agreed in the contract; or

(*c*) when the terms of the contract have been fulfilled.

There are special rules concerning the following.

(*a*) *Death*. The death, or, if a company, dissolution, of the principal terminates the agency. Except in the case of a power of attorney the agent is then personally liable for his acts. The death of the agent also terminates the agency.

(*b*) *Bankruptcy*. The bankruptcy of the principal terminates the agency. The bankruptcy of the agent terminates the agency if it renders him unfit to perform his duties.

(*c*) *Insanity*. X employed T as solicitor to sue Y. T commenced the action and brought the case to court. Unknown to T, X had gone insane in the meanwhile. HELD: T's agency was automatically terminated, and he was therefore liable to Y for damages for breach of warranty of authority: *Yonge* v. *Toynbee* (1910).

DUTIES OF PRINCIPAL AND AGENT

11. Duties of agent. Apart from the obvious duty to obey the principal's instructions, these are as follows:

(*a*) *To exercise due care and diligence* on the principal's behalf, plus any special skill he professes to have: *Keppel* v. *Wheeler* (1927).

(*b*) *To disclose* to the principal any material information he may receive in execution of his task.

(*c*) *Not to disclose confidential information* entrusted to him by his principal. There is a distinction between the information acquired and the experience gained by the agent in the course of his employment. The information remains the property of the principal and must not be divulged; the agent may, however, make use of his experience.

(*d*) *Not to delegate performance of his duties.* (*Delegatus non potest delegare:* a delegate cannot delegate.) But this prohibition is not strictly applied, and the agent may delegate performance where required by commercial necessity or ordinary usage.

(*e*) *Not to make any secret profit.* If, beyond his commission, he receives any extra profit in the course of his duties, he must disclose this to the principal.

If he fails so to disclose such additional profit:

(*i*) The principal can sue him for the amount kept secret;

(*ii*) The principal can refuse to pay the agent's commission, and can terminate the agency without notice;

(*iii*) The principal can sue the agent and the third party for damages to compensate him for any loss he has sustained: *Salford Corpn.* v. *Lever* (1891).

(*f*) *To avoid any conflict of interests.* "No agent who has accepted an employment from one principal can in law accept an engagement inconsistent with his duty to the first principal from a second principal, unless he makes the fullest disclosure to each principal of his interest and obtains the consent of each principal to the double employment": *Fullwood* v. *Hurley* (1928) *per* Scrutton L.J. In practice, of course, commercial agents (*see* 3) have many principals at any one time.

12. Duties of principal.

(*a*) *To pay any agreed commission* or remuneration, and not to prevent or hinder the agent from earning this: *Rhodes* v. *Forwood* (1876).

The agent has a *lien* over goods belonging to the principal,
enabling him to hold such goods until his commission is paid.

When commission becomes payable depends on the contract
between principal and agent, e.g. when the agent is employed to
sell goods or land, his commission may become payable:

(*i*) when he introduces a client (whether sale results or not):
or

(*ii*) on completion of the sale, and payment of the price.
The signing of an agreement "subject to contract" does not
amount to completion: *Luxor* v. *Cooper* (1941).)

(*b*) *To idemnify the agent* against liabilities properly incurred
n the discharge of his duties: *Christoforides* v. *Terry* (1924).

As against third parties the principal is liable for torts and
breaches of contract committed by his agent in the course of his
employment if the agent is in the position of a servant. This liabi-
ity is vicarious, i.e. indirect liability for the actions of another.

The extent of the vicarious liability depends on whether the
agent is a servant or an independent contractor, i.e. on whether
he is under the control of his employer as to what and how to do
his work, or merely, as in the case of an independent contractor,
as to what he is to do. Most commercial agents fall into the latter
category, and the principal's vicarious liability is therefore
restricted.

Vicarious liability is primarily important in the law of torts,
and is dealt with more fully later (*see* XIV, **14–17**).

THE AUTHORITY OF THE AGENT

3. The authority of the agent. The extent of the agent's authority
depends:

(*a*) *on his contract* with his principal, or

(*b*) *on the law*, where this implies a particular authority for
particular kinds of agency.

Thus, the law attributes special authority to auctioneers,
factors (professional selling agents), brokers, and bank managers.
(*see* 3). For example, the manager of a public house was forbidden
to order tobaccos by his principal, but did so. HELD: The principal
was liable to pay the seller, since a manager of a public house
would usually have authority to make orders of this kind, and
the seller could therefore rely on the agent's ostensible authority

in the absence of express knowledge of the limitation imposed by the principal: *Watteau* v. *Fenwick* (1893).

14. Breach of warranty of authority. Every person professing to act as agent for another impliedly warrants that he has authority to make binding contracts on behalf of his principal.

If therefore an agent lacks the authority he professes to have he is liable to action for damages for breach of the implied warranty of authority, brought by the person with whom he has been dealing: *Collen* v. *Wright* (1857).

The agent is still liable for damages, even if he was acting in good faith, genuinely believing he had the authority he claimed e.g. where his authority has been terminated without his knowledge by his principal's death or insanity: *Yonge* v. *Toynbee* (1910).

But he is not liable if his lack of authority was known to the third party at the time of making the contract, or if the third party agreed to exclude the liability: *Lilly* v. *Smales* (1892).

(Where a dishonest agent deliberately claims authority he knows he does not possess, he is also liable to an action for *fraud* by the third party.)

15. Relations between principal and third parties. Generally, once he has made a contract on behalf of his principal, the agent drops out of the transaction and privity of contract exists between the principal and the third party (*see* VI, 6, 7).

But the results of an agent's contract differ slightly depending on whether:

(*a*) he has disclosed the name of his principal and the fact of the agency (*see* 16); or

(*b*) he has concealed his principal's identity (and also perhaps the fact of the agency) (*see* 17).

16. Agent acting for named principal. Here the agent generally incurs neither rights nor liabilities under the contract, and drops out as soon as it is made: *Gadd* v. *Houghton* (1876).

EXCEPTIONS: (1) If the agent signs a deed he is personally liable thereon and the principal incurs no liability *unless* the agent was himself appointed by deed (a *power of attorney*)—in which case the agent drops out and the principal is liable in the ordinary way.

(2) If he signs a bill of exchange in his own name the agent is personally liable thereon. (To avoid this he should make it

clear that he is signing merely as agent, e.g. by signing "for & on behalf of" a named principal. A director signing a cheque on behalf of his company should always take this precaution.)

(3) Where trade custom makes the agent personally liable, e.g. in some cases where the agent is contracting on behalf of a foreign-based principal: *Miller, Gibb & Co.* v. *Smith & Tyrer* (1917). This custom no longer applies: *Teheran-Europe Ltd.* v. *S.T. Belton (Tractors) Ltd.* (1968).

17. Agent acting for unnamed principal. This covers cases where the agent conceals the identity of the principal, while admitting that he is acting merely as agent.

Here the agent drops out in the normal way, providing he makes it clear he is acting as agent. If he fails to do so he is personally liable on the contract. (The exceptions stated under **16** apply here also.)

The doctrine of the undisclosed principal covers cases where the agent conceals both the identity of the principal and also the fact that he is merely acting as agent. In this situation the third party can enforce the contract against either the agent or against the principal, when he discovers his existence.

The third party thus has an option whether to regard the agent as primarily responsible on the contract or, as soon as he knows of his existence, to transfer liability to the principal.

BUT NOTE:

(1) He cannot enforce the contract against both. If he sues one, he cannot later sue the other also.

(2) He may be estopped from suing the principal, if he allows the principal to think that he has settled matters satisfactorily with the agent, e.g. by unreasonably delaying action against the principal after discovery of his existence: *Heald* v. *Kenworthy* (1855).

PROGRESS TEST 11

1. Define agency, and explain what sorts of agency can occur 1, 2)

2. Explain how a factor differs from a broker. (3)

3. In what ways can an agent be appointed? (4–7)

4. A, B and C are partners. A and B run the business and C is "sleeping partner" who plays no active part in the management f the firm. Ostensibly on behalf of the firm, C borrows a large

sum of money from X and then decamps with the money. X now wishes to sue the firm for the return of the money. Advise A and B. **(5, 13, 14)**

5. In what circumstances may agency occur: (*a*) by ratification; and (*b*) by necessity? **(5, 7)**

6. A, a minor, is married to B. B pledges her husband's credit for the purchase of necessary groceries, knowing that her husband has forbidden her to do so. C, the grocer who supplies the goods, has in the past let Mrs. A have similar goods on credit and does not know that her husband has revoked her authority. Can C enforce a claim for compensation against A? **(5, 13, 14)**

7. A (a minor) owns a car which he regularly allows his friend B (also a minor) to drive. While B is driving a tyre bursts, and B commissions C's garage to fit a new tyre. B now refuses to pay for the tyre. Can C claim damages against A? **(5)**

8. Explain how an agency may be terminated: (*a*) by act of the parties; and (*b*) by operation of law. **(8, 10)**

9. What are the duties of an agent towards his principal? **(11)**

10. What are the duties of a principal towards his agent? **(12)**

11. What is meant by vicarious liability? **(12)**

12. What is the difference between actual and ostensible authority in agency? **(13)**

13. In what circumstances may a person acting as agent for another be liable for breach of warranty of authority, and what does this mean? **(14)**

14. In what circumstances may an agent be personally liable on a contract which he has made on behalf of his principal? **(14, 16)**

15. Explain what is meant by the doctrine of the undisclosed principal. **(17)**

16. A employs B, the owner of a ship, to carry a small cargo of rice from Bombay to London. On the way the rice is damaged by water and expands, presenting a threat to the safety of the ship. B stops at Lagos and sells the rice for much less than could have been obtained in London. A wishes to sue B for loss of profit. Advise B. **(5, 11)**

CHAPTER XII

Mercantile Law

ASSIGNMENT

1. Transfer of contracts. Rights and liabilities under a contract can be transferred in some cases. In this case, in accordance with the doctrine of privity if, in a contract between A and B, B transfers his contract to X, B drops out and the contract now subsists between A and X; B generally has no further rights or obligations.

(*a*) *Rights* can be transferred by assignment (*see* **2, 3**).

(*b*) *Liabilities* can only be transferred by agreement of the parties (for novation *see* IX, **5**) or where the contract expressly provides.

In a contract between A and B, if performance is not a personal matter B can always delegate performance to some other person e.g. his employee. This does not involve transfer of duties, and privity still exists between A and B.

2. Methods of assignment. A right or benefit arising under a contract is called a chose (or thing) in action, i.e. a personal right of property which can be enforced only by suing (by action) and not by taking physical possession: *Torkington* v. *Magee* (1902).

Contrast a chose (thing) in possession, which is a piece of property capable of actual physical possession.

Choses in action can be assigned in two ways.

(*a*) *Under the Law of Property Act* 1925, *s.* 136. (*see* **3**).

(*b*) *Equitable assignments.* This means any assignment which, though valid, fails to comply with the requirements of the Law of Property Act 1925, s. 136, e.g. an oral assignment.

In an equitable assignment the assignee (X) cannot sue in his own name, but must join the assignor (B) as co-plaintiff in any action against the debtor or other obligee (A), or as co-defendant if he refuses. Thus the action will be either X and B. v. A, or X v. B and A.

ESSENTIALS:

(*i*) Intention to assign (no particular form is necessary).

(*ii*) Notice is necessary to the obligee to prevent him, e.g. paying the assignor: *Dearle* v. *Hall* (1823).

(*iii*) Value is necessary only in assignments of future rights, e.g. the assignor's expectations under a will.

3. Statutory assignments. Assignment under the Law of Property Act 1925, s. 136 transfers

(*a*) the full legal obligation;

(*b*) the right to enforce it; and

(*c*) powers to give a full discharge.

(*a*) *Requirements.*

(*i*) The assignment must be absolute, e.g. not by way of loan.

(*ii*) It must be of the whole debt or other obligation.

(*iii*) It must be in writing, signed by the assignor, but it need not be for value: *Re Westerton* (1919).

(*iv*) Express notice in writing must be given by the assignee to the other party to the contract, i.e. the debtor or other obligee, to avoid him performing the contract in favour of the assignor.

Thus, if A owes B £100, B can sell his rights to collect payment to X (in the form set out above), and this will entitle X to enforce the debt against A. But X should notify A in writing of the transfer, to prevent any possibility of A paying B.

(*b*) *Effect.*

(*i*) The assignee (X in the above example) can sue in his own name to enforce the chose, e.g. by suing A for debt.

(*ii*) The assignee (X) takes subject to equities having priority over his assignment, e.g. if A has paid off part of his debt to B before receiving notice of the assignment X cannot compel A to pay the full amount (but must try and recover the money from B).

NEGOTIABLE INSTRUMENTS

4. Negotiable Instruments. Certain classes of chose in action (*see* XIX, 9), called negotiable instruments, can be transferred or negotiated without the formalities and restrictions affecting most choses in action under the Law of Property Act 1925, s. 136 (*see* **3**) or the rules of equity (*see* **2**).

(*a*) *Characteristics*.

(*i*) Title passes by delivery (or by delivery + indorsement); whereas a legal assignment of an ordinary chose in action must be in writing under the Law of Property Act 1925, s. 136.

(*ii*) No notice is necessary to the debtor or other obligee; whereas in assignments of ordinary choses notice is necessary either under the Law of Property Act 1925, s. 136 or the rule in *Dearle* v. *Hall*.

(*iii*) The holder can sue in his own name; whereas an assignee of an ordinary chose in action cannot so do if the assignment is merely equitable.

(*iv*) A bona fide transferee for value takes free of any defects in the transferor's title; whereas an assignee of an ordinary chose gets no better title than his assignor.

(*v*) A transferee in due course (*see* 7) takes free of any defences which could have been raised by the debtor against the transferor; whereas any defence available against an assignor can be raised against the assignee of an ordinary chose in action.

(*b*) *Examples*. A chose in action may become negotiable either by statute or by mercantile custom. Instruments negotiable by statute include bills of exchange and promissory notes. Instruments negotiable by custom include bank notes, share warrants, bearer debentures, and exchequer bills.

Note that the following are *not* negotiable instruments: bills of lading, Post Office orders, share certificates, IOUs, and receipts.

The most important class of negotiable instruments are bills of exchange (including cheques).

(BANKING STUDENTS: A special Appendix containing The Bills of Exchange Act 1882, is included at the end of this book for students doing examinations in banking, in which there are usually compulsory questions on bills and cheques. Other students should not need to consult the Appendix unless their examiners insist on a detailed knowledge of this subject.)

5. Bills of exchange. A bill of exchange is

(*a*) an unconditional order in writing,

(*b*) signed by the drawer, and

(*c*) addressed to a drawee,

(*d*) ordering the drawee

(*e*) to pay a fixed sum of money

(*f*) on demand or at a fixed or determinable future time

(g) to, or to the order of, a specified payee or to bearer: Bills of Exchange Act 1882, s. 3(i).

NOTE: (1) *Three parties*. There are usually three parties to a bill at its outset, the drawer, drawee and payee. (A cheque is a bill of which the drawee is a bank.)

(2) *Unconditional order*, e.g. not merely payable in certain circumstances such as "providing the war is over". But a Bill may validly indicate a particular fund out of which the money is to be paid, e.g. where a cheque stipulates a particular account.

(3) *Fixed sum*. The sum is regarded as sufficiently certain even if it is payable with interest, or by instalments, or is made subject to fluctuations of international rates of exchange.

(4) *Date*. An undated or wrongly dated bill is not necessarily invalid. If undated, a holder may himself fill in the date of issue or acceptance. Any date appearing on a bill is presumed to be the right one unless the contrary is proved. Ante-dating, post-dating, or Sunday dating do not affect the validity of a bill.

Bills of exchange require to be supported by consideration like other contracts, but note the following.

(a) Consideration is presumed, i.e. the presumption is in favour of any holder seeking to enforce a bill (whereas in ordinary contracts it is for the plaintiff to prove that he has given consideration).

(b) Past consideration will suffice, i.e. any antecedent debt or other obligation: Bills of Exchange Act 1882, s. 27.

6. Cheques. These are bills of exchange

(a) drawn on a banker, and

(b) payable on demand.

The relationship of banker and customer is basically that of debtor and creditor, and the rules laid down by the Bills of Exchange Act 1882 for ordinary bills apply to cheques save where they are incompatible.

The Cheques Act 1957 makes slight modifications in the law relating to cheques, mainly for the protection of bankers.

7. Position of holders. Any holder can enforce a bill against the drawer or, once the drawee has accepted liability, against the drawee.

(*a*) A *holder for value* is a person who holds a bill for which valuable consideration has at some time been given, not necessarily by him. Thus, if A pays a debt to B by cheque and B gives the cheque to X as a present, X is holder for value.

(*b*) A *holder in due course* is a person who has taken a bill:
- (*i*) complete and regular on the face of it;
- (*ii*) before it was overdue;
- (*iii*) without notice of any previous dishonour;
- (*iv*) in good faith;
- (*v*) for value;
- (*vi*) without notice of any defect in his transferor's title.

The law relating to negotiable instruments is largely designed to protect a holder in due course, and the law presumes that every holder is in this category. Such a person can enforce the bill against the drawer (or against the acceptor, i.e. a drawee who has accepted liability) as though he had a perfect legal title, notwithstanding any defects in the transferor's title. Thus, if B fraudulently obtains a cheque for £100 from A, and then negotiates it to X for value in the ordinary course of business, X, as a holder in due course, can insist on payment of the cheque by A.

NEMO DAT QUOD NON HABET

8. The *nemo dat* rule. *Nemo dat quod non habet* means "no one can give what he has not got". It expresses a basic rule of law: a transferor of property (real or personal) cannot transfer a better right to that property than he himself has at the time of transfer.

Thus, a thief cannot normally transfer to a purchaser the legal ownership of the thing stolen. And a borrower of goods cannot normally transfer the legal ownership of the goods to a purchaser if he attempts to sell them in defraud of the lender.

In the following cases the *nemo dat* rule does not apply, and the transferor can give a better title than he himself possesses.

(*a*) *Negotiable instruments.* A person who purchases a negotiable instrument which is complete and regular on the face of it, in good faith and in ordinary course of business, without notice of any defect in the instrument or in the transferor's title, is a holder in due course.

Such a holder obtains a valid title even though the transferor's title was defective: Bills of Exchange Act 1882, s. 29.

(b) *Sale under court order*, e.g. where the court orders an official to sell a debtor's property to satisfy an unpaid creditor.

(c) *Sale by a factor*. A factor in possession of goods can give a good title to a bona fide purchaser, even though he is exceeding his authority in selling the goods: *Factors Act* 1889, ss. 1, 2.

(d) *Sales under the Sale of Goods Act* 1893, *s*. 25. Under the Sale of Goods Act 1893, wherever a purchaser gets possession of goods without paying for them, or a seller remains in possession after sale, they can give a valid title to a bona fide purchaser who is unaware of the previous sale.

(e) *Sales under voidable title*. Where the seller has merely a voidable title to the property sold, he can nevertheless give a good title to a bona fide purchaser from him, providing his title has not already been avoided at the time, e.g. where X obtains goods by misrepresentation from P and sells them to B for value, B gets a good title: *see Phillips* v. *Brooks* (1919).

(f) *Owner estopped from denying seller's title*. If the true owner of goods allows another to act as though he had a right to dispose of property, he cannot later object if such a person sells the property to an innocent purchaser: *Pickard* v. *Sears* (1837).

(g) *Under the Hire-Purchase Act* 1964, *s*. 27, a hirer who disposes of a hired motor vehicle to a private purchaser (i.e. not a motor dealer or finance company) may make a good title provided the purchaser takes in good faith and without notice of the hire-purchase agreement. This provision of the Hire-Purchase Act 1964 has not been repealed (*see* **22, 23**).

(h) *Sales in market overt* (*open market*). Where goods are sold in any well-established market overt the purchaser will get a good title notwithstanding any defect in the seller's title, provided he has not notice of such defect: Sale of Goods Act 1893, s. 22(1).

NOTE: (1) *Market overt means:* (*i*) Any shop in the City of London, where such goods are normally sold, and (*ii*) any open market elsewhere in England or Wales established by royal charter, statute, or ancient custom.

(2) *Time of sale* must be between the hours of sunrise and sunset on the appointed market day (or, in the City of London, on any day save Sunday).

(3) *Place of sale* must be in the public part of any shop or stall, in view of passers-by, and the market-dealer must be the seller not the purchaser.

(4) *Things sold* include any form of *personalty*, except horses.

(5) *Protection of purchaser* covers any defect of title in the seller, except where the goods are stolen and the thief has been convicted. After conviction the goods revest in the true owner, notwithstanding any sale in market overt: Sale of Goods Act 1893, s. 24.

SALE OF GOODS

9. Sale of Goods Act 1893. The law relating to the sale of goods is now contained in the Sale of Goods Act 1893 which is based on ancient rules of common law and the law merchant, as expanded and modernised by the judges. The 1893 Act has been amended by the Supply of Goods (Implied Terms) Act 1973 and the Unfair Contract Terms Act 1977.

The term goods includes all chattels personal or other choses in possession, e.g. severed crops, ships, goods in process of manufacture, etc. It does not cover sales of work and materials, e.g. a sale in which the purchaser is buying materials worked upon by the vendor to produce a completed article, where the element of work outweighs the value of the actual materials. Thus, the purchase of a portrait from the painter otherwise than by a dealer is not covered by the Act: *Robinson* v. *Graves* (1935).

Contracts for the sale of goods can be made in any form. If the purchaser desires definite proof of purchase he may ask for a bill of sale (*see* XXII, 15).

10. Ascertained and unascertained goods. Specific or ascertained goods are identified and agreed upon at the time the contract is made. Unascertained goods are goods which exist when the contract is made, but are not specifically identified, e.g. are merely referred to by description, such as "500 tons of coal from your mine". Future goods are goods not yet manufactured.

If specific goods perish before the contract is made the contract is automatically void. The same will apply if they perish after the contract is made, provided they perish without the fault of either party and before the legal property in them has passed to the purchaser.

In the case of specific goods the ownership or legal property in them passes to the purchaser whenever the parties intend that it shall do so, e.g. in a sale to which no special conditions are attached, the legal property in the goods will pass as soon as the contract is made (even though delivery is not to take place until some later time): Sale of Goods Act 1893, s. 17.

In the case of unascertained goods the property in them passes only when:

(a) they have become ascertained; and

(b) the buyer has been notified of this: Sales of Goods Act 1893, s. 18.

If goods are damaged or destroyed after the contract has been made but before the property in them has passed to the purchaser the seller bears the loss. But after the property has passed to the purchaser, if the goods are destroyed (even though they are still in the possession of the seller) the risk falls on the purchaser, in the absence of contrary agreement.

The seller may let the buyer have goods on approval ("on sale or return"). Here the property in the goods passes to the purchaser when he signifies acceptance, or adopts the goods as his own (e.g. by using them), or retains them unreasonably long, or at such other time as the contract may provide.

11. Implied conditions and warranties. The Sale of Goods Act 1893 as amended by the Supply of Goods (Implied Terms) Act 1973 provides for the following terms to be implied into any contract for the sale of goods.

(a) *Implied undertakings as to title: s. 12.*

(i) A condition that one seller has the legal right to sell the goods or will have at the time the property is to pass.

(ii) A warranty that the goods are free from any charge or encumbrance not disclosed or known to the buyer, and that they will remain free until the time when the property is to pass.

(iii) A warranty that the buyer will enjoy quiet possession of the goods.

These terms cannot be excluded from any contract for the sale of goods.

(b) *Implied condition as to description: s. 13.* A condition that in a sale by description, where the buyer merely describes the type of goods he wants and leaves it to the seller to provide them, the goods shall correspond with the description.

(c) *Implied undertaking as to quality and fitness: s. 14.*

(i) A condition that goods sold in the course of a business are of merchantable quality. Goods are of merchantable quality if they are as fit for the purpose for which goods of that kind are commonly bought as it is reasonable to expect having regard to any description applied to them, the price, and all other relevant circumstances.

(*ii*) A condition that goods supplied for a particular purpose are reasonably fit for that purpose.

(*iii*) An implied warranty or condition may be incorporated by the custom of a particular trade.

(*d*) A condition, in sales by sample, that the bulk will correspond with the samples on which the order was based, and that the buyer will have a reasonable opportunity to compare the bulk with sample and that the goods will be reasonably free of any defect not likely to be apparent on such examination (*see* the Sale of Goods Act 1893, s. 15(2)).

NOTE: The terms implied in paragraphs (*b*), (*c*) and (*d*) cannot be excluded from a consumer sale and can only be excluded from a non-consumer sale so far as is fair and reasonable. A consumer sale means a sale of goods, other than by auction or by competitive tender, by a seller in the course of a business where the goods:

(*i*) are of a type ordinary brought for private use or consumption; and

(*ii*) are sold to a person who does not buy or hold himself out as buying them in the course of a business.

12. Rights of the seller.

(*a*) *Seller's lien.* A seller is entitled to retain possession of the goods until payment has been made or tendered, unless the contract excludes the lien. This lien is merely a right to retain possession, and the seller can only resell the goods to recover his money in certain exceptional circumstances.

(*b*) *Stoppage in transit.* The seller may order the stoppage of goods in their transit to the buyer, if the buyer becomes insolvent before the goods are delivered to him (or his agent) and before he has paid for them: Sale of Goods Act 1893, s. 44.

13. Ex post facto warranties.
The buyer may treat any breach of condition by the seller as grounds for repudiating the contract, or he may elect to treat it as merely a breach of warranty, go on with the contract and sue for damages, i.e. may treat it as a breach of an ex post facto warranty (*see* VII, 4 IX, 9).

He must treat a breach of condition in this way wherever he has accepted a substantial part of the goods, and it is impossible

to separate those accepted from those rejected: Sale of Goods
Act 1893, s. 11(1).

GIFTS

14. Gifts. A gift is a transfer of property from one person to
another without consideration. Gifts may be made as follows.

(*a*) By will (*see* XXIV).

(*b*) *Donatio mortis causa* (*see* **15**).

(*c*) *Inter vivos*. It is generally sufficient if the donor hands the
present to the donee, but where a special form of transfer is
legally required for the particular type of property (e.g. shares,
or land), this form of transfer must be used, e.g. a deed.

A promise to make a gift cannot be sued upon (unless it is
made under seal), since it is not supported by consideration.
Even if made under seal, the court will not order specific performance of such a promise because of the absence of mutuality.
(*see* XXIII, **6**).

Gifts may be made subject to a condition, precedent, or subsequent. Thus, giving an engagement ring to one's fiancée is
subject to an implied condition subsequent that the parties shall
marry; if the marriage does not take place, the ring normally
is returned.

15. Donatio mortis causa. This is a gift by delivery of property in
contemplation of the donor's imminent death, upon a condition
(express or implied) that the gift is not to take effect unless the
donor dies.

Requisites of a valid donatio mortis causa are as follows:

(*a*) *Contemplation of death.* The donor must be *in extremis*, i.e.
in imminent peril of death, either by illness or otherwise. It would
be enough if a donor knew he had cancer, even if he actually died
of some other cause: *Wilkes* v. *Allington* (1931).

(*b*) *Conditional upon death.* It is a present gift, but it ceases
to be effective if the donor in fact recovers and does not die.
Because it takes effect immediately, it pre-dates any gift by will
(which does not become effective till death), and therefore if
jewels are given to A by will made a year before death, and to B
by *donatio* a week before death, the gift by will lapses.

(*c*) *Delivery essential.* Words of intention to make a gift are
insufficient, without delivery, actual or constructive, e.g. by

handing the donee the keys to a safe where the property is kept. Mere delivery for safe keeping is not enough: there must be actual intention to transfer ownership: *Trimmer* v. *Danby* (1856). Delivery must be to the donee or someone on his behalf.

(*d*) *Property which can pass.* All pure personality can be made the subject of a D.M.C., e.g. promissory notes, cheques drawn in favour of the donor by a third party, bonds, saving certificates. But cheques drawn by the donor himself are automatically revoked by death and therefore cannot be the subject of a valid D.M.C.

Also there can be no D.M.C. of realty or leaseholds. If a chose in action is given, the gift will be ineffective unless the proper method of transfer is used.

16. Imperfect gifts. If the donor retains the property given, but states before witnesses or in writing that he will hold the property in trust for the donee, an enforceable trust may arise. (*see* XXIII, **19, 7**). The normal rule is that an imperfect gift will not be enforced.

In the following exceptional cases an imperfect gift will nevertheless be enforced:

(*a*) Where the donee is subsequently appointed personal representative of the donor, he may assert a valid claim after the donor's death: *Strong* v. *Bird* (1874).

(*b*) Where any conveyance of land is made to a minor this automatically operates as though it were an agreement for valuable consideration for the grantor to hold the land as trustee for the minor until he reaches eighteen: Settled Land Act 1925, s. 27.

BAILMENT

17. Bailment. A bailment is a delivery of goods by one person to another for some limited purpose, on condition that when the purpose has been accomplished the goods shall be returned.

The consideration in a contract of bailment is the bailor's parting with possession of his goods. Consequently, a bailment is an enforceable simple contract, even if no money changes hands.

There are various types of bailment:

(*a*) *Deposit.* Means goods are deposited for safe custody, e.g. in a cloakroom. The bailee cannot use the goods and must (subject to the contract) exercise reasonable care of the goods while in his possession. He must return them to the bailor, and no exclusionary clauses guarding him against consequences of negligence will protect him if he returns the goods to some person other than the bailor or the bailor's agent: *Alexander* v. *Railway Executive* (1951).

(*b*) *Loan for use*. The bailee is entitled to use the goods loaned and is not liable for fair wear and tear, unless he deviates from the conditions of the loan.

(*c*) *Hire*. Here the bailor impliedly warrants the fitness of the goods for the purpose hired. The bailee must take reasonable care of the goods and use them in accordance with the terms of the contract. He is not liable for loss by robbery, or accidental fire occasioned without negligence.

Hiring is automatically determined if the hirer attempts to sell the goods: *Helby* v. *Mathews* (1895).

(*d*) *Innkeepers*. They are responsible for the safety of their guests' belongings in certain cases (*see* **21**).

(*e*) *Pawn or pledge* of chattels as security for a loan (*see* **XXII**).

18. Duties of bailee.

(*a*) *To take reasonable care* of the goods bailed to him. What is reasonable depends on the type of bailment. If the bailee has been paid to provide safe keeping for goods his duty is higher than if he received no payment.

Contracts of bailment frequently contain clauses restricting the duty of care or excluding it, but if the bailee returns the goods to the wrong person he has no protection from such clause: *Alexander* v. *Railway Executive* (1951).

Where a bailee seeks to take advantage of an exclusion clause (*see* **VII, 11–13**) the burden of proof is on him to show that the loss has not occurred as a result of a fundamental breach of the contract: *Levison* v. *Patent Steam Carpet Cleaning Co.* (1977).

(*b*) *To return the goods* in accordance with the contract. If he fails to do so he is liable for loss or damage, notwithstanding the exercise of reasonable care: *Shaw* v. *Symmons* (1917).

NOTE: By the Unsolicited Goods and Services Act 1971, where a person becomes an "involuntary bailee" (e.g. has unsolicited goods delivered to him by post, so that he cannot easily refuse to take delivery) the following rules apply:

(1) the goods become the property of the recipient (*a*) after thirty days, if notice has been given to the sender with a

demand for their removal, or (b) after six months if no notice has been given to the sender.

(2) these rules do not apply if the goods were sent (a) on sale or return, or (b) for the purposes of the recipient's trade or business, or (c) if accompanied by a reply-paid coupon.

19. Duty of bailor. If the goods are bailed for a particular purpose of which the bailor knows (e.g. hire of a car) he is under a duty to disclose any defect rendering the goods unsuitable for that purpose. He impliedly warrants the fitness of any goods hired in this way, and owes a duty of reasonable care in this respect.

In other bailments the bailor generally owes no duty of care, save to warn the bailee if goods are dangerous, e.g. where explosives are deposited in a cloakroom.

20. Innkeeper and guests. A hotel or innkeeper is one who holds himself out as ready to receive all travellers who:

(a) are willing to pay a reasonable price for the accommodation offered, and

(b) come in a condition fit to be received: Hotel Proprietors Act 1956, s. 1.

An innkeeper must accept all travellers provided he has enough room and they are willing to pay and in a fit condition to receive. Failure to accept reasonable travellers renders him liable to damages: *Browne* v. *Brandt* (1902).

Any person is a traveller who calls for a meal or a drink: *Williams* v. *Linnett* (1952). But he is only entitled to protection of his luggage if he stays the night. The innkeeper has a right to retain all a guest's luggage for non-payment of his charges. This lien (*see* 27) does not extend to things over which the innkeeper owes no duty of care, e.g. the guest's car or pet animal.

By the Innkeepers Liability Act 1878, the hotelier is given a statutory right to sell such goods as are subject to his lien, and reimburse himself for his charges out of the proceeds of sale. The right to sell becomes exercisable when the goods have been retained for six weeks; and one month's notice of the sale must be given to the guest to give him a final chance of paying his bill.

21. Innkeeper's liability. The innkeeper is responsible for his guests' luggage (but not their pet animals, cars, etc.), and can only evade liability on the grounds that damage or loss was caused by:

(*a*) Act of God;

(*b*) the Queen's enemies;

(*c*) the guest's own negligence;

(*d*) inherent vice in the goods.

By the Hotel Proprietors Act 1956, the innkeeper's liability is restricted to £50 for any one article, or £100 in respect of any one guest, unless:

(*a*) loss or damage was caused by the wilful default or negligence of the innkeeper or his servants; or

(*b*) the goods were deposited with the innkeeper for safe custody in some place specially provided, e.g. the hotel safe.

A notice of these restrictions on liability must be given to the guest before or at the time of registering (when the contract is made), and a notice placed in the room is therefore inadequate: *Olley* v. *Marlborough Court Hotel* (1949).

HIRE-PURCHASE

22. The Consumer Credit Act 1974. The law on hire-purchase has been extended to other credit transactions by the Consumer Credit Act 1974, which replaces

(*a*) the Pawnbrokers Acts 1872 and 1960;

(*b*) the Moneylenders Acts 1900–27; and

(*c*) the Hire-Purchase Act 1965.

The new Act regulates all consumer credit agreements under which

(*a*) the creditor provides the debtor with credit not exceeding £5,000; and

(*b*) the debtor is an individual.

Credit includes a cash loan or the credit for a hire-purchase agreement. Advertisements to provide credit are also subject to regulation by the Act.

Part III of the Act deals with the licensing of credit businesses. A licence is required to carry on a consumer credit business. The licensing system is administered by the Director-General of Fair Trading, whose job it is to superintend the working and enforcement of the Act.

23. Hire-purchase. There are three different types of instalment agreements.

(a) *Hire-purchase*, where a person hires goods for a specified period (by monthly or weekly instalments) and has an option to purchase the goods hired at the expiry of the period of hire (usually with the last scheduled payment). During the period of hired, he is a mere bailee of the goods.

(b) *Credit-sale*, where goods are sold to a purchaser (who obtains both possession and title) by instalments.

(c) *Conditional sale*, where a person agrees to buy goods and obtains immediate possession, but the transfer of title is postponed until the fulfilment of a condition, e.g. the completion of stated instalments of purchase price.

24. The agreement. Parts V and VI of the Consumer Credit Act 1974 deal with the agreement. Under s. 61 a consumer credit agreement is not properly executed unless:

(a) a document in the form prescribed by regulations is signed by both creditor and debtor;

(b) the document embodies all the terms of the agreement other than the implied terms;

(c) the document, when presented to the debtor for signature, is legible and complete. A copy of the document must be supplied to the debtor.

An agreement which is the result of oral representations made to the debtor can be cancelled by the debtor within a cooling–off period of five days.

The agreement contains implied terms similar to those implied into a contract for the sale of goods (*see* 11).

25. Dealer as agent. In many hire-purchase transactions there are in fact three parties involved. Thus A wishes to obtain a car and arranges to take one stocked by B, a dealer, who arranges hire-purchase through C, a finance company. The resulting hire-purchase contract will be between A (the hirer) and C (the owner, who will have purchased the car for cash from B).

Under s. 56 of the Consumer Credit Act 1974, representations made by a dealer will be deemed to have been made by him as agent for the owner (C). Thus if B has misunderstood the age or condition of the car in the above example A may be able to sue C for misrepresentation.

26. Right to end the agreement. Under the Consumer Credit Act 1974, ss. 99, 100, the debtor can terminate the agreement by giving notice to the creditor and, as well as returning the goods, paying:

(a) all instalments due before termination;

(b) any damages for failure to take reasonable care of the goods;

(c) a minimum payment up to one half of the hire-purchase price.

Thus if the hirer paid less than half at the date of termination, he can be compelled to make up the difference; if he has paid more than a half, he cannot recover any of the money he has paid.

LIENS

27. Liens. A lien is a right over the chattels of another, arising by operation of law (independently of any contract), and giving the lienor a right to retain the goods until the owner has settled some debt connected with the chattels, or, in the case of some liens, unconnected with the chattels.

(A lien should be distinguished from the deposit of chattels by way of security for a loan, where the lender's right of retention depends on contract, i.e. a pawn or pledge (*see* XXII, **14–19**).)

Liens are of three kinds.

(a) Common law or possessory (*see* **28**).

(b) Maritime (*see* **29**).

(c) Equitable (*see* **30**).

28. Common law or possessory liens. These arise where the creditor has actual possession of some of the debtor's property, and has a right to retain such chattels until an outstanding debt is paid.

NOTE:

(1) A common law lien cannot arise independently of possession, i.e. the creditor is not entitled to obtain possession solely for the purpose of claiming such a lien (cf. equitable liens).

(2) A common law lien is exercisable only by detaining the goods until the debt is paid, i.e. there is no right of sale, save in exceptional cases where such a right is given by statute.

(3) A statutory right of sale is given to innkeepers (Innkeepers Liability Act 1878), unpaid sellers of goods who have remained in possession (Sale of Goods Act 1893), and repairers

(Torts (Interference with Goods) Act 1977 (for which *see* XV, 19)).

(4) A common law lien is extinguished by: (*i*) agreement, express or implied, (*ii*) payment of the debt; (*iii*) loss of possession; (*iv*) taking security for the debt, etc.

A common law lien **may** be general or particular.

(*a*) *A general lien* **is** available against the owner of the goods in respect of any charges owing to the creditor, who may retain for this purpose any goods of the debtor coming into his possession at the time the lien arises, e.g. stockbrokers' and factors' liens.

(*b*) *A particular lien* is available only against the particular goods in connection with which charges have been incurred, e.g. a carrier's lien for his freight charges.

29. Maritime liens. A maritime lien is a lien attaching to a ship in favour of the shipmaster (for disbursements), seamen (for their wages), salvors (for charges in connection with salvage), etc.

The lien is exercised against the ship, not against the owners. If owners sell a ship subjected to a lien the purchasers will take the ship with the lien attached. The method of exercise is generally to attach a notice of lien to the mast of the ship; port authorities may then refuse to let the ship sail until the debt is paid.

30. Equitable liens. Unlike common law liens, these are not founded on possession, and can be exercised by obtaining a court order for sale. But like all equitable rights, they are extinguishable by sale of the property to a bona fide purchaser for the value without notice of the lien.

They arise mainly in connection with the sale of land, e.g. a vendor of a house who has given up possession to the purchaser has a lien over the house and land for any unpaid purchase money. Similarly, a purchaser of land who has paid a deposit has a lien over the land for the amount of his purchase money.

PROGRESS TEST 12

1. Define a chose in action and explain how it can be assigned. (1–3)

2. What is the effect of a statutory assignment of a chose in action? (3)

3. What is meant by "negotiability"? What are the characteristics of a negotiable instrument? (4)

4. Define a bill of exchange. How does an ordinary bill of exchange differ from a cheque? (5, 6)

5. Explain what is meant by: (a) a holder for value; and (b) a holder in due course of a bill of exchange. (7)

6. How far is it true to say that the doctrine of consideration does not apply fully to bills of exchange? (5)

7. Explain what is meant by *nemo dat quod non habet*, and summarise the exceptions to this rule. (8)

8. Explain the rules governing sales in market overt. (8)

9. Define goods. How does a contract for the sale of goods differ from a contract for work and materials? (9)

10. Distinguish between ascertained and unascertained goods, and explain when the property in unascertained goods will pass to the purchaser under a contract for sale of goods. (10)

11. Summarise the conditions and warranties implied by the Sale of Goods Act 1893. (11)

12. Write explanatory notes on the following: (a) sale or return; (b) seller's lien; (c) stoppage in transit; (d) *ex post facto* warranty. (10, 12, 13)

13. Explain the distinction between gifts *inter vivos* and *donationes mortis causa*. (14, 15)

14. What is meant by the maxim "There is no equity to perfect an imperfect gift." (16)

15. A nursed B during B's last illness. On his death-bed B gave A his bank deposit book, a cheque signed by C in favour of B (and endorsed by B to A), and the lease of his flat. After B's death can A enforce these gifts? (15)

16. Define bailment and explain the duties of bailor and bailee in a contract of bailment. (17–19)

17. Outline the liability of an innkeeper for his guest's luggage. (21)

18. Define a lien and explain the extent of an innkeeper's lien. (20, 27)

19. What is hire-purchase and how does it differ from: (a) conditional sale, and (b) credit sale? (23)

20. Summarise the statutory requirements as to the form of most hire-purchase contracts. (24)

21. A door-to-door salesman persuaded Mrs. A to sign a hire-purchase agreement for a suite of furniture she could not afford. For some days she was afraid to tell her husband about the contract but has now done so, and A and Mrs. A wish to avoid the contract. Discuss. (24, 26)

22. B, a motor dealer, persuaded A to take a car on hire-purchase from C, a finance company. B did not explain to A that the car was second-hand. A now finds that the car is in such bad condition that it is almost unusable, and claims to be entitled to damages for misrepresentation against C and/or rescission of the contract on the grounds of breach of condition. Discuss.   (25)

23. In what circumstances can a hirer determine a hire-purchase agreement?   (26)

24. Distinguish between possessory and equitable liens, and explain the difference between general and particular liens.   (28–30)

THE LAW OF TORTS

CHAPTER XIII

Nature of Tortious Liability

1. Meaning of tort. The Norman–French word **tort** means simply a wrong. In English law it is used to denote a wrong which is actionable at the suit of the party injured (though, as shall be seen, the "injury" may be merely notional). Such wrongs are redressible by an award of damages to the injured person—we speak, therefore in relation to torts, of civil wrongs, to distinguish them from criminal wrongs. Initially, no such distinction was made.

2. Historical background. Early English law made no distinction between crimes and civil wrongs. Generally speaking, a wrong committed by X upon Y would only come to the attention of the early courts if the peace of the community was threatened. As the Norman and Plantagenet kings developed strong central government, so the punishment of those wrongs which threatened the peace of the realm fell to royal courts. Such wrongs formed the basis of our crimes, and were known generally as felonies. Those lesser wrongs which, although involving a breach of the peace, nevertheless did not ostensibly threaten law and order, but only affected the party complaining of the wrong, formed the basis of torts, and were known generally as trespasses.

By the thirteenth century, such wrongs were actionable in the royal courts, but only at the suit of the injured party upon the issue of a writ purchased by him from the Chancery (*see* I, 13).

The fourteenth century saw a new development in the form of the action on the case, related to trespass, but differing from it in one important respect; whereas trespass was concerned with direct, forcible injuries (a vestigial form of breach of the peace), the action on the case covered consequential injuries (i.e. those which did *not* involve a direct application of force).

These two "branches" were important, because it was necessary for a plaintiff to "fit" his claim into one or another of these categories, known as "forms of action".

The forms of action, of which there were many, apart from trespass and case as it is commonly known, defined and regulated the availability of litigation in the common law courts in respect to most branches of the law.

The Common Law Procedure Act 1852, effectively abolished the forms of action, thus enabling the courts to admit of actions in a much wider variety of circumstances—the case of *Rylands* v. *Fletcher* (1868) for example, was an innovation of this kind.

On the other hand, the stranglehold which the forms of action had can be seen in the persistence of the categorisation of torts, in the old style, into trespass, nuisance, negligence, etc.

3. Torts distinguished from other wrongs—Torts defined. No one would disagree that torts differ from other legal wrongs—crimes, breaches of contract, etc. However, there is considerable disagreement as to how, if at all the notion of a *tort* should be defined.

It is considered appropriate to deal with the two problems together, because one definition—that of Sir John Salmond—seeks to define tort by reference to the differences between a tort and other wrongs, viz: "a tort is a civil wrong for which the remedy is a common law action for unliquidated damages, and which is not exclusively the breach of a contract, or the breach of a trust or other merely equitable obligation": Salmond.

These differences can be briefly summarised as follows:

(*a*) *Tort and crime distinguished.*

(*i*) Crimes are offences—they are prosecuted and punished by the state, and the action takes place in a criminal court (before a magistrate, or judge and jury).

(*ii*) Torts are not punished at all; the party injured sues the guilty party (called a tortfeasor) in a civil court (usually a judge, but seldom with a jury).

(*b*) *Tort and breach of contract distinguished:*

(*i*) The right to sue in contract depends not on the plaintiff's being injured, but on the existence of a contract between himself and the guilty party (defendant).

(*ii*) Such rights and duties as are involved (*see* V) are devised by the parties making the contract, and are not, as in the case of tort, fixed by the law.

(*iii*) A person who is not a party to contract cannot sue for breach of it, even if he suffers injury as a direct result.

If breach of a *duty fixed by law* (i.e. a duty in tort), causes injury to anyone, that person will have a right to sue. This can be seen in the important case of *Donoghue* v. *Stephenson* (1932), where A bought a bottle of ginger beer from B, and gave it to C to drink. Somehow, a snail had been allowed to get inside the bottle contaminating its contents, and C suffered food poisoning as a result. Notwithstanding the fact that C was a party to no contract, either with B, or with the manufacturers of the ginger beer, she successfully sued the latter in tort, in what has come to be a momentous decision (*see* XVI, 4).

On the other hand, a situation may give rise to liability in both contract and tort. Thus, if A privately hires Doctor X to attend Mrs. A, and X negligently causes harm to Mrs. A:

(*i*) A may sue X for breach of contractual duty; and

(*ii*) Mrs. A may sue X for the tort of negligence.

(*c*) *Tort and breach of trust distinguished.*

(*i*) As with contracts, the duties arising under a trust are the creations of the trust itself—in tort, they are fixed by the law.

(*ii*) Trusts are governed by that branch of the law known as equity (*see* XXIII) whereas torts are common-law wrongs.

The other definition of the field of the law of tort is that of Sir Percy Winfield. Whilst Winfield's definition has regard to the distinctions between torts and other wrongs (above), he seeks not to define "a tort", but rather, "tortious liability", viz: "tortious liability arises from the breach of a duty primarily fixed by law: such duty is towards persons generally, and its breach is redressible by an action for unliquidated damages": Winfield.

The fact that torts are different from breaches of contract, crimes, etc., is implicit in this definition (e.g. duty *primarily fixed by law* and *not by the parties* etc.), as is the fact that "breach is redressible by... damages".

Where Winfield's definition differs substantially from Salmond's is in his refusal to define a *tort* as such. His definition, therefore, is at the heart of the theory that we have a law of *tort*, based on some general principle of liability, and dealing with all instances (including any which may not, as yet, have been brought to the courts' attention) of unjustifiable harm.

Salmond on the other hand, lends his definition to the theory that we have a law of *torts*, concerned with a series of limited and separate wrongs.

It is fair to say that the historical development of the law tends to lend support to Salmond's view; Winfield's, however, is possibly currently favoured, as least amongst some academics. Whichever definition is accepted, the student will have to accommodate several difficult concepts; these will not invariably serve to support his chosen view of the subject as a whole.

4. Damnum sine injuria (harm without legal injury). Despite the objections of Winfield's supporters, it is well settled that not all unjustifiable harm is actionable. In order to succeed in an action for tort, the plaintiff must show:

(*a*) that he has suffered harm; and
(*b*) that the defendant has violated a legal right of the plaintiff.

Where there is harm without violation of a legal right, i.e. *damnum* without *injuria*, the plaintiff has no redress.

Thus, if a trader is ruined by the legitimate competition of his rivals he has no redress in tort: *Mogul Steamship Co. Case* (1892) H.L. Similarly, if the owner of land legitimately digs wells on his own land, with the result that water, percolating under the land, is diverted from the reservoir owned by a neighbouring town, the town has no remedy: *Mayor of Bradford* v. *Pickles* (1895) H.L. This is so even if the defendant maliciously dug the wells for the express purpose of interrupting the flow of water to the reservoirs, since he was only doing what he was legally entitled to do (*see* 7 and XV).

EXAMPLE: A's lorry, negligently driven, damaged B's fire hydrant near C's factory, and as a result the water supply was cut off and C's factory lost a day's work, C sued A for negligence. HELD: C had suffered *damnum*, but the *injuria* was B's. Therefore C had no claim: *Electrochrome Ltd.* v. *Welsh Plastics Ltd.* (1968).

5. Injuria sine damno. By contrast, a plaintiff may be able to sue for an infringement upon his rights even though he has suffered no harm at all. Here there is *injuria* (legal injury) irrespective of *damnum* (actual harm).

Such instances constitute a number of particular torts which are said to be actionable *per se*—i.e. without proof of harm or damage. Trespass and libel are examples of such torts. The reasons for their being actionable *per se* are historical (*see* **2**: since trespass involved a direct and forcible interference with the plaintiff, harm could be presumed).

6. Protection of rights or redress for wrongs? In the light of **4** and **5** it may seem impossible to answer this question in relation to torts. Certainly, a tortious claim is based upon the commission of a wrong, actual or alleged. On the other hand, there is much to be said for the view that the law of tort seeks to uphold rights, equally.

Thus, it could be said that one's right to a good name is protected by the defamation laws. A defendant who has attacked the plaintiff's reputation will be required to justify his attack, and if he can do so, then the court will uphold *his* right to comment on the subject of the plaintiff, even if it is embarrassing or damaging to the latter. Thus to speak of say, libel as a "wrong" pure and simple, is to risk over-simplification, given the various "rights" which the court must consider and the complex issues involved (*see* XVIII).

7. Motive, malice and intention in tort. In general, the law is not concerned with the motive with which an act is done, in determining whether than act is tortious or not. Thus, a good motive will not excuse a wrongful act. As a corollary, a bad motive (i.e. malice) will not make an otherwise lawful act unlawful: *Mayor of Bradford* v. *Pickles* (1895) H.L. (*see* XV).

In some cases, however, malice is an essential ingredient; these are:

(*a*) malicious prosecution;
(*b*) injurious (or malicious) falsehood;
(*c*) conspiracy (sometimes).

Malice serves a notional function in other torts (e.g. publication of defamatory material must be malicious in the sense of being not innocent (*see* XVIII, **6**)), and may also defeat the defences of fair comment and of qualified privilege in actions for libel (*see* XVIII, **12**).

Intention is not normally a necessary ingredient, in the sense that it is not strictly necessary to prove that the defendant intended the consequences of his act, though proof that he did will obviously be cogent evidence of fault (*see* **8**).

On the other hand, it must be shown that the defendant's conduct was volitional. Thus, if X seizes Y's arm, and with it strikes Z, Y is guilty of no tort. Inevitable accident, or occasion-ally Act of God, may also be good defences to actions in tort (*see* XVII, 7)

8. Fault, negligence and strict liability. We have seen (*see* 7) that whilst it is not normally necessary to prove that the defendant intended the consequences of his act, if intention can be proved, then fault can be attributed to the defendant. It is, then, generally necessary to prove that the defendant is at fault. In the absence of intention, proof of negligence will suffice: e.g. *Stanley* v. *Powell* (1891).

NOTE: Negligence is also the name of an important, but complex *tort* (*see* XVI). Here, however, it is used in the relatively straightforward sense of indicating a want of care on the defendant's part—a failure to take reasonable steps to avoid causing harm.

There are, however, certain areas where proof of fault in the sense of intention or negligence, is not necessary. Such instances, which result from historical accident, requirements of policy, or a combination of these, are known as cases of strict liability. Examples of the doctrine of strict liability are:

(*a*) breaches of certain strict duties (*see* XXVII);

(*b*) the principle which makes an employer liable for the torts of his employee (vicarious liability; *see* XIV, **15**);

(*c*) liability for the harm done by dangerous animals (Animals Act 1971);

(*d*) the rule in *Rylands* v. *Fletcher* (1868) H.L. which says that the occupier of land who, for his own purposes brings on to his land anything which is not naturally there, and which is likely to do mischief if it escapes, must keep it at his peril. If he fails to do so, he is liable for all the direct consequences of its escape.

Liability is said to be *strict*, however, and not *absolute*. Thus, Act of God is a good defence to an action in the rule in *Rylands* v. *Fletcher*; a person injured by a dangerous animal has no cause of action if he consents to the risk of injury: *Cummings* v. *Granger* (1977) (*see* XVII, **12**).

9. Liability for omissions. So far, liability for the defendant's *conduct* has mainly been discussed. Mention has been made, however, of the failure to take reasonable care. Whilst this may be evidence of *fault*, this is not what is meant by an omission as such. In general, one will only be liable for failing to act (i.e. an omission) where one is under a positive duty to act, (e.g. a man, who is an excellent swimmer, fails to prevent his young child from drowning), or where the defendant has failed to remedy a dangerous state of affairs for which he is, for one reason or another, legally responsible: *Goldman* v. *Hargrave* (1967) P.C.

10. Causation. Clearly, a defendant should not be (and is not) liable for harm to the plaintiff of which his act or omission is not the cause. In practice, however, situations are not always so simple as to admit of only one cause; the court will seek to establish therefore, whether the defendant's act is a sufficiently proximate cause as to incur responsibility (the terms operative or effective, are sometimes used rather than proximate).

If the term proximate cause is adopted, however, it should be remembered that this does not necessarily refer to the "last event" before the injury is suffered, in a situation where more than one act or omission is involved.

11. Concurrent causes. Where two or more events can be seen to be causative in relation to the plaintiff's injuries both may be found to be operative or proximate: *Baker* v. *Willoughby* (1970) H.L. In that case, the House held that the two causes involved had led to *separate* injuries. On the other hand, concurrent causes may be found to contribute equally to the *same* injury: *Rouse* v. *Squires* (1973).

12. Independent causes. Sometimes an event other than the defendant's act can be said to "reduce the defendant's act to mere history". Such an event is referred to as a *novus actus interveniens*, (new intervening act) and has the effect of "breaking the chain" of causation which might otherwise place responsibility at the defendant's doorstep.

Such an act may be committed:

(*a*) by a third party (in which case it must normally be shown that the third party could foresee the consequences of his or her act): *Philco* v. *Spurling* (1949);

(*b*) by the plaintiff himself: *McKew* v. *Holland, Hannen & Cubitts* (1969) H.L., where the plaintiff's act, though foreseeable, was unreasonable in the circumstances; or

(*c*) by a natural event: *The Carslogie* (1952) H.L.

The danger of seeing the principle of novus actus interveniens in a rigid way, involving a strict time–sequence of

(a) an act by D; followed by

(b) an independent cause (novus actus interveni then)

(c) harm to the plaintiff;

is shown by the case of *Liesbosch Dredger* v. *Edison* (1933) where a *predisposing* cause was sufficient to break the chain of causation.

13. Remoteness of damage: 1. This problem differs from that of causation in that it assumes that the defendant's act has caused the plaintiff's injuries, and that, in every other respect, the defendant is guilty of a wrong (i.e. he has committed a tort); the question of remoteness looks at the extent of the defendant's liability. It can be said then, that the rules relative to remoteness of damage are rules which limit the damages which the plaintiff will eventually recover.

14. Remoteness of damage: 2. The principle, generally, is that the defendant to an action in tort is not liable for all the consequences of his actions, but only for those consequences which the law regards as proximate.

Two main tests have been devised to meet the problem.

(a) *Direct consequences*. The leading case is *Re Polemis* (1921) (C.A.). The facts were that a stevedore employed by the charterers of a ship dropped a plank into the hold of a vessel, where it caused a spark, igniting gas which had leaked from cargo, and vaporised in the hold. It was HELD that the fire was the direct consequence of the charterers' employee's negligence, and that the charterers (defendants) should be liable for all such consequences as flowed directly from this negligent act (though it was agreed that foresight was a factor in determining the innocence or otherwise of their acts).

(b) *Reasonable foresight*. The main test is the *Wagon Mound* test: *Overseas Tankship (U.K.)* v. *Morts Dock (The Wagon Mound No. 1)* (1961) P.C. (an appeal from the Australian High Court). A allowed oil to escape from their ship the Wagon Mound, where it was anchored. The oil floated across the water to B's wharf, where it was ignited by a spark. The wharf was destroyed in the ensuing fire. It was found that the destruction of the wharf by fire was not reasonably foreseeable and, accordingly, A was not liable since a defendant should be liable only for those consequences of his act which can be said to be reasonably foreseeable. The Judicial Committee in utilising this test, rejected the older rule in *Re Polemis*.

The reasonable foresight test has been followed in United Kingdom cases such as *Hughes* v. *Lord Advocate* (1963) in the House of Lords, and by the Court of Appeal in *Doughty* v. *Turner* (1964).

15. Scope of the rules relating to remoteness. In *The Wagon Mound* (*No.* 2) (1967) P.C., a different plaintiff (this time the owner of the docks; in *Wagon Mound* (*No.* 1) it was the charterer of a ship) brought an action in nuisance arising out of the same situation as the earlier case. It was HELD that the same test (reasonable foresight) applied. Thus, the test as to remoteness of damage in relation to the torts of negligence and nuisance can be stated as being that of reasonable foresight.

On the other hand, the Court of Appeal has ruled that the *Polemis* test (direct consequences) applies in cases of the tort of deceit.

No strict rule has as yet been formulated, though, it could be argued that the trend is to use the *Wagon Mound* test in those torts which, invariably, or, in the event, involve negligence, and the *Polemis* test in those torts where negligence is not in issue.

No problem as to remoteness of damage exists in relation to cases where harm is intended—the defendant will be liable for all such harm as results.

NOTE: Some text-books deal with both causation and remoteness of damage in the context of the tort of negligence. Whilst the vast majority of cases doubtless involve that tort, they are important issues in relation to tortious liability generally. Students are therefore advised, in reading such books, to be prepared to look for discussion in these topics within the chapters on negligence.

PROGRESS TEST 13

1. Outline the history of the law of tort(s). **(1, 2)**
2. How would you seek to define "a tort"? Distinguish torts from

(*a*) crimes;

(*b*) breaches of contract. **(3)**

3. Explain what is meant by "*damnum sine injuria*" and "*injuria sine damno*". **(4, 5)**

4. Of what relevance is motive in the law of tort? **(7)**

5. Explain "fault" in relation to liability in tort. When may a person be so liable without any fault on his part? **(8)**

6. Explain the terms:

(a) proximate cause;

(b) concurrent causes;

(c) "break the chain of causation". (10, 11, 12)

7. What is a *novus actus interveniens*? (12)

8. Outline the rules relating to remoteness of damage in tort (13, 14)

9. A negligently spills gasoline into the drain. Two blocks away, some workmen are repairing a gas main. One of them lights a cigarette, and the match ignites gas which has accumulated due to vaporisation of the gasoline in the drain, which has been carried along underground. The ensuing fire causes the gas main to explode. X and Y are injured. Discuss the problems as to causation and remoteness of damage which may apply in their cases. (10, 11, 12, 13, 14)

CHAPTER XIV

Capacity and Defences in Tort

CAPACITY IN TORT

1. Capacity. This refers to the question who may sue in tort?; also (and perhaps more usually) to the question who may be liable? (or, more specifically, whether a given party, where a tort has been committed, can be said to be responsible in law for the tort). Accordingly, the general question, "who may sue?" is dealt with first, then specific instances; the question of liability is dealt with in the context of each of these instances.

The general rule is that anyone may sue in tort. This includes minors (though procedure requires that an adult represent them as "next friend"), aliens (so long as they are not enemies) and even convicted criminals. Since the Law Reform (Husband and Wife) Act 1962, husband and wife may sue each other (*see* 9(*a*)).

Locus standi (the right to bring an action) in certain torts depends on particular qualifications: e.g. to bring an action in the tort of nuisance, a person must normally have some title to the land affected (*see* XV, 28).

Whilst it is not quite the same, one might well consider, in dealing with particular situations, whom the law seeks to protect in permitting an action in a particular case. For example, the Congenital Disabilities (Civil Liability) Act 1976 permits an action against a person whose breach of duty owed to a parent results in a child being born disabled. The passing of this Act, however, along with settlement out of court of many cases arising out of the thalidomide affair, meant that the courts did not pronounce definitely whether or not a duty could be said to be owed to an unborn child directly.

CAPACITY—SPECIFIC INSTANCES

2. The Crown. At common law the maxim "the Crown can do no wrong" prevented actions against the Crown or its servants. This maxim now applies only to the Queen in her personal capacity. Under the Crown Proceedings Act 1947, the Crown, in the sense of "the state", (but not the Queen herself) can be made liable in tort as if it were a person of full age and capacity in most cases (*see* IV, **51**).

3. Foreign sovereigns and diplomats. They can always sue for tort, but they cannot be sued unless they waive their diplomatic immunity either by entering an appearance to defend an action against them or by commencing proceedings themselves (in which case the defendant can raise any appropriate counterclaim against the diplomat). General provisions on these matters are contained in the Diplomatic Privileges Act 1964 and the State Immunity Act 1978.

4. Corporations. They can sue and be sued in their own names; but since they can act only through human agents, their liability in tort is necessarily vicarious (*see* **15**).

5. Trade Unions. They can sue in their registered name (if any).
   In general, no action in tort will lie against a trade union. The Trade Union and Labour Relations Act 1974 (as amended by the Trade Union and Labour Relations (Amendment) Act 1976) provides that the liability of trade unions will be limited to liability for breaches of duty resulting in personal injuries, or "in connection with . . . property", and then, only in so far as the union concerned is not acting "in contemplation or furtherance of a trade dispute": s. 14.

6. Minors. They are fully liable for their torts, providing they are old enough to possess any necessary element of intent; though in practice, actions are seldom brought against minors.
   Where the tort directly arises from a breach of contract the minor cannot be sued for tort if this would involve indirect enforcement of the contract, e.g. a minor fraudulently mis-representing his age to induce a void contract of loan cannot be sued for the tort of fraud: *Leslie* v. *Sheill* (1914). But where the tort arises independently of the contract he is fully liable, e.g. where a minor obtains a radio on a void hire-purchase contract and subsequently sells it, thus committing conversion by a bailee, he is fully liable: *Ballett* v. *Mingay* (1943). Where negligence is an ingredient of the tort, then the minor will be judged, in all probability, according to the standards which can reasonably be expected of a child of the age of the child in question. Certainly where contributory negligence is concerned, this is the standard used: *Gough* v. *Thorne* (1966).

7. Parent. A parent is not liable for the torts of his children except where:

(a) he is vicariously liable, by having commissioned the tort: or

(b) he is personally liable for the tort of negligence by reason of allowing his child unreasonable opportunity of doing mischief, e.g. by giving a very young child a loaded gun: *Bebee* v. *Sales* (1916).

8. Mentally disordered and drunken persons. They are generally fully liable, save where intent is a necessary element and their condition is such as to negative the intent: *Morriss* v. *Marsden* (1952).

9. Husband and wife.

(a) *They can now sue each other* for torts, even though these were committed after the marriage: Law Reform (Husband and Wife) Act 1962. The court may stay the action, however, if it appears that no substantial benefit will accrue to either party, or that the issue is one which could more conveniently be dealt with summarily in accordance with the Married Women's Property Act 1882, s. 17 (which provides for disposal of matrimonial property).

(b) *Liability of married women to third persons.* A married woman is now fully liable for her own torts: Law Reform (Married Women and Tortfeasors) Act 1935.

10. Executors and administrators. At common law, the general rule was that tortious rights and liability were extinguished by death (*actio personalis moritur cum persona*).

The Law Reform (Miscellaneous Provisions) Act 1934 abolished the common law rule, however, and provided that all causes of action subsisting against a (deceased) person or vesting in him shall survive. Thus actions by or against a deceased person subsist for or against his estate under the Act (with the notable exception of actions for defamation, which die with the party).

In the event that the action concerned results from a tort which is itself the cause of death, a cause of action is said to vest in the deceased at the instant of death: *Rose* v. *Ford* (1937). Thus, his estate can recover to the extent that the deceased can be said to have suffered loss.

As well as the rule *actio personalis moritur cum persona*, however, there was another rule at common law, to the effect that "the death of a human being could not be complained of as an in-

jury": *Baker* v. *Bolton* (1808) (i.e. the death of A, in itself, is not
a form of harm to B which the law recognises as actionable). This
harsh rule was mitigated firstly by the Fatal Accidents Act 1846,
and later by the Fatal Accidents Act 1976. These statutes have
created a new category of persons with capacity to sue (*see* **11**).

11. Dependants. The 1846 Act (*see* **10**) allowed actions by dependants of a person who was killed by another's tort. This was the
major exception to the general rule (*see* **10**). The 1976 Act
provides that the executors or administrators may bring an
action on behalf of the deceased's dependants: these are defined
as:

    (*a*) *wife or husband of the deceased*;
    (*b*) any person who is a *parent or grandparent* of the deceased;
    (*c*) *children or grandchildren*; and
    (*d*) *brother, sister, uncle or aunt* of the deceased: Fatal Acci-
dents Act 1976, s. 1(3). Such persons may sue in circumstances
"where death is caused . . . such as would (if death had not
ensued) have entitled the person injured to maintain an action":
Fatal Accidents Act 1976, s. 1(1).

12. Joint tortfeasors. These are wrongdoers who concert a common action, i.e. "a joint act done in pursuance of a concerted
purpose": *Brooke* v. *Bool* (1908). Their liability is *joint and
several*, i.e. the person injured may sue any one of them for the
whole amount of the damages, or may sue them jointly in one
action; and among themselves they are bound to contribute fair
shares of damages payable, even if one of their number has been
compelled to pay all.
    Joint tortfeasors are persons who:

    (*a*) commit the same wrongful act; and
    (*b*) cause the same harm, e.g. where A and B together assault
C.

    But where there are two distinct torts causing the same damage
the doers are not joint tortfeasors, e.g. where A and B independently driving separate cars both negligently hit and injure C.
    The Civil Liability (Contribution) Act 1978, provides that any
person liable in respect of damage suffered by another person
may recover contribution from any other person liable in respect
of the same damage, whether that other person's liability arises by
tort, breach of contract, breach of trust or otherwise. (This Act
completely replaces earlier provisions on this topic contained in

the Law Reform (Married Women and Tortfeasors) Act 1935, s. 6, which were repealed by the 1978 Act.)

13. Employers. An employer may be liable in tort:

(*a*) *at common law* (in negligence) for breach of his duty to provide:

    (*i*) a safe system of work;

    (*ii*) a competent staff;

    (*iii*) adequate plant, machinery, etc: *Wilson & Clyde Coal Co*. v. *English* (1938).

(*b*) for breach of a specific statutory duty: e.g. under the Factories Acts.

Some such duties are said to be *strict* in the sense that liability follows automatically from a breach of duty, irrespective of negligence: *Groves* v. *Wimborne* (1898) (on the Factory Acts). Sometimes, a statutory duty may overlap with a common law duty: e.g. Health & Safety at Work Act 1974 (relates to dangerous machinery (*see* **13** (*a*) (*i*));

(*c*) vicariously (*see* **14–17**).

VICARIOUS LIABILITY

14. The Rule. "He who acts through another, acts for himself" (Latin: *qui facit per alium facit per se*). Thus, a person who authorises the commission of a tort, expressly or impliedly, by another, is liable in damages just as if he himself had committed that tort. Liability so arising is called *vicarious liability*: it is indirect.

Vicarious liability is said to consist of "the liability A may incur towards C for the negligence or other tort of B where a *special relationship* exists between A and B, and B's tort is *referable to that relationship*.": Sir Percy Winfield.

15. Special Relationship. In practice the most common relationship which gives rise to vicarious liability is that of master (employer) and servant (employee). Whether this relationship exists or not is a question which is decided by reference to the following tests.

(*a*) Is the alleged servant employed under a *contract of service*? (or is it one *for services*, in which case he will probably be an independent contractor, for which *see* **17**).

(*b*) Is he *under the control* of another in the sense not only of what he must do, but also how he should do it? (the *control* test) *Mersey Docks* v. *Coggins & Griffiths* (1947).

(*c*) Is he an *integral part* of the other's business? This is a useful test in cases involving experts, such as surgeons, who cannot be said to be "controlled": *Cassidy* v. *Minister of Health* (1951).

(*d*) Is there provision for *another* to arrange for payment of national insurance contributions, wages, income tax, etc., and what is the extent of the power of dismissal?: *Ready Mixed Concrete* v. *Minister of Pensions* (1968).

Not all these tests are necessarily applied in a given case. The first one is the *basic* test; the rest are guidelines which have been used in the cases cited and elsewhere.

As well as in the master/servant relationship, vicarious liability arises in the case of *partner and co-partner* and *principal and agent*. However, there is not normally vicarious liability in cases of casual delegation. An example is given by *Morgans* v. *Launchbury* (1972). Here, A regularly used his wife's car to drive to and from work, frequently arriving home intoxicated. He agreed that in future he would get a friend to drive should he get drunk again; one night A asked B to drive the car to A's home, but an accident occured whilst B was driving towards a restaurant. HELD: Mrs. A (the car-owner) was not liable for B's negligence, since B was not acting on her instructions (B was not her agent).

If there is delegation of a *particular task*, however, even without reward, the person committing the tort will be treated as the other's agent, and vicarious liability will be incurred by that other: *Ormrod* v. *Crossville Motor Services* (1953).

16. Referability. This generally equates with the question: Was the tort committed by the servant (or agent) *in the course of his employment*? (i.e. was the servant doing improperly what he was employed to do). There is no universal rule applicable in every case. Whilst, obviously, no servant is legitimately employed to commit crimes, a fraud *has* been held to have been perpetrated in the course of a clerk's employment: *Lloyd* v. *Grace Smith* (1912). Perhaps the closest to a rule we can get is: Is the servant (employee/agent) at the material time engaged in the furtherance of his master's business, or is he on a "frolic of his own"? *Joel* v. *Morrison* (1834). With this in mind it can be seen that:

(*a*) it is irrelevant whether the servant is doing something for his own convenience, whilst engaged at his job.

EXAMPLE: A's employee B was delivering petrol to a garage. While the petrol was flowing from the lorry to a tank B lit a cigarette, and negligently caused an explosion by throwing away the match. HELD: A was vicariously liable, since at the time of disposing of the match B was in the course of his employment: *Century Insurance* v. *Northern Ireland Road Transport Board* (1942);

(b) it *may* even be irrelevant if the servant is expressly *forbidden* from doing something: *Limpus* v. *London General Omnibus Company* (1862).

Whether or not it is relevant will depend upon whether the prohibition is such as "*in itself and by itself delimits the scope of the servant's employment*" or not: *Rose* v. *Plenty* (1976).

For example, an instruction that "bus conductors must not drive buses." *delimits* the job of conductor; he is thereby confined to conducting, and any torts committed in the course of driving will *not* be in the course of his employment: *Beard* v. *London General Omnibus Company* (1900); *cf. Ricketts* v. *Tilling* (1915). On the other hand, a prohibition may be such that, if a servant disregards it he is deemed merely to be *doing improperly what he is employed to do*; i.e. he *is* in the course of his employment: *Rose* v. *Plenty* (1976).

17. Independent contractors. Generally, a master is not liable for the torts of his independent contractors. There are, however, several exceptions, including the following.

(a) Where the wrong committed by the contractor amounts to a tort of strict liability: *Rylands* v. *Fletcher* (1868).

(b) Where work is done over or on a highway: *Tarry* v. *Ashton* (1876), or involves fire: *Balfour* v. *Barty-King* (1957), or involves "extra-hazardous" activities: *Honeywill & Stein* v. *Larkin* (1934).

(c) Where the employer is a carrier or bailee for reward, and injury is suffered by charges or goods in his safe-keeping.

These are examples of "*non-delegable*" *duties*—in other words, it could be said that the employer is *personally*, rather than vicariously liable. An employer of independent contractors will be liable in any case if he himself is guilty of a breach of duty—as by hiring a contractor to commit trespass.

GENERAL DEFENCES IN TORT

18. Volenti non fit injuria. (Consent negates legal injury.) To be effective as a defence, the *consent* must be to the full risk of the injury—mere knowledge (*sciens*) of that risk is not enough: *Dann* v. *Hamilton* (1938).

(*a*) But such consent as *is* offered *need not be express*—indeed, it is sometimes said that consent *as such* is not necessary, and that the defence consists of the *voluntary assumption of the risk* (on the part of a plaintiff) of the injury of which he complains.

EXAMPLE: A and B were professional shotfirers, who chose to disregard certain instructions as to the use of explosives. Both were injured in the process of blasting. HELD: The defence of *volenti* applied: *I.C.I.* v. *Shatwell* (1965).

Similarly, it can be inferred that spectators of dangerous sports are *volens* with regard to the risk of accidents: *Hall* v. *Brooklands Auto-Racing Club* (1933); though probably not to unusual risks, not normally incidental to the sport in question: *Payne* v. *Maple Leaf Gardens Ltd.* (1949) (a Canadian case).

(*b*) *Consent* (*or assumption of risk*) *must be real and freely given.* The plaintiff must have a real choice: *Burnett* v. *B.W.B.* (1972); consent must not be induced by threats or the pressure of duty.

EXAMPLE: A policeman was injured in stopping a runaway horse in pursuance of his duty. HELD: He had not consented to injury: *Haynes* v. *Harwood* (1935).

But where an ordinary citizen, under no duty, was injured in stopping a horse he was *volens* (i.e. had consented) to his injuries: *Cutler* v. *United Daries* (1953).

NOTE: these cases can be distinguished by virtue of the fact that in the former, some children were nearby and there was therefore a strong likelihood of injury to someone had the horse not been stopped. It is arguable that, had the facts been similar in the *Cutler* Case, the plaintiff could have been said to have been under a *moral duty* to assist—the law is generally unwilling to allow the defence of *volenti non fit injuria* against a *rescuer*: *Baker* v. *Hopkins* (1959).

(*c*) *Employers' liability.* It is often said that *volenti* is not a defence in cases of breaches of employers' duties to their employees: *Smith* v. *Baker* (1891). It is submitted, however, that in so far as this is true, it is by virtue of the fact that an employee will normally have *no choice* in the matter (except, of course, to risk the loss of his job): *Burnett* v. *B.W.B.* (1973). If a *free choice* clearly exists and an employee submits himself to injury, there seems to be no good reason why the defence of *volenti non fit injuria* should not apply (*cf. I.C.I.* v. *Shatwell*).

(*d*) *A related topic is that of exclusion of liability.* Prior to the Motor Vehicles (Compulsory Insurance) Act 1971, a notice repudiating liability for accidents to passengers caused by the negligent driving of an uninsured driver was held to amount, on the part of the passenger to *volenti non fit injuria*: *Buckpitt* v. *Oates* (1968). The 1971 Act, however, has made any "antecedent understanding between driver and passenger . . ." of no effect. It is a nice question whether or not in such cases the injured passenger can still be said to consent to the *injury*; but certainly, he can no longer be said to have *waived his right to sue* by agreement. This provision has been embodied in the Road Traffic Act 1972, s. 148(3).

In similar, but broader vein, is the Unfair Contract Terms Act 1977, s. 2, which provides:

"(1) A person cannot by reference to any contract term or to a notice given to persons generally or to particular persons exclude or restrict his liability for death or personal injury resulting from negligence" (the section goes on to restrict exclusions for other loss or damage to reasonable exclusions).

Section 1(3) provides "where a contract term or notice purports to exclude or restrict liability for negligence, a person's agreement to or awareness of it is *not* of itself to be taken as indicating his *voluntary acceptance of any risk*".

Note that these sections relate to "business liability". *See also* XVI and VII, 13.

Thus, whilst the possibility of the defence of *volenti*, in cases involving contract terms or notices, remains, a defendant cannot rely on such a term or notice to support the defence, but will have to provide evidence that the injured plaintiff *did actually consent* (submit) to the risk of injury *quite apart* from his agreement to or awareness of the term or notice purporting to exclude liability (*cf. White* v. *Blackmore* (1972)).

19. Mistake. Generally mistake is no defence in tort, whether it is mistake of fact or of law, except in the following torts.

(*a*) Malicious prosecution.
(*b*) False imprisonment.
(*c*) Torts requiring malice as a constituent element, e.g. injurious falsehood.
(*d*) Deceit.

20. Accident. This can *only* be a defence where the *accident is inevitable*, i.e. where the consequences of an act are not foreseen and are not intended and could not have been avoided by any reasonable care by the defendant. (Contrast mistake, where the consequences are foreseen, but the defendant wrongly imagines that his act is still justified.)

"*Act of God*" is a special form of inevitable accident and arises where damage is caused by the operation of natural causes without human intervention which are *so unforeseeable that a reasonable man could not be expected to foresee or guard against them.*

The element of unforeseeability characterises both the defences of inevitable accident and Act of God and makes them a rare application.

EXAMPLES:

(1) X, while out shooting, fired at a bird, but his shots ricocheted off a tree and injured the plaintiff. HELD: This was inevitable accident and not actionable: *Stanley* v. *Powell* (1891).

(2) Unprecedented rainfall caused artificial pools on X's land to overflow and flood the plaintiff's land. HELD: Act of God, since wholly unforeseeable because of the unprecedented rainfall: *Nichols* v. *Marsland* (1875).

Act of God is a defence to torts of strict liability, such as *Rylands* v. *Fletcher*, whereas an inevitable accident, such as was involved in *Stanley* v. *Powell* probably is not.

Necessity (where a tort is committed to prevent some greater evil) is seldom invoked nowadays.

21. Statutory authority.

(*a*) *Absolute authority.* Acts done in pursuance of an express command of Parliament are not torts, and harm caused thereby is not actionable, unless it is caused by negligence. Thus, where the building of a railway under authority of statute causes harm to neighbouring land-owners, they have no remedy. But if the harm to them were caused by *negligence* of the railway company, e.g. by allowing sparks to escape and cause fires, liability would arise: *Smith* v. *L. & S.W. Rail Co.* (1870).

(*b*) *Statutory permission.* Where the legislature gives *mere permission* to do something, it must be done in as harmless a manner as possible. Thus, where permission was given to erect a smallpox hospital, it was held that nuisance caused by the hospital was actionable: *Metropolitan Asylum District* v. *Hill* (1881).

22. Limitation of actions. Not a "defence" as such but the rules limiting the period during which an action may be brought may serve to prevent a successful action from being brought, just as much as the general defences proper.

(*a*) *The Limitation period.* Laid down in the Limitation Act 1939, s. 2(1) as six years from the time when the cause of action accrues (*see* (*b*)) (twelve years in actions to recover land).

By the Limitation Act 1975, however, in cases of "negligence, nuisance or breach of statutory duty . . . where damages . . . consist of or include personal injuries", the period is set at three years (adding to the 1939 Act) and this period runs "from the date the cause of action accrues or the date (if later) of the plaintiff's knowledge".

(*b*) *Accrual of actions.* Generally, this occurs when the tort is committed. In cases involving torts of a continuing nature (e.g. nuisance) an independent action arises on each day on which the wrong continues, so that the limitation period runs from the time the wrong is discontinued.

Most of the problems which arose under the old legislation in cases of "delayed" diseases have been dealt with by the Limitation Act 1975 by allowing the limitation period to run from the time "of the plaintiff's knowledge". Thus, in cases of pneumoconiosis, asbestosis, and other diseases which are slow to develop, the limitation period now runs from the time that the plaintiff first has knowledge of the significance of his injury, amongst other things, rather than the time when he may, in fact, have first contracted the disease. Where the injury is in fact death, the limitation period is fixed by the Fatal Accidents Act 1976, and is three years from death, or from the date of knowledge of the person on whose behalf the action is brought (*see* **10, 11**).

PROGRESS TEST 14

1. Explain the tortious liability of:

(*a*) a foreign sovereign or representatives;
(*a*) the British Crown. **(2, 3)**

2. Outline the capacity (in tort) of:

(*a*) minors;
(*d*) their parents. **(6, 7)**

3. A, who is twenty years of age, gives his three-year-old-son the use of his air-pistol. The child accidentally shoots B, an adult, and B wishes to sue A. Advise B.   (6, 7, 14, 15, 20)

4. What are joint tortfeasors? What is their capacity in tort? (12)

5. Explain:

(*a*) vicarious liability;

(*b*) a contract of service;

(*c*) an independent contractor.   (14, 15)

6. In what circumstances will an employer be liable for torts committed by:

(*a*) independent contractors?

(*b*) agents or servants?   (16, 17)

7. A takes his car to B's garage. B hands the car over to C, his employee, and tells him to effect the repairs. Having done the repairs C takes the car out to test it, but whilst out, decides to go joy-riding. In the course of his joy-ride he collides with D's car. Advise A and D as to whether they can bring actions vicariously against B.   (16)

8. Explain what is meant by *volenti non fit injuria*. When is this defence available in tort?   (18)

9. Distinguish *volenti non fit injuria* from a situation where a defendant purports to exclude his liability. What legal effect do such exclusions have?   (18)

10. When, if ever, can (*a*) accident; and (*b*) necessity, be a defence to an action in tort?   (20)

11. Summarise the statutory rules relating to the limitation of actions in tort.   (23)

CHAPTER XV

Trespass and Nuisance

GENERAL

1. Trespass. This is probably the oldest form of tortious liability. The ancient writ of trespass dates back to a time when criminal and civil liability had not yet been recognised as separate. Consequently, some forms of trespass are still both crimes and torts, e.g. assault and battery. Trespass means direct interference with the person, goods or land of another. Trespass is actionable *per se*, i.e. without proof of actual damage suffered on the part of the plaintiff. Nor does it require intention on the part of the defendant; volition is, however, necessary (*see* XIII, 7).

2. Early developments. The early writ of trespass was confined to actions whereby a "breach of the King's Peace" was occasioned (Latin: *vi et armis et contra pacem regis*: with force of arms and against the King's Peace).

From the time of Edward I (1272–1307), however, two other varieties of trespass existed:

(*a*) trespass *quare clausum fregit* (i.e. trespass to land); and

(*b*) trespass *de bonis asportatis* (i.e. the unlawful taking of chattels).

During the thirteenth century, the scope of the action of trespass was further extended, as was the scope of other forms of action; in part at least by virtue of the statute *In Consimili Casu* 1285. Thus the extension of common law writs by analogy became possible, and the restrictions which had been imposed by the Provisions of Oxford 1258, were overcome.

The writ of trespass proved the most "fertile mother of actions": F. W. Maitland (1850–1906). Mediaeval lawyers, without creating entirely new writs, managed to extend trespass to cover indirect injuries to property and person. Such analogous claims were called "actions of trespass on the case". They differed from ordinary trespass in that:

(a) the plaintiff had to prove that he had suffered actual damage, but

(b) which did not involve the direct application of force.

3. Actions on the case. These lay for "consequential" (indirect) injuries not amounting to trespass, and included the following.

(a) *Nuisance.* Indirect interference with property of another, i.e. interference with his enjoyment of his property.

(b) *Negligence.* Injury of another's person or property unintentionally by carelessness amounting to breach of a legal duty to take care.

(c) *Assumpsit.* This action lay where one person had voluntarily undertaken a duty to another not previously imposed on him by law, and committed a breach of this duty. (This action on the case is the ancestor of the law of contract.)

TRESPASS TO THE PERSON

4. Scope of tort. This tort really comprises three separate heads:

(a) assault (*see* **5**);

(b) battery (*see* **6**); and

(c) false imprisonment (*see* **7**).

5. Assault. An attempt or threat to apply force to another whereby that other is reasonably put in present fear of violence, e.g. shaking your fist at someone or pointing at him a gun which he reasonably believes to be loaded, and thinks you may fire: *R.* v. *St. George* (1840).

Thus the following points are important.

(a) Mere threats are sufficient. If actual force is applied then the tort of battery is committed.

(b) The essence of the tort is fear. Therefore mere abuse is not enough. But a false alarm could amount to assault if it causes fright.

(c) A threatening act may be so qualified as to negative reasonable grounds for fear, e.g. where X put his hand on his sword and said, "If it were not assize time" he would resort to violence. HELD: No assault: *Tuberville* v. *Savage* (1669).

(d) Assault is also a crime. A certificate of acquittal or proof of punishment is a bar to later civil proceedings for tort: Offences against the Person Act 1861, s. 45.

5. Battery. This means the intentional application of force upon the person of the plaintiff, against his will; this force, in practice, need only be nominal: "The least touching of another in anger is a battery". Holt C.J., in *Cole* v. *Turner* (1704).

Battery is often combined with assault in civil actions. It is a crime, as well as a tort; the following points should be noted.

(*a*) The touching must be voluntary—accident will be a defence to an action for battery: *Stanley* v. *Powell* (1891).

(*b*) It must also be intentional. Whereas formerly a "negligent" battery was actionable, such unintentional touchings, where they cause injuries, are now actionable in the tort of negligence: *Letang* v. *Cooper* (1964). (An unintentional touching, such as that which may occur in a crowd jostling to get on to a bus, will not give rise to liability where no injury is caused, and is regarded as accidental.)

6. False imprisonment. The total deprivation of the freedom of another for any period, however short, without lawful justification.

(*a*) Restraint may be "physical" (e.g. a locked room), or "practical" (e.g. where P. is surrounded by threatening persons).

(*b*) Restraint must be total. So long as the plaintiff has a means of egress, no imprisonment has taken place (even if he is inconvenienced): *Bird* v. *Jones* (1845).

(*c*) The imprisonment must be occasioned by an act of the defendant. It is no tort that he failed to free the plaintiff (unless he is under a duty to that person (*see* XIII, 9): *Herd* v. *Weardale Steel Co.* (1915)).

(*d*) It is still false imprisonment even if the plaintiff is not aware of the fact that he is not free to go as he pleases: *Meering* v. *Grahame-White Aviation Co.* (1919).

7. Defences to trespass to the person.

(*a*) *Self defence* (in assault or battery). This is a valid defence where it is used to protect one's person or property. But force used must be reasonable in the circumstances, e.g. you may not stab a man who merely slaps your face: *Cook* v. *Beal* (1697). Reasonable force may also be used to eject a trespasser from land, and will not then constitute battery: *Collins* v. *Renison* (1754).

(*b*) *Exercise of parental authority.* This may be delegated to a schoolteacher or anyone else *in loco parentis*: *Cleary* v. *Booth* (1893). Any force used must be reasonable. A husband no longer has a legal right to chastise his wife by force or imprisonment: *R* v *Jackson* (1891).

(c) *Judicial authority.* Arrest or imprisonment is obviously justifiable if under judicial authority, providing the authority is properly given, e.g. arrest under a justices' warrant.

(d) *Arrest of criminals.* Any private citizen is entitled (without obtaining a justices' warrant) to arrest any person whom he believes on reasonable grounds to have committed, or to be in the process of committing, an arrestable offence: Criminal Law Act 1967, s. 2. A police constable may also arrest without warrant in the above circumstances; otherwise generally he must have a warrant.

(e) *Consent* and *inevitable accident.*

9. Criminal proceedings. Assault and battery constitute crimes as well as torts; so, in some circumstances, may trespass to chattel (goods).

Generally, if D has been tried summarily, for assault, and has been convicted and punished, or the case against him dismissed, then no further proceedings, either criminal or civil may be brought against him in respect of the same act: Offences against the Person Act 1861, s. 45.

TRESPASS TO LAND

10. Trespass. This means entering or remaining on land in the possession of the plaintiff, or depositing material thereon, without lawful justification. Trespass therefore consists in interference with possession (as distinct from nuisance, which is interference with enjoyment of occupation). Consequently, the plaintiff must be the possessor of the land, not necessarily the owner; in fact the possessor may have an action for trespass against the owner if his lawful possession is interfered with by the owner.

Like other forms of trespass, trespass to land is theoretically actionable *per se.* It may be committed by entering on land, sitting on a fence, dumping rubbish, allowing cattle to stray, etc. The tort is technically called trespass *quare clausm fregit*, since the ancient writ of trespass began with these words (meaning whereas he has broken the "close" or boundary) (*see* 2).

1. Notes on trespass to land.

(a) It is a tort, not a crime. Notices saying "Trespassers will be prosecuted" are therefore incorrect, as a trespasser cannot be prosecuted, since it is not a crime.

(b) It may be commiteed unawares, e.g. by walking across land which is private, in the mistaken belief that there is a public right of way across it.

(c) Unauthorised use. A person on land with permission of the occupier may commit trespass if he exceeds the scope of his permission, e.g. where a person used a public footpath across land for the purpose of spying on the owner's race-horses in training: *Hickman* v. *Maisey* (1900).

(d) It may be perpetrated through a non-human agency, e.g. cattle, rubbish, missiles, roots of trees, etc. Thus, where A's horse kicked B's mare through the fence separating A's land from B's, A was held liable for trespass: *Ellis* v. *Loftus Iron Co.* (1874).

(e) The tort is not confined to trespassers to "land" in the sense of the land-surface. Thus, trespass to land may be committed by interfering with the airspace above P's land, as with a sign: *Kelsen* v. *Imperial Tobacco Co.* (1957); or by burrowing underneath it. The Civil Aviation Act 1949, provides a defence to such trespasses as may technically be committed whenever aeroplanes fly over P's land, though it also provides that if anything should fall out of the 'plane, or any damage caused by the aircraft in some other way, then liability will be strict.

2. Trespass *ab initio*.
A person entering the plaintiff's land with permission may become a trespasser if the permission is withdrawn, or if he exceeds the scope of permission, e.g. by doing an unlawful act: *Hickman* v. *Maisey* (1900).

A distinction is drawn between private permission and public licence.

(a) *Private permission* from the occupier. If the permission is revoked, e.g. because of unruly conduct, the defendant becomes a trespasser from the moment of revocation (and must be given a reasonable time to leave, before force can be used to eject him).

(b) *Public licence*, e.g. where the law gives to the public a right of entry, such as the right of travellers to enter inns. If a person entering the plaintiff's land or premises under such a public right abuses his right he becomes a trespasser.

(i) If the abuse consists of non-feasance, i.e. not doing something he should do, he becomes a trespasser from that moment. Thus, where customers at an inn became rowdy and refused to pay for drinks, their licence to remain was revoked and they became trespassers at that time: *Six Carpenters' Case* (1610)

(*ii*) If the abuse consists of a misfeasance, i.e. doing something wrongful, he becomes a trespasser from the moment of entry (i.e. *ab initio*). Thus, a hotel guest who after a week at a hotel does something positively tortious, loses his licence to be there and can be sued for seven days' trespass, as though he had never had such a licence.

> NOTE: The doctrine of trespass *ab initio* has recently been doubted by the C.A. as largely inapplicable to modern circumstances, and doubt has been thrown on the validity of the decision in the *Six Carpenters' Case* (above): *Chic Fashions (West Wales)* v. *Jones* (1968). The doctrine will certainly not apply so as to make someone a trespasser for the purpose of the law of burglary (*see* XXVIII, 6).

13. Trespass by relation back. A person's possession of land dates back in law to the time when he became entitled to possession, even though he did not actually take possession until some time later. He can therefore sue for trespass committed any time after he became entitled to possession, e.g. where the heir to land returns from abroad to discover that a trespasser has been occupying the land since the death of the owner some years before. This is called "trespass by relation back" to the date of entitlement to possession.

14. Trespass by severance. Trespass can also be committed by severance, i.e. by detaching something attached to the land, such as fruit, crops, flowers, timber. In such cases the plaintiff may sue for the value of the thing severed, or for compensation for the diminution in the value of the land by reason of the severance.

15. Trespass and incorporeal rights. A person who, whilst not the possessor of the land as such nevertheless is the owner of something attached to the land (such as in **14**) may sue in respect of this thing. Interference with servitudes, such as rights to light, or to the use of land, are protected not by the tort of trespass, but that of nuisance.

16. Who can sue? Notice that trespass is a tort against possession, not against ownership. Therefore any person in possession of land can sue for trespass.

It is no defence to show that the plaintiff's right of possession is

defeasible by a third person, e.g. where the trespasser proves that
the plaintiff holds the land under a lease which is void for some
reason. This principle is technically expressed by saying that *jus
tertii* (the right of a third party) is no defence.

17. Remedies for trespass.

(a) *Damages.* This is usually the amount necessary to compensate the plaintiff for any diminution in the value of the land, or
for any loss caused to him by interrupted possession.

(b) *Injunction.* This forbids continuation or repetition of the
trespass.

(c) *Animals.* The Animals Act 1971, s. 1, entitles the occupier
of property to detain livestock which strays on to his land, subject to compensation being paid for any damage caused thereby.
He must, however, take reasonable care of detained animals, and
must report their detention to the police within forty-eight hours.

(d) *Re-entry and ejection.* Under the Statute of Forcible Entries
1381, it was an offence to use force to enter property, even if the
person using such force was an occupier who had been dispossessed by a trespass (e.g. a holidaymaker whose house is
"squatted" in during his absence). If the occupier could re-enter
peaceably, he could use reasonable force to eject the trespasser—
as, indeed he could where he had not been dispossessed at all:
Hemmings v. *Stoke Poges Golf Club* (1920).

The Criminal Law Act 1977, however, repealed the Statute of
Forcible Entries 1381, and substituted two offences:

(i) "using or threatening violence for the purpose of securing
entry into any premises . . . without lawful authority . . . provided there is someone present . . . on the premises who is
opposed to the entry" (s. 6); and

(ii) by s. 7; "failing to leave premises, having entered as a
trespasser on being required to do so" by a "displaced residential
occupier."

Whilst the offence under s. 6 may still, prima facie, be committed by the occupier himself (as in the example given above),
s. 6(3) provides for the defence that he is a "displaced residential
occupier". Thus the owner of a dwelling house may now re-enter
his premises, by force if necessary, and eject trespassers therein,
the common-law remedy of ejectment being unchanged.

18. Defences. The general defence is justification of entry, e.g. by
showing that it was made with the consent of the possessor or

under process of law, e.g. by court order, as where a bailiff enters to seize the occupier's property in pursuance of a court order. Necessity may also be a defence in some cases (*see* XXVI, **10**).

WRONGFUL INTERFERENCE WITH GOODS

19. Wrongful interference with goods. This is a general term, given to a number of possible varieties of torts, by the Torts (Interference with Goods) Act 1977. Section 1 of this Act defines "wrongful interference with goods" as involving any of the following:

(*a*) conversion of goods (known formerly as trover);

(*b*) trespass to goods (trespass *de bonis asportatis* (*see* **2**));

(*c*) negligence, in so far as it results in damage to goods; and

(*d*) any other tort, in so far as it results in damage to goods.

Then s. 2 abolishes the tort of detinue (unlawful detention of goods). Negligence and "any other torts" are dealt with elsewhere; this leaves trespass and conversion to be considered.

20. Trespass to goods. Trespass *de bonis asportatis* lay originally, like trespass to the person, for direct interferences—this time, though, to goods rather than to the person. This may include causing direct injury to the goods (such as throwing acid on to P's clothing, burning it); or it may involve the removal of the goods from P's possession. The following features can be stated.

(*a*) The action is founded on possession, and not ownership. Thus the plaintiff need only be the borrower of goods, or bailee: *The Winkfield* (1902).

(*b*) Like trespass generally, trespass to goods is actionable *per se* (without any need for actual damage).

(*c*) The interference (or touching) must be intentional or negligent.

(*d*) A finder of lost chattels (goods) does not commit trespass, unless the owner is known, or could be easily ascertained, and he keeps them nevertheless. In fact, the finder of goods has a title to sue anyone other than the owner himself (since the action is based on possession): *Armory* v. *Delamirie* (1722).

21. Trespass and detinue. The tort of detinue has now been abolished. Detinue derived in fact from the old action of debt. It differed from that action in that it referred, not to a sum of money owed by D, but to chattels owned by P, which were in D's possession and which D wrongfully detained. Thus, D may have acquired the chattel (goods) quite innocently (e.g. by a loan), and was not, therefore, guilty of any trespass, but may still be liable for their retention.

The Torts (Interference with Goods) Act 1977, s. 2, has extended the definition of conversion so as to include the wrongful detention of goods, as well as other dealings with goods which are inconsistent with the plaintiff's title (*see* 22).

22. Conversion. This action was once known as "trover" since it relied on a fictitious "finding" of the goods (trover=to find).

It may nowadays be defined as any dealing with goods which is adverse to the plaintiff's right to them. Thus the taking of goods may amount to conversion; so, however, might the destruction of goods which are lawfully in the defendant's possession as bailee, and their unauthorised sale by the defendant: *Consolidated Co.* v. *Curtis* (1892). The following main points therefore emerge.

(*a*) Like trespass, conversion is based on possession: There is also sufficient *locus standi* (title to sue) if the plaintiff has an immediate right to possession.

(*b*) Whereas formerly loss or destruction of goods, to constitute conversion, had to be intentional, the Torts (Interference with Goods) Act 1977, s. 2, provides that an action will lie in conversion for loss or destruction of goods which a bailee has *allowed to happen* in breach of his duty to his bailor. In allowing an action for unintended loss or destruction the Act has filled a gap which would otherwise have resulted.

(*c*) "Innocent" interference is no defence. Thus, so long as D acts intentionally, ignorance as to the owner's rights will not excuse him: *Hollins* v. *Fowler* (1875). So a woman was guilty of conversion even where she moved another's goods, as she said, because she feared a burglary: *Kirk* v. *Gregory* (1876) (*see* XXIII).

(*d*) Defences are, basically:

(*i*) that the defendant is the owner, or has the owner's authority to detain the goods;

(*ii*) that the defendant had the consent of the possessor of the goods.

23. Trespass and conversion: remedies. Generally, the remedies for trespass and for conversion were (and remain) the same. They include the following.

(a) *Damages*, assessed as the value at the time of the interference with the goods.

(b) *Recaption and replevin*: where goods are not damaged or destroyed, the plaintiff may retake them, by reasonable force if necessary.

(c) *Injunction*. This is appropriate to prevent further use by D, in a manner which is inconsistent with P's rights.

The Torts (Interference with Goods) Act 1977, s. 3, has retained the possibility that the return of goods to the plaintiff may be ordered by the court instead of, or as well as, damages.

The Act has also removed the old anomaly whereby, since both the actual possessor and anyone who had a right to immediate possession (e.g. an owner of goods who has bailed them to P) could sue, a defendant may be liable twice in respect of the same goods.

Section 7 provides that if a converter of goods pays damages to the possessor, and then to the owner, then the possessor is accountable to the owner, who, in turn, should re-imburse the converter.

NUISANCE

24. Nature of nuisance. Nuisance is an action on the case. It consists of the unlawful interference with the use or enjoyment of another's land. Unlike trespass, it is not actionable *per se*, but, because of its nature, does not normally require physical injuries such as may be involved in cases of negligence: *Fay* v. *Prentice* (1845). In this case the corner of the defendant's house projected over the plaintiff's land; HELD: that to establish nuisance it was *not* necessary to show that rain fell from the overhang, so damaging the plaintiff's land. Thus, dumping rubbish on your neighbour's land, being direct, is trespass. Dumping rubbish on your own land, causing a smell, inconveniencing your neighbour, is indirect, and therefore a nuisance. It is not necessary (in order for it to be a nuisance) that your neighbour should become ill as a consequence.

25. Varieties of nuisance.

(a) *Public nuisance*. The definition of nuisance given above refers primarily to private nuisance. A public nuisance may be said to have occurred where the interference is with the enjoyment of property whose use is shared by the public or a large number of public, and is therefore defined as a nuisance which "materially affects the reasonable comfort and convenience of life of a class of Her Majesty's subjects who come within the sphere of its operation": Winfield. Thus, obstruction of the highway or of a waterway used by the public is a public nuisance: *Rose* v. *Miles* (1815).

(*b*) *Private nuisance*. As defined above, consists generally of an unlawful interference, with the use of enjoyment of another's land. Such an interference may be:

(*i*) an interference with a corporeal hereditament (i.e. the land itself, or use thereof) such as pollution; or

(*ii*) an interference with an incorporeal hereditament or servitude (i.e. particular rights attaching to the land).

This last variety is an ancient form of wrong, since the particular right concerned is proprietary in nature, and may be "natural" (e.g. the right to use of a stream: *Young* v. *Bankie Distillery Co.* (1893)); or may be "acquired" (e.g. the right to light: *Colls* v. *Home and Colonial Stores* (1904)).

26. Public nuisance. This is a crime as well as a tort, since its effects are such as to go beyond a single person's interests. A person committing a public nuisance can therefore be prosecuted in the criminal courts, or sued, by the Attorney-General acting on behalf of the public, to secure an injunction to prevent continuance of the nuisance.

A private individual may sue on his own behalf, but only if he suffers some special damage; that is some loss or harm *over* and above that suffered by the public at large. (For example, where the defendant obstructed a waterway, and, whereas the public were thereby inconvenienced, the plaintiff, who was dependent on the access provided by the waterway in order to deliver goods by barge, suffered considerable additional expense in having his goods carried overland: *Rose* v. *Miles* (1815)).

27. Private nuisance.

(*a*) The interference must be "unlawful". Thus a landowner was not liable when he abstracted percolating water from underneath his own property, and subsidence was caused in his neighbour's, even though he acted maliciously: HELD that, since he had a legal right to abstract the water, no action could lie: *Bradford* v. *Pickles* (1895) H.L.

(*b*) Where actual damage to the property, or things on the

property is suffered, the defendant will not be able to claim his own use of land was reasonable: *St. Helen's Smelting Co.* v. *Tipping* (1865): but;

(c) Though it is not normally necessary for the plaintiff to show the defendant's conduct is unreasonable, the defendant may not be liable if he can show he acted reasonably having regard to to all the circumstances, including the following.

(i) *the locality*: "that may be a nuisance in Grosvenor Square which would be none in Smithfield Market": *per* Pollock C. B., in *Bamford* v. *Turnley* (1862).

(ii) *sensibility of plaintiff*: if the alleged interference is only such as would affect a sensitive user of land, and not normally reasonable use no nuisance is committed: *Robinson* v. *Kilvert* (1889).

(iii) *defendant's intention*: where D created a noise purely to annoy his neighbours, whose music-making he disliked, he was liable: *Christie* v. *Davey* (1893). Had he merely been making "reasonable noise" such as turning up his television set purely in order to hear it above the noise from next door, doubtless he would not have been liable.

NOTE: This situation should be carefully distinguished from that in *Bradford* v. *Pickles* (above); there D had a legal right to abstract water: here, we cannot speak of a "legal right" to make a noise.

28. Parties to an action in private nuisance.

(a) *Who can sue?* Generally, the plaintiff must have a proprietary interest—he must be the occupier of the land affected. Thus, when C's wife was injured by broken glass falling from his kitchen ceiling which had been broken by D's gutter collapsing, the wife had no remedy in nuisance: *Cunard* v. *Antifyre* (1933). (This case is also cited to support the proposition that private nuisance cannot be brought for personal injuries unless negligence can be proved.)

(b) *Who can be sued?*

(i) The creator of a nuisance—even if he is no longer in occupation of the land from where the nuisance emanates: *Roswell* v. *Prior* (1701).

(ii) The occupier of the land from whence the nuisance emanates. This is so even if he is not the creator of the nuisance, so long as he has "adopted" or "continued" the nuisance:

Sedleigh-Denfield v. *O'Callaghan* (1940) (either knowingly or negligently: *Barker* v. *Herbert* (1911)).

(*iii*) A landlord who retains the power to inspect premises let by him: *Wilchick* v. *Marks* (1934).

29. Strict liability. Where the nuisance involves premises adjacent to a highway, and which fall into disrepair, then the occupier is strictly liable for all consequences, including personal injuries, not only to passers-by: *Tarry* v. *Ashton* (1876); but to adjoining occupiers also: *Wringe* v. *Cohen* (1940).

30. Defences to nuisance actions. Apart from the general defences of consent and statutory authority, several defences exist to an action in nuisance.

(*a*) Where D's act is lawful and reasonable (*see* 27(*c*)).

(*b*) Prescription: where P has "suffered" the nuisance for twenty years without complaint. It is no defence, however, that D has conducted himself in the same way for twenty years, if P has not in fact felt the effects and condoned them: *Sturges* v. *Bridgeman* (1879).

(*c*) Generally, a lack of intention or negligence, to do the act which causes the nuisance: thus, if a tree collapses on to P's car due to rot, undiscoverable by reasonable inspection: or where a "latent defect" in building materials causes the collapse of a wall, D will not be liable: *Noble* v. *Harrison* (1926).

NOTE: such instances are sometimes called "secret unobservable processes of nature". Act of God, similarly, will be a defence for the same reasons.

(*d*) Though not strictly a defence, D may show that the harm suffered by P was the result not of a continuous state of affairs, but an isolated event. This is not a nuisance, though of course, it is open to P to attempt to prove negligence on someone's part: *Salisbury* v. *Woodland* (1970).

31. Remedies for nuisance. In addition to the normal remedies of damages and injunctions, the plaintiff has the self-help remedy of abatement.

Abatement consists in the plaintiff terminating the nuisance himself, without going to court, e.g. by cutting off overhanging branches of his neighbour's trees which are impinging on the air-space above the plaintiff's own ground. If life or property are endangered, or the nuisance can be abated without entering the defendant's land, the plaintiff can exercise his right of abatement without prior notice to the defendant: *Lemmon* v. *Webb* (1894). But if he will need to enter the defendant's land to abate the nuisance, he must give notice of his intention to do so, and if then refused permission to enter, he must sue in the normal way.

PROGRESS TEST 15

1. Define trespass and explain its origins. **(1–3)**

2. Define assault and battery. How would you distinguish them? **(5–6)**

3. What is meant by false imprisonment? Can such a tort be done negligently, e.g. by omitting to act? In what circumstances may such imprisonment be justified? **(7, 8)**

4. Define trespass to land. What is meant by trespass by relation back? In what circumstances may the occupier of land use force to prevent trespass? **(10–17)**

5. A was motoring correspondent for a newspaper and was interested in a new "secret" racing car being developed by B. Having been given permission by B to look at standard models in production at B's factory, he took the opportunity to sneak into B's "secret" workshop and take photographs of the new racing car. B has applied for an injunction to prevent A publishing the photographs, on the grounds that A was a trespasser. Discuss. **(10–18)**

6. Summarise the remedies and defences appropriate in an action for trespass to land. **(17, 18)**

7. Define (*a*) trespass to goods; (*b*) wrongful interference with goods, giving examples of both, including examples of how they developed. **(19, 20)**

8. Outline the remedies available in cases of wrongful interference with goods. **(23)**

9. Distinguish public and private nuisance. **(25)**

10. Distinguish trespass to land from nuisance. Who is liable in cases of the latter? **(24, 28, 29)**

11. A has a clothes-line, supported by a tall post in his garden. One night, a boy climbs the post to steal apples from A's nearby tree. The next morning the post collapses, flattening B's greenhouse next door and injuring B's visitor C. Advise B and C. **(28–30)**

CHAPTER XVI

Negligence

THE TORT OF NEGLIGENCE

1. The meaning of negligence. The word negligence has two meanings in the law of torts:

(*a*) a "state of mind" which may be such as to form the basis of liability in several torts, e.g. nuisance, trespass (*see* XIII, **8**);

(*b*) a separate tort consisting of the breach of a specific duty, recognised by the law, and owed to the plaintiff.

The separate tort of negligence is a comparatively recent development: whilst the failure to take care in relation to others was recognised in 1676 (*Mitchil* v. *Alestree*); the tort itself was only formulated in the nineteenth century (*Blyth* v. *Birmingham Waterworks Co.* (1856)), where the notion of the "reasonable man' first appears. The tort derives from trespass by way of the action on the case. Therefore, like all actions on the case, it is actionable only on proof of actual damage (i.e. is not actionable *per se*). It is said to lie for "consequential" or "indirect injuries", also (*see* **9**).

2. The tort of negligence. As a separate tort negligence has been defined as "something more than heedless or careless conduct, whether in omission or commission: it properly connotes the complex concept of duty, breach and damage thereby suffered by the person to whom the duty was owing": *per* Lord Wright in *Lochgelly Iron & Coal Co.* v. *M'Mullan* (1934).

The necessary ingredients of actionable negligence therefore are:

(*a*) a legal duty of care owed to the plaintiff;
(*b*) breach of that duty; and
(*c*) consequent damage.

3. Legal duty of care. A general definition of the legal duty of care is difficult to state: there is no general duty to take care. Indeed, I may be as careless as I wish, so long as I do not cause anyone else harm; and even then may not be liable, if the harm caused is not a foreseeable consequence of my carelessness. On the other hand, the law certainly requires a reasonable degree of care of us in our dealings with others and that degree of care, and the extent to which we are required to exercise it will, in fact, vary from case to case. Thus, where a sick person seeks the aid of a doctor, more is expected of him than the passer-by who just happens to find someone injured on the road. The "notional" duty of care may be expressed as a duty to take such care *as is reasonable* to avoid acts or omissions which it can *reasonably be foreseen* are likely to *cause injury* to someone.

4. The duty in fact. Whilst a "notional" duty may be elusive, whether or not a duty exists in a given case can be established more or less as a fact.

The means whereby this may be established is nowadays by an application of the "neighbour test" formulated by Lord Atkin in *Donoghue* v. *Stephenson* (1932) H.L.:

> "You must take reasonable care to avoid acts or omissions which you can reasonably foresee would be likely to injure your neighbour. Who, then is my neighbour? The answer seems to be—those persons who are so closely and directly affected by my act that I ought reasonably to have them in contemplation as being so affected."

The question, whenever a person suffers injury, then, is whether this can be said to have been reasonably foreseeable on the part of the person whose act (or omission) has, prima facie, caused the injury. Thus, where a pregnant woman hearing the noise of a road accident some distance away, sustained nervous shock, inducing a miscarriage, it was HELD that she was outside the scope of D's duty, and could not recover damages: *Bourhill* v. *Young* (1943) H.L. (To be actionable at all, "nervous shock" must be more than mere upset.)

5. The standard of care. Even given the fact that D could have reasonably foreseen that P may suffer as a consequence of his act or omission, he may not be liable if his conduct was reasonable in the circumstances. Thus, the law "exacts a degree of care commensurate with the risk created": *per* Lord Macmillan in *Read* v. *Lyons* (1947). The test, therefore, is whether a reasonable man would have foreseen the risk to the plaintiff in the circumstances of the case, and if so, whether he would have done (or desisted from doing) anything other than that which the defendant in fact did to avert the danger.

Thus, where P was injured when a cricket ball was struck out of D's ground during the course of a match, it was HELD that although this was foreseeable, the risk of injury was so small that a reasonable man would have taken no further measures to prevent such an occurence: *Bolton* v. *Stone* (1951).

NOTE: the ground was, in fact, fenced off from the surrounding area, and the spot where the ball was struck was a considerable distance from the spot where the plaintiff was struck.

On the other hand, where an employer endangered the sight of a one-eyed employee by failing to provide him with safety goggles, he was liable when the man was blinded, since he was aware of the great risk involved and could, quite reasonably, have provided the goggles: *Paris* v. *Stepney Borough Council* (1951).

6. Normal practice. One rule of thumb which the courts have adopted, in order to determine the standard of care required of a defendant, is what practice is normal in such circumstances. Thus, the do-it-yourself householder is required, when fixing a handle to a door, to use the same screws as would be used by a competent carpenter, in order to avoid liability if his visitor is injured by the handle coming off: *Wells* v. *Cooper* (1958). This is not a binding rule, however, and the courts have been known to find D liable even where he can show that he behaved "perfectly in accord with normal practice": *Cavanagh* v. *Ulster Weaving Co.* (1960).

The implication is that "normal practice" in a particular trade or practice simply may not be good enough, in the event that injury is caused!

7. Unforeseen dangers. Following from 5 and 6 it is obvious that, where the injury incurred by P results from a danger of which D could not reasonably be expected to be aware, then D should not be liable.

EXAMPLE: P was paralysed as a consequence of being injected with a contaminated chemical. This had been stored in phials in a bath of phenol. The contamination had been caused by phenol penetrating hair-line cracks in the phials and going into solution in the chemical. HELD: D was not liable, since this was not a risk which was known to the medical profession at the time: *Roe* v. *Minister of Health* (1954).

Perhaps it is fair to say, however, that once such a case occurs, the risk can no longer be said to be unknown. Thus, if the same thing were to recur, the defendant in a case of this kind would probably be liable.

8. Specific duties. Certain duties are sufficiently well established as to amount to what are virtually separate torts: e.g. the duty owed by an occupier of premises; the duty owed by a bailee of goods.

Two specific duties which have developed recently and which have become of considerable importance are:

(a) the duty to prevent economic loss to the plaintiff; and

(b) the duty to avoid negligent statements.

9. Economic loss. The traditional view is that the tort of negligence arises in the event of personal injuries or damage to property only. Thus, injuries "to the plaintiff's pocket" fell outside its scope. From the nineteenth century at least, the courts were willing to award damages in respect of economic loss so long as that loss was "immediately consequential upon injury to the plaintiff's person or property": *Cattle* v. *Stockton Waterworks* (1875). Thus, if D's negligence causes damage to A's property, but, for some reason, P suffers financially, P cannot recover damages: *Weller* v. *Foot and Mouth Institute* (1966).

No duty of care exists to protect P from purely financial loss.

On the other hand, when due to D's negligence, power was cut off to P's factory, wherein molten metal had to be discarded lest it solidified as the temperature dropped, it was HELD that:

(a) P could recover not only the value of the molten metal, but also such economic loss as was consequential upon its loss (i.e. the profit he would have made on the finished product); but

(b) P could not recover the loss of profit occasioned by the lack of power, since this was not consequential upon any damage to his property: *Spartan Steel* v. *Martin* (1973).

10. Negligent statements. Until 1963 the courts were only willing to allow liability in tort in respect of statements where:

(a) The statement was made fraudulently (in which case the tort of *deceit* was committed): *Derry* v. *Peek* (1889); or

(b) If made negligently, the consequences of the statement were physical injuries (i.e. to the person or to property): *Clayton* v. *Woodman* (1962).

In *Hedley Byrne & Co.* v. *Heller & Partners Ltd.* (1964), it was held by the H.L. that liability would attach for negligent false statements, resulting in pecuniary (financial) loss to the plaintiff, so long as certain conditions applied. These conditions were:

(a) P must rely on the advice sought by him, and given by D.

(b) D must know, or be in a position such that he ought to know of P's reliance.

(c) The circumstances must be such that P's reliance is reasonable.

These three conditions, if fulfilled, constitute a "special relationship" between P and D, which is the basis of liability. Over and above these, however, it is necessary that:

(a) D should not have disclaimed responsibility (though such disclaimers are now only valid if they satisfy the requirements of "reasonableness": Unfair Contract Terms Act 1977, s. 2);

(b) the defendant should not enjoy any special immunity.

EXAMPLE: R was defended by W, a barrister, on a criminal charge. R was convicted, but claimed that this was due to W's negligence. HELD: Counsel enjoy an immunity from liability in negligence since public policy requires that persons involved with the administration of justice should enjoy freedom of action: *Rondel* v. *Worsley* (1967). This decision was followed in *Arenson* v. *Arenson* (1972), where an arbitrator enjoyed a similar immunity. Clearly, this is desirable, since if a convicted criminal could bring such an action, it would, in effect, involve a complete retrial of the criminal action in circumstances where no grounds for a normal appeal exist. This immunity is not a complete one; it is confined to such work done by counsel as is intimately connected with the conduct of the case in court: *Saif Ali* v. *Sydney Mitchell* (1978) (*see* III, 55).

The three conditions which amount to a "special relationship" are given in their vaguest form. The courts have sometimes attempted to be more restrictive; thus, the requirement that P's reliance on D's advice must be reasonable has been seen in one case to mean no less than the fact that D is actually in the business of giving advice professionally: *Mutual Life Assurance Co* v. *Evatt* (1971) P.C. On the other hand, in the most recent case of this kind, it was thought enough that D was in a position to have all the facts.

EXAMPLE: P took on the franchise of a petrol station owned by D. D represented to him that the station was assured of a particular turnover: the rerouting of a highway meant that motorists seldom used the station in fact. HELD: D was liable, since, being in the petrol station business, it was his business to know of highway plans such as these, which were bound to effect sales, and therefore was negligent in making representations to P which failed to take account of such plans: *Esso Petroleum Ltd.* v. *Mardon* (1976).

11. Negligent mis-statement: a new tort? Recent decisions have sufficiently defined and extended the principle begun in *Hedley Byrne* (**10**) to give rise to the question: is this now a new, separate tort? Apart from the need for a special relationship, which is unique, the following developments should be considered.

EXAMPLES

(1) D (a local authority) approved the foundations of a house which was later sold by the builder to X, who, in turn, sold it to P. Some time later cracks appeared in the walls, and it was discovered that the foundations were, in fact, unsound, being built on an old rubbish tip. HELD: P could recover damages in respect of both the cost of repairing her house, and the fall in value suffered: *Dutton* v. *Bognor Regis U.D.C.* (1972).

NOTE: this case extends the duty of care to third parties, i.e. persons other than those to whom the statement is actually made, as is the case in negligence generally.

(2) D leased to P a warehouse, and covenanted to maintain insurance cover against fire, and, in the event of a claim, re-instate the premises. P therefore left all insurance matters to D. Later D was bought out, and the purchasing company ceased to take out cover. A fire occurred and P sought to recover the cost of re-instatement from D. It was HELD that P could not recover on the basis of D's failure to inform him of this change in circumstances: *Argy Trading Co.* v. *Lapid Developments Ltd.* (1977).

Thus liability arises in respect of acts (or, more accurately, positive statements) but not omissions: in this negligent mis-statement differs from negligence generally.

(*Dutton's case* has been followed in several decisions, e.g. *Anns* v. *Merton* (1977); *Batty* v. *Metropolitan Property Ltd.* (1978).)

12. Proof of negligence: *res ipsa loquitur* (the facts speak for themselves). Whereas, to establish a breach of duty, the plaintiff must normally prove a want of care on the party of the defendant, in some circumstances negligence can be presumed, on the grounds that:

(a) the defendant had sole control of the cause of mischief; and
(b) the accident which occurred was such as could not normally happen without negligence.

Thus, where P is injured, whilst walking in the road, by panels falling from D's window, a presumption of negligence on D's part is raised: *Byrne* v. *Boadle* (1863); or where P slips on yoghurt on the floor of D's shop: *Ward* v. *Tesco Stores* (1976).

The effect of this presumption is effectively to shift the burden of proof away from the plaintiff and on to the defendant (to try to prove that the incident was not caused by his negligence). Such explanations as he offers, therefore, must be consistent with the taking of reasonable care on his part. Thus, where a wall collapses on to P, the burden of rebutting the presumption of negligence falls on to D. If D can show that his work was carried out in accordance with stringent safety regulations, he will have discharged that burden: *Walsh* v. *Holst* (1958).

On the other hand, the defendant's explanation, whilst perhaps revealing how the accident in fact occurred, may fail to satisfy the court that he was not negligent, after all.

EXAMPLE: P was injured when the bus in which he was a passenger crashed. D (the bus company) showed that the accident was due not to negligent driving on the part of their driver, but to a fault in a tyre, which burst, causing the crash. It was HELD, that they had nevertheless been negligent in failing to detect and remedy the fault: *Barkway* v. *S. Wales Transport Co.* (1950).

13. **Contributory negligence.** At common law, a defendant could normally escape liability if he could show that, despite his negligence, the harm complained of would not have occurred if the plaintiff had not contributed to the accident by his own negligence: *Butterfield* v. *Forrester* (1809).

The Law Reform (Contributory Negligence) Act 1945 has effectively abolished that rule, and provides that, where a plaintiff suffers injury "as the result partly of his own fault and partly of the fault of any other person . . .", then he can still recover damages, but the damages must be reduced "to such extent as the court thinks just": Law Reform (Contributory Negligence) Act

1945, s. 1(1). The word "fault" includes negligence, of course, but it is not necessary to show that the plaintiff is himself negligent, in the sense of being in breach of a duty of care, in order to establish contributory negligence. It is often said, then, that contributory negligence today consists of a failure on the part of the plaintiff, to take reasonable care for his own safety. Thus, where P was riding on the tow-bar of a "traxcavator" vehicle which was involved in a collision with another vehicle which was being negligently driven, he was guilty of contributory negligence, since the tow-bar was obviously a dangerous place to ride in the event of such a collision: *Jones* v. *Livox Quarries* (1952).

It is also accepted now that a plaintiff may be found to have been contributorily negligent not only if his failure to take care for his own safety is actually, somehow, a contributory cause of the accident whereby he is injured, but also, where his conduct is such that, although in no way a factor which causes the accident, it nevertheless results in his injuries being greater than they would otherwise have been. Thus, where P fails to wear a seat-belt and is injured when the driver of the car in which he is a passenger negligently collides with something, and he is thrown through the windscreen: *Froom* v. *Butcher* (1976).

NOTE: the court must of course be satisfied that, had he worn a belt, P would in fact have been spared at least some of his injuries, though if the wearing of seat-belts becomes compulsory, they may not be free to question this.

14. Particular applications of negligence. There are several further areas where the tort of negligence has been utilised to meet particular requirements, which can be regarded separately.

(*a*) Liability for nervous shock (*see* 15).
(*b*) Liability for defective chattels (*see* 16).
(*c*) Liability for premises (*see* 17–25).

15. Nervous shock. For a long time, nervous shock was not actionable at all, unless it stemmed from some actual injury, resulting from physical impact.

Where the shock was intentionally inflicted, however, the courts allowed the recovery of damages in *Wilkinson* v. *Downton* (1897). And later the possibility of recovery for nervous shock in circumstances where the plaintiff was in genuine fear of physical injury was mooted: *Dulieu* v. *White* (1901).

In *Hambrook* v. *Stokes* (1925) it was considered enough if the ear was that felt by a mother for the safety of her children, and after 1932 (*Donoghue* v. *Stephenson*) the courts tended to consider nervous shock in the same way they did physical injuries: i.e. is it reasonably foreseeable that the plaintiff will suffer nervous shock as a consequence of the defendant's acts?

EXAMPLE: P suffered nervous shock as a result of witnessing the carnage, after a railway disaster caused by D's servants' negligence: *Chadwick* v. *British Transport Commission* (1967).

The rule has persisted, however, that to recover, the plaintiff must prove something more than anxiety or upset; it must amount to injury, though a "recognisable psychiatric illness" will suffice: *Hinz* v. *Berry* (1970).

16. Defective chattels. It was for long the case that liability would attach in respect of things which were dangerous *per se*. A person was also liable in respect of the dangerous condition of chattels, which was known to him, but of which he failed to warn their recipient, *Farrant* v. *Barnes* (1862).

Donoghue v. *Stephenson* (1932) created the possibility of liability in respect of defects which were not known, but which ought to have been known by the supplier of the defective chattels. Thus the manufacturer of defective underwear was liable when their wearer got a rash from them: *Grant* v. *Australian Knitting Mills* (1936). Whilst it may have been thought that the liability hereby created was confined to "consumer goods" (in *Donoghue* v. *Stephenson* it was a bottle of ginger beer) subsequent developments have shown that such liability goes further than this. Thus, when a dangerous chemical was mistakenly supplied to a school laboratory, resulting in an explosion, the suppliers were liable: *Kubach* v. *Hollands* (1937).

17. Defective premises and land. In general, liability (if any) in respect of defective premises and land will be incurred by the occupier of the premises or land concerned. We speak, therefore, of occupier's liability. Non-occupiers may be liable in negligence if they render land dangerous without fault on the part of the occupier himself (*see* **22** (*c*)).

OCCUPIERS LIABILITY

18. Occupiers Liability Act 1957. This statute "codified" the common law, and restated it adding little new material. In studying the subject, however, it is necessary to look at pre-Act cases for definitions, etc.

19. Who is an occupier? Defined as the person who has overall control of the premises. Thus, he may be absent, leaving someone else on the premises. Such a situation may give rise to more than one occupier: *Wheat* v. *Lacon* (1966). Indeed, the owner of premises, in employing independent contractors to work on the premises may relinquish control to the contractors, so as to make them occupiers for the purposes of the Act: *Bunker* v. *Brand* (1969).

20. What are the premises? Liability may attach in respect of anything which is, in effect, capable of being occupied; thus a hole: *Bunker* v. *Brand*; a wall: *Latham* v. *Johnson* (1913); and a lift: *Haseldine* v. *Daw* (1941), have all been held to be premises. Thus, if A is injured whilst riding in B's car, liability would be in negligence if the injuries are due to B's negligent driving, but under the Occupiers Liability Act if the injuries are caused by, say, the seat collapsing and breaking A's leg.

21. To whom is the duty owed? The Occupiers Liability Act is explicit on this. Section 2(1) provides that an occupier owes the same duty, the "common duty of care", to all his visitors.

The term "visitors" includes everyone who enters the premises with the express or implied invitation of the occupier, i.e. are not trespassers, who are not included in the provisions of the Act at all, and must therefore be dealt with separately.

Where the visitor enters the premises in pursuance of a contract, the occupier may regulate his liability, or even exclude it altogether, by the terms of the contract. If the situation amounts to one of "business liability", then liability for death or personal injury cannot be excluded or restricted, and liability for other loss or damage can only be excluded in the extent that such terms or notice, which purports to bring the exclusion clause to the plaintiff's attention "satisfies the requirements of reasonableness": Unfair Contract Terms Act 1977, s. 2.

22. The common duty of care. This is defined (Occupiers Liability Act 1957, s. 2(2)) as a duty "to take such care as in all the circumstances of the case is reasonable to see that the visitor will be reasonably safe in using the premises for the purposes for which he is invited or permitted by the occupier to be there".

(a) *All the circumstances of the case.* These may include the vulnerability of the visitor; for example, if he is a child; and whether the risk involved is one which is normally incidental to the visitor's trade or calling.

EXAMPLE: A window-cleaner was injured when a window sash broke, and the window fell on his hand. HELD: the occupier was not liable, since the cleaner should appreciate and guard against such dangers (though P's employers were liable for not providing a window-stop to protect him): *General Cleaning Contractors* v. *Christmas* (1952).

(b) *Knowledge of danger on the part of the visitor.* If the visitor knows of the danger and willingly accepts it, then the occupier will not be liable. Where the occupier attempts to bring the fact of a danger to the visitor's attention, his liability (or lack of it) will depend upon whether such a warning was "enough to enable the visitor to be reasonably safe". Thus, when the attention of two sweeps was drawn to the fact that the flue they had been hired to clean was faulty, and should not be swept whilst the fire was alight, the occupiers were not liable for the sweep's death: *Roles* v. *Nathan* (1963).

On the other hand, mere knowledge on the part of the visitor does not absolve the occupier from liability: *Bunker* v. *Brand* (1969).

(c) *Independent contractors.* An occupier is not liable for damage caused to a visitor by a danger which results from the negligent work of an independent contractor, unless he is in some way negligent (e.g. in hiring a disreputable contractor, or failing to check the work where he may reasonably have done so).

EXAMPLES: (1) Where a piece of plaster fell from the ceiling of a store, injuring P, the store-owners were not liable, since the ceiling had been recently repaired by independent contractors: *O'Connor* v. *Swan & Edger* (1963).

(2) Where a cleaner negligently failed to clear ice from a doorstep, the occupier was liable when P slipped and was injured, since no more than a glance was required to ensure the work had been properly done: *Woodward* v. *Mayor of Hastings* (1945).

23. Defences. The occupier may raise any of the defences to torts generally (e.g. consent, statutory authority). In addition, the considerations dealt with above (warnings, independent contracts, etc.) may operate as defences, subject to the qualifications given.

24. Liability to trespassers. Trespassers are not covered by the Occupiers Liability Act at all: liability, if any, to trespassers exists at common law only.

Such duty as is owed by an occupier to trespassers was defined by the House of Lords in *British Railways Board* v. *Herrington* (1972) where it was decided that the occupier of premises owes to a trespasser a duty of "common humanity". The standard of care involved in this extraordinary duty was defined as being that standard which may reasonably be expected from the "sensible and humane" man who finds himself in the situation of the defendant, having regard to the defendant's actual (subjective) "knowledge, skill and resources". The case, in fact, involved a child who was injured when he strayed on to D's live railway line through a hole in a fence, the existence of which was known to D.

The decision was followed in *Pannett* v. *McGuinness* (1973), but in *Penny* v. *Northampton Borough Council* (1975) the principle was applied so as to withhold recovery by a child trespasser. Here a boy was injured, whilst playing on a rubbish tip occupied by the defendant council, when a friend threw an empty aerosol-spray can on to a bonfire, causing an explosion. It was HELD that the council could not be expected without a considerably larger budget than that available to them, to guard against such dangers, even if they were foreseeable.

The duty owed to a trespasser is therefore partly, at least, subjective in the sense that it is not entirely dependent on an objective "reasonable man" standard, but takes account of the subjective (actual) knowledge and available resources of the defendant. Although many of the cases to reach the superior courts involve child trespassers, the rule basically applies to adults, too, though presumably the factors which may create a duty towards children (e.g. whether something on the land is an "allurement" to children) would not apply in respect of adults.

It has always been the case, and still is, that an occupier may not inflict intentional harm on trespassers: *Bird* v. *Holbrook* (1828).

25. Defective Premises Act 1972. This Act provides that any person who undertakes work for (or in connection with) the provision of a dwelling owes a duty of care:

(*a*) to the person who commissions the work; and

(*b*) to any person who subsequently acquires an interest in the dwelling e.g. a subsequent purchaser (*see Dutton* v. *Bognor Regis U.D.C.* discussed at **11**).

PROGRESS TEST 16

1. What is meant by the word "negligence" in English law? What are the main ingredients of the tort of negligence? (**1, 2**)

2. Define, as nearly as possible the duty of care owed in negligence. What is meant by "standard of care"? (**3–6**)

3. A visits B. On his way out of B's house, he pushes the gate open; the gate, however, collapses. B has recently repaired the gate with "superglu" adhesive. A suffers grazes; on his admission to hospital, he is injected with anti-tetanus serum. Unfortunately, owing to an allergy unknown to medicine, he suffers brain damage. Discuss. (**6, 7** and **18–25**)

4. What specific duties are owed in particular situations in the tort of negligence? What are the rules relating to

(*a*) economic loss;

(*b*) negligent mis–statement? (**8–11**)

5. What is meant by *res ipsa loquitur*? (**12**)

6. Outline the rules relating to

(*a*) contributory negligence;

(*b*) cases involving nervous shock;

(*c*) liability for defective chattels. (**13–16**)

7. What is meant by the common duty of care owed by an occupier of premises? What factors will effect this duty? (**22**)

8. X is a sewerage expert, who goes on to Y's land at Y's request to improve Y's drainage and sewerage system. Whilst checking out a drain, X is overcome by noxious fumes, and becomes seriously ill. The fumes are the result of a blockage in Y's plumbing, which had recently been overhauled by Z, a well-known plumber. Discuss. (**21, 22**)

9. What duty is owed by the occupier of premises to trespassers? (**24**)

CHAPTER XVII

Strict Liability

MEANING AND SCOPE OF STRICT LIABILITY

The term "strict liability" refers to those exceptional situations where a defendant is liable irrespective of fault on his part (*see* XIII, 8). As a result, a plaintiff who suffers harm in certain circumstances can successfully sue without having to prove intention or negligence on D's part.

The term "strict liability" is, however, preferred to "absolute liability" since, generally, certain defences are available. Occasionally, statutes may create "absolute" duties whereby liability will attach irrespective of how the breach of duty was brought about, and these defences may not be available here. The main examples of strict liability are set out below.

THE RULE IN RYLANDS V. FLETCHER

1. The rule. "The person who, for his own purposes, brings on his land and collects and keeps there anything likely to do mischief if it escapes, must keep it in at his peril, and if he does not do so, is prima facie answerable for all the damage which is the natural consequence of its escape": *per* Blackburn J. in *Rylands* v *Fletcher* (1868). In the House of Lords, Lord Cairns L.C. referred to the defendant's "non-natural" user of the land as being essential to his liability. Liability under the rule will be limited by the following requirements by virtue of the formulation of the rule itself.

2. Dangerous objects. The defendant is liable only for things "likely to do mischief". A thing may fall within the rule because it is inherently dangerous (explosives, fire, etc), or because it transpires in the particular circumstances to be dangerous.

> EXAMPLE: A's horse died when it ate the poisonous leaves of a tree which projected out of B's land into A's. B was liable under the rule in *Rylands* v. *Fletcher*: *Crowhurst* v. *Amersham Burial Board* (1878).

3. It must be for D's "own purpose". It is enough, however, if he shares this purpose with a third party (though he will not be liable if the thing is for the benefit of both the defendant and the plaintiff); *Carstairs* v. *Taylor* (1871) (*see* 7).

4. There must be an actual escape. Thus, when R visited C's factory, and was injured by an explosion which occurred *within* the works there, the rule did not apply: *Read* v. *Lyons* (1947).

On the other hand, the rule is not confined to adjoining land-owners. In *Miles* v. *Forest Rock Co.* (1918) the rule applied where escape was to a highway. What is necessary is that the escape should be "to a place not subject to (the defendant's) control" *per* Viscount Simon.

5. Non-natural user/brought on to land. These are separate. That user is "natural" will negate liability.

The term "natural" is nowadays taken to refer to "normal": therefore artificial things may well not be non-natural: e.g. domestic water supply: *Rickards* v. *Lothian* (1913).

Certainly the thing must be brought on to the defendant's land. Natural accumulations are outside the scope of the rule (even if they are dangerous): *Pontardawe R.D.C.* v. *Moore-Gwyn* (1929).

6. Defendant is answerable for all damage. *Rylands* v. *Fletcher* is not actionable *per se* (i.e. proof of actual damage is necessary). Personal injuries have been held to fall within the rule: *Shiffman* v. *Order of St. John* (1936).

7. Defences.

(*a*) *Plaintiff's default.* If the plaintiff brought the injury on himself he has no cause of action.

(*b*) *Plaintiff's consent.* Where, for example, the plaintiff freely consented to the existence on the defendant's land of the source of the mischief. In *Peters* v. *Prince of Wales Theatre* (1943), the idea of "shared benefit" (between plaintiff and defendant (*see* 3)) was regarded as an element of this defence.

(*c*) *Act of God.* This is where the escape was caused by a completely unforeseeable natural catastrophe, of which "human prudence is not bound to recognise the possibility": *Nichols* v. *Marsland* (1875).

(*d*) *Uncontrollable act of a stranger.* For this defence to apply the escape must be caused by the intervention of someone over whom the defendant has no control: *Perry* v. *Kendricks* (1956).

Such an intervention must also be unforeseeable: *Box* v. *Jubb* (1879).

(e) *Statutory authority*. Where liability under the rule is expressly or impliedly excluded: *Green* v. *Chelsea Waterworks Co* (1894).

LIABILITY FOR FIRE

Whilst fires may be, naturally enough, the subject of the rule in *Rylands* v. *Fletcher*, liability may exist independently of that rule.

8. Fires intentionally started. A person who keeps a fire "keeps it at his peril". This is an ancient principle, and we hear of liability for fires negligently allowed to spread as early as 1401: *Beaulieu* v. *Finglam*. If the fire is, in itself, dangerous, then liability will be strict under the rule in *Rylands* v. *Fletcher*: *Balfour* v. *Barty-King* (1957). On the other hand, if the fire is merely a domestic one in a grate, negligence must be shown: *Sochaki* v. *Sas* (1947).

9. Accidental fires. The Fires Prevention (Metropolis) Act 1774 provides that no action will lie against anyone on whose property a fire is accidentally begun (this is not confined to London). If the fire, once started, is negligently allowed to spread, the defendant will be liable (but not strictly): *Musgrove* v. *Pandelis* (1919). This applies even if the fire is started by a natural event or Act of God: *Goldman* v. *Hargrave* (1967)

10. Combustibles. The rule in *Rylands* v. *Fletcher* will apply to situations where combustibles are stored in such a manner that they are likely to do mischief by igniting: *Mason* v. *Levy* (1967)

LIABILITY FOR ANIMALS

11. Ordinary liability in tort. A person may be liable in negligence for failing to control his animal: *Mitchil* v. *Alestree* (1676); or in nuisance, where, for example, a stench is caused by animals: *Aldred's* Case (1610). A man can assault another through the agency of his dog, and he could even be liable in slander by teaching his parrot to recite defamatory words.

12. Dangerous animals. The law imposes a more specific liability on owners of animals in addition to the possibilities mentioned in **11**. The law divides animals according to whether they belong to "dangerous species": Animals Act 1971, s. 1. There are now three main areas of concern.

(*a*) *Section* 6 defines a "dangerous species" as one

(*i*) which is not usually domesticated in the British Isles; and

(*ii*) whose fully grown members have such characteristics that they are likely to cause severe damage unless restrained.

The keeper of such an animal is strictly liable for any damage it causes.

(*b*) On the other hand (apart from normal liability in tort: *see* 11) the keeper of a "non–dangerous" species as defined in s. 2. is only liable, according to that section if:

(*i*) the damage is of a kind which the animal was likely to cause unless restrained; and

(*ii*) the damage was the result of characteristics peculiar to the particular animal; and

(*iii*) these characteristics were known, or ought to have been known, by the keeper.

The keeper of an animal is its owner or the head of a household where it is normally kept.

NOTE: Before the Animals Act a similar liability existed, and was known as *scienter* (liability based on D's knowledge).

(*c*) *Defences.* The following are available under the Act.

(*i*) Plaintiff's fault: s. 5(1).

(*ii*) *Volenti* (consent): s. 5(2).

EXAMPLE: *Cummings* v. *Granger* (1977), where P was aware that a guard dog was in D's property, but nevertheless entered (as a trespasser) and was bitten. (But see the Guard Dogs Act 1975, s. 1, which makes it an offence to permit the use of an unrestrained guard dog, unless it is secured; and requires a notice containing a warning to be exhibited.)

(*iii*) Plaintiff is a trespasser: s. 5(3). This defence is only available if either the animal is not kept on the premises for protection of persons or property, or, if it is, then where such keeping is reasonable: *Cummings* v. *Granger*.

(*iv*) Contributory negligence: s. 10.

13. Liability for particular species.

(*a*) *Cattle trespass.* At common law, whenever cattle strayed on to land possessed by someone other than their owner, liability was strict.

The Animals Act 1971, s. 4, provides that where damage is done by straying livestock to the land or to any property on it, or if the landowner (or occupier) on to whose land the livestock stray reasonably incurs any expenses in keeping the livestock while it cannot be restored to its owner, the person to whom the livestock belongs is liable for the damage or expenses. "Livestock" is defined in s. 11 as "cattle, horses, asses, mules, hinnies, sheep, pigs, goats and poultry, and also deer not in the wild state".

(*i*) The person to whom the livestock "belongs" need not necessarily be the owner: s. 4(2).

(*ii*) Damage must now be proved—the tort is not actionable *per se*.

(*iii*) The Animals Act 1971, s. 8, allows for liability in respect of any animals, if they stray on to a highway and do damage there, where, for instance, the owner fails to fence the land (unless the area is one where fencing is not customary).

(*b*) *Dogs.* The Animals Act 1971, s. 3, provides for strict liability on the part of the keeper of a dog which causes damage by killing or injuring livestock.

STATUTORY TORTS

14. Nature of liability. Where a statute imposes a duty on someone, the liability (if any) in tort which will result from a breach of this duty will depend on the exact wording of the statute. Thus certain duties imposed by statute are said to be absolute.

EXAMPLES: Factories Acts: *Groves* v. *Wimborne* (1898); Employers Liability (Defective Equipment) Act 1969 (which assumes negligence on the part of an employer whose employee is injured by defective equipment supplied (but not made) by him, where the defect is attributable to the fault "of a third party").

In neither case is an injured person guaranteed a cause of action: he must prove:

(*a*) that there was, in fact, a breach of the statutory duty (whether absolute or qualified);

(*b*) that his damage was caused by the breach. In *McWilliams* v. *Sir William Arrol & Co.* (1962), the Factories Acts required provision of safety belts for "spidermen" when climbing up scaffolding. No belts were provided, but in an action on behalf of a man who had fallen to his death, it was found that he had not worn belts when they were available. It was therefore not his employer's breach of duty which caused his death, but his own practice of not wearing a belt;

(c) that he was a member of a class the statute was intended to protect: *Groves* v. *Wimborne* (1898);

NOTE: The Guard Dogs Act 1975, s. 5 (*see* 12), provides "the provisions of this Act shall not be construed as conferring a right of action in any civil proceedings";

(d) that the injury complained of was one the statute was intended to prevent.

EXAMPLE: A failed to keep sheep penned whilst in transit aboard his ship. Some of the sheep were washed overboard in rough weather. HELD: The purpose of the Order requiring pens (made under the Contagious Diseases (Animals) Act 1869) was to prevent the spread of disease amongst the animals, not to guard against animals being washed overboard. The sheep-owner's claim failed: *Gorris* v. *Scott* (1874).

15. Defences. This will depend on whether the duty is absolute or qualified.

If the duty is, indeed, absolute, then no defences will be available (even Act of God).

Most duties admit of some defences, however, and are to that extent at least, qualified. Thus, where the defendant properly delegated performance of the duty to the plaintiff himself, and the injury was caused by the plaintiff's own conduct, the defence of volenti non fit injuria applied: *I.C.I.* v. *Shatwell* (1965) (*see* XIV, 18). In other cases normal defences may be available, including contributory negligence (*see* XVI, 13).

16. Other instances of strict liability. These occur, particularly, in specific cases of *nuisance* (*see* XV, 24–31) as well as in relation to extra-hazardous activities other than those involving fire or *Rylands* v. *Fletcher*: *Honeywill & Stein* v. *Larkin* (1934). Cases of vicarious liability may also be said to be "strict" in the sense that, although negligence may have to be proved on the part of an employee, his employer may be liable without fault on his own part (*see* XIV, 14–16).

PROGRESS TEST 16

1. Explain what is meant by strict liability.
2. Outline the rule in *Rylands* v. *Fletcher*. What are the limits to this rule? **(1–6)**

3. What defences are available in answer to a claim in *Rylands* v. *Fletcher*? (7)

4. In what circumstances will a person be liable for damage caused by fire? How does this differ from *Rylands* v. *Fletcher*? (8–10)

5. What practical difference results from distinguishing animals which are "dangerous" from others in the law of torts? (11–13)

6. A's bull escapes from his field. It rams B's car, denting it, and frightened by the noise charges into C's china shop, damaging much of his stock. It finally gores D. Discuss the liability of A. Would it make any difference if the bull was one specially reared for bullfighting as opposed to stud? (11–13)

7. What factors must be established to bring a successful action for breach of statutory duty? (14, 15)

8. When will a statutory tort involve strict liability? (14, 15)

CHAPTER XVIII

Defamation

GENERAL REQUIREMENTS AND DEFINITIONS

1. Meaning of defamation. To defame someone is to attack their reputation (or in other words detract from their justified fame: *de*fame). A defamatory statement is one which involves an imputation against a living person (*see* XIV, **10**) which is "injurious to that person in his trade, or holds him up to hatred, ridicule or contempt": *per* Blackburn J. in *Capital & Counties Bank* v. *Henty* (1882)) or "tends to lower the plaintiff in the estimation of right-thinking members of society generally": *per* Lord Atkin in *Sim* v. *Stretch* (1936).

2. Libel and slander. Such statements may be in permanent form, in which case they are referred to as libel, or in transient form, in which case they are known as slander.

In fact, a "statement" is not necessarily required—a picture or combination of words and pictures may constitute libel: *Garbett* v. *Hazell, Watson* (1943). Indeed a wax effigy has been held to constitute a libel in certain circumstances: *Monson* v. *Tussauds* (1894). No doubt gestures may constitute slander. On the other hand, radio and television are media for libel: Defamation Act 1952, s. 1; as are words spoken in plays: Theatres Act 1968, s. 4. Thus "statements in permanent form" must be liberally interpreted.

The main result of this distinction between libel and slander is an historical one. Libel is actionable *per se* (without proof of damage); slander, on the other hand, requires proof of special damage. (Special damage here means simply actual damage—more than the mere loss of face: *Lynch* v. *Knight* (1861).)

To this general rule (that slander is not actionable *per se*), however, there are the following four exceptions.

(*a*) Slander imputing a criminal offence punishable by imprisonment: *Gray* v. *Jones* (1939).

(*b*) Imputation of unchastity on the part of a woman: Slander of Women Act 1891: *see Kerr* v. *Kennedy* (1942).

(*c*) Imputation that the plaintiff suffers from a contagious disease (such as would cause others to "shun and avoid him").

(*d*) Imputing professional incompetence against the plaintiff: Defamation Act 1952 s. 2 (refers to words "calculated to disparage the plaintiff in any office, profession, calling, trade or business").

NOTE: The Report of the Committee on Defamation (1975) (Cmnd. 5909) (the Faulks Committee) recommended, amongst other things, the assimilation of the law relating to slander to that of libel, thus removing for practical purposes the effect of the distinction.

3. The elements of defamation. To succeed in an action for libel or slander a plaintiff must prove three things.

(*a*) That the statement complained of was defamatory (*see* **4**).

(*b*) That it could reasonably be understood to refer to the plaintiff (*see* **5**).

(*c*) That it was published to a third party (*see* **6**).

These are dealt with below, and the problems associated with these issues discussed.

4. Defamatory statements and innuendos. A statement may, on the face of it, be defamatory in the sense outlined above (**1**). On the other hand, a statement may not be expressly defamatory but only by implication. Such a statement is said to consist of, or include an innuendo. There are two kinds of innuendos.

(*a*) *The true or legal innuendo.* This is where words which are innocent in themselves derive a defamatory meaning from some extraneous facts.

EXAMPLE: A newspaper published a photograph of X with a woman, C, with a caption stating them to be engaged. It was held that Mrs. X could recover damages from the newspaper. Although she was not even referred to, the suggestion that X was engaged might have led people who knew that she lived with X to believe that she was not, in fact, married to him: *Cassidy* v. *Daily Mirror* (1929).

(*b*) *The popular or false innuendo.* This really consists of an extension of the ordinary meaning of words: *Allsop* v. *Church of England Newspapers* (1972) (reference to plaintiff as "obsessed with the bent"). Whether a statement is claimed to be expressly defamatory, or to depend upon an innuendo, it is for the judge to decide whether the words are reasonably capable of bearing the defamatory meaning alleged by the plaintiff: *Lewis* v. *Daily Telegraph* (1964). If he decides that they are so capable, it is for the jury (if any) to decide whether the statement is so understood by "right thinking members of society" (*see* 5).

5. Reference to plaintiff. It is necessary that the statement:

(*a*) might reasonably be understood to refer to the plaintiff; this is a question for the judge; and

(*b*) is so understood by reasonable people; this is a question for the jury (*see* 4).

At common law it was irrelevant that the defendant did not intend to refer to the plaintiff but had someone else in mind: *Newstead* v. *London Express Newspapers* (1940); or even a fictitious person: *Hulton* v. *Jones* (1910).

It is not necessary for the plaintiff to be referred to by name (*see* 4 (*a*)), but it is not enough if the defendant makes a statement which is so general that a particular plaintiff cannot be identified: *Knuppfer* v. *London Express* (1944).

The Defamation Act 1952, s. 4, however, provides for a defence in cases of unintentional defamation (applicable where the defendant publishes innocently in relation to the plaintiff, as in *Newstead* v. *London Express Newspapers* (1940)). For these provisions *see* 13.

6. Publication and repetition. This is the basis of liability: the defamatory statement must be published to a third person. The term "third persons" does not include the defendant's spouse: *Wenhak* v. *Morgan* (1888); but does include the plaintiff's spouse: *Theaker* v. *Richardson* (1962).

Publication need not be intentional; it is enough if the circumstances are such that someone other than the plaintiff (or his spouse) is likely to read the statement: *Huth* v. *Huth* (1915). Indeed the law presumes that statements made in the form of telegrams etc. are published to Post Office officials though, obviously, not intended for them to read.

Each publication of a defamatory statement gives rise to a separate cause of action, and repetition of such a statement, even by someone who is not aware of its defamatory nature, constitutes a publication.

Innocent dissemination, however, does not amount to publication. Thus whilst the newsagent, bookseller, etc, is prima facie liable when he sells a paper or book which is defamatory, it is a defence for him to show:

(a) he did not know, and;

(b) could not be reasonably expected to know (i.e. was not negligent in failing to know)

that the material circulated by him is defamatory. In *Vizetelly* v. *Mudies Select Library* (1900) a library was liable, since its failure to ascertain the defamatory nature of books was negligent.

DEFENCES

7. Special defences. Defamation by its nature is subject to various special defences, apart from the defences available in torts generally; (*see* XIV, **18–21**)

8. Justification. This is a plea that the statement complained of is substantially true. To be defamatory, a statement must be false. "Truth will out!": *M'Pherson* v. *Daniels* (1829).

Justification is a complete defence to the tort of defamation but is not a defence to an action in criminal libel (*see* XXIX, **14**).

Since the Defamation Act 1952, s. 5, was passed, it is possible, in cases where the statement complained of contains more than one charge (or imputation), for the defence to succeed, even if the truth of some of the imputations is not proved; what is necessary, however, is that "the words not proved to be true do not materially injure the plaintiff's reputation having regard to the truth of the remaining charges".

A price attaches to an unsuccessful plea of justification: the defendant may be liable to increased damages: *Associated Leisure Ltd.* v. *Associated Newspapers* (1970).

Formerly, a conviction in a criminal court was not sufficient evidence upon which to base a plea of justification: *Hinds* v. *Sparks* (1964). Since the Civil Evidence Act 1968, s. 13, the conviction of P will now support the plea of justification.

9. Fair comment. This must be on a matter of public interest. Thus politicians, actors and other public figures must expect their conduct to be commented on. Provided such comments are fair they have no cause for complaint. The term "fair", however, here assumes a rather complex meaning. Whilst generally the prime requirement is that such views as are expressed by the defendant are honestly held, the following factors are also relevant.

(*a*) The facts, upon which the comment is made, must themselves be substantially true: *Broadway Approvals* v. *Odhams Press* (1965) (though they do not necessarily have to be stated: *Kemsley* v. *Foot* (1952)). On the other hand, if the facts are not stated, certain types of comment, particularly those that impute corruption or dishonesty to the plaintiff, will have to be proved substantially true (i.e. are the subject only of justification): *Campbell* v. *Spottiswoode* (1863).

(*b*) Malice defeats the defence. Implied malice, in the sense of a lack of honest belief in the statement, will suffice to defeat the defence; actual or express malice, in the sense of spite or "ill will", will also render a comment "unfair": *Thomas* v. *Bradbury, Agnew & Co.* (1906).

(*c*) It is for the judge to decide whether the matter is one of "public interest": such matters need only be of interest to the public—it does not have to be in the public interest in the sense of "for the public good" that the statement should be published: *London Artistes* v. *Littler* (1968).

(*d*) To support the defence, such facts as are relied upon as a basis for the comments must be true at the time the statement was made, it is not enough if these facts subsequently came to light: *Cohen* v. *Daily Telegraph* (1968).

10. Privilege. Circumstances require that on certain occasions, the right to reputation should be subordinated to requirements of freedom of speech and/or comment. Such occasions are said to be privileged; statements made on such occasions are protected by law, and proof that the statement was, in fact, made on such an occasion will found a defence to an action in defamation. There are two kinds of privilege: absolute (*see* **11**) and qualified (*see* **12**).

11. Absolute privilege. No action whatever can be brought in respect of statements made on occasions which are absolutely privileged, even if the statement is not only untrue but made maliciously. Such occasions are.

(*a*) Statements made in Parliament (Bill of Rights 1689, Article 9);

(*b*) Statements made in the course of judicial proceedings (e.g. by judge, juror, witness): *Addis* v. *Crocker* (1961).

(c) State communications (e.g. made by a Minister to the Crown or to another officer of State): *Chatterton* v. *Secretary of State for India* (1895).

(d) Publications made by, or addressed to the Parliamentary Commissioner: Parliamentary Commissioner Act 1967, s. 10.

(e) Communications between a solicitor and his client so long as they relate to the subject on which the solicitor has been retained: *More* v. *Weaver* (1928).

12. Qualified privilege. This differs from absolute privilege in that it is destroyed if it can be shown that the defendant was actuated by express malice (such as spite or ill will, for which *see* 9): *Horrocks* v. *Lowe* (1974). Examples of occasions which are the subject of the defence are as follows.

(a) Fair and accurate reports of Parliamentary proceedings.

(b) Fair and accurate reports of judicial proceedings.

(c) Fair and accurate reports of other public bodies; e.g. the United Nations, domestic tribunals, local authorites (the modern basis of these privileged occasions is found in the Defamation Act 1952, ss. 7–9 and Scheds.).

(d) Statements made in performance of a duty. This is restricted, as stated by Lord Atkinson in *Adam* v. *Ward* (1917): "where the person who makes a communication has an interest or a duty, legal, social, or moral to make it and the person to whom it is made has an interest to receive it. This reciprocity is essential."

EXAMPLE: A wrote to A and B's employer and to Mrs. B. that B was misbehaving whilst abroad. HELD: publication to the employer was privileged since the relationship of employer/employee created the necessary reciprocity. No such reciprocity existed as between A and Mrs. B. and A was liable in respect of the publication: *Watt* v. *Longsdon* (1930).

On the other hand, an employer can give unfavourable references concerning an employee to a prospective employer: *Jackson* v. *Hopperton* (1864).

(e) Statements made in protection of an interest are also privileged provided that reciprocity exists (*see* (d)).

NOTE: Whilst malice destroys the defence of qualified privilege, proof of malice on the part of one of several joint defendants does not deprive the others of their usual defences: *Eggar* v. *Chelmsford* (1965).

13. Apology and amends. These are not normally a defence except in the following circumstances.

(*a*) *Defamation Act* 1952, *s*. 4. Apology and offer of an amends is a necessary element of the defence for unintentional publication (*see* 5).

(*b*) *A newspaper* has a defence under the Libel Act 1843, if it can show:

(*i*) a lack of malice or gross negligence in publishing;

(*ii*) that a full apology has been made; and

(*iii*) that a sum of money has been paid into court in lieu of damages (by way of amends).

PROGRESS TEST 18

1. What is meant by "defamation?" Distinguish "libel" and "slander". **(1, 2)**

2. What elements must be established to succeed in an action for defamation? Explain what is meant by an innuendo? **(3–6)**

3. Distinguish: (*a*) justification; (*b*) fair comment; (*c*) qualified privilege. **(8–10, 12)**

4. Where may the defence of absolute privilege be used to meet a case of defamation? **(11)**

5. X Co. ask Y Co. for a reference for Honest, who is presently employed by Y Co., and has applied for a senior post with them. The reference is made by Nasty, one of the directors of Y Co. In it, he falsely states that Honest has been involved in embezzlement; copies of this reference are sent to X Co. and to Honest himself. The other directors of Y Co. are not aware that a reference has been given. Discuss. **(6, 12)**

PART FOUR

THE LAW OF PROPERTY

CHAPTER XIX

Real and Personal Property

INTRODUCTION

1. Meaning of property. Property fundamentally means anything which belongs to a person, i.e. which is *proper* to that person. (French *propre* = one's own.)

English law recognises *two kinds* of property:

(*a*) *real property*, i.e. freehold interest in land;

(*b*) *personal property*, i.e. any other kind of property, including leasehold interests in land.

2. Ownership and possession. The owner of property is the person who is entitled to *all legal rights* over that property, including the right to exclusive use and possession of it.

The owner may, however, part with possession, e.g. where the owner of a book lends it to another person. Hère ownership remains vested in the lender, but the borrower now has possession of the book.

Ownership therefore is a legal concept; *possession* is a matter of fact. Possession was recognised by the law before ownership. Thus, most of the older forms of tort relating to property relate to wrongful dispossession, and in order to sue in such an action the plaintiff had merely to prove that he was entitled to possession of the property (and not that he was the owner). Even today a plaintiff suing for trespass to land has merely to prove that he is entitled to possession of the land. In some cases the possessor of land may even maintain an action for trespass against the owner (*see* XV, **10, 16**).

3. Importance of possession. Possession in law connotes two things:

(*a*) *control* over the property possessed; and

(*b*) *intention* to exert *exclusive* control.

Control may be exercised through others, e.g. servants and agents. And a person who has effective control of property may not be the possessor if he has no intention to exert exclusive control, e.g. where he is merely the custodian of goods for another.

The maxim that "possession is nine points of the law", means that the law protects the possessor of property, and presumes him to be the owner unless the contrary is proved. This protection may even be available against the true owner of the property.

4. Acquisition of ownership. Ownership may be acquired in the following ways.

(a) *Originally*, i.e. (i) by asserting ownership and possession over something *not previously owned* by anyone else, e.g. catching fish at sea, or (ii) by asserting ownership over something abandoned by the previous owner.

(b) *Derivatively*, i.e. acquiring ownership from a previous owner, either (i) with his consent (sale, gift, etc.) or (ii) without consent, e.g. where the court orders sale of a bankrupt person's property to pay his debts.

(c) *By succession*, i.e. by inheritance on the death of the former owner, either (i) in accordance with the deceased's will, or (ii) upon intestacy where there is no will.

5. Legal and equitable interests. Rights of property protected by common law were called legal rights, and included possession and ownership.

But where the owner of property was under a moral duty to hold it for the benefit of another (called a beneficiary), common law would not protect the beneficiary's rights. In such cases equity intervened to enforce the claims of morality, and compelled the owner of the property to hold it as trustee for the beneficiary. (The right of such beneficiary was then called an equitable interest in the property.)

Since the Judicature Act 1873, both legal and equitable interests are enforced in all the courts, but they still exist separately. Thus, T, by will, may leave property to A and B, directing them to hold it as trustees for the benefit of X; here A and B will become the legal owners, and X will inherit merely an equitable interest in the property. (For a detailed account of the law of trusts *see* XXIII.)

KINDS OF PROPERTY

6. Realty and personalty. Real property means freehold interests in land, and personal property means moveable property and leasehold interests in land.

These two kinds of property are so called because in the Middle Ages a person wrongfully dispossessed of property had a choice of two types of action.

(*a*) *A real action* (action *in rem*), i.e. an action for recovery of the thing itself. (Latin, *res* = thing.) Such actions were available only in relation to what would now be called freehold land.

(*b*) *A personal action* (action *in personam*), i.e. an action for damages against the dispossessor personally, without any claim for recovery of the property. This was originally the only type of action available where the property involved was something other than freehold land.

Eventually property recoverable by a real action came to be called realty, or real property, i.e. freehold land. All other property was personalty.

7. Chattels real: leases. Although leasehold interests in land were originally classed as personalty for the reasons stated above, the courts from the fifteenth century onwards allowed a dispossessed tenant to bring a real action called an action for ejectment against a dispossessor. Thus, leases came to have some of the quality of real property, and were called chattels real (i.e. personal property recoverable by a real action).

The Law of Property Act 1925 laid down that from 1st January 1926 leases were to be treated like freehold land, i.e. were to be treated as realty in all respects. Freehold and leasehold are now the only two legal estates allowed by the law (*see* **XX, 10**).

8. Kinds of personalty.

(*a*) *Chattels real*, i.e. leases (now treated as realty (*see* **7**)).

(*b*) *Chattels personal*, i.e. items of moveable property such as furniture, clothes, cars, ships, books, paintings.

9. Choses in possession and in action. The word *chose* (French) means a thing, and all property whether land or chattels is classed as choses in possession or choses in action.

(*a*) *Choses in possession*, i.e. tangible things capable of physical possession, such as land, books, cars, pianos.

(b) *Choses in action*, i.e. intangible rights which can be enforced only by action in the courts and are not capable of physical possession, e.g. debts, patents, copyrights, cheques, shares in companies. Choses in action can be sold like choses in possession, but the assignment must be in a certain form (*see* XII, 2).

Thus, if A owns a car he has a chose in possession. But if he hires the car to B for twelve months, A now has only a chose in action, i.e. a right to sue B for recovery of the car at the end of the twelve months.

10. Methods of transfer inter vivos. The method required to transfer property *inter vivos*, i.e. during the life of the transferor, depends on the type of property:

(a) *Real property*.

(i) *Transfer upon sale* is affected by a deed of conveyance; transfers not by deed may be void: Law of Property Act 1925, s. 52.

(ii) *Leases* must be granted under seal (if for more than three years).

(iii) *Gifts* of land must also be by deed.

Note that this refers to the actual transfer. A contract to transfer at some future time must be evidenced in writing, but need not be by deed: Law of Property Act 1925, s. 40 (*see also* V, 7).

(b) *Personal property*.

(i) *Choses in possession* can normally be transferred by mere delivery, whether such delivery is actual (handing over the chose itself) or constructive (handing over the means to obtain it, e.g. a key to the place where it is kept).

(ii) *Choses in action* must be assigned as laid down by the Law of Property Act 1925, s. 136, the rules of equity or of some particular statute. Negotiable instruments are transferable by mere delivery.

11. Kinds of proprietary rights. A man may have a right over his own property or over the property of another. A right over one's own things is called a *jus in re propria*. A right over property of another is called a *jus in re aliena*.

(a) *Jura in re propria* include choses in possession such as land (immoveable property) and chattels (moveable property), and choses in action, such as debts, shares, patents.

(b) *Jura in re aliena* include:

(i) leases of land belonging to other people;

(*ii*) rights of way, etc., across the land of another;

(*iii*) rights over property of another by way of security, e.g. mortgages, pledges. *See* XXII.

For detailed rules on succession *see* **12** and XXIV.

12. Succession upon death. When a man dies, his property remains to be disposed of by his personal representatives. The method of succession to the deceased's property will be governed:

(*a*) *by his will* (if any) and distribution will be arranged by his executors, i.e. personal representatives appointed by the will;

(*b*) *by the law of intestacy* (if there is no will) and distribution will be arranged by his administrators, i.e. personal representatives appointed by the court.

The method of transfer of property by personal representatives is basically the same as in **10**, save that land is usually transferred by a document called a vesting assent, which need not necessarily be a deed.

For wills and intestacy *see* XXIV.

13. Bankruptcy. Where a person is insolvent, he or his creditors may apply for his affairs to be administered under the supervision of the court, and distributed among the creditors as fairly as may be.

Administration by the court in this way is called bankruptcy and is usually effected by a trustee in bankruptcy appointed by the creditors and supervised by the court and/or the Department of Trade.

Insolvency means that a man is unable to pay his debts as they fall due, or has insufficient funds to meet his liabilities. It does not always result in bankruptcy (*see* XXIV, **26**).

14. Securities. A lender of money may insist on being given some security for his loan, e.g. possession, or the right to possession or sale, of some property belonging to the debtor. The lender's rights to the property in question are generally suspended so that they will become operative only if the borrower fails to repay the loan as agreed.

Security for loans may take the following forms.

(*a*) *Mortgage* (of realty or personalty).

(*b*) *Pawn* or pledge (of personalty).

(*c*) *Conditional bills of sale* (for personalty).

(*d*) *Assignment of a chose in action* (subject to a condition that the lender will assign it back to the borrower when the loan is repaid).

The law relating to securities is dealt with in XXII.

THE 1925 LEGISLATION

15. Need for reform. The English law of property is largely feudal in origin, and by the beginning of this century it had developed from comparatively simple beginnings into a highly complex and comprehensive system containing many anachronisms.

The need for reform became apparent in the nineteenth century, and several Acts were passed effecting piecemeal improvements. But it was not until 1925 that a full-scale overhaul was made of the law relating to both real and personal property.

Nineteenth century reforms had included:

(*a*) *the Administration of Estates Act* 1833, which made land available for payment of a deceased's debts (previously only personalties could be claimed by ordinary creditors).

(*b*) *the Settled Land Act* 1882, which reformed the law relating to settlements (trusts) of land.

(*c*) *the Land Transfer Act* 1897, and *the Conveyancing Act* 1881, attempted to simplify methods of transferring land.

16. The 1925 legislation. After a preliminary Law of Property Act 1922, Parliament passed a series of Acts overhauling the law of real and personal property, its transfer, incidents and inheritance.

(*a*) *The Law of Property* 1925 (the L.P.A.), brought real and personal property into line in many respects, and simplified land law.

(*b*) *The Settled Land Act* 1925 (the S.L.A.), codified the law relating to settlements, and removed many restrictions on the powers of the tenant for life.

(*c*) *The Trustee Act* 1925 (the T.A.), codified the rules relating to the appointment, retirement and duties of trustees.

(*d*) *The Land Charges Act* 1925 (the L.C.A., now replaced by the Land Charges Act 1972 and the Local Land Charges Act 1975), and the *Land Registration Act* (the L.R.A.) provided for the registration of certain types of interest in land at a central land registry, and made some such interests void unless so registered.

(*e*) *The Administration of Estates Act* 1925 (the A.E.A.), laid down the rules governing the payment of a deceased person's debts and the distribution of his property on intestacy.

17. Purposes of the Property Acts.

(a) *Abolition of anachronisms.* Several ancient forms of feudal tenure, such as copyhold (*see* XX) were abolished. Complicated rules of feudal law were also swept away, such as the "old rule against perpetuities": the rule in *Whitby* v. *Mitchell* (1890) (*see* XX, 23).

(b) *Assimilation of real and personal property.* The law relating to realty and personalty was brought into line as far as possible, mainly by subjecting land to the rules which formerly had applied only to personalty.

(c) *Simplification of conveyancing.* The methods of transferring land were simplified, e.g. by providing for the registration of estates in land and transfer merely by changing the entry in the register. Registration on a compulsory basis has been substantially extended in recent years so that about three-quarters of all conveyancing is done under the L.R.A.

18. The Law of Property Act 1925.

This, the most important of the Property Acts, provided for the following main matters.

(a) *Legal estates were reduced to two,* namely freehold and leasehold (*see* XX, 10).

(b) *Legal interests were reduced to six,* including easements, profits, rentcharges, and mortgages charge (*see* XX, 18).

(c) *Equitable interests are overreached* on sale of the legal estate, i.e. when the legal owner of land sells it, the sale operates to cancel (overreach) any equitable rights attaching to the land, except in certain cases (*see* XX, 24).

(d) *Anachronistic feudal systems of tenure were abolished* (*see* XX, 2).

(e) *Feudal methods of transferring land were abolished,* and it was provided that transfer should by by *grant* only, i.e. by deed.

PROGRESS TEST 19

1. Define property and explain the distinction between: (a) real and personal property, and (b) ownership and possession. (1, 2)

2. Summarise the ways in which ownership of property may be acquired. (4)

3. Explain the distinction between legal and equitable interests in property. (5)

4. A borrows a suitcase from B, to take on his holiday. He fills the suitcase with his (A's) clothes, and at the airport hands the

case to C, a porter. C loses the case. A and B wish to sue C for conversion. Advise A and B.   (XV, 22; 3)

5. Explain the historical origins of the distinction between realty and personalty.   (6)

6. Why are leases of land technically classed as personalty? (7)

7. Distinguish between choses in possession and choses in action, and explain how each can be transferred.   (9, 10)

8. Summarise the methods by which property can be transferred *inter vivos*.   (10)

9. Distinguish between *jura in re propria* and *jura in re aliena*. (11)

10. Summarise the forms of succession to property on death of the owner.   (12)

11. What are the principal forms of security for loans of money?   (14)

12. Summarise the chief reforms effected by legislation in English property law in the nineteenth century.   (15)

13. List the principal property statutes enacted in 1925, and explain their purposes.   (16, 17)

14. Summarise the main provisions of the Law of Property Act 1925.   (18)

CHAPTER XX

Estates and Interest in Land

TENURE AND ESTATES

1. Meaning of tenure. Under the old feudal system of law, all land in England belonged to the king, and all land-holders were therefore merely tenants (*see* I, 11). Tenancies were granted in return for services to be rendered as follows.

(*a*) *To the king*, if the king was the landlord. (Tenants holding directly under the king were called tenants *in capite*.)

(*b*) *To a mesne landlord* by tenants to whom tenants *in capite* or other major land-holders made sub-grants by the process of sub-infeudation.

The relationship of the tenant to his immediate landlord was called tenure.

2. Kinds of tenure: freehold.

(*a*) *Chivalric tenures*, e.g. knight service, where the tenant was required to perform military duties for his mesne lord. such as the provision of armed retainers. (Military tenures of this kind were abolished in 1660.)

(*b*) *Socage tenure*, involving non-military services, such as fixed agricultural work (or, in the later Middle Ages, rent in lieu of labour).

(*c*) *Spiritual tenure*, where the church held land, e.g. in return for saying masses for the landlord's soul after his death.

3. Villeinage and copyhold. Agricultural workers (called villeins) were allowed to live on a tenant's land in return for labour. Villeins originally had no rights in the land, could not marry without their lord's consent, could not leave the land, and could be sold with the land.

Shortage of labour in the later Middle Ages enabled villeins to force an improvement in their status by:

(*a*) substituting money payments called rent for the services formerly required; and

(b) obtaining recognition as tenants of the land on which they lived.

These tenancies were evidenced by copies of the rolls or records of the landlord's manorial court, and this type of tenancy came to be called copyhold.

4. Meaning of estate. Tenure means the relationship existing between a tenant and his lord, and estate means the nature of the tenant's rights in his land.

Estates are basically of *two types*:

(a) freehold; and
(b) leasehold.

5. Estates of freehold before 1925.

(a) *Fee simple*: a grant of land to a tenant and his heirs for ever (or until sold or otherwise disposed of).

(b) *Estate tail*: an estate entailed so as to descend to specified heirs of the tenant, e.g. a tail male ("to A and the heirs male of his body"), or a tail female ("to A and his heirs female").

NOTE: (a) and (b) above were classed as *estates of inheritance* (*fees*), i.e. were capable of passing at the tenant's death to his heirs, instead of ceasing automatically.

(c) *Estate for life*: e.g. a grant "to A for life."

(d) *Estate pur autre vie* (for the life of another), e.g. a grant "to A during the life of B."

NOTE: (c) and (d) above were called *mere freeholds*, because they could not be inherited by the heirs of the tenant.

6. Interests in land. An interest in land is a right in or over the land of another, e.g. a right of way across a neighbour's land.

7. Equitable estates and interests. In addition to the legal estate and interests described above, parallel equitable estates and interests (orginally recognised and enforced only in the equity Court of Chancery) might exist simultaneously in the same piece of land.

Thus, where land was granted "to A in fee simple on trust for B", A (the *trustee*) had the legal estate in fee simple, subject to an equitable fee simple vested in B (the beneficiary) (*see* XXIII).

Since 1873 equitable interests are recognised and enforced in all courts (*see* I, **26**).

8. Future interests. These are rights to obtain land at some future date, e.g. when the present owner dies.

A future interest is *vested* if the person entitled to it is ascertained, and his interest will take effect immediately on determination of the previous interest, e.g. a grant "to A for life, remainder to B",—a *vested* remainder.

A future interest is *contingent* if the person entitled is not yet known, or the vesting of the interest is dependent on the happening of some future event which may not occur, e.g. a grant "to A for life, *if* he shall attain twenty-one". Such a grant will become vested as soon as A reaches his twenty-first birthday, but if he dies before that date the grant will lapse and revert to the grantor.

9. Reversions and remainders. A *reversion* is a future interest arising by operation of law, e.g. where on the expiry of a lease the land reverts to the landlord. Thus, a person who grants a lease always has a reversionary interest in the land, and the land will automatically revert to him in due course.

A *remainder* is an estate which is granted so as to commence after the termination of an earlier grant, e.g. "to A for life, remainder to B". Here on A's death B will obtain the land. If the remainder is dependent on an uncertain future event it is called a contingent remainder (*see* 8).

LEGAL ESTATES IN LAND

10. L.P.A. 1925, s. 1. Only two legal estates can now exist in land.

(*a*) *Fee simple absolute in possession* (commonly called *freehold*).

(*b*) *Term of years absolute* (commonly called leasehold).

The characteristic of freehold is that it may last for an indefinite time, possibly for ever, while a lease is for a fixed period.

11. Fee simple absolute in possession. Fee is a technical word indicating an estate of inheritance, i.e. an estate capable of passing to the tenant's heirs at his death.

(*a*) *Simple* means it can pass to the general heirs, i.e. it is not entailed to a particular class of heirs.

(*b*) *Absolute* means that the grant is not qualified, e.g. by provision for a gift over to another person in certain circumstances.

(*c*) *In possession* means that the tenant is entitled to physical possession, though he may contract to part with possession in return for a rental, e.g. where he grants a lease of the land.

12. Creation of a fee simple. Contracts to sell or otherwise dispose of land or any interest therein must be evidenced in writing: Law of Property Act 1925, s. 40 (*see* V, 7).

Such a contract is performed by the grantor executing a deed of conveyance, which operates to transfer the fee simple to the purchaser.

No special words are needed to create a fee simple, whether the grant is inter vivos or by will. The grantee automatically receives full estate or interest which the grantor had power to convey, unless a contrary intention appears in the conveyance: Law of Property Act 1925, s. 60. Thus if the grantor wishes to reserve for himself certain rights over the land, he must do so expressly in the conveyance.

13. Position of the fee simple owner. He is the virtual owner of the land (subject to the Crown's theoretical overlordship). He is entitled to everything above, below, or on the land, e.g. the air above the land, minerals or water below it, and buildings or crops upon it.

In theory "an Englishman's home is his castle", i.e. he can do what he likes with his land. But in practice recent legislation has curtailed his rights considerably.

EXAMPLES:

(1) *The Town and Country Planning Act.* Consent of local planning authorities is required for all building, mining, or engineering operations and for any material change in use of the land: Town and Country Planning Act 1971, s. 1.

(2) *Ownership of minerals.* At common law gold and silver found under land belong to the Crown. And by Act of Parliament iron, coal, and petroleum belong to the state also.

NOTE: Water percolating under land in *undefined channels* belongs to the owner of the soil, and he can take it all if he wishes, even though by so doing he deprives neighbours of their share: *Bradford* v. *Pickles* (*see* XIII, 4). If the water flows through *defined channels* (whether above or below the land), he can take as much as he wants for *normal purposes*, such as farming, even though he exhausts the supply to the detriment of his neighbours. But if the water is to be used for *extra-*

ordinary purposes, such as supplying a factory, he must usually replace what he has taken.

14. Term of years absolute. This description includes leases for any period, even though this may be for less than a year, provided the lease has a certain duration.

Tenancies for uncertain periods are not legal estates, but are equitable only, e.g. tenancies at will (*see* XXI, **2**).

Leases are dealt with fully in XXI.

CO-OWNERSHIP

15. Co-ownership of land. Where land is granted to several people simultaneously, they are either tenants in common or joint tenants.

Tenancies in common can now only exist in equity. Therefore if land is granted to A and B as tenants in common, they will hold as joint tenants on trust for sale (*see* **16**).

16. Tenancies in common. These arise wherever land is granted in such a way as to suggest that the grantor intends the tenants to have distinct shares, though the land remains physically undivided, e.g. a grant "to A and B equally" or "to A and B in undivided shares". Words conveying such a suggestion are called "words of severance".

Since 1925 a grant to tenants in common operates only in equity. The grantees will be regarded as legal joint tenants, but they will hold the land on trust for sale (with power to postpone indefinitely). When the statutory joint tenants then sell (or when the survivor sells), the proceeds will be divided between them (or between the last survivor and the heirs of the deceased tenants). Thus if land is granted to A and B as tenants in common, they will hold as joint tenants on trust for sale. If B dies, A will become solely entitled (under the rules of survivorship (*see* **17**) but will have to sell the land at some date and share the proceeds of sale with B's heirs.

17. Joint tenancies. Wherever land is conveyed to two or more persons without words of severance, they hold it as joint tenants and each is theoretically entitled to the whole land. Such a grant might take the form of: "to A and B jointly" or simply "to A and B".

Note the following points.

(a) *Joint tenants are all entitled to the whole land.* They cannot claim any section of the land as their own private shares. If there is a house, then theoretically each is fully entitled to use of all parts of the house simultaneously with all the other joint tenants.

(b) *Not more than four joint tenants.* There cannot be more than four legal owners of land simultaneously: Trustee Act 1925, s. 34. If land is conveyed to more than four persons, the first four named will hold as joint tenants (trustees) on trust for sale for the benefit of themselves and the remaining grantees.

(c) *The right of survivorship applies* (the *jus accrescendi*). On the death of one joint tenant, the survivors inherit his share. Thus, if land is granted to A, B and C jointly and B and C die, A will become sole owner and trustee for the heirs of B and C.

(d) *The statutory trust for sale.* After 1925, whenever, land is conveyed to joint tenants beneficially, or to "tenants in common" (who are now treated as joint tenants), they will hold the land on trust for sale (with power to postpone sale indefinitely) and after sale they, or the survivor of them, must distribute the proceeds of sale equally among all the tenants and/or their heirs.

LEGAL INTERESTS

18. Legal interests since 1925. The only interests which can now be created as legal interests (as distinct from merely equitable) are the following.

(a) *Easements and profits à prendre* (*see* **19** and XXI, **16–22**).

(b) *A charge by way of legal mortgage* (*see* XXII).

(c) *Land tax or other charge on land* imposed by law, and not by agreement of the parties.

(d) *Rights of entry* exercisable over or in respect of a legal rentcharge (*see* **20**).

19. Easements and profits. An easement is a right or privilege which the owner or occupier of one piece of land (the dominant tenement) has over the land of another (called the servient tenement), e.g. a right of way, light, or support.

A profit à prendre is a right to take something from the land of another, e.g. to fish in his river.

Easements and profits are examples of rights *in alieno solo*, i.e. over the land of another (*see* XXI, **16–22**).

20. Rentcharges. A rentcharge is rent (money payable from land) which is payable out of the profits of land to a person who has no tenurial interest in the land, e.g. where a tenant charges his land with an annual payment to his widowed mother until her death. (Where the recipient has a tenurial interest, e.g. a right of occupation, such money is called rentservice, e.g. the rent payable under a lease.)

Rentcharges could formerly be created by deed, will, or statute. They can be extinguished by deed of release executed by the person entitled, or by lapse of twelve years non-payment without objection from the person entitled.

The owner of the rentcharge can enforce payment by:

(*a*) suing for debt;

(*b*) distraining (if the money is twenty-one days in arrear or more), i.e. by entering the land and seizing the tenant's chattels;

(*c*) taking possession of the land until the charge is paid, or, in some cases,

(*d*) appointing a receiver to take possession on his behalf.

The Rentcharges Act 1977, s. 2, prohibits the creation of new rentcharges. Under s. 3, every rentcharge will be extinguished at the expiry of sixty years from

(*a*) the passing of the Act; or

(*b*) the date on which the rentcharge first became payable; whichever is the later.

EQUITABLE INTERESTS

21. How they arise.

(*a*) *Express creation.*
Where A grants property to B to hold on *trust* for C, B becomes the legal owner and C acquires merely an equitable interest in the land (*see* **XXIII**).

(*b*) *Implied creation.*
   (i) *An informal grant* of a fee simple, lease, or any of the interests listed in **18** operates to create an equitable estate or interest (which may be converted into legal estate or interest under the rule in *Walsh* v. *Lonsdale* (*see* **22**)). A formal grant is one made by deed: an informal grant is one made in any other way, e.g. by letter.

   (ii) *Any grant*, whether formal or informal, of an estate or interest not mentioned in the Law of Property Act 1925, s. 1 operates to create an equitable interest only, e.g. grants of entails and remainders (*see* **5**).

22. The rule in Walsh v. Lonsdale (1882). Legal estates and interests can be created only by deed or by will, and an informal grant will create merely an equitable interest.

But in such cases equity will compel the grantor to execute a proper deed, and so convert the equitable interest or estate into a proper legal interest or estate. This is done by ordering specific performance against the grantor: *Walsh* v. *Lonsdale*.

Specific performance will only be ordered in such a case if:

(*a*) there is a binding written consent between the parties; or

(*b*) the equitable doctrine of part performance is applicable (*see* V, **7**).

Where such a situation arises, the rule in *Walsh* v. *Lonsdale* lays down that the parties shall be treated as if their relationship was already formalised by deed. Thus, a binding agreement to create a lease is usually as effective as a formal lease, i.e. the same covenants will apply on both sides. But since the relationship of the parties pending the order for specific performance is equitable only, the grantee's interest is capable of being overreached on sale of the legal estate by the grantor (*see* **24**).

23. Entails and future interests. These can now only exist as equitable interests, even though created by deed: Law of Property Act 1925, s. 1.

Consequently, after 1925, where there is an express grant of an entailed interest or a vested or contingent remainder, the grantee will obtain only an equitable interest.

Under the perpetuity rule a grant of a future interest was void if there was any possibility that it might fail to vest in the grantee within twenty-one years after the death of a living person or persons, e.g. a grant "to A for life, remainder to such of his children as become priests": here the grant to the children was void since none of them may ever decide to become priests.

The Perpetuities and Accumulations Act 1964 introduced a "wait and see" rule whereby a gift is void only if circumstances make it clear that it *can only vest* outside the perpetuity period. A period of eighty years may be substituted for the life of a living person.

Accumulations of income are subject to similar restrictions.

24. Overreaching of equitable interests. In order to simplify conveyancing, the Law of Property Act 1925, provides that wherever a legal owner of land sells it, he can convey a good title notwithstanding the equitable claims of any other person attaching to the land. Such equitable claims are said to be *overreached* or extinguished.

Thus if A and B are trustees of land for the benefit of C, they can sell the land without the concurrence of C and if they do, C's interest in the land is overreached. His only claim will then be against the trustees for breach of trust (*see* XXIII, **31**).

In such cases the equitable or beneficial owner can sue to recover the land from the purchaser only if it can be shown that the purchaser knew, or should have known, of the equitable interest of C at the time he purchased the land. But if he is a bona fide purchaser for value of the legal estate, without notice of such equitable claim, his purchase will overreach all equitable interests attaching to the land.

STRICT SETTLEMENTS AND TRUSTS FOR SALE

25. Strict settlements and trusts for sale.

(*a*) *Strict settlement.* This is a trust the purpose of which is to secure the enjoyment of property by successive generations of beneficiaries, e.g. where a man wishes to prevent his heirs selling family heirlooms. The trustees in such a settlement are instructed to *retain* the property, not to sell it.

But the Settled Land Act 1925, now enables the tenant for life of settled land, i.e. the principal beneficiary, to sell the property or otherwise dispose of it himself without the concurrence of the trustees.

(*b*) *Trust for sale.* These are trusts in which the trustees are placed under a positive duty to sell the trust property, though they are generally given power to retain it for as long as seems advisable. After sale they must usually distribute the proceeds among the beneficiaries, or invest the proceeds for their benefit.

(*c*) *Other types of trust.* There are several intermediary types of trust between the two above extremes, and the general rules stated in chapter XXIII apply to all trusts except where the trust instrument lays down special rules.

26. Creation of strict settlements.

(*a*) *Inter vivos.* Where the settlor creates a settlement during his life-time, he must do two things:

(*i*) vest the property by the appropriate form of legal transfer in the trustees as legal owners;

(ii) inform the trustees of their duties, and the purposes of the trust.

Where the trust is of land, two documents are required to achieve these objects:

(a) *a vesting deed*, conveying the legal estate to the trustees;

(b) *a trust instrument*, which sets out the conditions of the trust. A purchaser of land from the trustees is concerned only with the vesting deed, and since he need not peruse the trust instrument (and can be prevented from doing so), he is not fixed with notice of the trust: thus, the interests of the beneficiaries in the land can be more easily overreached (*see* XXIII, 3).

In trusts of personalty a trust instrument is required but not a vesting deed (unless the personalty is such as should be transferred by deed, e.g. transfer of shares in a ship). Chattels can be transferred by mere delivery, and the vesting in this case can therefore be oral.

(c) *By will*. Here the will is treated as the trust instrument and the property is conveyed to the trustees by the executors of the will signing a written authorisation called a vesting assent.

27. Creation of trusts for sale. These most commonly arise by operation of law, rather than by express creation.

By statute a trust for sale arises automatically:

(a) wherever land is held by joint tenants;

(b) where executors hold property undisposed of by will;

(c) in cases of intestacy (*see* XXIV, 20).

PROGRESS TEST 20

1. Explain what was meant by tenure in mediaeval law. (1, 2)

2. Distinguish between an estate and an interest in land. (4, 6)

3. How do equitable estates and interests differ from legal estates and interests? (7)

4. What are future interests? Define: (a) reversion, and (b) remainder. (8, 9)

5. How may a fee simple be created, and how far is it true to say that the fee-simple owner is the absolute owner of everything above, below, or on his ground? (12, 13)

6. What is a term of years absolute, and how does it differ from a fee simple? (10, 11, 13, 14)

7. Explain the meaning of the following terms: (*a*) words of severance; (*b*) undivided shares; (*c*) *jus accrescendi*; (*d*) joint tenants. **(15–17)**

8. Define: (*a*) easement, and (*b*) *profit à prendre*. How does an easement differ from a profit? **(19)**

9. What is a rentcharge? How can it be created and how can it be enforced? **(20)**

10. Explain how an equitable interest may arise. **(21)**

11. State the rule in *Walsh* v. *Lonsdale*, and explain its significance. **(22)**

12. What is the perpetuity rule? **(23)**

13. Explain how equitable interest can be overreached. **(24)**

CHAPTER XXI

Leases, Covenants and Servitudes

LEASES

1. Definition. A term of years absolute or lease means a tenancy of land for a period of time having certain duration. A lease is one of the two legal estates recognised by modern law: Law of Property Act 1925, s. 1.

2. Kinds of tenancy.

(*a*) *Tenancy for fixed term.* This is a tenancy which is:
   (*i*) created by express agreement, and
   (*ii*) having a definite commencement and duration.

(*b*) *Periodic tenancies.* Here the tenant takes possession for an indefinite period but agrees to pay rent calculated on a yearly, quarterly, monthly, weekly basis. The tenancy so created is either yearly, quarterly, monthly, or weekly according to the period over which rent is calculated. Thus a grant "To A at £400 per year" would be a yearly tenancy.

NOTE: The period of notice required to terminate such periodic tenancy would be, normally: (*i*) six months for a yearly periodic tenancy; (*ii*) three months for a quarterly tenancy; (*iii*) one month for a monthly tenancy; (*iv*) one week for a weekly tenancy. (These periods are subject to variation by agreement.)

(*c*) *Tenancy at sufferance.* This can only arise by implication of law where a tenant under a lease stays in possession ("holds over") after expiry of his lease. He can be compelled to pay rent for as long as he remains, but the lessor can eject him at any time.

(*d*) *Tenancy at will.* May arise by express agreement (rare) or by implication and may be determined at any time by either party, expressly or impliedly, e.g. on death of either. Such a tenancy arises where possession is granted (with or without payment of rent) for no fixed period. Where rent is accepted a tenancy at will often becomes a periodic tenancy, weekly, monthly, or yearly depending on how the rent is calculated.

3. Creation of leases.

(a) *Leases for more than three years* must be created by deed in order to become a legal estate: Law of Property Act 1925, s. 52. But a merely written lease creates an equitable interest capable of being converted into a legal estate by an order for specific performance: *Walsh* v. *Lonsdale* (1882) (*see* XXX, 22). And even if merely oral, it may be enforced by equity in the same way if the equitable doctrine of part performance applies (*see* V, 7).

(b) *Leases for not more than three years* need not be by deed. If supported by written evidence, these are legally enforceable provided they:

    (i) take effect in possession; and

    (ii) are at the best rent obtainable.

4. Determination of leases.

(a) *By effluxion of time.* A lease for a fixed period terminates automatically on the last day of the term without any notice being necessary.

(b) *By notice.* A periodic tenancy requires to be determined by notice by lessor or tenant to coincide with the last day of any period. Length of notice may be fixed by agreement; otherwise it is implied by law, i.e. six months for yearly tenancies, one month for monthly tenancies, one week for weekly.

(c) *By surrender* to the tenant's immediate landlord.

(d) *By merger* where the tenant himself obtains a transfer of his immediate landlord's interest.

(e) *By forfeiture*, but only where the lease contains an express proviso that if the tenant breaks any of the covenants in the lease it shall be forfeited (*see* 5).

NOTE: The *Leasehold Reform Acts* 1967 and 1979 provide that where a dwelling having a rateable value of not more than £200 (£400 in London) has been leased for more than twenty-one years and has been occupied by the leaseholder for five years or more, the leaseholder will have the right: (1) to enfranchise (i.e. buy the freehold), or (2) to extend the lease for 50 years. Failing agreement between the parties, the price for the freehold or rent for the fifty years can be fixed by the Lands Tribunal.

5. Protection against forfeiture.

(a) *Breach of covenant to pay rent.* The court will grant relief provided that (*i*) the tenant pays all arrears of rent and costs, and

(*ii*) it is just and equitable that relief should be granted, and

(*iii*) the tenant applies for relief within six months of the landlord taking possession of the land.

(*b*) *Breach of other covenants*. The landlord cannot forfeit until he has given reasonable notice (usually three months) specifying the breach complained of and requiring the tenant to remedy the breach and/or pay compensation if appropriate: Law of Property Act 1925, s. 146. The tenant may then apply for relief, at any time before the landlord has taken possession and relief may be granted on such terms as the court thinks just.

COVENANTS IN A LEASE

6. Express or implied covenants. In any lease the lessor may require the tenant to sign certain express covenants, e.g. to insure against fire. Where no covenants are expressed, the following covenants are implied by lessor and lessee (*see* **7, 8**).

7. Implied covenants by lessor.

(*a*) *Covenant for quiet enjoyment*, i.e. that the tenant's possession will not be directly interfered with by the lessor or persons claiming under him.

(*b*) *Covenant not to derogate from the grant*, i.e. that the lessor will not interfere with the tenant's enjoyment indirectly (in ways not amounting to breach of (*a*) above), e.g. by using adjoining premises in a "manner inconsistent with the purpose of the lease".

(*c*) *Fitness for habitation*. This is only implied in:

(*i*) furnished lettings, or

(*ii*) unfurnished lettings at low rents.

8. Implied covenants by lessee.

(*a*) *To pay the rent*.

(*b*) *To pay rates and taxes*, except those which are legally the landlord's personal obligation.

(*c*) *Not to commit waste*, i.e. not to damage the property or permit it to depreciate unreasonably by neglect.

(*d*) *To repair*. This obligation is primarily the landlord's and a tenant impliedly covenants merely to let the landlord enter and view the property to see what repairs are necessary. But if the lease is agreed subject to "the usual covenants" the obligation to repair is transferred to the tenant.

9. Express covenants. In a formal lease the above covenants are usually set out expressly, plus the following additional covenants by the tenant.

(*a*) *Not to assign or underlet* without the landlord's consent. (The consent must not be unreasonably withheld: Landlord and Tenant Act 1927, s. 19.)

(*b*) *To repair.*

(*i*) Long leases: the tenant usually covenants to repair outside and inside.

(*ii*) Short leases: landlord covenants to repair outside and tenant inside.

(*c*) *To insure against fire.*

10. Enforceability of covenants. The original landlord and tenant are contractually liable on the covenants in the lease. Where the tenant assigns his lease (or himself takes a subtenant) or the landlord assigns his reversion, the binding effect of the covenants will depend on the law relating to restrictive covenants (*see* **11–15**).

RESTRICTIVE COVENANTS

11. Definition. Restrictive covenants are promises restricting the use of land, and which may be enforceable not only between the original promisor and promisee, but also between their assigns.

The enforceability of such covenants differs slightly:

(*a*) at law; and

(*b*) in equity.

12. Enforceability at common law.

(*a*) *Benefit of the covenant.* This would pass to an assignee and be enforceable by him if the covenant touched and concerned land, and was for the benefit of the land (not of the original covenantee personally), and the legal estate in the land had been obtained by the assignee.

(*b*) *Burden of the covenant.* This usually did not pass to the assignee—thus an assignee of a lease would not be bound by the tenant's obligations in the original lease.

13. Enforceability in equity.

(*a*) *Benefit of the covenant.* This would pass to an assignee if it touched and concerned land and the assignee had obtained an interest in the land which the covenant was intended to benefit.

(b) *Burden of the covenant*. This would pass to an assignee under the rule in *Tulk* v. *Moxhay* (1848) if:

(i) the covenant is *negative* in nature; and

(ii) the assignee owns land capable of being *benefited*; and

(iii) the burden of the covenant was *attached to the land* against which the claim is made and not merely against the assignee personally.

Thus equity followed the law in its attitudes to the benefit of covenants, and applied the more progressive *Tulk* v. *Moxhay* rule where the dispute involved the enforcement of the burden of a covenant.

EXAMPLE: A sold land to B, exacting a covenant that B would not build on the land (the covenant to be enforceable against any person to whom B sold the land). B sold the land to C, who sold it to D (who took the land with notice of the covenant). D decided to build on the land, and A sued for an injunction to prevent building. D relied on the doctrine of privity of contract (*see* VI, **6, 7**) and claimed he was not bound by the covenant, since he was not a party to it. HELD: The injunction was granted, since the convenant "touched and concerned" the land and had more than contractual implications: *Tulk* v. *Moxhay* (1848).

14. Position now. The modern rules (following *Tulk* v. *Moxhay*) relating to covenants and their enforceability can be summarised as follows.

(a) The covenant must be for the benefit of a dominant tenement, which must be identifiable.

(b) An assignee *of the whole* of the dominant or quasi-dominant tenement may enforce the covenant.

(c) An assignee *of part* of the quasi-dominant tenement may enforce the covenant if:

(i) the intention in the original covenant appears to be that it shall pass for the benefit of part tenants;

(ii) the original intention was to benefit part only of the land, and the person claiming to enforce is the tenant of that part.

15. Discharge of covenants.

(a) *By waiver.*

(b) *By order of the court.*

(c) *By the Lands Tribunal* on the grounds that:

(*i*) the covenant has become obsolete; or

(*ii*) the persons benefited agree to the discharge; or

(*iii*) that discharge will not injure the persons benefited: Law of Property Act 1925, s. 84.

EASEMENTS AND PROFITS

16. Jura in re alieno (rights in the property of another). Servitudes or rights over another's land are primarily of two kinds.

(*a*) *Easements:* privileges without profit, e.g. rights of way, light, air support, water.

(*b*) *Profits à prendre:* privileges giving a right to take something from another's land, e.g. hunting, shooting, fishing rights, grazing rights.

17. Nature of easements. These are privileges for the benefit of land rather than for the benefit of the owner of land, i.e. they are always appurtenant to land.

(*a*) *Easements cannot exist in gross:* they cannot exist independently of ownership of land, i.e. cannot be personal rights. They must be appurtenant to land, i.e. must benefit a piece of land (and consequently the owner or tenant).

(*b*) *There must be dominant and a servient tenement*, i.e. a piece of land to be benefited (the dominant tenement) and a piece of land burdened (the servient tenement).

(*c*) *They must be capable of definition*, i.e. must be capable of forming the subject-matter of a grant.

EXAMPLES:

(1) A, B and C bought new houses overlooking a park, and the owners of the park (who had provided the land on which the houses were built) covenanted not to allow building on the park. The park was sold to X, who decided to build. A, B, and C claimed an easement to view the unbuilt park and to walk over it. X claimed that the rights claimed were too vague to constitute easement. HELD: Easement established: *Re Ellenborough Park* (1956).

(2) Two separate but adjoining houses, Nos. 14 and 16 Market Street, were owned by A and B. No. 14 was demolished, leaving the wall of No. 16 exposed to the weather. The wall was not weatherproof, since it had adjoined the wall of No. 14 and was not designed to be weatherproof. No. 16 sustained

damage, and B sued for infringement of an *easement of protection*. HELD: There was no such easement known to land: *Phipps* v. *Pears* (1964).

18. Nature of profits.

(*a*) *They may exist in gross*, i.e. independently of the ownership or occupation of land. (But note (*c*) and (*d*) below.)

(*b*) *They may be several or common*, i.e. belonging to one person (several) or shared by a group (common).

(*c*) *A profit appurtenant* is one attached by agreement to land (and therefore similar to an easement) and only to be enjoyed by the owner of a particular piece of land.

(*d*) *A profit apendant* is one attached by law to a piece of land, i.e. a common or pasture, e.g. certain village greens.

19. Acquisition of easements and profits.

(*a*) *By Act of Parliament*, e.g. where a local authority is given a right to build roads across lands.

(*b*) *By express reservation or grant*. (Note that the Law of Property Act 1925, s. 62 provides that a grant of land carries with it all privileges and easements attaching to the land, whether the grant mentions them or not, unless a contrary intention appears.)

(*c*) *By implied grant or reservation*, e.g. where an easement of necessity is implied in favour of a grantor who has retained a plot of land entirely surrounded by the land sold and therefore needs a right of way to enter and leave his land. (But the courts are reluctant to imply such reserved easements even in such exceptional circumstances, the maxim being, "a grantor must not derogate from his grant.") Easements will be readily implied in favour of a grantee wherever necessary for reasonable enjoyment of the land.

(*d*) *By prescription* (presumed grant). The court may presume an easement or profit in favour of any person who can show he has exercised the right claimed provided:

(*i*) the enjoyment has been continuous for the period proved; and

(*ii*) has been exercised "*as of right*" (i.e. without the consent of the owner of the land) *nec vi, nec clam, nec precario* (not by force, not secretly, not merely by permission).

20. Methods of prescription.

(*a*) *At common law:* by proof of user from "time immemorial", i.e. since 1189. In practice, any long user will suffice to raise a presumption that the right has existed since 1189. But this presumption may be rebutted by proof that the right did not or could not have existed at some time since 1189 (*see* II, **5**).

(*b*) *Lost modern grant*. Because of difficulty of proving use since 1189, the courts will sometimes presume that a grant was made at some time since then but has since been lost, provided long use can be proved, e.g. twenty years.

(*c*) *Under the Prescription Act* 1832. This Act aimed at making prescription easier than under (*a*) and (*b*), though both those methods still exist.

21. Prescription Act 1832.

(*a*) *Profits*.

(*i*) If the claimant can show thirty years uninterrupted enjoyment his claim cannot be defeated merely by showing that user must have commenced since 1189.

(*ii*) On proof that the profit was enjoyed for sixty years continuously, the profit is indefeasible save by showing that it was enjoyed only under a written consent.

(*b*) *Easements other than light*. The same principles apply as to profits, but in the case of easements the periods are:

(*i*) twenty years, and

(*ii*) forty years.

(*c*) *Easements of light*. If the right was actually enjoyed for twenty years it becomes absolute, and can be defeated only by showing it was derived from a written consent.

The Rights of Light Act 1959 makes the period twenty-seven years in some cases, and also enables the owner of land over which light passes to forestall prescription by registering with the local authority a notice which operates as an automatic infringement.

22. Extinguishment of easements and profits.

(*a*) *By Act of Parliament*.

(*b*) *By release*, express or implied.

(*c*) *By union of dominant and servient tenements in the ownership of one person*.

PROGRESS TEST 21

1. Define a lease and explain the various forms a lease can take. (**1, 2**)

2. Distinguish: (*a*) between a yearly and a monthly tenancy,

and (b) between a tenancy at sufferance and a tenancy at will. (2)

3. How may a lease: (a) be created, and (b) be determined? (3, 4)

4. What protection has a tenant against forfeiture of his lease? (5)

5. What covenants are generally implied in leases: (a) by the lessor, and (b) by the lessee? (7, 8)

6. What is meant by a restrictive covenant, and how far is such a covenant enforceable today? (11, 13, 14)

7. State the rule in *Tulk* v. *Moxhay* (1848) and summarise the facts of the case. (13)

8. How may a restrictive covenant be discharged? (15)

9. Define easements and *profits à prendre*. Give examples of each. (16, 17, 18)

10. How do easements differ from profits? (16–19)

11. How may an easement be acquired, and how may it be extinguished? (19, 22)

12. Explain the rules governing the prescription of easements and profits. (19–21)

CHAPTER XXII

Securities

SECURITIES GENERALLY

1. Meaning of security. A security is some right or interest in property given to a creditor so that, in the event of the debtor failing to pay the debt as and when agreed, the creditor may reimburse himself for the amount of the debt out of the property charged.

Both real and personal property may be charged with repayment of a debt in this way.

2. Kinds of security.

(*a*) *Mortgages.* A mortgage is an assurance to the creditor of the legal or equitable interest in property as security for the discharge of a debt or other obligation, subject to a proviso that on repayment the mortgage shall become void. (Norman-French: *mort/gage* = dead pledge.)

The characteristic of this type of security today is that possession of the thing mortgaged remains vested in the mortgagor (until the debt is overdue).

(*b*) *Pledge or pawn.* A pledge is a deposit of chattels with a lender as security for repayment of a loan. If the pledgee is a professional lender upon this type of security the pledge is called a pawn and the lender a pawnbroker.

A pledge thus differs from a mortgage in that the pledgee has possession of his security, while ownership remains vested in the borrower. In a mortgage, the mortgagee does not get possession but does obtain a legal or equitable interest in the property subjected to the mortgage, which he can enforce by selling the property, etc., if the debt is not paid.

(*c*) *Liens.* A lien is a right which a creditor may acquire over property of a debtor, real or personal, either to retain the property until the debt is paid (a possessory lien) or to seek a court order for sale of the property if the debt is unpaid (an equitable lien) (*see* XII, **27**).

A lien differs from a mortgage or pledge in that it arises by

275

operation of law, and not from any agreement between the creditor and debtor.

3. Mortgages of real and personal property. Real property can be mortgaged, and personalty can be mortgaged or pledged. Mortgages of land are dealt with in **5–13** below, and mortgages and pledges of personalty in **14–19.**

4. Legal and equitable mortgages. Since a mortgage consists of the transfer or assurance to the mortgagee of an interest in the property charged, it follows that the interest so conferred may be either legal or equitable.

A legal mortgage is one under which the creditor receives a legal interest in the property. Thus, a legal mortgage of land must be created by deed, since a legal estate or interest in land can only be created in this way: Law of Property Act 1925, ss. 51, 52.

An equitable mortgage is one under which the creditor receives only an equitable interest in the property, e.g. a mortgage of land made otherwise than by deed.

MORTGAGES OF LAND

5. Legal mortgages before 1925. Mortgages of land were generally created by conveying to the mortgagee the entire estate or interest of the mortgagor in the land, subject to a promise by the mortgagee to reconvey the property on repayment of the loan on a certain date (normally six months from the date of the mortgage).

After the date for repayment (the legal date for redemption), the mortgagor lost his legal right to the land. From this time onwards, however, equity recognised him as possessing an equitable right to redeem (and so to recover his land). The mortgagor's possession of both (*a*) a legal right to redeem on the contracted date, and (*b*) an equitable right to redeem later, was called his equity of redemption and was an equitable interest in land, which he could sell, mortgage, leave by will, etc.

Since, after expiry of the legal date for redemption, the mortgagor would have only an equitable interest in the land, any second mortage created by him could only be an equitable mortgage, even though created by deed.

6. Legal mortages since 1925. The mortgage by conveyance was abolished by the Law of Property Act 1925, which provided that legal mortgages can now take only the following forms.

(*a*) *By lease to the mortgagee* for a long term of years, subject to a proviso for cesser on redemption, i.e, that the lease shall cease automatically on repayment of the loan plus interest. (Mortgages of freehold are usually by lease for 4,000 years, and mortgages of leasehold by a lease for the maximum period possible, e.g. the period of the tenant's lease less ten days. Thus, if A has a lease for 99 years, of which 67 years remain unexpired, he may create a mortgage in favour of B by granting him a lease for 66 years plus 355 days.)

(*b*) *By charge by deed expressed to be by way of legal mortgage*: Law of Property Act 1925, s. 85.

(The mortgagee acquires the same rights and remedies in both types of mortgage. The legal charge is fundamentally an invention of the L.P.A. 1925, is simpler than the mortgage by lease, and is becoming increasingly popular.)

NOTE: Any attempt to create a mortgage by the old method of conveying the fee simple to the mortgagee operates as a grant of a mortgage lease for 4,000 years subject to cesser on redemption: L.P.A., 1925 s. 85.

7. Equitable mortgages.

If the mortgagee receives merely an equitable interest in the land his mortgage is said to be equitable. This may occur in the following ways:

(*a*) *Any mortgage of an equitable interest*, whether by deed or otherwise.

If the mortgagor himself has only an equitable interest in the property (e.g. as beneficiary under a trust) he can only confer a like interest on the mortgagee.

Such a mortgage may be by lease, or charge (as in legal mortgages) which must be in writing (whether by deed or not) signed by the mortgagor or his agent: L.P.A. 1925, s. 53, or by mere deposit of title deeds.

(*b*) *Any informal mortgage of a legal estate or interest*. Thus, an attempt to create a legal mortgage otherwise than by deed, operates to create an equitable mortgage. Similarly, a binding contract to grant a legal mortgage in the future immediately creates an equitable mortgage, which may be converted into a proper sealed legal mortgage by an order for specific performance under the rule in *Walsh* v. *Lonsdale*: (*see* XX, **22**). In order for there to be a binding contract there must be: (*i*) written evidence of the contract, or (*ii*) sufficient part performance (*see* V, **7**).

Such a mortgage can therefore be created by informal lease or charge, binding contract to grant a legal mortgage, or by mere deposit of the title deeds to the land (with the mortgagee) by way of security. Banks often accept equitable mortgages by deposit of title deeds, as security for short term loans.

8. Remedies of a legal mortgagee. The remedies are the same whether the mortgage is by lease or by charge: L.P.A. s. 87. The remedies are available for non-payment of loan and/or interest as and when due, or for breach of some other covenant in the mortgage.

(*a*) *To sue for debt* on the mortgagor's covenant to repay. This is the basic remedy, and is open to all creditors (whether secured by mortgage or not).

(*b*) *To take possession of the land.* A mortgagee who takes possession must account to the mortgagor for any loss to the property occasioned by his default, and because of this liability the remedy of possession is rarely exercised: *White* v. *City of London Brewery* (1889).

(*c*) *To foreclose*, i.e. to obtain a court order extinguishing the mortgagor's equitable right to redeem and vesting the full legal estate in the mortgagee. The courts are often reluctant to grant this remedy, and will first give the mortgagor a warning (called a foreclosure order nisi) allowing him a further six months in which to redeem. If he fails to redeem by the end of this period, the order is made absolute: L.P.A. 1925, s. 88.

(*d*) *To sell the land*, under the power implied in all mortgages by deed (whether legal or equitable), unless a contrary intention is expressed: L.P.A. 1925, s. 101.

NOTE: The power of sale arises as soon as the legal date for redemption has passed, but it cannot be exercised until: (*i*) three months' notice has been served requiring repayment of the loan, and the notice has expired, or (*ii*) interest on the loan is in arrear for two months, or (*iii*) there has been a breach of some other covenant in the mortgage than the covenant to repay: L.P.A. 1925, s. 103.

A mortgagee cannot buy the land for himself, but he is not bound to obtain the best price possible. After sale he is a trustee of any surplus moneys (after deducting the amount of his loan + interest) and must pay them to the mortgagor (or any subsequent mortgagees: *see* below).

(*e*) *To appoint a receiver*, under the power implied in all mortgages by deed (whether legal or equitable), unless a contrary intention is expressed: L.P.A. 1925, s. 101.

The receiver is appointed to collect all profits of the land and to use them in paying:

(*i*) rates, taxes, etc.;

(*ii*) his own charges;

(*iii*) the mortgage under which he is appointed:

(*iv*) residue to the mortgagor.

Legally the receiver is treated as agent for the mortgagor, who is therefore responsible for his defaults (unless the mortgage provides to the contrary). Consequently, it is more beneficial to the mortgagee in most cases to appoint a receiver than to take possession himself.

The mortgagee's remedies are concurrent, so he can appoint a receiver, and order sale at the same time.

9. Remedies of equitable mortgagees.

(*a*) *To sue for debt*.

(*b*) *To sell*, if the mortgage is by deed (otherwise only if the mortgage contains an express power of sale).

(*c*) *To appoint a receiver*, if the mortgage is by deed (otherwise only if the mortgage contains an express power).

(*d*) *To foreclose*. (But this remedy is not available if the mortgage is by charge and not by lease.)

An equitable mortgagee cannot take possession, unless an express power is given by the mortgage deed or contract.

10. Mortgagee's other rights.

(*a*) *To consolidate*, i.e. to insist that several mortgages must be redeemed simultaneously or not at all. Today consolidation is only allowed where:

(*i*) Consolidation is expressly reserved in both or all the mortgages to be consolidated: L.P.A. 1925, s. 93.

(*ii*) The legal date for redemption has expired.

(*iii*) The same mortgagor created both or all the mortgages.

(*iv*) The same mortgagee has at some time acquired all the mortgages to be consolidated: *Pledge* v. *White* (1896).

(*b*) *To tack further advances*. If A borrows money from X on a first mortgage, and from Y on a second mortgage, X is entitled to repayment in priority over Y. But if X makes a further loan to A, Y is entitled to repayment of his mortgage before the further mortgage to X, unless X is entitled to tack his second mortgage on to his first, so gaining overall priority. Today tacking is only allowed where: (L.P.A. 1925, s. 94)

(*i*) any intervening mortgagee agrees; or

(*ii*) an obligation to make further advances is imposed on X in the first mortgage, i.e. where in effect loans are to be made by instalments as part of the same mortgage; or

(*iii*) no notice of the intervening mortgage is available to X when he makes his further advance. (Registration of the intervening mortgage constitutes notice for this purpose (*see* 13)).

(*c*) *Other rights of the mortgagee.* A first mortgagee is entitled to take possession of the title deeds to the property. And any mortgage created by deed (whether a first or later mortgage) gives the mortgagee power to insure the property against fire, up to two-thirds of its value: L.P.A. 1925, s. 101.

11. Redemption of mortgages. *At common law* the mortgagor was only entitled to redeem on the legal date fixed by the contract. After expiry of this date his rights in the land were terminated, and the mortgagee became absolutely entitled.

Equity, however, applied the maxim "once a mortgage, always a mortgage" and gave the mortgagor a secondary, equitable right to redeem even after expiry of the legal date for redemption. The two rights of redemption together, legal and equitable, were called the equity of redemption.

The equity of redemption is an equitable interest in land and can be sold, mortgaged, devised by will, etc. Any person who obtains the equity of redemption in a piece of land can redeem the mortgage, e.g. where the mortgagor's heir inherits it by will or upon intestacy.

The equity of redemption is extinguished by:

(*a*) sale or foreclosure by the mortgagee;

(*b*) the mortgagor releasing it to the mortgagee; or

(*c*) by lapse of time under the Limitation Act 1939, s. 16, i.e. by the lapse of twelve years from the date on which the mortgage went into possession of the mortgaged land.

(Mortgages of personalty are governed by the Limitation Act 1939, s. 18, which provides that no action may be brought to recover the principal money secured on any property more than twelve years after the right to receive it accrued).

12. Clogs on the equity of redemption. Any agreement which attempts to bar the mortgagor's right to redeem is void. Similarly, provisions in a mortgage which would mean that after redemption the mortgagor would not get back his property free of the mortgagee's claims, are also void.

Such stipulations in a mortgage are called "clogs on the equity", since they attempt to defeat the equity of redemption.

The general rule is that laid down by Lord Parker in *Kreglinger* v. *New Patagonia Meat Co.* (1914): "There is now no rule in equity which precludes a mortgagee, whether the mortgage be made upon the occasion of a loan or otherwise, from stipulating for any collateral advantage, provided such collateral advantage is not either (1) unfair and unconscionable, or (2) in the nature of a penalty clogging the equity of redemption, or (3) inconsistent with or repugnant to the contractual and equitable right to redeem". This point was recently emphasised by Browne Wilkinson J. in *Multisernice Bookbinding* v. *Marden* (1978): "in order to be freed from the necessity to comply with all the terms of the mortgage, the plaintiffs must show that the bargain, or some of its terms, was unfair and unconscionable; it is not enough to show that in the eyes of the court, it was unreasonable".

Many of the cases involve a type of solus agreement, that is, a mortgage granted on an undertaking by a garage owner to buy all his petrol or by a publican to buy all his beer from the mortgagee. The courts have decided that:

(*a*) *a mortage cannot be made irredeemable*. But it is legitimate for the mortgagee to insist that redemption shall be postponed for a reasonable period, e.g. that the mortgagor may not redeem within twenty years: *Knightsbridge Estates Trust Ltd.* v. *Byrne* (1939).

(*b*) *the mortgage must not be in restraint of trade*. A garage was mortgaged, the mortgage to be repaid in instalments over 21 years. The garage owner also undertook to sell only the mortgagee's petrol for the same 21 year period. This period was too long and the agreement was in restraint of trade (*see* VIII, 21): *Esso* v. *Harper's Garage* (1968).

(*c*) *After redemption*, the mortgagor must get back his property unfettered, i.e. free of all claims by the mortgagee. Thus, where a mortgagor of an inn covenanted to buy all his beer from the mortgagee, even after redemption, the covenant was void: *Noakes & Co. Ltd.* v. *Rice* (1902).

(*d*) *Collateral advantages* given to the mortgagee in the mortgage must cease upon redemption. Thus, if, in addition to promising to repay the loan, a publican covenants to buy all his beer from the mortgagee until redemption, such a provision is valid: *Biggs* v. *Hoddinott* (1898). But the covenant must cease to be binding as soon as the loan is repaid.

13. Priority of mortgages. The mortgagor may create several mortgages on the same property. Where there are several mortgages, the value of the property (when sold) may not be sufficient to pay all the mortgagees. In this case it is necessary to ascertain which mortgagees have the first claim on the proceeds of sale. The equitable rules governing priorities are now augmented by the L.P.A. 1925, s. 97, and the Land Charges Act 1972, s. 4 as follows:

(a) *Legal or equitable mortgages* protected by deposit of title deeds. These rank for priority from the date of creation.

(b) *Puisne mortgages* (i.e. legal mortgages not protected by deposit of title deeds). These rank from the date of registration as Class C land charges, and are void against a purchaser (including mortgagee or chargee) unless so registered.

(c) *Equitable mortgages* not protected by deposit of title deeds. These are called *general equitable charges*. Like puisne mortgages they rank from date of registration and are void against a purchaser of the land unless so registered.

A first mortgagee will normally insist on receiving title deeds, and consequently registration is mainly necessary in the case of subsequent mortgages.

NOTE that where tacking of further advances is allowed, this may alter the order of priorities, even among registered mortgages (*see* **10**).

Sub-mortgages may be created by a mortgagee who wishes to borrow money on the security of a mortgage he holds himself. If his mortgage is by lease he may create a sub-mortgage by sub-leasing to his creditor for a shorter term than he himself holds from the mortgagor. If the mortgage is by charge he must assign his charge to his creditor subject to a proviso for re-assignment on repayment of the loan.

MORTGAGES OF PERSONALTY

14. Kinds of mortgage. A mortgage of personalty may be created by *assigning* to the mortgagee the legal interest in the personalty, on condition of reassignment on repayment of the loan. The type of assignment will depend on the means required by the law for transferring title to the particular kind of personalty involved. Thus, shares, copyrights, insurance policies, etc., need a written assignment. Chattels may be assigned by mere delivery, so that no document is required to mortgage them.

This method, however, is too informal for most cases. The lender may require documentary proof of his rights (especially as the chattels may be left in the possession of the mortgagor), and if he parts with possession the mortgagor may also require documentary proof.

The two principal methods of mortgaging chattels are:

(a) *by conditional bill of sale*, where the mortgagor is to remain in possession (*see* 15);

(b) *by pledge*, where the mortgagee obtains possession until redemption. (Lenders who make their business out of this sort of loan are called pawnbrokers and their transactions pawns (*see* 16, 17).)

There are also special forms of company charges (*see* 18).

15. **Conditional bills of sale.** A bill of sale is "a document given with respect to the transfer of chattels, and is used in cases where possession is not intended to be given": *Johnson* v. *Diprose* (1893) *per* Lord Esher M.R.

An *absolute* bill of sale is a documentary assignment of chattels, giving title without delivery. Since most goods are sold by delivery, absolute bills of sale are rare. They are appropriate, e.g. where a ship is sold while at sea.

A *conditional* bill of sale is one used where chattels are given as security for a loan, i.e. it transfers ownership to the lender, but subject to a condition that the chattels shall be reassigned to the borrower on repayment.

Conditional bills of sale must comply with the requirements of the Bills of Sale Acts 1878 and 1882, as follows:

(a) The bill must be *registered* at the Central Office of the Supreme Court within seven days of creation, and is void unless so registered.

(b) It must be *attested* by at least one witness, otherwise it is void.

(c) *Consideration* for the bill must be truly stated.

(*d*) *Interest* payable and *date of repayment* must be stated, together with any additional conditions.

(*e*) *The chattels comprised* in the bill must be inventoried.

A conditional bill take its priority from the date of registration.

The lender's remedy is seizure of the goods on grounds of failure to repay the loan as agreed, bankruptcy of the debtor, or fraudulent dealing with the goods so as to remove them from the lender's power.

16. Pledges. A pledge involves actual or constructive delivery of the chattels to the pledgee. Constructive delivery might be by giving the pledgee the key to a warehouse in which the goods are stored.

The pledgor remains the legal owner of the goods, and the pledgee becomes a bailee who must return the goods on repayment as agreed. The pledgor is entitled to demand a receipt for deposit of the goods.

The pledgee owes a duty of care for the goods, and if through his negligence they are damaged or stolen he must make good any loss. (But if the goods were taken from him by robbery, i.e. theft with violence, he is excused from liability.) The pledgee generally has no right to use the goods deposited. Even if there is no written agreement, he still has a possessory lien over the goods until payment of his loan.

17. Pawnbrokers. They are professional pledgees, licensed under the Pawnbrokers Act 1872, to carry on business by lending money on security of goods pawned to them.

The Pawnbrokers Acts 1872 and 1960 (applying to loans of £50 or less) lay down the following rules.

(*a*) A pawn-ticket must be given for the pledge.

(*b*) Pawns are to be redeemable any time within six months plus seven days.

(*c*) Pledges not redeemed within the statutory period: (*i*) if for less than £2, belong absolutely to the pawnbroker, and (*ii*) if more than £2, must be sold by public auction. (Surplus moneys to go the pledgor.)

(*d*) Pledges for more than £2 are redeemable any time before sale by auction.

(*e*) If the loan exceeds £5 a contract may be made with special conditions defining the pawnbroker's rights, provided copies are signed by both parties.

(*f*) The pawnbroker must deliver up the goods on presentation of the pawn-ticket and repayment. (He is entitled to presume that the person presenting the ticket is lawfully justified in taking the goods.)

(*g*) If the goods are destroyed by fire the pawnbroker is responsible for making good the loss.

The Consumer Credit Act 1974 provides for the repeal of the Pawnbrokers Acts from a date yet to be appointed. The 1974 Act deals with all consumer transactions for credit under £5,000 (*see* XII, 22–26) and in the case of pawn provides for pawn receipts.

18. Company charges. Company charges are void against the liquidator and creditors unless registered with the Registrar of Companies. The types of company charges are listed in the Companies Act 1948, s. 95. They fall into two categories.

(*a*) *Fixed charges.* These are charges over a specific asset.

(*b*) *Floating charges.* "A floating security is an equitable charge on the assets for the time being of a going concern. It attaches to the subject charged in the varying condition in which it happens to be from time to time. It is of the essence of such a charge that it remains dormant until the undertaking charged ceases to be a going concern, or until the person in whose favour the charge is created intervenes": *Government Stock Co.* v. *Manila Railway* (1897) *per* Lord Macnaghten.

19. Suitability of pledges, etc. Whether personalty is mortgaged by assignment or by pledge depends largely on the type of property (as well as upon the question of who is to receive possession of the goods).

Thus, *choses in action*, such as shares, insurance policies, etc., are generally mortgaged by assignment in due form. (But they can also be pledged if so desired, and stockbrokers frequently raise money be depositing share certificates with a bank by way of pledge.)

Small chattels are generally pawned (or otherwise pledged), e.g. jewels, watches, clocks, clothing, musical instruments.

Large chattels, or large quantities of chattels, will generally not be accepted by a pawnbroker or other pledgee because of difficulties of storage, and therefore must generally be mortgaged by conditional bills of sale, e.g. collections of paintings, household furniture, grand pianos. Conditional bills of sale are unpopular because of the publicity involved in registration (*see* **15**).

A borrower will therefore usually try to pledge his chattels, if he can find a lender willing to accept them. Otherwise he will try to borrow without security.

PROGRESS TEST 22

1. What kinds of security are recognised in English law? **(1, 2)**

2. Distinguish between a legal and an equitable mortgage **(4)**

3. Explain the distinction between the legal date for redemption of mortgages of land and the equitable right to redeem. What is the equity of redemption? **(5, 11)**

4. What forms may be taken by legal mortgages after 1925? **(6)**

5. How may an equitable mortgage occur? **(7)**

6. Summarise the remedies open to a legal mortgagee where the mortgagor has failed to repay principal or interest. **(8)**

7. What remedies are available to equitable mortgagees? **(9)**

8. In what circumstances may a mortgagee today be able to apply the remedies of consolidation and tacking? **(10)**

9. How may the equity of redemption be extinguished and what is meant by a "clog" on the equity? **(11, 12)**

10. Summarise the rules governing the priority of mortgages. **(13)**

11. How can chattels be mortgaged? **(14)**

12. What is a bill of sale, and how does an absolute bill differ from a conditional bill of sale? **(15)**

13. Summarise the main provisions of the Pawnbrokers Acts with regard to pledges to pawnbrokers. **(17)**

14. What would be the most appropriate ways of using the following properties as security for a loan: (*a*) a grand piano; (*b*) a collection of valuable paintings; (*c*) an expectation under a will; (*d*) a leasehold house; (*e*) an interest under a trust fund? **(19)**

PART FIVE
EQUITY AND TRUSTS

CHAPTER XXIII

Equity

INTRODUCTION

1. Nature and scope of equity. Since the fusion of law and equity (*see* I, 26) all courts have been able to apply equitable rules and to award equitable remedies. Equity was never a complete system of law. It filled the gaps in the common law. Whereas the courts must apply the rules of common law and statute where appropriate, they have always had a discretion whether or not to apply an equitable rule or award an equitable remedy. In exercising this discretion the courts have traditionally applied the maxims of equity (*see* 2), which are a set of principles of fairness. Where the rules of law and equity conflict, equity prevails.

The importance of equity today is in six areas of law:

(*a*) *Equitable doctrines* (*see* 4).

(*b*) *Equitable remedies* (*see* 5–7).

(*c*) *Equitable protection.* Equity has always protected persons at a disadvantage such as women, infants, or the victims of fraud. Examples of such protection are the rules of estoppel (*see* VI, 5) or rescission for fraud (*see* VIII, 9).

(*d*) *Trusts.* The trust (*see* 8–31) is the great creation of equity.

(*e*) *Securities.* The mortgage was a creation of the common law but its development has been by equity (*see* XXII).

(*f*) *Succession.* The rules governing administration of the assets of a deceased have also been developed by equity (*see* XXIV).

2. Maxims of equity. These maxims still express the spirit of equity, although they do not really cover all the technical rules now applicable.

(*a*) *Equity will not suffer a wrong to be without a remedy.* An example is the enforcement of trusts, which were not recognised at common law.

287

(b) *Equity follows the law.* This really means two things.

(i) Equity will not interfere where a rule of law applies unless that rule is unconscionable.

(ii) Equitable interests follow the model of legal ones; thus we have equitable mortgages or assignments as well as legal mortgages or assignments (*see* XII, 2; XXII, 4).

(c) *He who seeks equity must do equity.* Equitable relief will not be granted to a plaintiff who is not prepared to act equitably himself. This is the basis of estoppel (*see* VI, 5). This maxim applies to the present or future conduct of the plaintiff.

(d) *He who comes into equity must come with clean hands.* This maxim differs from (c) in that it applies to the plaintiff's past conduct. A woman was entitled to trust money when she came of age. She fraudulently misrepresented to her trustees that she was of age and they paid the money. She could not then obtain the money again when she really did come of age: *Overton* v. *Bannister* (1844).

(e) *Delay defeats equity* or *equity aids only the vigilant.* Unreasonable delay in bringing a claim will defeat it. This is the equitable doctrine of *laches.*

(f) *Equality is equity.* Thus in matrimonial cases the basic inference may be that the parties should divide the property equally. It has been said, however, that "the decision of cases of this kind has been made more difficult by excessive application of the maxim 'Equality is Equity' ": *Gissing* v. *Gissing* (1970) *per* Lord Pearson. The courts try to award a share proportionate to the parties' contributions.

(g) *Equity looks to the intent rather than the form.* Equity will, for example, treat a transaction as a mortgage, if that is its intention, even though it may describe itself as a conveyance.

(h) *Equity acts in personam.* The essence of equity is the enforcement of moral obligations owed by the defendant to the plaintiff personally. Where T acquires property from G by promising to use it for the benefit of B, even if the promise is unsupported by consideration equity will compel T to carry out his bargain. But B's right is a personal, moral right against T only. Therefore if T sells the property to X, who has no notice of the trust, B cannot enforce the action against T for breach of trust (*see* 31). Equitable remedies operate against the defendant personally (*see* 5–7)

(i) *Equity looks on that as done which ought to be done.* This is the basis of the rule in *Walsh* v. *Lonsdale* (1882) (*see* **XX, 22**) and of the doctrine of conversion (*see* **4**(*a*)).

(*j*) *Equity imputes an intention to fulfil an obligation.* Thus, where a man is under a duty and does something capable of being construed as performance of that duty. Where A dies owing B £1,000 and in his will leaves a legacy of £1,000 to B, equity will not allow B both to take the legacy and to sue A's executors for the debt. "Equity presumes that a man intends to be just before he would be generous." This is the basis of the doctrines of performance and satisfaction (*see* **4**(*c*), (*d*)).

(*k*) *Where there is equal equity, the law shall prevail.* Where plaintiff and defendant have equally sound moral claims, strict legal rules will decide between them.

(*l*) *Where the equities are equal, the first in time shall prevail.* Where two persons make equally sound competing claims to property equity will usually decide in favour of the person whose claim arose first.

3. The limits of equitable protection. Where T acquires property from G by promising to use it for the benefit of B (*see* **2**(*h*)) both T and B have some interest in the property.

(*a*) T is the legal owner.

(*b*) B is equitable or beneficial owner.

Legal and equitable interests in property may thus exist side by side in the same property.

(*a*) The *legal owner* is in a stronger position.

(*i*) He can sell the property so as to defeat or *overreach* any equitable interests attaching to it.

(*ii*) He can recover the property from any person who wrongfully dispossesses him. His rights are *in rem*, fixed to the property itself.

(*b*) The *equitable owner* is in a weaker position.

(*i*) His rights in the property itself (as opposed to the value of the property) can be destroyed or overreached by sale by the legal owner.

(*ii*) His rights are enforceable only against persons who acquire legal ownership of the property with knowledge of his equitable interest.

Under the rule in *Pilcher* v. *Rawlins* (1871) such equitable interests are overreached by the *bona fide purchaser of the legal estate for value without notice*.

Each of these four elements is important.

(*a*) *Bona fide*. The purchaser must act in good faith and make reasonable inquiries to see if any person has equitable claims upon the property.

(*b*) *Purchaser . . . for value*. The purchaser must give valuable consideration (*see* VI, 1) and not merely receive it as a gift or for illusory consideration.

(*c*) *Of the legal estate*.

(*d*) *Without notice*. If the purchaser has failed to make the reasonable inquiries which would give him actual notice of equitable interests he may be deemed to have constructive notice.

EQUITABLE DOCTRINES

4. Equitable doctrines.

(*a*) *Conversion*. "Money directed to be employed in the purchase of land, and land directed to be sold and turned into money, are to be considered as that species of property into which they are directed to be converted; and this in whatever manner the direction is given; whether by will, by way of contract, marriage articles, settlement or otherwise, and whether the money is actually deposited, or only covenanted to be paid, whether the land is actually conveyed or only agreed to be paid. The owner of the fund or the contracting parties may make land money or money land": *Fletcher* v. *Ashburner* (1779) *per* Sewell M.R. This is the principle behind the trust for sale (*see* XX, 25).

(*b*) *Election*. The doctrine of election was carefully discussed by Buckley L.J. in *Re Gordon's Will Trusts* (1978). He distinguished two classes.

(*i*) *Dual gifts*. A by the same will confers beneficial interests on both B and C. The gift to B is valid; that to C is not as the property involved in fact belongs to B. B may then elect. Either he does not give effect to the will at all, or he takes his own benefit and gives effect to A's gift to C.

(*ii*) *Mutual settlements*. Here A and B each make a settlement in favour of each other (or of C). B cannot both enforce the trust under which he benefits and repudiate the other.

(*c*) *Performance*. "Where a man covenants to do an act, and he does an act which may be converted to a completion of this covenant, it shall be supposed that he meant to complete it":

Sowden v. *Sowden* (1785) *per* Kenyon M.R. The covenant may be
of two kinds

    (*i*) Covenant to purchase and settle land.

    (*ii*) Covenant to leave personalty by will or on intestacy.

    (*d*) *Satisfaction*. This doctrine differs from performance only in
one way. The act done is different from the act agreed to be done.
It will amount to satisfaction if such was the intention of the
party acting.

    (*e*) *Subrogation*. This doctrine applies, for example, in a con-
tract of insurance. After the insurer has met a claim he acquires
all the rights the claimant had against third parties. Many legal
actions are brought by insurers in the name of an insured under
the doctrine of subrogation.

EQUITABLE REMEDIES

5. Equitable remedies. One of the chief ways in which equity
supplemented the law was by granting auxiliary or additional
remedies where the common law remedy of damages proved
inadequate. Equitable remedies have two characteristics.

    (*a*) Equity acts *in personam*.

    (*b*) Equitable remedies are discretionary. They are only
awarded when the maxims of equity are met (*see* **2**).

There are six remedies to consider.

    (*a*) *Specific performance* (*see* **6**).

    (*b*) *Injunction* (*see* **7**).

    (*c*) *Receivers*. A receiver may be appointed to collect and pre-
serve all the profits of a property on behalf of a mortgagee,
creditor, shareholder, or the beneficiary under a trust.

    (*d*) *Rescission*. Rescission allows an innocent party to escape
from his obligations under a contract on the ground of fraud or
mistake (*see* VIII, **2**, **9**). Under the Misrepresentation Act 1967, s.
2(2) damages may sometimes be awarded instead of rescission
(*see* VIII, **8**).

    (*e*) *Rectification*. Equity will rectify a document which wrongly
records the intentions of the parties to it (*see* VII, **9**).

    (*f*) *Account*. A financial statement or account may be ordered
where a fiduciary relationship exists. Thus an agent may be
required to account to his principal, or a trustee to his beneficiary,
or one partner to another.

6. Specific performance. This is a remedy for breach of contract and consists of a court order compelling the defendant to perform his side of the contract. Specific performance is always discretionary and will only be awarded:

(*a*) *where damages would be inadequate.* Examples are as follows.

(*i*) Contracts for the sale or leasing of land, provided the requirements of writing or part performance are fulfilled (*see* V, 7).

(*ii*) Contracts to deliver specific or ascertained goods: Sale of Goods Act 1893, s. 52.

(*iii*) Contracts for the sale of valuable and unique chattels. Specific performance may be awarded in addition to or instead of damages.

(*b*) *where the enforcement of the order would not require constant supervision by the court.* Specific performance will not be awarded to enforce a building contract or a contract of employment. It may, however, be awarded where the court can tell the defendant exactly what he must do and has been used to enforce a covenant to repair property under a lease. "The real question is whether there is a sufficient definition of what has to be done in order to comply with the order of the court": *Tito* v. *Waddell* (No. 2) (1977) *per* Megarry V.-C.

(*c*) *where the contract is mutually enforceable.* A minor plaintiff cannot obtain specific performance of a contract which would not be binding on him (*see* VI, **10**), since it would be impossible for the adult defendant to claim specific performance against the infant.

(*d*) *where the plaintiff has himself acted inequitably.*

7. Injunction. An injunction is a court order. Usually it is *negative* or *prohibitory*, and forbids a person from doing something. In rare circumstances it may be *mandatory*, and command a person to do something. Mandatory injunctions are rare because the courts will not make an order which requires supervision.

Injunctions may take different forms.

(*a*) A *quia timet* injunction may be awarded to prevent an apprehended injury before it has occurred, but only where there are strong grounds for supposing it to be imminent, and where the court can tell the defendant exactly what he must do: *Morris* v. *Redland Bricks* (1970).

(*b*) An *interim* or *interlocutory* injunction may be granted pending the decision of a case.

(*c*) A *perpetual* injunction may be granted when a dispute has finally been settled and where damages are useless. An interim injunction forbidding interference with a right of light is made perpetual when the right of light has been finally proved in court.

An injunction may be appropriate in a wide variety of cases.

(*a*) *Contract*. Whereas specific performance may enforce the performance of a contract (*see* 6), an injunction may restrain a breach. Sometimes an injunction can do in a negative manner what could not be done by specific performance. In *Warner Bros. v. Nelson* (1937) a film star under an exclusive contract was forbidden by injunction from making films with any other company.

(*b*) *Tort*. An injunction may be granted to prohibit continuance of a nuisance or to forbid a trespass.

(*c*) *Trusts*. An injunction may be granted to forbid a trustee from selling trust property to the detriment of beneficiaries.

An injunction will not be granted unless the party seeking it has sufficient interest in the matter. An injunction to enforce a public right can only be sought with the consent of the Attorney-General in a *relator* action. This was restated by the House of Lords in *Gouriet* v. *Union of Post Office Workers* (1977). The refusal of the Attorney-General to give his consent to a relator action is not subject to review by the courts.

TRUSTS

. The nature of trusts. A trust is a relationship in which a person called a *trustee* is compelled, as legal owner, to hold real or personal property for the benefit of another person, called the *beneficiary* or *cestui que trust*. There may be several trustees in any trust and several beneficiaries. A trustee may himself be one of the beneficiaries. A trustee of property may be thought of as the legal owner, and the beneficiary as the beneficial or equitable owner.

There are four matters to consider.

(*a*) *Classification*. Trusts are of two kinds, as follows.

(*i*) A private trust is for the benefit of a specified group of beneficiaries (*see* 10–13).

(*ii*) A charitable or public trust is for a general charitable purpose, such as the advancement of education, which is for the benefit of a large and fluctuating group of people (*see* **14–17**).

(*b*) *Creation.* A person who creates a trust is called the settlor. Trusts can arise in three ways.

(*i*) A private or public trust can be created by *express* words of the settlor (*see* **11**).

(*ii*) A private trust may be presumed from the intentions of the settlor. It is then called an implied or *resulting* trust (*see* **19**).

(*iii*) A private trust may arise independently of express words or intention. It is then called a *constructive* trust (*see* **20, 21**).

(*c*) *Variation of trusts.* (*see* **22, 23**).

(*d*) *Trustees.*

(*i*) Appointment (*see* **24–26**).

(*ii*) Duties and powers (*see* **27–31**).

9. Discretionary trusts and powers of appointment. There are three different situations to consider.

(*a*) The settlor S leaves property to the trustee T on trust for A, B and C. T must then divide the property equally between A, B and C. This is an ordinary trust.

(*b*) The settlor S leaves property to the trustee T on trust for such of A, B and C as T may decide. This is called a discretionary trust.

(*c*) The settlor S leaves property to such of his children A, B and C, as his widow W shall appoint with a gift over to D. This is called a power of appointment.

There is one great difference between a discretionary trust and a power of appointment. The trustee of a discretionary trust must exercise his discretion. The property will go to such of A, B and C as T may decide, but it must eventually go to at least one of them. If T fails to decide, the court will intervene. As Lord Wilberforce said in *McPhail* v. *Doulton* (the *Baden* case) (1970) "the court, if called on to execute the trust power, will do so in the manner best calculated to give effect to the settlor's or testator's intentions. It may do so by appointing new trustees, or by authorising or directing representative persons of the classes of beneficiaries to prepare a scheme of distribution, or even should the proper basis appear, by itself directing the trustees so to distribute." In the case of the power of appointment, however, W may never exercise it at all. There the property will eventually pass to D and there is nothing A, B or C can do about it.

There was formerly a second great difference, that of the test or certainty of objects. Since the decision in the *Baden* case, however, the tests have been assimilated (*see* 12).

EXPRESS PRIVATE TRUSTS

0. Express creation. An express private trust is one expressly created by a settlor, *inter vivos* or by will, for the benefit of a particular person or group of persons and not for some institution or public purpose. To create an express private trust the following conditions must be satisfied.

(*a*) *The three certainties.* There must be:

(*i*) *certainty of subject-matter.* The trust property must be sufficiently identified, and the shares which the beneficiaries are to receive.

(*ii*) *certainty of words* (*see* 11). If there is no certainty of subject-matter or words the trust fails and the grantee takes the property absolutely.

(*iii*) *certainty of objects* (*see* 12). If there is no certainty of objects the particular trust will fail but the grantee will be compelled to hold the property on trust for the settlor or his heirs.

(*b*) *Proper constitution* (*see* 13).

(*c*) *Perpetuity and inalienability.* The trust must not infringe:

(*i*) the rule against perpetuity (when the property *vests*); or

(*ii*) the rule against inalienability (the *duration* of the trust).

These rules are considered elsewhere (*see* XX, 23).

(*d*) *Avoidance of voluntary settlements.* Where a person conveys property to a trustee with intent to defraud his creditors, the settlement may in certain circumstances be avoided. Voluntary conveyances, for which no consideration has been given in return, can be avoided and the property recovered from the trustees if the settlor goes bankrupt within two years of making the settlement: Bankruptcy Act 1914, s. 42.

If all the terms have been completely defined by the settlor and the property has been conveyed to the trustees the trust is executed. If some further document is necessary to convey the property to the trustees the trust is executory. A completely constituted trust (*see* 13) will be enforced whether it is executed or executory. Revocation of the trust is impossible once it has been completely constituted, unless

(*a*) the settlor expressly reserved the power to revoke; or

(b) the trust was procured by fraud; or
(c) the trust was created by mistake.

11. Certainty of words. The words of the grant must be clear and impose a definite duty on the trustee to carry out the trust. The test is the settlor's intention derived from the words used. No particular words need to be used, although the courts will more readily infer a trust where the word "trust" has been used. A trust will not normally be inferred where the words are only precatory, that is merely requesting performance of the trust. A grant of property by will to the testator's widow "in full confidence that she will do what is right as to the disposal thereof between my children" was found to be insufficiently commanding and the trust failed: *Re Adams & Kensington Vestry* (1884). A Lopes L.J. said in *Re Hamilton* (1895), "The court will not allow a precatory trust to be raised unless on the consideration of all the words employed it comes to the conclusion that it was the intention of the testator to create a trust." It has recently been said, however, that simple people are not expected to use "stilted lawyers' language". The court may even be satisfied with the repeated words, "This money is as much yours as mine": *Paul v Constance* (1977).

12. Certainty of objects. Certainty of objects means that the beneficiaries must be sufficiently identified. In the case of power of appointment (*see* 9) the House of Lords decided in *Re Gulbenkian's Settlement Trusts* (1968), that a power was valid if it could be said with certainty whether any given individual was or was not a member of the class of objects of the power and that the power did not fail simply because it was impossible to ascertain every member of the class. In the *Baden* case (1970) a majority of the House of Lords decided that the same test was to be applied to ascertain the validity of a trust. The trust in that case was established to benefit the staff of a company. The trust deed authorised the trustees to make "at their absolute discretion grants to or for the benefit of any of the officers and employees or ex-officers or ex-employees of the company or to any relatives or dependants of any such persons". The House decided that this was capable of constituting a trust. Lord Wilberforce, delivering the majority speech, assimilated the tests of trust and power. "The trust is valid if it can be said with certainty that any individual is or is not a member of the class." Lord Wilberforce also mentioned the case where "the meaning of the words used i clear but the definition of beneficiaries is so hopelessly wide as not to form 'anything like a class' so that the trust is administratively unworkable or in Lord Eldon L.C.s words one that cannot be executed (*Morice* v. *Bishop of Durham* (1805)). I hesitate to give examples for they may prejudice future cases, but perhaps 'all the residents of Greater London' will serve. I do not think that a discretionary trust for 'relatives' even of a living person falls within this category."

13. Completely and incompletely constituted trusts. A trust is not completely constituted until

(*a*) the property has actually been *vested* in the trustees; or

(*b*) there is a *binding contract* so as to vest the property in them; or

(*c*) the settlor has made a binding *declaration of trust* to the effect that he will hold the property himself as trustee for some other person.

In creating the trust any necessary formalities must be observed. Under the Law of Property Act 1925, s. 51(1)(*b*), (*c*), a declaration of trust respecting land must be proved by writing and the disposition of an equitable interest or trust subsisting at the time of the disposition must be in writing. A valid will, of course, must observe other formalities (*see* XXIV, 1–3). If the settlor has failed to observe the necessary formalities a resulting trust will arise (*see* 19(*d*)).

EXPRESS PUBLIC TRUSTS (CHARITIES)

14. Charities. The first attempt to define charities was in the preamble to the Charitable Uses Act 1601. That Act has now been repealed, but the Charities Act 1960, s. 38(4) provides: "Any reference in any enactment or document to a charity within the meaning, purview and interpretation of the Charitable Uses Act 1601, or of the preamble to it, shall be construed as a reference to a charity within the meaning which the word bears as a legal term according to the law of England and Wales." It is not altogether clear what this means, but the definition of charities in current use is that of Lord Macnaghten in *Commissioners of Income Tax* v. *Pemsel* (1891): " 'Charity' in its legal sense comprises four principal divisions: trusts for the relief of poverty; trusts for the advancement of education; trusts for the advancement of religion; and trusts for other purposes beneficial to the community, not falling under any of the preceding heads." In considering these four categories it is necessary to remember two things. First that changing social values render some of the old cases on education and religion unsafe. Secondly, in all cases it is necessary "that the trust is one the administration of which the court itself could if necessary undertake and control": *Re Hummeltenberg* (1923) *per* Russell J.

(*a*) *Trusts for the relief of poverty.* Poverty is a relative term. A gift for "ladies of limited means" may be charitable whereas one to provide housing for "the working classes" may not be. Trusts under this head are an anomalous exception to the rule that a charitable trust must benefit the public or a section thereof: *Re Scarisbrick* (1951).

(*b*) *Trusts for the advancement of education. Re Hopkins' Will Trusts* (1965) raised the issue whether a gift to the Francis Bacon Society for "finding the Bacon–Shakespeare manuscripts" could be for the advancement of education. In deciding that it could be, Wilberforce J. considered the meaning of "education". He thought that it "must be used in a wide sense, certainly extending beyond teaching, and that the requirement is that, in order to be charitable, research must either be of educational value to the researcher or must be so directed as to lead to something which will pass into the store of educational material, or so as to improve the sum of communicable knowledge in an area which education may cover—education in this last context extending to the formation of literary taste and appreciation". A majority of the Court of Appeal has decided that the preparation of law reports is for the advancement of education, in spite of the commercial use to which they are put: *Incorporated Council of Law Reporting* v. *Attorney-General* (1971). An educational trust must be for the public benefit within the terms outlined by Lord Simonds in *Oppenheim* v. *Tobacco Securities Trust Co. Ltd.* (1951).

(*i*) The possible beneficiaries must not be numerically negligible; and

(*ii*) the quality which distinguishes them from other members of the community must be a quality which does not depend on their relationship to a particular individual.

(*c*) *Trusts for the advancement of religion.* "As between different religions the law stands neutral, but it assumes that any religion is at least likely to be better than none": *Neville Estates Ltd.* v. *Madden* (1965) *per* Cross J. Again there must be some element of public benefit: in *Gilmour* v. *Coats* (1949) a trust for the benefit of a Carmelite convent of strictly cloistered and purely contemplative nuns was found not to be charitable.

(*d*) *Trusts for other purposes beneficial to the community*. Other purposes within the "spirit and intendment" of the 1601 preamble are charitable: for example relief of the aged, repair of churches, the preservation of places of historic interest. Other worthy and improving purposes may be charitable, but there are three conditions they must meet.

(*i*) *Non-political object*. A trust whose main object requires legislation is not charitable since its purpose is primarily political: *National Anti-Vivisection Society* v. *I.R.C.* (1948).

(*ii*) *Charitable purpose primary*. A trust for a police athletic association is not charitable as its main purpose is merely recreational: *I.R.C.* v. *Glasgow City Police Athletic Association* (1953).

(*iii*) *Public benefit*. It was said *obiter* by Lord Simonds in *I.R.C.* v. *Baddeley* (1955) that "a trust cannot qualify as a charity within the fourth class in Pemsel's case if the beneficiaries are a class of persons not only confined to a particular area but selected from within it by reference to a particular creed".

15. Advantages of charities. The great advantage to a trust in qualifying as a charity is that it is exempt from income and other taxes. This is why so many of the relevant cases involve the I.R.C. (*see* **14**(*d*)). There are a number of other advantages attaching to charitable status.

(*a*) *Certainty of objects*. If the settlor's general intention appears to be charitable the gift will not fail merely because the particular object named has ceased to exist. The *cy-près* rule will apply (*see* **16**).

(*b*) *Perpetuity*. A charitable trust will fail if it does not vest within the perpetuity period: *Re Lord Stratheden and Campbell* (1894). On the other hand, if a gift is made to Charity A with provision for the property to pass to Charity B if the first charity ceases to exist, the gift over will be valid even though it may not vest within the perpetuity period.

(*c*) *Inalienability*. Charities are not subject to the rule against inalienability.

(*d*) *Purpose trusts*. Charitable trusts are valid purpose trusts (*see* **18**).

16. Cy-près. If the particular object of the trust fails but the donor has shown a general charitable intention the court will apply the property to some similar charitable object. This is called application *cy-près*. The doctrine *cy-près* applies where two conditions are met.

(*a*) *General charitable intention.* This is "a paramount intention on the part of a donor to effect some charitable purpose which the court can find a method of putting into operation". It is contrasted with a particular charitable disposition to take effect if, but only if, it can be carried into effect in a particular specified way: *Re Lysaght* (1966) *per* Buckley J.

The Charities Act 1960, s. 14 deems a general charitable intention to exist whenever

(*i*) the donor of property cannot be identified or found, for example because he donated to a collecting box; or

(*ii*) the donor of property has disclaimed in writing all rights to the return of the property if the object of the trust fails.

(*b*) *Failure of original purpose.* This is now defined in the Charities Act 1960, s. 13. Trust property may be applied *cy-près* in any of the following situations.

(*i*) When the original purpose has been fulfilled or is incapable of fulfilment;

(*ii*) When the original purpose required only part of the property;

(*iii*) When the property can more efficiently be used in conjunction with other property applicable for similar purposes;

(*iv*) When the original purpose was defined by reference to a geographical area or class of persons which is no longer appropriate;

(*v*) When the original purpose has been adequately provided for by other means or has ceased to be regarded as charitable.

17. Administration. Most charities have to be registered with the Charity Commissioners, who as constituted under the Charities Act 1960 have general powers of supervision over the administration of such trusts. This power is shared with the courts. Registration is conclusive proof of charitable status. The enforcement of charitable trusts could formerly only be at the suit of the Attorney-General, but the Charities Act 1960 enables the Charity Commissioners to authorise the trustees and certain other persons to commence proceedings for enforcement where necessary.

PURPOSE TRUSTS

18. Purpose trusts. Public charitable trusts are purpose trusts. An express private trust can never be a purpose trust for three reasons. In the case of a purpose trust:

(*a*) there is no certainty of objects (*see* **12**);

(*b*) there are no beneficiaries and therefore there is no one able to enforce the trust under the rule in *Saunders* v. *Vautier* (1841) (*see* **22**);

(*c*) the court can control the exercise of the trust, "for an uncontrollable power of disposition would be ownership, and not trust".

These three reasons were given by Sir William Grant M.R. in *Morice* v. *Bishop of Durham* (1804).

A number of old cases, however, have allowed non-charitable purpose trusts. Trusts for the maintenance of tombs and monuments, which lack the element of public benefit necessary to be charitable, or for the maintenance of animals have been allowed where they have arisen "under wills and are intimately connected with the deceased". Such trusts, said Roxburgh J. in *Re Astor's Settlement Trusts* (1952), can "properly be regarded as anomalous and exceptional and in no way destructive of the proposition which traces its descent from or through Sir William Grant".

Sir William Grant's proposition has recently been amended in two types of case.

(*a*) *Purpose for ascertainable beneficiaries.* In *Re Denley's Trust Deed* (1968) land was conveyed to trustees "for the purpose of a recreation or sports ground for the benefit of the employees of the company". Recreational purposes are not charitable (*see* **14**(*d*)(*ii*)). Goff. J. decided that the trust was nevertheless valid. The beneficiaries, as employees of the company, were sufficiently ascertainable. The court could control the trust by restraining any improper use of the land. "Where the trust, though expressed as a purpose, is directly or indirectly for the benefit of an individual or individuals, it seems to me that it is in general outside the mischief of the beneficiary principle."

(*b*) *Unincorporated associations.* In *Neville Estates* v. *Madden* (1962) Cross J. distinguished three types of gift to an unincorporated association.

(*i*) A gift to the present members as joint tenants so that any member can sever his share and take it if he ceases to be a member.

(*ii*) A gift to the present members subject to their contractual rights and liabilities towards each other. Then a member cannot sever his share, and on his death or resignation it will accrue to the then existing members.

(*iii*) A gift for the purposes of the association. Cross J. thought that a gift in this category would fail unless the association were a charity. In *Re Lipkinski's Will Trusts* (1977), however, Oliver J. found otherwise. He decided, in the case of a gift for the construction of new buildings for an association, that such a gift was valid where it was for a purpose within the association's powers. The members were the beneficiaries and as such were "able to enforce the trust or, indeed, in the exercise of their contractual rights, to terminate the trust for their own benefit".

RESULTING TRUSTS

19. Resulting trusts. A resulting trust is one where the court infers that the settlor intended to create a trust in favour of himself or of his heirs or nominees, and the benefit results to the donor. This is sometimes called an *implied* trust.

A resulting trust arises in four situations.

(*a*) *Failure to exhaust beneficial interest.* The problem in *Re West Sussex Constabulary's Fund Trusts* (1970) arose out of the amalgamation of the Sussex police forces. What was to be done with the money remaining in the West Sussex Widows, Children and Benevolent Fund, which was not a charitable trust? Goff J. distinguished between:

(*i*) Money raised by collecting boxes, raffles and sweepstakes. Here the donor's intention was to part with the money absolutely. As the trust was not a charity the *cy-près* rule (*see* **16**) could not apply, so the money would go to the Crown as *bona vacantia*.

(*ii*) Money representing donations and legacies. This was given for a purpose which had failed and would be held on resulting trust for the donors and their estates.

(*b*) *Failure of trust.* If A vests property in B as trustee for an object which fails, for example because the beneficiary is dead, B will hold the property as trustee for A or his heirs.

(*c*) *Purchase in the name of another.* If A buys property with his own money but has it conveyed to B, it will be presumed that he intended not to make a gift to B, but that B should hold the property as trustee for A or his heirs. Where B is the wife or child of A the *presumption of advancement* arises: that is, that A intended to advance the interests of his wife or child, and the purchase will be treated as an absolute gift to B unless there is clear evidence to the contrary.

(*d*) *Voluntary transfer.* In *Vandervell* v. *I.R.C.* (1967) the issue was whether the trust was completely constituted (*see* 13). The settlor directed the trustees of a trust he had established to transfer shares to X with an option for the trustees of a second trust, in favour of the settlor's children, to repurchase. Before the option was exercised a high dividend was to be declared on the shares and this would constitute the benefit to X. No doubt the transfer was effective to give X the legal estate in the shares. The I.R.C., however, maintained that the settlor had failed to transfer the beneficial interest since he had not executed a document under the Law of Property Act 1925 s. 52(1) (*c*) and that there must be a resulting trust in favour of the settlor on which he could be taxed. By a majority the House of Lords rejected this. "If the intention of the beneficial owner in directing the trustee to transfer the legal estate to X is that X should be the beneficial owner, I can see no reason for any further document or further words in the document assigning the legal estate also expressly transferring the beneficial interest: the greater includes the less": *per* Lord Upjohn.

CONSTRUCTIVE TRUSTS

20. Constructive trusts. "A constructive trust is one which arises when a stranger to a trust already constituted is held by the court to be bound in good faith and in conscience by the trust in consequence of his conduct and behaviour." It is "a trust to be made out by circumstances": *Soar* v. *Ashwell* (1893) *per* Bowen L.J. A constructive trust arises by operation of law in the following circumstances.

(*a*) *Vendor's lien.* If the vendor of land transfers possession to the purchaser before the purchase price is wholly paid he has a lien over the land until he is paid in full. Until then the purchaser holds the land as constructive trustee for the vendor.

(*b*) *Purchaser's lien.* A similar situation arises where a purchaser has paid a deposit on land and the sale is called off for some reason other than the purchaser's default. Here the pur-

chaser has a lien over the land for his deposit and the vendor i
a constructive trustee for that amount.

(c) *Trustee profiting from his trust*. Trustees must not profi
from their trust, and if one receives a benefit for himself as a resul
of his position he can be compelled to hold the benefit as con
structive trustee on the same trusts as if it were part of the expres
trust: *Keech* v. *Sandford* (1726) (*see* 29).

(d) *Mortgagee's power of sale*. A mortgagee who exercises hi
power to sell the mortgaged property holds any surplus money:
after deducting the amount of his loan plus interest, on con
structive trust for the mortgagor (*see* XXII, 8).

(e) *Transferee of trust property*. Where a person buys trus
property from a trustee knowing that it is being sold in breach c
trust, he holds the property on constructive trust for the bene
ficiaries. Similarly, if trust property is transferred to an agent, suc
as a solicitor, with notice of the trust, he will hold on constructiv
trust and will be liable if he misapplies funds: *Soar* v. *Ashwe*
(1893).

(f) *Fraudulent conveyance of property*. If property is conveye
with an oral arrangement that X can continue to live there it ma
be held on constructive trust to allow X to remain there: *Ba*
nister v. *Bannister* (1948).

21. Secret trusts. Secret trusts are a form of constructive tru
in that they are imposed by the courts. The principle was e>
plained by Lord Sumner in *Blackwell* v. *Blackwell* (1929): ".
court of conscience finds a man in the position of an absolu
legal owner of a sum of money, which has been bequeathed to hi
under a valid will, and it declares that, on proof of certain fac
relating to the motives and actions of the testator, it will n
allow the legal owner to exercise his legal right to do what he wi
with his own. This seems to be a perfectly normal exercise c
general equitable jurisdiction." This will arise in two types c
case:

(a) *Fully secret trusts* where no trust is disclosed at all.

(b) *Half secret trusts* where the fact of a trust is disclosed br
not the nature of the trust nor the identities of the beneficiarie

A secret trust arose in *Ottaway* v. *Norman* (1971). T lived wit
his housekeeper H. T's son by his former wife, S, often visite
them. T told S that when he died the house would go to H and c
her death she would leave it to S. T duly left the house to H an
died. Later H also died, but she left the house to X. Brightman

decided that X was bound by a secret trust in favour of S. "It will be convenient to call the person on whom such a trust is imposed the 'primary donee' and the beneficiary under that trust the 'secondary donee'. The essential elements which must be proved to exist are:

(*i*) the intention of the testator to subject the primary donee to an obligation in favour of the secondary donee;

(*ii*) communication of that intention to the primary donee; and

(*iii*) the acceptance of that obligation by the primary donee either expressly or by acquiescence."

VARIATION OF TRUSTS

22. Variation before 1958. Under the rule in *Saunders* v. *Vautier* (1841) the beneficiaries entitled to the whole beneficial interest if all of full age can join together to put an end to the trust. Apart from this rather drastic step, it is possible in some circumstances to vary the terms of a trust whilst keeping it in existence. The main power to vary is contained in the Variation of Trusts Act 1958 (*see* **23**). There are four other powers of variation which, although not repealed or limited by the 1958 Act, have in practice been superseded by it. There is also a power to vary trusts on divorce under the Matrimonial Causes Act 1973.

(*a*) *Common law.* The common law jurisdiction to vary trusts was reviewed by the House of Lords in *Chapman* v. *Chapman* (1954). It may arise in four exceptional circumstances.

(*i*) To allow *conversion* (*see* **4**(*a*)) of the property of a beneficiary who is a minor.

(*ii*) To allow *salvage* in cases "not foreseen or anticipated by the author of the trust where the trustees are embarrassed by the emergency that has arisen": *Re New* (1901) *per* Romer L.J.

(*iii*) To allow the property to be used for the *maintenance* of a beneficiary.

(*iv*) To approve a *compromise* arrangement where there is genuine dispute about rights.

(*b*) *Trustee Act* 1925 *s.* 57. This allows the court to give trustees (other than the trustees of a settlement: *see* (*c*)) power to sell, lease, mortgage or purchase property where this is desirable for the "management or administration" of the property if the court thinks this expedient but the trust does not give the trustee such power. "The object of s. 57 was to ensure that trust property should be managed as advantageously as possible in the interests of the beneficiaries, and, with that object in view, to authorise specific dealings with the property": *Re Downshire's Settled Estates* (1953) *per* Lord Evershed M.R.

(*c*) *Settled Land Act* 1925, *s.* 64. This enables the court to authorise any transaction concerning settled land (*see* XX, 25) "which in the opinion of the court would be for the benefit of the settled land".

(*d*) *Trustee Act* 1925, *s.* 53. This enables the court to order the conveyance of property to which a minor is beneficially entitled "for the maintenance, education or benefit" of the minor.

23. Variation of Trusts Act 1958. The Variation of Trusts Act 1958 enables the court to approve any variation. There are three aspects to consider.

(*a*) *Extent of the Act.* The Act applies to:
  (*i*) any property, real or personal;
  (*ii*) any trust arising before or after the passage of the Act;
  (*iii*) any will, settlement or other disposition.

(*b*) *Extent of the variation.* The Act applies to "any arrangement (by whomsoever proposed, and whether or not there is any other person beneficially interested who is capable of assenting thereto) varying or revoking all or any of the trusts, or enlarging the powers of the trustees of managing or administering any of the property subject to the trusts".

(*c*) *Extent of the approval.* The court may approve on behalf of
  (*i*) a beneficiary who is a minor or other person incapable of assenting.
  (*ii*) any person, whether ascertained or not, who may at some future date become a beneficiary.
  (*iii*) any unborn person.
  (*iv*) any person with an interest under a protective trust. (A protective trust is a trust under the Trustee Act 1925 s. 33 whereby on the bankruptcy or other default of the principal beneficiary the property is held on a discretionary trust.)

Except under head (*iv*) the court may not approve a variation on behalf of any person unless it is for the benefit of that person.

Under the rule in *Saunders* v. *Vautier* (1841) (*see* 22) beneficiaries of full age and understanding acting together can revoke the trust. The Act authorises the court to give approval either to revoke or to vary the trust on behalf of beneficiaries who are not of full age and understanding or who are not ascertained. The Act is used to vary trusts in order to reduce liability to taxation. It gives the courts a discretion whether or not to approve any proposed variation, and although they normally allow schemes to avoid tax they may decline to do so if the variation is not otherwise advantageous to the beneficiaries. In *Re Weston's Settlements* (1969), Lord Denning M.R. summarised the court's attitude:

"(*i*) In exercising its discretion, the function of the court is to protect those who cannot protect themselves: it must do what is truly for their benefit;

(*ii*) it can give its consent to a scheme to avoid death duties or other taxes;

(*iii*) the court should not consider merely the financial benefit to the minors or unborn children, but also their educational and social benefit."

In that case a proposal to transfer the trust to Jersey, although it would avoid English taxes, was found to be not sufficiently advantageous. "There are many things in life more worth while than money. One of these things is to be brought up in this our England, which is still 'the envy of less happier lands'. I do not believe it is for the benefit of children to be uprooted from England and transported to another country simply to avoid tax . . . Children are like trees: they grow stronger with firm roots."

APPOINTMENT AND RETIREMENT OF TRUSTEES

24. Capacity. A trustee may be:

(*a*) *any sane person of full age.* Appointment of a minor is void.

(*b*) *a trust corporation.* A trust corporation means the Public Trustee or any corporate body empowered by law to conduct trustee business: Trustee Act 1925, s. 68. The *Public Trustee* is a state official established by the Public Trustee Act 1906 as a corporation sole. If he accepts appointment he can be sole trustee or one of several. The advantages of the Public Trustee are

(*i*) being a trust corporation he never dies;

(*ii*) the state is responsible for any breach of trust.

The disadvantages of the Public Trustee are:

(*i*) he cannot act for a charitable trust;

(*ii*) he cannot run a trust business without the consent of the Treasury.

In trusts of personalty there may be any number of trustees. In trusts of land the maximum number is four and in practice receipts must be given by at least two: Trustee Act 1925, ss. 14, 34.

25. Appointment.

(*a*) *Under the trust*. The settlor usually appoints the first trustees when the trust is created. Once the trust is established he has no further power of appointment unless such a power is expressly reserved in the trust instrument. The trust instrument may alternatively give express power to some other person.

(*b*) *Under the Trustee Act* 1925, *s*. 36. Trustees are usually appointed under this statutory power. It is exercised by:

(*i*) the person nominated by the trust instrument; or

(*ii*) the last surviving trustee or his personal representatives.

The statutory power can be exercised to replace a trustee who
(*i*) is dead;

(*ii*) remains out of the United Kingdom for more than twelve months;

(*iii*) desires to be discharged;

(*iv*) refuses to act;

(*v*) is unfit to act, for example owing to bankruptcy;

(*vi*) is incapable of acting, for example owing to age or insanity;

(*vii*) is a minor;

(*viii*) is removed under a power in the trust instrument.

(*c*) *By the court*. The court has two powers to appoint trustees.

(*i*) *Trustee Act* 1925, *s*. 41. The court can appoint a new trustee when it is found "inexpedient, difficult or impracticable so to do without the assistance of the court". Application to the court may be made by any beneficiary or trustee: s. 58.

(*ii*) *Judicial Trustees Act* 1896. Here the court appoints some court official such as the Official Solicitor to act as a judicial trustee under the supervision of the court.

26. Termination of trusteeship.

(*a*) *Disclaimer*. A trustee may always disclaim a trust provided he has not already done something to signify his acceptance, such as taking possession of part of the trust property. Disclaimer is usually effected by deed.

(*b*) *Retirement*. A trustee can retire:

(*i*) under a court order.

(*ii*) with the consent of the beneficiaries if they are all of full age and capacity.

(*iii*) under a power in the trust instrument.

(*iv*) under the Trustee Act 1925, s. 39. To retire under these provisions the trustee must execute a deed and (1) leave a trust corporation or two persons to carry on the trust; (2) obtain the consent by deed of his co-trustees; and (3) sign a vesting declaration transferring the property to the new or continuing trustees.

(*c*) *Replacement* (*see* 25(*b*)).

(*d*) *Removal* (*see* 25(*c*)).

DUTIES AND POWERS OF TRUSTEES

27. Duties. The trustees are under a duty to obey the court when it intervenes and in certain circumstances (*see* 22) to obey the directions of the beneficiaries. The trustees are also subject to certain general duties.

(*a*) *To obtain control of the trust property.*

(*b*) *To take care of the trust property.* There are two elements to this.

(*i*) Trustees must take such care as an ordinary prudent man would take of his own property. They are liable for losses occasioned by breach of such duty.

(*ii*) Trustees must invest in securities authorised by the Trustee Act 1925 and the Trustee Investments Act 1961.

(*c*) *To sell wasting assets.* Under the rule in *Howe* v. *Dartmouth* (1802) it is presumed that the settlor's intention was for his trustees to convert (*see* 4(*a*)) wasting assets and hazardous or otherwise unauthorised investments.

(*d*) *To keep accounts* (*see* 5(*f*)).

(*e*) *To distribute the trust property to those entitled.*

(*f*) *Not to delegate performance of their duties* (*see* 28).

(*g*) *Not to profit from the trust* (*see* 29).

28. Delegatus non potest delegare ("a delegate must not delegate"). A trustee cannot delegate his duties. He can, however, in certain circumstances perform those duties through agents:

(*a*) where authorised by the *trust instrument*;

(b) where this is necessary in the *ordinary course of business*, for example employing a builder to do necessary repairs;

(c) where authorised by *statute*.

(i) *Professional services*. A trustee may employ professional people such as solicitors, accountants, bankers and stockbrokers for specialised work. He is not liable for their default provided he has selected them with care: Trustee Act 1925, s. 23.

(ii) *Surveyors*. Where a trustee lends money on the security of a mortgage he may employ a surveyor to value the property. If it is later found that the value of the mortgage advance exceeds the true value of the property the Trustee Act 1925, s. 8 provides that the trustee will not be liable if (1) he lent the money on the advice of the surveyor; and (2) he did not lend more than two-thirds of the valuation.

(iii) *Deputies*. A trustee going overseas for more than one month may by power of attorney appoint a deputy to act for him in his absence. He remains personally liable for the acts or default of such a deputy: Trustee Act 1925, s. 28.

29. Duty not to profit from the trust. Profit must be distinguished from indemnification and remuneration.

(a) *Profit*. A trustee must not make any profit from his office, unless expressly authorised by the trust instrument, and can be made to refund any unauthorised profit.

(i) A trustee cannot generally buy trust property: *Fox* v. *Mackreth* (1788).

(ii) If a trustee cannot obtain renewal of a trust lease for his own use: *Keech* v. *Sandford* (1726).

(iii) If a trustee speculates in unauthorised investments (*see* 27(b) (ii)) the trust is entitled to any profit while the trustee is personally liable to make good any losses: *Docker* v. *Somes* (1834).

(b) *Indemnification*. A trustee may reimburse himself for expenses properly incurred in performance of his duties: Trustee Act 1925, s. 30(2).

(c) *Remuneration*. Remuneration is either

(i) under the trust instrument; or

(ii) awarded by the court.

The principles of remuneration were discussed by Walton J. in *Re Duke of Norfolk's Settlement Trusts* (1978).

(i) The court's jurisdiction to award remuneration is wholly exceptional, to be exercised sparingly.

(*ii*) Normally the court only awards remuneration when this is necessary to obtain the services of a particular trustee or of some particular kind of trustee such as a trust corporation. The Public Trustee has a statutory right to charge for his services.

(*iii*) Possibly the court will award remuneration where an implied promise to pay on behalf of the beneficiaries is found.

(*iv*) If the level of remuneration is fixed by the trust instrument the court will not alter it.

(*v*) The court is reluctant to award remuneration unless application is made promptly.

30. Powers of trustees. The Trustee Act 1925 gives trustees various powers which they can exercise at their discretion.

(*a*) *Maintenance.* Trust money may be used for the maintenance, education or benefit of a beneficiary who is a minor: s. 31.

(*b*) *Advancement.* Trust money can also be used for purposes such as the purchase of a house for a beneficiary: s. 32.

(*c*) *Sale* or *mortgage* of trust property: ss. 13, 16.

(*d*) *Insurance* of trust property up to three-quarters of its value: s. 19.

(*e*) *Settlement of claims* by or against the trust: s. 15. Before distributing trust property the trustees should advertise for claimants in the London Gazette and a local newspaper giving at least two months' notice of the last date for submission of claims, and they will then be under no liability to claimants coming forward after that date: s. 27.

(*f*) *Investment* authorised by the Trustee Act 1925 and the Trustee Investments Act 1961.

31. Breach of trust. A trustee is liable to compensate the trust for his own or his agent's breach of trust. He is only liable for the breach of a co-trustee if he has contributed to it by his own wilful default: Trustee Act 1925, s. 30(1). A trustee is in wilful default if "he knows that he is committing, and intends to commit, a breach of his duty, or is recklessly careless in the sense of not caring whether his act or omission is or is not a breach of his duty": *Re City Equitable Fire Insurance Co. Ltd.* (1925) *per* Romer J. Thus a trustee would be liable for loss occasioned by improperly leaving it: *Townley* v. *Sherborne* (1634). Where a breach had been committed beneficiaries have two remedies:

(*a*) To sue the trustees personally for damages for breach of trust.

(*b*) To obtain a tracing order to pursue and recover trust property wrongfully held by any person: *Re Diplock* (1950). Land cannot be recovered from a bona fide purchaser for value without notice (*see* **3**).

Under normal principles of contribution, a trustee who has compensated the trust may claim for contribution from his co-trustees. In addition, a trustee must indemnify others where:

(*a*) all are made liable for a breach which he alone committed;
(*b*) he was a solicitor and counselled the breach; or
(*c*) he was a beneficiary as well as a trustee: *Chillingworth* v. *Chambers* (1896).

A trustee may be relieved from liability where:

(*a*) the court so orders using its powers under the Trustee Act 1925, s. 61;
(*b*) the Limitation Acts debar an action; or
(*c*) an adult beneficiary releases the trustee from liability with full knowledge of the facts.

PROGRESS TEST 23

1. Define the nature and scope of equity. (**1, 3**)
2. Briefly summarise the maxims of equity and illustrate the modern working of the maxims by discussing a case in which one of the maxims applied. (**2**)
3. What are the equitable doctrines? (**4**)
4. In what circumstances will the remedy of specific performance be awarded for a breach of contract? (**6**)
5. In what situations is an injunction available? (**7**)
6. Distinguish a trust from a power of appointment. (**9**)
7. What are the requisites of an express private trust? (**10–13**)
8. What is a charitable trust? (**14, 15**)
9. Describe the operation of the *cy-près* doctrine. (**16**)
10. In what circumstances can a purpose trust exist? (**18**)
11. A buys Blackacre and has it conveyed into the joint names of his solicitor X and Mrs. A. What trust will arise here? (**19**)
12. What is a secret trust? (**21**)
13. In what circumstances may trusts be varied? (**22, 23**)
14. Who can be a trustee? How are trustees appointed? (**24, 25**)
15. What duties are imposed on trustees by law, in the

absence of anything to the contrary in the trust instrument?
(27–29)

16. What powers are given to trustees by the Trustee Act
1925? (30)

17. When is a trustee liable for breach of trust? (31)

PART SIX
LAW OF SUCCESSION

CHAPTER XXIV

Law of Succession

REQUISITES OF A VALID WILL

1. Characteristics of a will. A will is a declaration made by a person during his lifetime of his intentions concerning the disposal of his property after his death. The maker of the will is called the *testator*. The basis of the modern law is the Wills Act 1837.

A will has certain characteristics.

(*a*) *Ambulatory.* A will has no effect until the death of the testator.

(*b*) *Revocable.* A testator cannot make his will irrevocable.

(*c*) *Sole expression of testamentary wishes.* "The law, on a man's death, finds out what are the instruments which express his last will. If some extant writing be revoked, or is inconsistent with a later testamentary writing, it is discarded. But all that survive this scrutiny form part of the ultimate will or effective expression of his wishes about his estate. In this sense it is inaccurate to speak of a man leaving two wills; he does leave, and can leave, but one will": *Douglas-Menzies* v. *Umphelby* (1908) *per* Lord Atkinson.

A supplement to a will is called a *codicil*.

(*d*) *Proper law of the will.*

(*i*) Wills of land are governed by the law of the country in which the land is situated, i.e. the *lex situs*.

(*ii*) Wills of personal property, i.e. moveables, must be made in accordance with the law of the testator's domicil at his death; a will is not necessarily revoked by a change of domicil after its execution: Wills Act 1837, s. 3.

2. Testamentary capacity. By virtue of the Wills Act 1837, s. 7, and later Acts any person of full age and sound mind may make a valid will provided it is made in the proper form (*see* **3, 4**).

The only exception to this is that the will of a soldier or sailor "being in actual military service" is valid even though the soldier or sailor is under age or his will is not in proper form: Wills Act 1837, s. 11. This provision is explained and extended to airmen by the Wills (Soldiers and Sailors) Act 1918. A soldier, sailor or airman is on "actual military service" if he is serving with forces who are or have been engaged in military operations, or who are believed to be about to so engage. Seamen on shore-leave, and airmen training overseas for military operations are therefore included: *Re Wingham* (1949). The court can order a *statutory* will for an adult patient under the Mental Health Act 1959 s. 103.

3. Formalities of a valid will. Under the Wills Act 1837 s. 9 no will or codicil is valid unless the following conditions are observed.

(*a*) The will must be in writing. Any document will suffice, e.g. a letter. And a will may incorporate other documents, providing such other documents were existing at the time the will was made and are referred to in the will. Parol (oral) evidence may be used to identify such other documents if they are clearly referred to in the will.

(*b*) It must be signed by the testator, or by someone acting on his behalf. That other person must be acknowledged by the testator and must sign in his presence.

(*c*) The will must be signed at the foot or end of it. It is sufficient if the signature follows after a blank space, or is at the side or on an opposing page, or follows the signature of a witness provided it is clear that it was intended by the testator to give effect to the will as a whole: Wills Act Amendment Act 1852.

(*d*) The signature must be attested by at least two witnesses (*see* 4).

"It is undoubted law that whatever may be the form of a duly executed instrument, if the person executing it intends that it shall not take effect until after his death, and it is dependent upon his death for its vigour and effect, it is testamentary": *Cock* v. *Cooke* (1866) *per* Lord Penzance.

4. Witnesses. The testator's signature must be attested by at least two witnesses who must be present when the testator signs or acknowledges his signature: *Re Olding* (1841).

A blind person cannot witness a will or codicil, since he cannot actually see the signature: *Re Gibson* (1949). But an illiterate person can be a witness, since he can see the signature, even if he cannot read it. And an illiterate witness can validly sign by a mark, thumbprint, etc., and his signature will be valid even if put against the wrong name in the attestation clause: *In the goods of Ashmore* (1843).

The testator must be in such a position that he can see the witnesses sign if he wishes to do so: *Newton* v. *Clarke* (1839). And he must be aware of what they are doing, e.g. not so near death that he cannot understand: *Jenner* v. *Ffinch* (1879).

If any beneficiary, or the husband or wife of a beneficiary, attests a will the attestation is valid, but the gift to the witness or his spouse will fail, and is void: Wills Act 1837, s. 15.

But executors and creditors can lawfully attest, even though the will directs payment to be made to them in the course of business: Wills Act 1837, ss. 16, 17.

PROPERTY WHICH MAY BE DISPOSED OF BY WILL

5. Disposable property. Under the Wills Act 1837, s. 3 a will can dispose of all the real and personal property to which the testator is entitled at his death, either in law or equity, and which if not so disposed of would descend upon his heirs or upon his executors or administrators.

In the case of a testator who dies domiciled in England, if the will fails to make reasonable provision for his dependants the court has power to make provision for those dependants under the Inheritance (Provision for Family and Dependants) Act 1975 (*see* 13).

Dispositions are either:

(*a*) *devises*, which are dispositions of freehold land; or

(*b*) *legacies*, which are dispositions of personalty including leases (*see* 6).

A general devise of all the testator's lands is presumed to include leasehold land: *Prescott* v. *Barker* (1874).

6. Legacies. Legacies are of four kinds.

(*a*) *General legacies.* No particular thing is given, e.g. *a* diamond ring, or a gift of £1,000, or *a* horse, or *a* thousand shares in I.C.I.

(b) *Specific legacies.* A particular thing is given, e.g. *my* diamond ring, *my* horse, *my* shares in I.C.I., *my* Rolls-Royce.

(c) *Demonstrative legacies.* A gift which is directed to be taken from a particular source, e.g. £1,000 *out of* my deposit account.

(d) *A residuary gift* is a gift of the residue of the estate after payment of debts and funeral expenses, and the distribution of legacies and devises.

Differences between them are shown by the rules relating to abatement (*see* 7) and ademption (*see* 8).

7. Abatement of legacies. The testator's debts must be paid before his estate is distributed, and sometimes the property given by his will must also be used wholly or partly for this purpose. The rule is that general legacies are subject to abatement before specific or demonstrative legacies can be called upon. If a demonstrative legacy is abated in this way, by the fund out of which it is to be paid being used to pay debts, it is transformed into a general legacy to be paid out of any available residuary property.

8. Ademption of specific legacies. If a specific thing given to a legatee is not in the testator's possession at his death the gift is "*adeemed*", i.e. the legatee gets nothing. Here it is presumed that the testator has shown an intention to revoke the gift.

Ademption of a specific legacy will also occur where the thing given has been substantially changed before the testator's death, e.g. where the gift is of "my collection of valuable stamps" and the testator has sold his stamps and bought a collection of valuable books. A mere change in name or form, however, will not lead to ademption, e.g. where shares are specifically left and the company subsequently changes its name or undergoes reconstruction: *Re O'Brien* (1946). General legacies are not liable to ademption, and demonstrative legacies if adeemed are turned into general legacies.

9. Lapsed gifts. Where a legatee or devisee dies before the testator, the gift made to him lapses and the property so given falls into residue for the benefit of the residuary legatee.

Lapse does not occur where:

(a) there is a devise of an entailed interest and the devisee predeceases the testator but is survived by issue capable of inheriting the entailed interest. Here the gift endures for the benefit of such issue: Wills Act 1837, s. 32. For example, where the gift is "to A and his heirs male", if A dies before the testator but leaves a son, the son will get the land.

(b) there is a devise or bequest of more than a life interest in property to a child of the testator and such person predeceases the testator, but leaves issue surviving the testator, the bequest or devise endures for the benefit of the issue: Wills Act 1837, s. 33. For example, where property is left to a son of the testator who predeceases his father, but himself leaves a daughter or son; here the grandchild will inherit.

REVOCATION OF WILLS

10. Revocation and revival. A will cannot be revoked by any presumption of an intention on the ground of an alteration in circumstances: Wills Act 1837, s. 19. A's will can only be revoked under the following provisions:

(a) *Wills Act* 1837, *s.* 18. A will is automatically revoked by the subsequent marriage of the testator, whether the testator is male or female: Wills Act 1837, s. 18. Wills made after 1925 expressly in contemplation of a marriage which does take place are not revoked by the solemnisation of that marriage: Law of Property Act 1925, s. 177.

(b) *Wills Act* 1837, *s.* 20 (*see* **11**). A revoked will can be revived only by being re-executed, or by a freshly executed codicil expressing a clear intention to revive the will.

11. Wills Act 1837, s. 20. "No will or codicil, or any part thereof, shall be revoked otherwise than as aforesaid (i.e. s. 18: see 10(a)), or by another will or codicil, executed in manner herein before required, or by some writing declaring an intention to revoke the same, and executed, or by the burning, tearing, or otherwise destroying the same by the testator, or by some person in his presence and by his direction, with the intention of revoking the same." This section provides three ways in which a will can be revoked.

(a) *Subsequent will or codicil*. A will usually commences with a clause revoking all former wills, and if such a clause is not inserted the later will (or codicil) does not revoke the former will except in so far as it is inconsistent therewith.

If a testator revokes his will, intending to make a new one, but then fails to make a new will, or makes a will which is void for any reason, the original will remains valid. Here the revocation of the first will is regarded as being dependent on the validity of the later one. Thus, if a man destroys his will under the mistaken belief that all his property will pass automatically to his wife at his death, and that a will leaving all his property to her is therefore unnecessary, a copy of the will can be admitted to probate: *In the Estate of Greenstreet* (1930).

(*b*) *Writing executed like a will.* A will may be revoked by a writing which, though not a will itself, is signed and attested and shows a clear intention to revoke all former wills, e.g. a letter, signed by the testator and attested by two witnesses, requesting the addressee to destroy the will: *In the Goods of Durance* (1872).

(*c*) *Destruction.* There are three elements.

(*i*) Intention to revoke at the time of the revocation (*animus revocandi*). If a will is lost and the court is not satisfied that it was destroyed with intention to revoke, verbal evidence may be given as to its contents, e.g. by a witness who read the will and remembers the contents: *Sugden* v. *Lord St. Leonards* (1876).

(*ii*) Sufficient act of destruction. It is insufficient to write "cancelled" across the will: *Stephens* v. *Taprell* (1840); or to cancel the signature and throw the will in a waste-paper basket: *Cheese* v. *Lovejoy* (1877).

(*iii*) By the testator or in his presence and by his direction.

12. Mutual wills. The doctrine of mutual wills is an equitable doctrine developed to prevent an unconscionable revocation. For the doctrine to operate three requirements must be met.

(*a*) There must be an arrangement between two people, usually husband and wife, to execute mutual wills making provision for each other with remainder to a third party usually a child.

(*b*) There must be an agreement that the survivor would not revoke this arrangement.

(*c*) On the death of one party leaving his will unrevoked the arrangement becomes binding.

The survivor holds the property on implied (*see* XXIII, **19**) or constructive (*see* XXIII, **20**) trust for the third party. "The instrument itself is the evidence of the agreement; and he that dies first does by his death carry the agreement on his part into execution. If the other then refuses, he is guilty of a fraud, can never unbind himself, and becomes a trustee of course for no man shall deceive another to his prejudice. By engaging to do something that is in his power, he is made a trustee for the performance and transmits that trust to those that claim under him": *Dufour* v. *Pereira* (1769) *per* Lord Camden.

MAINTENANCE OF DEPENDANTS

13. Inheritance (Provision for Family and Dependants) Act 1975. Formerly a testator could dispose of his property by will in any way he chose, but the Inheritance (Family Provision) Act 1938 gave the court power to vary a will at the request of the testator's dependants if he fails reasonably to provide for them. The 1938 Act was extended to cover cases of total intestacy by the Intestates' Estates Act 1952.

In respect of a person who died in England or Wales after 31st March 1975 the court's powers are now contained in the Inheritance (Provision for Family and Dependants) Act 1975. Under the 1975 Act there are two things to consider:

(*a*) Dependants who may apply to the court (*see* **14**).

(*b*) The order of the court (*see* **15**).

The 1975 Act gives the court new powers to prevent evasion by ordering a donee to return property to the estate where it was given by the deceased with the intention of defeating the Act and not for full consideration.

14. Dependants. The following dependants of the deceased may apply to the court under s. 1 of the Act.

(*a*) *A wife or husband of the deceased.*

(*b*) *A former wife or husband who has not remarried.* A former wife or husband is one whose marriage to the deceased was annulled or dissolved.

(*c*) *A child of the deceased.* This includes a child of any age whether married or not and also extends to an adopted or illegitimate child.

(*d*) *A person treated by the deceased as a child of the family.* This includes a child who is not the deceased's child.

(*e*) *A dependant of the deceased.* This includes an elderly relative and also a person living with but not married to the deceased.

Application is made to the High Court or, if the deceased's

property does not exceed £15,000, to the county court, and must normally be made within six months from the date on which representation of the deceased's estate is taken out (*see* 18).

15. The order. The court considers the will of the deceased to see whether it makes reasonable financial provision for the applicant (*see* (*a*)). If the court considers that it does not, then the court goes on to consider what provision it should order (*see* (*b*)).

(*a*) *Circumstances in which the order may be made.* The Act provides two tests.

(*i*) For a surviving spouse the test is reasonable financial provision, whether or not the provision is needed for the spouse's maintenance.

(*ii*) For other dependants the provision must be such as would be reasonable for the applicant's maintenance.

In all cases the court applies an objective standard; the views and conduct of the deceased are irrelevant. In deciding whether reasonable financial provision has been made, s. 3 of the Act requires the court to consider a number of guidelines. General guidelines include:

(*i*)   the applicant's resources and needs;
(*ii*) the obligations of the deceased to the applicant;
(*iii*) the size of the deceased's estate;
(*iv*) any physical or mental disability of the applicant.

Further guidelines are laid down in relation to specific applicants. For example the court must consider:

(*i*) in the case of a surviving spouse, the age of the applicant and the duration of the marriage;

(*ii*) in the case of a child of the deceased, the manner in which the applicant expected to be educated or trained.

(*b*) *The court's order.* If the court decides that reasonable financial provision has not been made in the deceased's will, then it can order provision to be made out of the net estate of the deceased, which is widely defined under s. 25. Orders can be:

(*i*)   periodical payments;
(*ii*) lump sum payment;
(*iii*) transfer of property;
(*iv*) settlement of property;
(*v*)   acquisition of property for transfer or settlement;
(*vi*) variation of marriage settlement.

Under s. 6 only an order for periodical payments can be varied. The need for certainty in other cases is obvious.

PERSONAL REPRESENTATIVES

16. Executors and administrators. The persons who wind up and distribute a deceased's estate are called his personal representatives. Personal representatives are of two kinds.

(*a*) *Executors.* An executor is appointed by the testator in his will. The testator may appoint anyone as his executor and may appoint any number, but probate (*see* **18**) will not be granted to more than four executors nor will it be granted to a minor until he comes of age. Under the Administration of Estates Act 1925, s. 7 if a last surviving executor dies testate, then his executors will take his place. If a last surviving executor dies intestate, then the court will appoint an administrator *de bonis non* to take over his duties as executor.

(*b*) *Administrators.* An administrator is a personal representative appointed by the court under the Judicature Act 1925, ss. 160–3, in three situations

(*i*) *Administrator cum testamento annexo.* Where a will fails to appoint an executor, or an appointment of an executor fails (e.g. because the person appointed is incapacitated or refuses to act) the court will appoint a person to administer the estate "with the will annexed", i.e. to administer in accordance with the will, as though he were an executor. Such an administrator is called an administrator *cum testamento annexo.*

(*ii*) *Administrator on intestacy.*

(*iii*) *Administrator pendente lite.* Where legal proceedings concerning the validity of the will are pending, the court may appoint an administrator *pendente lite* (pending litigation) to safeguard the estate.

Except in the case of an administrator *pendente lite*, the court appoints between two and four administrators from the legatees of good character having the highest priority under the Non-Contentious Probate Rules 1954.

17. Executor de son tort. A person not named in the will to be an executor may be compelled by law to act as an executor if he interferes with the deceased's property before the proper executors take charge of it, e.g. a person who sells property belonging to the deceased, even if by mistake, would be compelled to hold the proceeds of sale as though he were an executor, i.e. in accordance with the terms of the will. Such a person is called an executor *de son tort* (executor by his own wrongdoing).

18. The grant. The court grants either:

(*a*) *probate*, which confirms the authority of the executor; or

(*b*) *letters of administration*, which confer authority on the administrator. This is either:

(*i*) administration with the will annexed; or

(*ii*) simple administration on an intestacy.

The word probate is often used to cover both probate and letters of administration.

Probate is of two kinds.

(*a*) *Non-contentious* business is assigned to the Family Division (*see* III, **17**). The will is proved in common form.

(*b*) *Contentious* business is assigned to the Chancery Division (*see* III, **16**). The will is proved in solemn form. Contentious business is of three kinds:

(*i*) questioning the validity of the will;

(*ii*) disputing the interest of a person claiming to be entitled to letters of administration;

(*iii*) seeking the revocation of probate or letters of administration.

A party who wishes to object to a will enters a *caveat*; probate will then not be granted without notice to the caveator.

19. Duties of personal representatives.

(*a*) To collect all the assets, e.g. by suing for debts if necessary.

(*b*) To pay all the deceased's debts in the following order.

(*i*) *Preferred debts:* funeral and testamentary expenses, rates and taxes for the last twelve months, wages of servants for the last four months and not exceeding £800.

(*ii*) *Ordinary debts* (whether special or simple contracts) in the order in which they were incurred (subject to the personal representatives' right to prefer one debt over another in certain cases).

(*iii*) *Deferred debts:* loans owing to a spouse, etc.

(The order of payment of debts is only important where the estate is insolvent. The property which the executors use to pay debts is generally undisposed of property, or residue, and then general legacy funds. Specific legacy funds are left to the last.)

(c) To distribute the remaining property among beneficiaries.

INTESTACY

20. Intestacy. Intestacy is of two kinds.

(a) *Total*.

(b) *Partial*. Where a testator has failed to dispose of all his property by his will, he is said to die partially intestate. The property undisposed of will be distributed by his executors according to the intestacy rules stated above.

Descent upon intestacy is now governed by the following Acts:

(a) the Administration of Estates Act 1925;
(b) the Intestates' Estates Act 1952 for deaths after 1952;
(c) the Family Provision Act 1966 for deaths after 1966;
(d) the Family Law Reform Act 1969 for deaths after 1969.

Under these Acts the intestate's property all vests in his personal representatives upon trust for sale (with power to postpone indefinitely) for distribution of the proceeds of sale according to the rules laid out below (*see* **21–23**).

Before distributing any property among beneficiaries, the personal representatives have to ascertain whether the deceased has left enough property to pay his debts in full. If there is insufficient property the estate is insolvent. In this case the personal representatives have to pay as many of the debts as they can, in a prescribed order of priority.

The rules governing the order in which debts are payable are the same as those applying in cases of bankruptcy (*see* the Administration of Estates Act 1925, s. 34). (The only difference from the order of payment in bankruptcy is that the personal representatives have to pay the funeral and testamentary expenses before all other debts.)

21. Where the intestate leaves a surviving spouse. The rights of the intestate's widow or widower depend largely on whether there are any children of the marriage or not.

(a) No issue, and no surviving parents, brothers or sisters of the whole blood: The estate passes absolutely to the surviving spouse.

(*b*) Issue. The surviving spouse takes:

(*i*) personal chattels, e.g. personal jewellery; and

(*ii*) a fixed sum free of death duty or costs (if possible), with interest at 4 per cent; and the sum is £8,750 if the intestate died after 1966, £15,000 if after June 1972, or £25,000 if after March 1977; and

(*iii*) a life interest in one half of the residue.

The remaining property then goes to the issue upon the *statutory trusts* (*see* 23).

(*c*) No issue, but a surviving parent, brother or sister of the whole blood: The surviving spouse takes:

(*i*) personal chattels; and

(*ii*) a fixed sum free of duty or costs with interest at 4 per cent; the sum is £30,000 if the intestate died after 1966; £40,000 if after June 1972, £55,000 if after March 1977; and

((*iii*) half the residue absolutely.

The remaining property, if there are parents, goes to the parents of the intestate absolutely. If there are no parents, then to the brothers or sisters on the statutory trusts.

22. Where the intestate leaves no surviving spouse, but leaves:

(*a*) *Issue.* The residue is held for them on the statutory trusts after paying debts, etc.

(*b*) *No issue but one or both parents.* The property passes to the parents absolutely.

(*c*) *No issue or parents but other relatives.* The property is distributed in the following order:

(*i*) brothers and sisters (or their issue) of the whole blood;

(*ii*) brothers and sisters (or their issue) of the half blood;

(*iii*) grandparents absolutely (if there are not of class (*i*) and (*ii*) above);

(*iv*) uncles and aunts (or issue) of the whole blood;

(*v*) uncles and aunts (or issue) of the half blood.

In cases (*i*), (*ii*), (*iv*) and (*v*) the property is held on the statutory trusts (*see* 23).

(*d*) *No relatives at all.* The property goes to the Crown absolutely as *bona vacantia* (unowned goods), but the Crown may make provision for any dependant or other person for whom the intestate could have reasonably been expected to provide.

23. The statutory trusts. The statutory trusts are set out in the Administration of Estates Act 1925, ss. 46, 47. The statutory trust to be carried out by the administrators is to divide the property equally among the persons entitled at the age of eighteen, or on prior marriage.

If a beneficiary under the above tables has predeceased the testator his share goes to his issue; if no issue, then it falls into the common fund.

BANKRUPTCY

24. Meaning of bankruptcy. Bankruptcy is a process where by all the property of an insolvent person is transferred to a trustee in bankruptcy (by a court order), for distribution among his creditors.

The objects of bankruptcy are:

(*a*) to ensure fair distribution among the creditors of as much property as is available; and

(*b*) to enable the debtor to settle as many of his debts as possible, by this means, and then to start off "with a clean sheet" after his discharge (*see* **29**).

Bankruptcy is thus a form of succession *inter vivos*, whereby the bankrupt's trustee becomes entitled to distribute all his property in a manner similar to succession of personal representatives on death of a person.

25. Grounds for bankruptcy. The Bankruptcy Act 1914 lays down various situations which are grounds for the court to order a person to be declared bankrupt.

(*a*) Assignment by the debtor of all his property to a trustee for the payment of his debts, under a deed of arrangement.

(*b*) Transferring property to any person in order to defraud creditors, i.e. by attempting to remove the property from his creditors' grasp.

(*c*) Giving notice to creditors of inability to pay debts, or of suspension of payment.

(*d*) Leaving the country to evade creditors, or hiding (even at his own home).

26. Procedure in bankruptcy. On the debtor committing any of the recognised acts of bankruptcy any creditor owed £200 or more can present a petition to the Chancery Division (or the local county court) asking that the debtor be declared bankrupt.

If satisfied that there are grounds the court will first make a receiving order which makes the Official Receiver (an officer of the Department of Trade who is attached to the court) receiver of all the debtor's property with power to make detailed inquiries into the debtor's financial situation.

The debtor must then prepare a statement of affairs to be submitted to a creditors' meeting. At the meeting the debtor may put forward any scheme for payment of his debts, or offer a composition (i.e. an offer to pay outright the best possible proportion of his debts that he can manage, e.g. 75p in each £1 owed). If the creditors accept the scheme or composition (and the court approves) no further proceedings in bankruptcy are taken.

If no scheme or composition is accepted the court will proceed to issue an adjudication order and the debtor then becomes bankrupt. The creditors will nominate some person to be his trustee in bankruptcy, with power to take over all the debtor's property (except necessary clothing, bedding and tools) and to sell or distribute it among all the creditors as fairly as possible.

27. Distribution in bankruptcy. The trustee in bankruptcy must pay all the debts as far as possible. Since there is unlikely to be enough money to pay all debts in full, he must follow a prescribed order of priorities.

(a) *Preferred debts:* include one year's rates and taxes, wages for employees (not exceeding £800), national insurance contributions, etc.

(b) *Ordinary debts:* this category includes all simple and special contract debts, damages for breach of contract, etc. (But not unliquidated damages demanded against the bankrupt for any tort.)

(c) *Deferred debts:* e.g. loans by a wife to her husband (or by husband to wife) for the purpose of trade, and loans to a partnership at a rate of interest varying with profits.

Certain debts are not payable in bankruptcy, e.g. debts contracted by any person after notice that the debtor has committed an act of bankruptcy. Debts payable must be proved (by the creditor submitting an account plus affidavit) and are called provable debts. (Debts not payable are called non-provable debts.)

28. Property available. Generally all the bankrupt's property can be taken in his bankruptcy, including:

(*a*) property acquired before or after the receiving order;

(*b*) trade goods in the bankrupt's reputed ownership (even though they in fact belong to someone else, if the true owner is estopped from asserting his claim);

(*c*) property transferred gratuitously by the debtor to some other person, in attempt to defeat his creditors.

Property not available in bankruptcy includes such as is held by the bankrupt as trustee for another, and necessary clothes, bedding and tools of his trade up to the value of £250.

29. Discharge in bankruptcy. At any time after he has been adjudicated bankrupt the debtor may apply to the court for his discharge. The court will grant discharge only if satisfied that the bankrupt has produced all his property to his trustee, and has discharged as many of his provable liabilities as he reasonably can. The court will generally refuse discharge if the bankrupt has paid less than 50p of each pound owed, and has not yet done everything possible to make good the deficiency.

The effect of discharge is to release the bankrupt from all debts provable in bankruptcy, except debts due to the Crown and debts incurred by reason of fraud or breach of trust, etc. (He is not released from liability for non-provable debts, i.e. these are merely suspended during bankruptcy, and he may be made to pay them after his discharge.)

PROGRESS TEST 24

1. What is a will? (1)
2. What is meant by the ademption and abatement of legacies, and to what forms of legacies do these terms apply? (6–8)

T by his will leaves half his property to his son, B, and the other half to "C and the heirs male of his body". B and C are killed in a plane crash and T dies on hearing the news. Will the gifts lapse? (9)

3. How may a will be revoked? (10–12)

T, a soldier, aged 20 in 1944, orally made a will leaving "all my things to my mother". In 1946 T married X, by whom he had two children. In 1948 T made a will in favour of X. X died in 1952 and in 1956 T married Y. T has now died. How will his property be distributed? (2, 9, 13–15, 21)

4. How may personal representatives be appointed by or for a

deceased person? What is meant by: (*a*) *cum testamento annexo*; (*b*) *pendente lite*; (*c*) *de bonis non*? **(16, 17)**

5. (*a*) You are appointed the sole executor of the will of T. On examining T's estate you discover:

(*i*) that he was insolvent,

(*ii*) that his will disposes of only half his property;

(*iii*) that the will makes no provision for his wife and his mentally defective son, aged 28.

What rules should guide you in administering his estate? **(20, 22)**

(*b*) What may be the effect of T's insolvency on general and specific legacies contained in his will? **(6–8)**

6. What are the main purposes of bankruptcy? What are the grounds for petitioning for a debtor's bankruptcy? Trace the procedure in bankruptcy up to the adjudication order. **(24–26)**

7. (*a*) You are appointed trustee in bankruptcy for X, a debtor. In what order should you pay his debts? **(27)**

(*b*) On commencing your duties you discover:

(*i*) that X has in his possession and use a van obtained on hire purchase from Y. Co. Ltd.,

(*ii*) that a month before the Receiving Order X made a gift of £5,000 to trustees to hold for the benefit of Mrs. X,

(*iii*) that X is himself trustee of valuable land for a minor.

How far are you entitled to claim any of the above items of property for the purpose of paying X's creditors? **(28)**

PART SEVEN
CRIMINAL LAW

CHAPTER XXV

Criminal Liability

1. The nature of crime. There is no statutory definition of crime, and it is even conceded that it "is not possible to discover a legal definition of crime which can be of value for English law": J. W. C. Turner, *Kenny's Outlines of Criminal Law*. For practical purposes, a crime may be defined as a public wrong whose commission will result in criminal proceedings, which may, in turn result in the punishment of the wrongdoer.

2. Public wrong. It is the chief characteristic of crimes, that, unlike torts or breaches of contract, it is not left to the individual affected to bring an action in court—though he may initiate such an action by reporting the commission of offences to the police. A criminal prosecution (as opposed to a civil action for damages) is therefore brought by the state (though private prosecutions are still possible in some cases). The corollary is that, whereas the plaintiff to a civil action may, if he so wishes, withdraw from his action, a criminal action can neither be terminated nor compromised (that is, the parties concerned cannot agree to stay proceedings).

3. Criminal proceedings. A definite distinction can be made between criminal and civil proceedings. In relation to the more serious offences, at least, a criminal case will involve a judge and jury, whereas in a civil action, the judge will normally sit alone. There is a presumption, in a criminal trial, that the accused person is innocent, and it is the task of his prosecutors to produce evidence which convinces the jury of his guilt "beyond all reasonable doubt". No such presumption exists in civil actions, the burden of proof being to establish one's case "on the balance of probabilities".

4. Punishment. Whereas the outcome of a successful civil action is normally the award of damages, a successful prosecution normally results in punishment. This may involve imprisonment, a fine, probation, or a combination of these. A prison sentence may be "suspended", or the accused may be discharged either absolutely, or conditionally, upon good behaviour. Whilst these are not exactly "let-offs", they do seem to depart from the traditional notion of punishment. There is a school of thought that criminal "punishments" should not be punitive at all, but should serve to deter others, or the offender himself, from committing similar crimes, by setting an example. In practice, judges seem to comply with both punitive and deterrent theories.

5. Crimes which are also torts. Some crimes may also be torts: e.g. assault and battery, public nuisance, libel. In fact, the requirements for criminal prosecutions often differ slightly from those necessary for civil liability: e.g. a public nuisance must affect a "class of Her Majesty's subjects", to be criminal. Whether in a given case the wrong is a tort or a crime will invariably depend on the nature of the proceedings which are taken, in any event. Thus, we may speak of a person being guilty of the crime of assault if he is successfully prosecuted in a criminal court; the same person will be liable for the tort of assault if the action is brought in the civil court (*see* XV, 5).

6. Classification of crimes. The earliest classification involved only felonies. These were the more serious offences, which were regarded as putting good order in jeopardy, and included murder, rape, etc. The most serious offences of all, in that they were directed at the state itself, constituted treason. A wrong which was in "breach of the king's peace" but which fell short of a felony was normally categorised as a trespass: this explains why several torts today either actually are crimes as well, or are similar to crimes in their nature (*see* 5).

From time to time, however, other offences were created to maintain order. These were often less serious, and were generally created by statute, though a number were introduced by the Court of Star Chamber, between 1487 and 1641, and were known generally as misdemeanours. This distinction, between felonies and misdemeanours, was important, because a person convicted of a felony was liable to forfeiture of his property, and in some cases, to the loss of his life (neither of these measures applied to misdemeanours). In 1870, forfeiture was abolished, and the death penalty removed for felonies other than murder: the distinction between felonies and misdemeanours persisted, however, until 1967.

7. Modern classification. Under the Criminal Law Act 1967, the following classification was introduced.

(*a*) The distinction between felonies and misdemeanours was abolished and replaced by the notions of "arrestable" and "non-arrestable" offences: arrestable offences were defined as those for which sentence is fixed by law; or for which "a person (not previously convicted) may . . . be sentenced . . . to five years imprisonment": ss. 1, 2(1). These offences are those for which arrest may be made without warrant.

(*b*) Section 2 defines the respective powers of arrest of a private individual and of a constable. Thus:

(*i*) any person may arrest without warrant anyone who is, or whom he, with reasonable cause suspects to be, in the act of committing an offence;

(*ii*) where an arrestable offence has been committed, any person may arrest anyone who is, or whom he, with reasonable cause, suspects to be guilty of the offence;

(*iii*) a constable can arrest anyone he reasonably suspects has committed an arrestable offence, provided only that he, with reasonable cause, suspects that such an offence has been committed.

8. Indictable and summary offences. A further classification, which has survived the Criminal Law Acts of 1967 and 1977, is that of indictable and summary offences. These terms refer to the mode and venue of trial involved; "indictment" is the process whereby an accused goes to trial before a judge and jury. "Summary" offences, on the other hand, may be dealt with by magistrates. On the whole, indictable offences are more serious.

The Criminal Law Act 1977 divides offences into three groups according to whether the offence is:

(*a*) indictable only; or triable only on indictment; or

(*b*) summary only; or triable summarily only; or

(*c*) triable "either way" (i.e. summarily or on indictment).

An offence may be tried "either way" if it is:

(*a*) expressly stated to be so either in the statute creating the offence or in some part of the Criminal Law Act 1977 (e.g. bigamy is made triable either way by the Criminal Law Act 1977, s. 16); or (*b*) listed in the Criminal Law Act 1977, Sched. 3.

In general it is for the magistrates to decide (in the case of offences triable either way) which form of trial to adopt: Criminal Law Act 1977, s. 20. The accused, however, has the right to a jury trial, of which he should be informed. If he exercises his right and elects jury trial the magistrates act only as examining justices (*see* III, 26). If the case is prosecuted by one of the law-officers (e.g. the Attorney-General), that officer may apply for the offence to be tried on indictment, irrespective of the wishes of the accused.

9. Elements of a crime. The maxim *actus non facit reum, nisi mens sit rea* (the act itself does not constitute guilt unless done with a guilty intent) applies to crimes generally. The prosecution must therefore prove beyond all reasonable doubt that the accused committed a prohibited act (*actus reus*) with a guilty intent (*mens rea*). Some offences do not require a guilty intent, as such, and are accordingly referred to as crimes of strict liability (*see* 11). Such offences are invariably the creation of statutes.

10. Actus reus. This may consist in an act or ommission. It also includes the consequences, and such "surrounding circumstances", if any be required, as are material to the definition of the crime.

(*a*) To be murder or manslaughter, the accused's blow or deed must result in the death of the victim; to be guilty of bigamy it is necessary that the accused is already married when undergoing a ceremony of marriage (Offences against the Person Act 1861, s. 57).

(*b*) Some offences do not require an act as such; a person may be convicted on the basis of "surrounding circumstances" alone.

EXAMPLE: D had been forbidden entry to the U.K., but was arrested in Ireland, and brought into the country in custody. HELD: she was guilty of an offence of "being an alien, to whom leave to enter has been refused, was found in the U.K.". The offence consisted of "being found", and not of the *act* of entering: Larsonneur (1933).

(*c*) On the other hand, if an act be required, then the act must be a voluntary one. Thus, a man was acquitted of murder when the jury believed he had been asleep at the time: *Boshears* (1961). An act may be involuntary as the result of an illness: *Quick* (1973) or an accident depriving D of his consciousness or faculties of volition: *Watmore* v. *Jenkins* (1962); it may even be involuntary if, through no fault of the driver, he loses control of his car due to mechanical failure, and injures a pedestrian: *Burns* v. *Bidder* (1967). (*See* XXVI, **7, 12.**) Duress, by depriving a man of choice, also renders his act involuntary.

(*d*) Liability for omissions, as in tort, arises where there is a positive duty to act. Such a duty may arise:

(*i*) by contract: *Pittwood* (1902);

(*ii*) in a parent and child, or similar relationship: e.g. *Stone and Dobinson* (1977) where a man and his mistress allowed his disabled sister to starve to death;

(*iii*) where the defendant himself creates a dangerous situation.

11. Mens rea. This means "guilty intent", or "blameworthy mind". In fact, intent as such is often not necessary at all, and what the law regards as blameworthy varies from one offence to another.

Mens rea may take any of the following forms.

(*a*) *Intention* to bring about the prohibited consequences.

(*b*) *Recklessness* as to those consequences, that is, foresight as to the consequences, but no desire or intention to bring them about.

(*c*) *Negligence* as to consequences, that is, failure to foresee the consequences in circumstances where the law requires foresight; generally, where the reasonable man would have foreseen them.

Certain offences are said to be crimes of strict liability. These are invariably created by statutes, and occur normally where the statute expressly or by necessary implication excludes the requirement for *mens rea*. In *Sweet* v. *Parsley* (1970) the H.L. held that D was not guilty of "being concerned in the management of premises" where drugs were used, merely by virtue of being the landlady; it was necessary that she had some knowledge of the drug use, at least. The dicta in *Tolson* (1889) to the effect that the absence of *mens rea* "really consists in an honest and reasonable belief in facts which, if true, would make the defendant's act innocent" has also been used to mitigate the harshness of strict liability. Nevertheless, in *Alphacell Ltd.* v. *Woodward* (1972), the H.L. HELD that D was guilty of an offence involving pollution of a river contrary to the Rivers (Prevention of Pollution) Act 1951, even without knowledge of the pollution they were causing. It would seem that considerations of public policy can sway the judges to maintain or to dispense with the presumption in favour of *mens rea*, in the face of a statute which remains silent on the matter.

12. Modes of participation. It is not only the person who actually "does the deed" (i.e. whose conduct is immediately connected with the *actus reus*) who is guilty of an offence. The Accessories and Abettors Act 1861, s. 8 says: "whoever shall aid, abet, counsel or procure the commission of a misdemeanour . . . shall be liable to be tried, indicted and punished as a principal offender".

The Criminal Law Act 1967, abolished the distinction between felonies and misdemeanours (*see* 7), so the 1861 Act now applies to all indictable (and some summary) offences. The Criminal Law Act 1967, ss. 4, 5, establish further offences relating to assisting and concealing offenders after the offence; persons guilty of such activities were formerly known as "accessories after the fact".

A participant in an offence may be:

(*a*) *the principal offender*. The person who commits the *actus reus* (with the necessary *mens rea*) or instigates an innocent agent to do so.

(*b*) *an aider and abettor*. A person who is present, assisting and encouraging the commission of an offence. Mere presence is not enough: *Coney* (1882); though applauding an unlawful performance probably is: *Wilcox* v. *Jeffrey* (1951).

(*c*) *a counsellor or procurer:* that is, one who, prior to the commission of an offence, incites its commission, or renders assistance for its commission. There is authority that such a person must be aware of the nature of the offence he is counselling and procuring: *Bainbridge* (1960), but it is no defence that he did not want it to occur. Thus, a person who lends a gun to a villain, knowing he is going to use it in a robbery, cannot escape liability on the grounds that he hoped no robbery would occur: *Bullock* (1955). If the villain killed someone, the lender of the gun would not be guilty of murder unless he actually contemplated that the gun would be used to cause grievous bodily harm or death. He may be guilty of manslaughter: *Betts and Ridley* (1930).

This last point applies equally to aiders and abettors. The general rule is that a secondary party (aider and abettor or counsellor and procurer) is guilty only to the extent of his own *mens rea*; thus, in a "gang-fight" D was not guilty of any offence, other than common assault, when his friend killed a boy with a knife, since he had no knowledge of the knife at all: *Davies* v. *D.P.P.* (1954). Had he known of the knife, and contemplated its use, to threaten, he would have been guilty of manslaughter (which requires recklessness) and murder, if he had contemplated use of the knife to inflict injury: *Betty* (1963).

(*d*) *One who impedes the arrest of an offender.* This category of offender was created by the Criminal Law Act 1967, s. 4: "Where a person has committed an arrestable offence any other person who, knowing or believing him to be guilty of the offence . . . does without lawful authority or reasonable excuse any act with intent to impede his apprehension shall be guilty of an offence." The offence replaces the old mode of participation whereby D could be an "accessory after the fact".

(*e*) *A concealer.* "Where a person has committed an arrestable offence, any other person who, knowing or believing that the offence . . . has been committed, . . . accepts consideration for concealing information which might assist in securing the prosecution or conviction if the offender is guilty of an offence": Criminal Law Act 1967, s. 5. (No prosecutions for this offence can be instituted without the consent of the Director of Public Prosecutions.)

13. Inchoate offences. "Inchoate" means "incomplete". These crimes are only incomplete in the sense that, apart from being themselves criminal offences, they are also steps towards the commission of another, complete offence, or in contemplation of such an offence. There are three varieties of "inchoate" offences: attempt, incitement and conspiracy.

(*a*) *Attempt.* To attempt to commit a crime is itself an offence. An attempt is a step towards the commission of a crime. Not all such acts are attempts; an act, to constitute an offence must be more than mere preparation: *Robinson* (1915). It must be proximate to the completed offence, thus approaching a haystack with a lit match is attempted arson: *Taylor* (1859).

To be guilty of a criminal attempt, it is necessary that the accused has the same *mens rea* as is required by the crime attempted: *Whybrow* (1951). If the act attempted by the accused is not criminal, or is impossible of achievement no criminal attempt will have taken place, whatever his *mens rea* (intention): *Haughton* v. *Smith* (1975) H.L.

(*b*) *Incitement.* It is an offence to incite another to commit a crime, whether or not the crime is actually committed. It is also an offence to attempt to incite someone to a crime, e.g. D posts a letter of incitement to X, but it is intercepted by the police. D is guilty of attempted incitement: *R.* v. *Banks* (1873). Incitement consists of any form of influence brought to bear on someone, in order to procure the commission of a crime including threats: *Race Relations Board* v. *Applin* (1973). As in attempts, an act can only be a criminal incitement if the act incited, if done, is itself criminal.

(*c*) *Conspiracy.* At common law an agreement to do an unlawful act, or a lawful act by unlawful means, was a conspiracy. The offence was a common-law misdemeanour (*see* **6**) which originated in Star Chamber (*see* I, **34**). The Criminal Law Act 1977 has resulted in a reclassification of conspiracies. Section 1 of that Act creates a new offence of statutory conspiracy; this consists of "an agreement between two or more persons that a course of conduct shall be pursued which will necessarily amount to or involve the commission of an offence or offences by one or more of the parties if the agreement is carried out". Statutory conspiracy therefore refers to a conspiracy to commit a crime. Section 2 of the Act exempts from liability a person who "conspires" *only* with:

(*i*) his or her spouse;

(*ii*) a person lacking criminal capacity (such as a small child); or

(*iii*) his intended victim.

Section 3 provides that a person convicted of statutory conspiracy must not be sentenced to a term of imprisonment greater than that which would have been imposed if he had been convicted of the offence conspired at. Section 5(1) provides for the abolition of the offence at common law, subject to s. 5(2), which provides for the retention of the common-law offence so far as it relates to conspiracy to *defraud*. If the purpose of a conspiracy is to rob, steal, or obtain property by deception, however, this is a statutory conspiracy, even though some measure of fraud is involved: *Duncalf* (1979).

At common law, apart from a conspiracy to commit an offence or a conspiracy to defraud, the following were criminal.

(*i*) Conspiracy to corrupt public morals: *Shaw* v. *D.P.P.* (1962).

(*ii*) Conspiracy to outrage public decency: *Knuller* v. *D.P.P.* (1972).

(*iii*) Conspiracy to effect a public mischief: *D.P.P.* v. *Withers* (1974).

Both (*i*) and (*ii*) remain criminal conspiracies since it is established that there are in fact offences which consist in the corruption of public morals and outrage on public decency. Type (*iii*), however, is no longer a criminal conspiracy. A conspiracy to commit a tort is not criminal conspiracy except in so far as the tort constitutes a crime as well as a tort (e.g. some sorts of trespass, by virtue of the Criminal Law Act 1977, s. 7 (*see* XXIX, 12)).

PROGRESS TEST 25

1. Define a crime. How would you distinguish a crime from a civil wrong? (1–5)

2. What is meant by a felony? What other categories of offences exist and to what extent is there overlap? (6–8)

3. What is meant by *actus reus*? Can a person be guilty of an offence by omitting to act? (9, 10)

4. Define *mens rea*. When might *mens rea* be dispensed with by the courts? (11)

5. In what ways may a person participate in a crime?

A and B go to visit C where B asks for the loan of C's pistol whilst A is in the bathroom. Later, they stop P in the street and ask for his wallet. When P refuses, B produces the gun and shoots P dead. Both A and B then hide in D's house. Discuss. (12)

6. What is meant by an "inchoate" offence? Discuss the main varieties of inchoate offences. (13)

7. Nasty and Dirty are heard discussing the security arrangements at Dick's shop. Later, Dirty is found outside Dick's shop with a crowbar. Discuss. (12, 13)

Would your answer be different if, due to the nylon stocking he uses as a mask, Dirty has difficulty seeing, and is in fact outside his own shop by mistake?

CHAPTER XXVI

Limitations on Criminal Responsibility

1. General. A number of issues arise in relation to criminal responsibility, quite apart from the considerations of *actus non facit reum, nisi mens sit rea*. Where an offence has been committed, there may be some reason why its perpetrator cannot be held responsible.

There are three categories of such reasons:

(*a*) jurisdictional limitations;

(*b*) incapacity or exemption;

(*c*) general defences.

2. Jurisdictional limitations.

(*a*) *Lapse of time.* Generally, lapse of time is no bar to criminal prosecution (contrast tort, contract: *see* IX, **11**, XIV, **23**).

The Limitation Acts do not, generally, apply to crimes, but in some cases, particular statutes bar prosecution for certain offences after prescribed periods, e.g.

(*i*) treason—three years: Treason Act 1695;

(*ii*) summary offences generally: six months: Magistrates' Courts Act 1952;

(*iii*) offences against the Trade Descriptions Act 1968: three years.

(*b*) *Territorial limits.* Generally, a person cannot be tried in British courts for an offence committed on land abroad. Again particular statutes create exceptions, whereby an offence committed by a British subject abroad is triable in this country, e.g. treason, murder, bigamy. Even where an offence has been committed in Britain, where the offender is residing in a foreign country, or has fled there, it is necessary to resort to extradition in order to bring him back to stand trial. This is a process which only exists as between states who have agreed an extradition treaty; if no such treaty exists between Britain and the country of refuge, the offender is effectively outside the scope of our jurisdiction. In the case of extradition from the U.K. our Extradition Acts preclude extradition for "offences of a political nature".

3. Incapacity and exemptions. Certain persons may be either incapable of criminal responsibility, or exempt, by virtue of belonging to a class of persons who are subject to special rules or privileges.

(*a*) *Incapacity*. The only persons who are effectively "incapable" of committing crimes are children under the age of ten years: Children and Young Persons Act 1963, s. 16. Even if such a child commits an act which would otherwise be an offence, no offence has been committed; thus, where a seven-year-old child "stole" a tricycle, his parents could not be guilty of receiving stolen goods when they took it from him: *Walters* v. *Lunt* (1951).

Children between the ages of ten and fourteen are capable of criminal acts; they are exempt unless it can be shown:

(*i*) they committed an *actus reus* with *mens rea*; and

(*ii*) they did so with a "mischievous discretion", i.e. knowledge that they were doing wrong. In a case of manslaughter, it was said that the child must know he was doing something "gravely wrong": *Gorrie* (1918).

A boy below the age of fourteen years cannot be convicted of rape or attempted rape but he can be convicted of indecent assault.

Children over the age of fourteen have full responsibility. They are, however, subject to different treatment from adult offenders, so that care orders, etc. may be utilised by the juvenile court, where most of the offenders between fourteen and eighteen are tried.

(*b*) *Exemptions*. Certain persons are exempted from criminal liability.

(*i*) The Sovereign: "the Queen can do no wrong" (though those who advise the Sovereign may be responsible for their acts);

(*ii*) Foreign Heads of State and Diplomats: as (*i*) (Diplomatic Privileges Act 1964 and State Immunity Act 1978).

4. Employers and corporations. Whilst neither of these categories are completely exempt or incapable, in practice, circumstances may be such that they cannot be responsible.

(*a*) *Employers*. A master is not, generally, liable for the crimes of his servant (for tortious liability *see* XIV, **15**). He may be liable, however, if:

(*i*) he counselled or abetted the offence; or

(*ii*) the servant's act can be attributed to the master in law, e.g. only the master can "sell" goods, legally or otherwise, since only he has legal ownership of the goods. Thus, an absent master was liable for the fraudulent sale of hams by his servant: *Coppen* v. *Moore* (1898); or

(*iii*) the master has delegated the running of his business to the servant:

EXAMPLE: D ran a café, which was managed in his absence by X. Unknown to him, X permitted prostitutes to meet there. D was guilty of an offence under the Metropolitan Police Act 1859, which forbade persons from "permitting such meetings": *Allen* v. *Whitehead* (1930); or

(*iv*) where the offence is one of strict liability (*see* XXV, **11**).

(*b*) *Corporations*. They are generally liable for crimes, but limitations are in fact dictated by their artificial nature. A corporation cannot commit certain offences (e.g. rape or burglary), and cannot be subject to certain punishments (e.g. death or imprisonment).

5. General defences. There are several such defences: they differ considerably in that some may amount to a deprivation, possibly temporary, of volition (therefore no *actus reus* can have voluntarily been committed); others may entail the absence of *mens rea*; others may arise from other factors.

6. Insanity. This is a complete defence, provided that the accused can show that at the time the offence was committed, he was "labouring under such defect of reason, from disease of the mind, as not to know the nature and quality of his act, or, if he did know it, that he did not know he was doing what was wrong": *M'Naghten* (1846).

(*a*) Everyone is presumed sane. It is up to the accused to prove insanity, but the burden of proof is not the same as that required of the prosecution in proving guilt (i.e. beyond all reasonable doubt). To justify a verdict of "not guilty by reason of insanity" (*see* (*e*)) the accused must prove he was (or is) insane on the balance of probabilities (i.e. more likely than not).

(*b*) There must be some actual disease of the mind. This is a legal, not a medical question: accordingly neither external factors, nor mere stupidity will suffice: *Kemp* (1957).

(*c*) D must be in such a condition as not to know the nature and quality of his acts; or not to know they are wrong. Strong impulse, even if uncontrollable is not enough, though it might amount to another defence such as automatism (involuntary conduct) or if the case is one of murder, diminished responsibility (Homicide Act 1957, s. 2) which, if successful, would mitigate so as to make the accused guilty only of manslaughter.

(*d*) Partial delusions may be sufficient, but only to the extent that D is to be judged "as if the facts with respect to which the delusion exists were real": thus, if D kills P thinking P to be attacking him, he may be acquitted. If, on the other hand he does so thinking he has been "divinely ordained", he is guilty of murder.

(*e*) If proven, a plea of insanity results in a verdict of "not guilty by reason of insanity": Criminal Procedure (Insanity) Act 1964, s. 1.

7. Automatism. An act is not punishable if it is done involuntarily, e.g. sleepwalking: *Boshears* (*see* **XXV, 10**). Such involuntariness may be the result of a recognised disease of the mind: thus, where a disease of the mind induces loss of control, we sometimes speak of "insane automatism".

Such automatism scarcely differs from the defence of insanity and in *Bratty* v. *A.-G. for Northern Ireland* (1963) H.L., it was suggested that, if D raised a defence based on a disease of the mind, and the jury rejected the defence of insanity, then "there could be no room for the alternative defence of automatism". The better view, therefore, is that, where D raises evidence of a disease of the mind, then the proper defence is insanity.

In cases where the defence raises the defence of diminished responsibility (and possibly also in cases involving the defence of automatism, where it depends upon some abnormality of mind) it is now open to the prosecution to lead evidence of insanity: Criminal Procedure (Insanity) Act 1964, s. 6.

Automatism is not available where the state of unconsciousness is self-induced: a driver charged with manslaughter when he fell asleep at the wheel of his car could not plead automatism since he could have stopped the car when he felt too sleepy to drive: *Kay* v. *Butterworth* (1945).

8. Intoxication. This includes both drunkenness and intoxication by drugs: *Lipman* (1970). Neither of these is a defence in itself: it might be the case, however, that the accused, through intoxication, is denying that he had *mens rea*. It is unlikely that he could establish automatism through intoxication; if intoxication is prolonged, though, it might cause a disease of the mind such as would form the basis of the defence of insanity.

The rules may be summarised as follows.

(a) *Involuntary intoxication.* An example is shown by D's drink being "laced" without his knowledge: this is a defence if it means that D has no *mens rea*.

(b) *Voluntary intoxication.*

(i) Where the intention to commit the offence is formed before intoxication, this is obviously no defence: *A.-G. for Northern Ireland* v. *Gallagher* (1963) H.L.

(ii) Intoxication and "specific intent". Self-induced intoxication may serve as a partial defence. In *D.P.P.* v. *Majewski* (1976), H.L., it was HELD: that when D was charged with an offence involving a "specific intent", then, by reason of his intoxication through drink and drugs, he should be acquitted of that offence, but should be convicted of a crime of "basic intent" only, if the facts permitted. "Specific intent" is a novel concept in the law. Certainly crimes involving ulterior intent, or whose definition specifically involves a particular intent fall within its scope—notably murder.

(iii) Where, on the other hand, a crime of "basic intent" (such as manslaughter) is charged, and D attempts to deny *mens rea*, then evidence of intoxication is likely to be fatal to his defence, since the intention to take the drink or drugs may, in itself, be sufficient *mens rea*: *Lipman* (1970). Accordingly, the Butler Committee has proposed that a statutory offence, that of "dangerous intoxication" should be created in cases where an intoxicated person causes death, or injury to the person or to property so as to endanger life. "Basic intent" has been defined as "the intention to do no more than the act which brings about the *actus reus*" (i.e. no need to intend or foresee any consequences): *per* Lord Elwyn-Jones L.C. in *Majewski* (1976).

9. Duress. It is a defence to show that the accused committed the offence against his will and under compulsion such as deprived him of choice (in other words, made his act effectively involuntarily)

(a) Superior orders are not, in themselves, sufficient to amount to duress.

(b) Where the compulsion amounts to threats, then these must be of physical violence, such as leaves D with no choice. It is traditional to maintain that threats to someone other than the accused himself (including his family) are not enough; recently this has been doubted (*see Abbot* v. *R* (1976)). The violence must also be to the person—destruction of property is not enough.

(*c*) Duress in murder cases. The traditional view is that duress is not available as a defence to murder. In *Lynch* v. *D.P.P. for Northern Ireland* (1975), however, the H.L. held that the question of duress should have been put to the jury where D was accused of aiding and abetting murder. In *Abbott* v. *R* (1976), the P.C. held that duress could not be relied upon by a principal offender: the question is not fully decided, however, since this decision is, of course, not binding on U.K. courts (but *see* III, **9**); and two law lords in *Lynch* v. *U.P.P. for N. Ireland* could see no reason for distinguishing between principals and aiders and abettors. Nevertheless, the rule at present is that duress is not available as a defence to the principal offender in a case of murder, though it now is available to secondary parties.

(*d*) Duress and treason. The old rule is that duress is no answer to treason. There are, however, various offences of treason, and duress has been allowed as a defence to several of these, such as: supplying food to the enemy: *Oldcastle*'s case (1419), and helping the enemy with propaganda: *Purdy* (1946).

(*e*) Marital coercion. A special defence of duress, whereby a wife can show that her offence was committed in the presence of and under the orders of her husband: Criminal Justice Act 1925, s. 47.

10. Necessity. This means the commission of an offence to prevent some graver occurrence or offence. It is usually only a defence in certain well-defined situations, such as under s. 3 Criminal Law Act 1967, where "reasonable force" may be used in preventing crimes (this would include self-defence) or making an arrest.

In *Buckoke* v. *G.L.C.* (1971), however, it was said that if a fire-engine driver "shot" the traffic lights in order to hasten to a dangerous fire, he should not be punished. It is possible, therefore, that an emergency may provide grounds for upholding the defence of necessity in cases of merely "technical" offences which do not themselves endanger people or property.

The defence is certainly not available to murder, on the ground that killing one person enables others to survive: *Dudley and Stephens* (1884).

Duress may in some cases be regarded as a modified form of the defence of necessity.

Statutes have occasionally adopted a modified form of the defence of necessity in circumstances not involving self-defence: e.g. the Abortion Act 1967 permits the carrying out of an abortion when it is thought necessary, two medical practitioners having to certify that they consider the operation necessary for (*inter alia*) the safety of the mother (*see* XXVII, 7) (in other circumstances the operation would be a criminal offence).

11. Mistake. It is now settled that, where a mistake of fact is such that it prevents D from having the required *mens rea*, then it is a defence.

Three situations may arise.

(*a*) Where the law requires intention or recklessness as to some element in the *actus reus*. Here, a mistake will be a good defence. Thus, where D persisted in having sexual intercourse with a woman, believing her to be consenting whereas in fact she was not, he was not guilty of rape: *Morgan* v. *D.P.P.* (1976) H.L. (*See* now the Sexual Offences (Amendment) Act 1976, s. 1, making this rule part of statute law.)

(*b*) Where the offence may be committed negligently: here, to be a defence, a mistake must be a reasonable one: *Tolson* (1889).

(*c*) Strict liability: here, mistake is no defence at all: *Woodrow* (1846).

Mistake of law, on the other hand, is no defence to crime.

12. Accident. This is only a defence in circumstances where D is not charged with a crime of negligence; nor is a defence that D intended to commit an offence, but his intended victim is not the person who is, in fact, affected. Thus, where A intended to strike B, but missed and struck C instead, he was still guilty of assault (known as the "doctrine of transferred malice"): *Latimer* (1886). Similarly, if D is mistaken as to the identity of his victim, this is no defence (see **11,** above). On the other hand, if no crime whatsoever is intended, as when D shoots at a rabbit, but hits A, he is not guilty of any crime (unless, in so doing, he was reckless or negligent).

PROGRESS TEST 26

1. What (*a*) jurisdictional limitations and (*b*) incapacities and exemptions might limit criminal responsibility? (**1–4**)
2. What is meant by:

(a) insanity; and

(b) automatism?

When might each provide a defence to a criminal charge?
(6, 7)

3. Soak goes out with his friends, A and B, for a drink. Soak is an alcoholic, but he has been trying to keep his consumption down. Whilst he is in the lavatory, and unknown to him, A slips neat spirit into his beer. Later, when all three are asked to leave, Soak goes berserk and assaults the barman. Discuss.   (6–8)

4. What is meant by duress? What would be the case if A forces B to take drugs, causing B to completely lose consciousness of what he is doing, and, whilst in that state kill C?   (8, 9)

5. In what circumstances might necessity be a good defence to a criminal charge? Where would it be true to say that necessity is sometimes known by other names, thus creating specific defences based on necessity?   (9, 10)

6. When might a mistake be a good defence to a criminal charge? X goes out with his gun, seeking to injure A. He mistakes B for A, and shoots at him. Unfortunately he misses and kills C. Discuss.   (11, 12)

CHAPTER XXVII

Offences Against the Person

FATAL OFFENCES

1. Homicide. This is the general term given to all unlawful killings, including murder and manslaughter. It is normal to deal with these offences separately.

2. Murder. This is the "unlawful killing of a reasonable creature in being and under the Queen's peace, with malice aforethought, so as the party wounded or hurt dies of the wound or hurt within a year and a day": Coke.

(*a*) "Unlawful killing" is necessary—killing an enemy in war, for instance, is not unlawful, so is not murder, even if done with malice aforethought.

(*b*) Reasonable creature, means a "human life in being". The difficulty here arises in the case of unborn or newly born children. It is not murder to kill a child in the womb (though it might be an offence (*see* **6, 7**)). To be the victim of murder the child must have an existence independent of its mother, though it is not necessary that it should have breathed: *Brain* (1834).

(*c*) Causation—the "year and a day rule". The rule itself is an ancient one, which acknowledges the difficulty of tracing causation when the interval (between the wound and eventual death) is a long one. Whatever the interval, however, there is no doubt that death must have been occasioned or expedited by the accused's act or ommission. Thus, when P was stabbed during a fight, and died, the fact that there was inadequate medical care available made no difference, so long as the stab wound was still an "operative cause of death": *Smith* (1959).

On the other hand, when P was wounded, but death was caused, not by the wound, but by the injection of a drug to which P was intolerant, then this was not murder: *Jordan* (1956).

(*d*) The Queen's peace protects both subjects and aliens, but not enemy aliens in time of war.

(*e*) Malice aforethought. This is the *mens rea* of murder—it is a technical term, which covers various states of mind. "Malice" in the sense of "ill will" is not necessary; nor is premeditation, in the sense of advance planning. Malice aforethought consists of:

(*i*) the intention to cause death in any person; or

(*ii*) the intention to do grievous bodily harm to any person; or

(*iii*) knowingly to expose the victim to the real and probable risk of death or grievous bodily harm.

Items (*i*) and (*ii*) are well-established; (*iii*) is a recent formulation derived from the decision in *Hyam* v. *D.P.P.* (1975) H.L. It requires that the act be "aimed" at someone (the victim), and the risk must, of course, be known to the accused (the Criminal Justice Act 1967, s. 8, requires that the jury must determine what was, in fact, known or foreseen by D; it is not enough that the circumstances are such that death is the "natural and probable consequence" of D's acts). In one case D became jealous when her lover started seeing Mrs. O. One night she went to Mrs. O's house, pushed some petrol-soaked material through her letter-box and ignited it, with the intention of frightening her away. The house caught fire, and Mrs. O's children, who were asleep, died. It was HELD that this was murder: *Hyam* v. *D.P.P.* (1975).

(*f*) Penalty. The death penalty having been abolished by the Murder (Abolition of Death Penalty) Act 1965, the penalty for murder is now life imprisonment.

3. Manslaughter. This is unlawfully causing the death of another but without malice aforethought. (The same rules relating to causation in murder apply here.)

4. Voluntary manslaughter. This is the term used for a situation where D may even intend to kill someone, but nevertheless be guilty only of manslaughter. There are three such situations.

(*a*) Where D acts under provocation (Homicide Act 1957, s. 3).

(*b*) Where D is suffering from diminished responsibility (Homicide Act 1957, s. 2).

(*c*) Where D kills in pursuance of a suicide pact (Homicide Act 1957, s. 4).

(*a*) *Provocation.* The Homicide Act 1957, s. 3, allows the question of provocation to be put to the jury where there is evidence of provocation by things done or said, or both; formerly, words alone were not normally regarded as sufficient. The question for the jury is whether, as a result of what was said or done, a reasonable man would have lost his self-control, and done as D did.

    (*i*) "Cooling-off" time. If D has had sufficient time to "cool-off" after being provoked, and before killing, it may be murder, not manslaughter: *Hayward* (1833).

    (*ii*) Whatever the rule before, it is now clear that provocation need not be given by the person killed; nor need it be directed at D: *Davies* (1975).

    (*iii*) "Reasonable man" is now to be interpreted as meaning a reasonable person of the age of the accused: *Camplin* (1978) H.L.

What matters is that D has actually lost his self-control at the time of killing, and that a reasonable man would have done likewise.

    (*b*) *Diminished responsibility*. This is defined in the Homicide Act 1957, s. 2, as "such abnormality of mind . . . as substantially impairs his mental responsibility for his acts and omissions". Unlike insanity the cause need not be a disease of the mind, but might include external factors, such as injury, as well as "irresistible impulse": *Byrne* (1960).

5. Involuntary manslaughter. This covers cases where killing is not intended, and includes:

    (*a*) *constructive manslaughter:* the intention to commit an unlawful and dangerous act from which death results. In one case D threw stones over the side of a railway bridge; one struck the guard of a passing train, killing him: *D.P.P.* v. *Newbury* (1977);

    (*b*) *gross negligence:* where an act, though otherwise lawful, is done with such disregard for the lives and safety of others as to amount to an offence: *Andrews* v. *D.P.P.* (1937);

    (*c*) *an unlawful omission*, such as neglecting to feed a child: *Lowe* (1973), or dependent adult: *Stone and Dobinson* (1977). (This is similar to gross negligence in that there must be obvious disregard for others; it differs, however, in that liability for any consequences of omissions can only occur where D is under a legal duty to act (*see* XXV, **10**).)

6. Infanticide. Where a woman wilfully causes the death of her child, whilst it is under the age of twelve months, but whilst the balance of her mind is disturbed by the after-effects of birth, she is guilty of infanticide, and not of murder: Infanticide Act 1938, s. 1. Infanticide is punishable as manslaughter.

7. Child destruction and abortion. It is not murder to kill a child as yet unborn. It is an offence, however, to destroy the life of an unborn child, unless the destruction is necessary for the preservation of its mother's life: Infant Life (Preservation) Act 1929, s. 1.

The Abortion Act 1967 legalises abortion in certain circumstances. By virtue of s. 1, a doctor may terminate a pregnancy where two doctors have certified that

(*a*) continuance of pregnancy might endanger the health of the mother or of her existing children; or

(*b*) there is a real risk that the child, if born, would suffer from such mental or physical abnormality as to be severely handicapped.

This does not affect the offence of child destruction since the Abortion Act 1967 specifically provides that it is not to affect the 1929 Act's provisions. Note that the 1929 Act deals only with an unborn child "capable of being born alive".

NON-FATAL OFFENCES

8. Assault and battery. Assault means any act which D causes P to apprehend an act of violence upon himself. Battery means actually applying force to another.

There are several degrees of assault, and we may speak of some of them as "aggravated" assaults, by virtue of the fact that they are regarded as more heinous (though not necessarily more dangerous).

Most varieties of assault are defined by the Offences against the Person Act 1861.

(*a*) Common assault: s. 47.

(*b*) Assault occasioning bodily harm: s. 47.

(*c*) Assault causing grievous bodily harm: s. 20.

(*d*) Unlawful or malicious wounding: s. 20.

(*e*) Wounding with intent to do grievous bodily harm: s. 18.

Aggravated assaults include:

(*a*) assault with intent to avoid arrest (s. 38);

(*b*) assaulting a clergyman in the discharge of his duties (s. 37).

9. Sexual offences.

(*a*) *Rape* This is now defined by the Sexual Offences (Amendment) Act 1976: "A man commits rape if he has unlawful sexual intercourse with a woman who, at the time, does not consent to it and, at the time, he knows she does not consent, or is reckless as to whether she consents to it." This effectively codifies the decision in *Morgan* v. *D.P.P.* (1976) H.L. Since the definition requires "unlawful sexual intercourse", a husband cannot be guilty of raping his wife, unless husband and wife are judicially separated: *Clarke* (1949). If he uses unreasonable force to obtain intercourse with his wife, a man may be guilty of another offence, such as assault: *Miller* (1954).

(*b*) *Other offences* involving sexual intercourse. It is an offence:

(*i*) to have intercourse with a girl under 16 years of age: Sexual Offences Act 1956, s. 6. A man is not guilty, however, if he reasonably believes the girl to be over 16, so long as she is, in fact, over 13, provided he has not been charged with "a like offence" previously and is under twenty-four years of age;

(*ii*) to administer drugs to obtain intercourse: Sexual Offences Act 1956, s. 4(1);

(*iii*) to procure intercourse by threats or false pretence: *ibid.*, s. 2;

(*iv*) to procure, for the purposes of intercourse with a third party, a girl under twenty-one years: *ibid.*, s. 23(1);

(*v*) to have intercourse with mental defectives, or to procure defectives;

(*vi*) to commit incest; i.e. to have intercourse with blood relatives.

(*c*) *Indecent assault.* Such an assault, upon either a man or a woman, is an offence under the Sexual Offences Act 1956, ss. 14, 15. Homosexual acts between consenting males over twenty-one years of age in private are no longer criminal: Sexual Offences Act 1967, s. 1.

(*d*) *Other sexual offences* include:

(*i*) offences connected with prostitution;

(*ii*) unnatural offences such as buggery;

(*iii*) indecent exposure: Vagrancy Act 1824, s. 4;

(*iv*) abduction of women.

10. Bigamy. It is an offence if anyone, being married "shall marry any other person during the life of the former husband or wife . . .": Offences against the Person Act 1861, s. 57.

(*a*) "Being married". No offence is committed if the previous marriage was, in fact, void, or if D has obtained a divorce.

(*b*) It is a defence to show that the accused's spouse has been continuously absent for seven years or more, and that, during that time the accused did not know that such spouse was alive: Offences against the Person Act 1861, s. 57. Note that under the Matrimonial Courts Act 1973, s. 19, it is possible to secure a court decree of presumption of death and dissolution of marriage.

(c) It is also a defence if, on reasonable grounds, the accused believes the former spouse to be dead. E.g.: D was reliably informed that her husband had died after 5 years of their living apart. She was acquitted of bigamy when, acting in good faith on this advice, she married X: *Tolson* (1889).

This defence of "honest and reasonable mistake" has been extended to include a belief that the previous marriage was dissolved: *Gould* (1968).

11. Motoring offences. Many offences under the Road Traffic Acts, of course, are not offences against the person. The principal offences which are, however, are the following:

(a) *Causing death by reckless driving.* The Road Traffic Act 1972, s. 1, makes it an offence to cause the death of another person by driving a motor vehicle on a road recklessly (*see also* (b)).

(b) *Reckless driving.* The Road Traffic Act 1972, s. 2, makes it an offence to drive a motor vehicle recklessly on a road. Both this provision and the one mentioned in (a) are the versions substituted into the 1972 Act by the Criminal Law Act 1977, s. 50.

(c) *Driving without due care and attention*, or *driving without due consideration for other persons using the road*: Road Traffic Act 1972, s. 3. These are separate heads of liability, though it is common to refer to both as "careless driving".

(d) A motorist whose driving causes death may be convicted of manslaughter: *Andrews* v. *D.P.P.* (1937).

PROGRESS TEST 27

1. Define and distinguish between murder and manslaughter. What is meant by "malice aforethought" in the former? (1–5)

2. Distinguish "voluntary" and "involuntary" manslaughter. Try to define these by reference to the origins of the offences involved. (4, 5)

3. A and B are man and wife. Eight months after the birth of their child, B kills the infant. On arriving home, A is so shocked that he immediately shoots B, and when their neighbour C arrives

to investigate the noise, he punches him in the eye, blinding him. Later A drinks fifteen whiskies, and drives to London. Discuss. **(4, 6, 8, 11)**

4. Distinguish between assault and battery. What is meant by "aggravated assault"? (Giving examples.) **(8)**

5. Define rape. What other offences involving sexual intercourse are there? **(9)**

6. What is the general nature of the crime of bigamy? What technical defences might be available to a person charged with bigamy? **(10)**

7. Outline the main offences connected with road traffic which may be said to constitute offences against the person. **(11)**

CHAPTER XXVIII

Offences Against Property

THEFT ACTS

1. Introduction. The law relating to offences now covered by the Theft Acts of 1968 and 1978 was formerly contained in the Larceny Acts 1861 and 1916.

The Theft Act 1968, substituted the offence of theft for that of larceny; and redefined and renamed many of the allied offences relating to frauds, etc. It was found, however, that one particular offence, that of "obtaining a pecuniary advantage by deception" (Theft Act 1968, s. 16) remained unnecessarily complicated; the Theft Act 1978 has replaced this section with other provisions.

Offences relating to forgery are under the Forgery Act 1913, which is still in force.

2. Theft. A person is guilty of theft if he: "dishonestly appropriates property belonging to another with the intention of permanently depriving that other of it": Theft Act 1968, s. 1(1).

The maximum punishment for theft is ten years imprisonment: Theft Act 1968, s. 7.

3. Actus reus of theft. The *actus reus* of theft is the "appropriation of property belonging to another".

(*a*) *Appropriation.* This is defined in s. 3 as "any assumption by a person of the rights of any owner".

(*i*) It is no longer necessary to move the property: "to destroy P's goods *in situ* would amount to an appropriation".

(*iii*) If D comes by the property innocently, but later decides to keep it, then he "appropriates" it at that later time: *Stein* v. *Henshall* (1976).

(*b*) *Property.*

(*i*) Section 4(1) defines property as "money and all property, real or personal, including things in action and other intangible property".

(*ii*) Things forming part of the land (such as plants) cannot be stolen, normally, unless "severed" from the land. Thus picking wild flowers, mushrooms, fruit or foliage is not theft, unless done for sale or commercial purpose: s. 4(2).

(*iii*) Wild creatures, on the other hand, may be stolen: s. 4(2).

(*c*) *Belonging to another.* The Theft Act 1968, s. 5(1), says: "property shall be regarded as belonging to any person having possession or control of it, or having any proprietary right or interest".

(*i*) Whilst, normally, property is stolen from its owner, in *Turner (No. 2)* (1971), where T had taken his car to a garage for repairs, it was held to be theft when he went back one night and removed it, using spare keys, to avoid paying the repair bills. An owner cannot normally be guilty of theft: where D removed his own car from a police pound, this was not theft: *Meredith* (1973). This was because the garage could refuse to return the vehicle (i.e. had control, as well as possession) until the repair bills were paid: the police did not have such a right.

(*ii*) Any proprietary right or interest will suffice: thus goods may be stolen from P whilst they are in the possession of X (though it is likely that the goods are effectively stolen from X too, since he is in possession). More significant, perhaps, is the case where D sells goods to P, and then fails to deliver them. This is theft from P, who, when he purchased the goods acquired a proprietary interest. It is also theft where a partner appropriates to his own use partnership property: *Bonner* (1970).

(*iii*) Property held for another, which is received for a particular purpose may be stolen by the holder or receiver in that it still belongs to that other person: s. 5(3). It is not enough that by receiving the money, D merely becomes indebted to P: *Hall* (1972).

(*iv*) Property obtained by mistake is regarded as belonging to any person entitled to restoration, and a failure to make restoration amounts to theft: s. 5(4). Not every case involving such a mistake involves an obligation to make restoration. If the mistake is induced by D, an offence under s. 15 may have been committed (*see* 9).

(*v*) Trust property, for the purposes of the Theft Act 1968, belongs to the person who is entitled to enforce the trust: s. 5(2).

4. Mens rea of theft. This is two fold: the appropriation must be both dishonest and accompanied by an intention permanently to deprive the person to whom the property belongs: s. 1(1).

(a) *Dishonest.* Dishonesty is not defined in the Act: instead three examples of where an appropriation is *not* to be regarded as dishonest are cited, though s. 2(2) makes it clear that a person's appropriation may be dishonest even if he is willing to pay for the property appropriated.

The following, therefore, are not dishonest appropriations.

(i) Where D believes he had a right in law to deprive the other of the property.

(ii) Where he believes that the other would have consented had he known of the circumstances.

(iii) Where he believes that the person to whom the property belongs cannot be discovered by taking reasonable steps; e.g. where D finds goods which are apparently abandoned.

(b) *The intention permanently to deprive.* A temporary borrowing of property, even if done dishonestly, does not amount to theft, unless it is done in circumstances "making it equivalent to an outright taking or disposal".

EXAMPLE: D takes P's season ticket for the opera and uses it for the remainder of the season, intending to return it afterwards. These would be "circumstances equivalent to an outright taking".

On the other hand, where D picked up a lady's handbag in the cinema to ascertain whether it contained anything he would have been interested in stealing, this was not theft, since it was only a "conditional" taking: *Easom* (1971).

(c) Whilst it is not theft if there is no intention permanently to deprive anyone, in the event that certain types of property are involved, other offences may be committed without such an intention. These are as follows:

(i) *Taking a conveyance without authority:* s. 12. Conveyance here includes cars, motor-cycles, or anything constructed for the purpose of conveying persons by land, sea or air. This is an arrestable offence. Taking a pedal cycle is a separate summary offence: s. 12(5).

(ii) *Removal of articles from a place open to the public:* s. 11. The place must be a building, or part of a building to which the public have access (if no access is permitted the remover may be

guilty of burglary (*see* **6**)). This offence carries a maximum
penalty of five years' imprisonment.

(*iii*) *Dishonestly abstracting, wasting or diverting electricity*.
s. 13. This offence is punishable by up to five years' imprisonment

5. Robbery. "A person is guilty of robbery if he steals and immediately before or at the time of doing so, and in order to do so
he uses force on any person, or puts or seeks to put any person
in fear of being then and there subjected to force": Theft Act
1968, s. 8(1).

(*a*) It is necessary that he steals. Robbery is therefore a form of
"aggravated theft". (As such, an offender risks life imprisonment.
It is not robbery, then, if D has any of the defences which would
be available to him on a charge of theft.

EXAMPLE: D takes a car by force, believing he has a right to
the vehicle: *Robinson* (1977).

(*b*) Force means more than mere physical contact. A well
executed pickpocketing is therefore not robbery, though a
clumsy one may be. It is certainly necessary that the force he used
or threatened in order to steal. Where some boys surrounded a
young man threateningly, and the young man, in fear for his
safety, offered money which was accepted, this was not robbery
since the threat was made gratuitously, and not with a view to
stealing: *Bruce* (1975).

6. Burglary. A person is guilty of burglary (punishable by
fourteen years' imprisonment) if:

(*a*) he enters any building or part of a building as a trespasser
and with intent to steal, inflict grievous bodily harm, or commit
rape therein, or to do any unlawful damage to the building or
anything therein; or

(*b*) having entered as a trespasser, he steals or attempts to steal
or inflicts or attempts to inflict any grievous bodily harm: Theft
Act 1968, s. 9.

7. Entry as a trespasser.

(*a*) It is crucial to determine whether at the time of entering
the accused was a trespasser.

EXAMPLE: D climbed up a ladder to a girl's bedroom-window
with the intention of having intercourse with her (regardless of
whether she consented). He was on the window-sill when he

was beckoned in by the girl. HELD: That it was *not* burglary because he had *not* effectively entered the house (not having crossed the window-sill) before the invitation to enter was made: *Collins* (1972).

(*b*) If D is given permission to enter for a particular purpose, but in fact enters for the purpose of stealing or some other purpose, he is a trespasser: *Jones and Smith* (1976). It is the same if his entry is made under false pretences: if, e.g., D pretends to be a gas-man come to read the meter, and once inside steals: *Boyle* (1954).

(*c*) It is irrelevant what time of day or night the offence is committed.

(*d*) If a person commits any burglary, and has with him any firearm, offensive weapon or explosive (or imitation firearm), he is guilty of aggravated burglary and liable to imprisonment for life: s. 10.

8. Offences involving deception. These were contained in the Theft Act 1968, ss. 15 and 16. They were defined as:

(*a*) dishonestly obtaining property by deception: s. 15 (*see* **9**);

(*b*) dishonestly obtaining a pecuniary advantage by deception: s. 16 (*see* **10**).

Section 16 has now been repealed by the Theft Act 1978. Section 15 of the Theft Act 1968 remains in force.

9. Obtaining property by deception. This offence is committed by anyone who "by any deception dishonestly obtains property belonging to another with the intention of permanently depriving that other of it". It carries a penalty of up to ten years' imprisonment: Theft Act 1968, s. 15(1).

The offence is similar to theft except that instead of an appropriation, an obtaining by deception must take place. Both offences may be committed on the same set of facts. In *Lawrence* (1971) H.L., a taxi-driver took a foreign student from Victoria Station to West London; the student, who did not understand English money, held out his wallet for the driver to take the correct fare; in fact the driver took considerably more. It was HELD that whilst this was an offence under s. 15, it might also have been charged as theft.

(*a*) Deception includes any deception whether by words or conduct. In *Lawrence* (1971), the conduct of the driver in taking an excessive amount constituted a deception (the taking, of course, also amounted to theft). Such a deception may involve a "deception as to present intention": s. 15(3).

(b) To constitute an offence, it must be shown that the deception was operative.

EXAMPLE: D, having acquired a stolen car, changed its number-plates and offered it for sale to P, who bought it. It was HELD that since P did not buy the car in reliance on the representation as to the registration number, no offence had been committed (though had it been proved that P had purchased the car only on the understanding that D was its owner, there might have been): *Laverty* (1970).

(c) Money counts as property for the purposes of this section.

(d) "Obtaining" includes the obtaining for oneself or for another: s. 15(2).

(e) The defences to theft (that D is not in fact "dishonest": s. 2(1); or does not in fact intend to permanently deprive: s. 6) apply: *Feely* (1973).

10. The Theft Act 1978. This Act was passed to replace the offence of "obtaining a pecuniary advantage by deception" formerly contained in the Theft Act 1968, s. 16. The new offences are as follows:

(a) By deception, dishonestly obtaining any services: s. 1(1). This offence carries up to five years' imprisonment, and s. 1(2) says that "it is an obtaining of services where the other person is induced to confer a benefit, by doing some act, or causing or permitting some act to be done, on the understanding that the benefit has been or will be paid for".

(b) Evading, by any deception, any liability: s. 2(1). This includes:

(i) the remission, in whole or in part, of any existing liability to make a payment;

(ii) with intent to default on payment, in whole or in part, inducing a creditor to wait for, or forgo payment;

(iii) dishonestly obtaining any exemption or abatement of liability.

"Liability" is defined as "any legally enforceable liability": s. 2(2); gambling debts are thereby still excluded.

It is still an offence to proffer a cheque, in order to induce a creditor to defer the date when payment of a liability falls due:

XXVIII. OFFENCES AGAINST PROPERTY 361

s. 2(3). Offences under this section carry a penalty of up to five years' imprisonment.

(c) Dishonestly making off without making payment, in circumstances where payment for any goods supplied or service done is expected or required on the spot: s. 3(1).

This covers the difficult decision which was invoked in such cases as *D.P.P.* v. *Ray* (1974) H.L. where D ordered a meal in a restaurant and having eaten the meal decided not to pay, and walked out without doing so. It was HELD that he was guilty of an offence under the Theft Act 1968, s. 16, but the logic used was cumbersome, the House having to regard the representation (that he intended to pay) which had been made when he ordered the meal as a "continuing one", which became false when he decided not to pay. Such "reasoning" is no longer necessary since the Theft Act 1978 has replaced the earlier provisions.

This offence carries a penalty of up to two years' imprisonment.

11. False accounting. This is proscribed by the Theft Act 1968, s. 17, and is committed "where a person dishonestly and with a view to gain for himself or with intent to cause loss to another

(*a*) destroys, defaces, conceals or falsifies any account, or any record or document made or required for any accounting purpose; or

(*b*) produces such a document in furnishing information for any purpose which, to his knowledge, is or may be misleading, false or deceptive in a material particular".

This offence carries a maximum penalty of seven years' imprisonment.

Related offences are:

(*a*) false statements by company directors etc.: s. 19 (seven years);

(*b*) suppression of documents, done dishonestly with a view to gain: s. 20 (seven years).

12. Blackmail. This is dealt with by the Theft Act 1968, s. 21, which provides that a person is guilty of blackmail if, with a view to gain for himself or intent to cause loss to another, he makes an unwarranted demand with menaces.

The offence carries a sentence of up to fourteen years' imprisonment: s. 21(3).

A demand with menaces is unwarranted unless the person making it believes:

(*a*) that he has reasonable grounds for making the demand; and

(*b*) that the use of menaces is a proper means of reinforcing the demand.

(*i*) *The thing demanded:* the nature of thing demanded is irrelevant; it need not be money.

(*ii*) *The menaces need not involve physical violence.* If they do, however, the offence of robbery may also be committed (*see* 4). A "menace" was defined in *Thorne* v. *Motor Trade Association* (1937) as "a threat of any action detrimental to or unpleasant to the person addressed" (*per* Lord Wright).

(*iii*) "Gain" here includes keeping what one has, as well as getting what one has not, and loss includes loss of an expectation, as well as losing what one already has: s. 34(2).

(*iv*) Blackmail is committed as soon as the demand is made; accordingly it is improbable that a person could be convicted of attempted blackmail (*see* XXV, 13); either his act is too remote, or the offence of blackmail itself is committed.

13. Handling stolen goods. A person is guilty of handling stolen goods if (otherwise than in the course of stealing), knowing or believing them to be stolen, he dishonestly receives the goods, or dishonestly undertakes or assists in their retention, removal, disposal or realisation by or for the benefit of another person, or if he arranges to do so: Theft Act 1968, s. 22(1). (This offence carries a maximum penalty of fourteen years' imprisonment.)

(*a*) Stolen goods include property which is obtained by theft, blackmail or deception: s. 24(4).

(*b*) Goods cease to be stolen if they are returned to their lawful possessor or to other lawful custody: s. 24(3). Thus, in *Haughton* v. *Smith* (1975) H.L. it was held that D could not be convicted of attempted theft, once the goods had been reduced to the custody of the police. Whether goods have been so reduced is a question of fact for the jury to decide.

(*c*) Evidence that the accused has been involved in handling goods within 12 months, or has them in his possession at the time, is admissible for the purpose of proving that he knew or believed the goods were stolen: s. 27(3). It is not, however, *conclusive* evidence: *Sloggett* (1972).

(*d*) An allied offence is contained in s. 23, which makes it an offence to publish an advertisement for the return of stolen goods which states that no questions will be asked, or that the person returning the goods will be safe from apprehension or inquiry; a person guilty of such an offence is liable to a fine of £100 on summary conviction.

14. Going equipped for stealing. Under the Theft Act 1968, s. 25, it is an offence for any person to have, when not at his place of abode, any article for use in the course of or in connection with any burglary, theft or cheat: s. 25(1). Proof that D had an article made or adapted for such a use is proof that he had it with him for such a use: s. 25(2). It has been held that where D had innocuous implements (screwdrivers and gloves) it was necessary to prove that they were to be used in the future: it was *not* enough that D was in possession of articles after a robbery, and was trying to get rid of them: *Ellames* (1974).

15. Husband and wife. Since the Theft Act 1968 came into force, a husband can be prosecuted for stealing from his wife, and vice-versa: Theft Act 1968, s. 30.

OTHER OFFENCES

16. The Forgery Act 1913. Under this Act, forgery is defined as the making of a false document in order that it may be used as genuine, or the counterfeiting of certain seals and dies (mentioned in the Act) with intent to defraud or deceive: s. 1(1).

(*a*) The seals and dies are listed in s. 5; these are official seals and dies. Forgery of these carries a maximum penalty of life imprisonment.

(*b*) Forgery is restricted to a document. "Documents" include letters, deeds, wills, banknotes, pictures or paintings, and many others. It is the document itself which must be false; it is not enough that a false signature is attached to a painting. To speak of this situation as involving a "forged painting" is wrong; sometimes the test is expressed as involving "that the document must tell a lie about itself": *Closs* (1858).

(*c*) It is also an offence to "utter" a forged document; that is, to issue a forged document knowingly, with intent to defraud, even where the utterer is not himself the maker of the forgery: s. 6. Possession of forged documents, if done knowingly and without lawful excuse, is also an offence: ss. 8, 9.

(*d*) Penalties: forgery of private documents carries a maximum penalty of fourteen years on indictment: s. 2; forgery of public documents carries a maximum penalty of life imprisonment: s. 3.

17. The Criminal Damage Act 1971. This Act now governs the main offences concerning damage to property. This Act therefore replaces the Malicious Damage Act 1861, and simplifies the law (as the 1968 and 1978 Theft Acts do in relation to the old Larceny Acts).

Under the Criminal Damage Act 1971, it is an offence punishable by up to ten years' imprisonment, without lawful excuse, to destroy or damage any property belonging to another intending to destroy or damage that property or being reckless as to whether any such property might be destroyed or damaged.

(a) Property to be damaged, has to be material—intangible property is (of course) excluded (*cf.* theft), whereas (again unlike theft) land is included: s. 10(1).

(b) Damage does not necessarily involve breaking: a completed jig-saw puzzle could be damaged by being dismantled.

(c) Lawful excuse includes "claim of right", similar to the denial of dishonesty in a charge of theft (*see* 4(a)), but also includes the defence that the accused destroyed or damaged the property in order to protect property, or a right to property belonging to himself or another (for the defence of necessity *see* XXVI, 10).

(d) The statute covers the offence known as arson; that is, to destroy or damage property by fire.

(e) It is also an offence to threaten to destroy or damage property without lawful excuse: s. 2. (This might constitute also blackmail, if done with a view to gain or causing loss and if a unwarranted demand is made.)

PROGRESS TEST 28

1. Define theft. What is meant by "property belonging to another"? (2, 3)

2. Shifty comes across Happy's mackintosh in a cloakroom. He decides to try it on to see if it will fit him. In fact, it is far too small. Has Shifty committed any offence? (4)

3. Distinguish between robbery and blackmail. (5, 12)

4. In how many ways might burglary be committed? Outline the differences between them. (6, 7)

5. Which offences involving deception arise under the Theft Acts? What are their main features? (8–10)

6. Sly sells goods cheaply to Stupid. The police raid Stupid's

home, and he is charged with handling, the goods having been the proceeds of a lorry hi-jacking. Stupid denies the offence, but has in fact been involved in a similar matter three months previously. Is he guilty? (13)

7. Define forgery. If I made good copies of Constable paintings and they were sold as Constables, would I be guilty of forgery? (16)

8. Outline what is involved in the offence of criminal damage. (17)

CHAPTER XXIX

Offences Against State Security and Public Order

OFFENCES AGAINST STATE SECURITY

1. Treason. Various statutes have created a number of offences of treason, the most important of which are the following.

(*a*) Compassing the death of the sovereign, or levying war against the sovereign in his realm or giving aid and comfort to the sovereign's enemies in the realm or elsewhere: Statute of Treasons 1351.

(*b*) Compassing or imagining or intending the sovereign's death, destruction, wounding or imprisonment: Treason Act 1795.

(*c*) Expressing intention to depose the sovereign, incite invasion or intimidate either House of Parliament: Treason Felony Act 1848.

NOTE: Treason is one of the most serious offences and is tried in the same manner as murder. The punishment for the more serious forms is still death.

2. Misprision of treason. This means concealing treason (without concurring in it) and is punishable with imprisonment for life.

3. Official Secrets Acts 1911 and 1920. These Acts seek to protect classified secrets, and prohibit any person from communicating (or receiving) such secrets relating to works of defence, arsenals, dockyards, camps, ships, offices, or any other prohibited place or any other form of secret information.

4. Perjury. This occurs where any person knowingly makes a false statement on oath in any judicial proceeding: Perjury Act 1911, s. 1. Related offences include the making of false statements relating to births, marriages, or deaths (whether under oath or not) and procuring some other person to commit perjury (subornation of perjury).

All forms of perjury are punishable by fine or imprisonment for up to seven years or both.

5. Sedition. This means any practices (short of treason) intended to promote disaffection among subjects, either against the state or among themselves, or to bring the sovereign or government into hatred.

OFFENCES AGAINST PUBLIC ORDER

6. Rout, riot and unlawful assembly. These have already been dealt with in connection with the citizen's right of freedom of assembly (*see* IV, 49).

7. Incitement to racial hatred. It is an offence to publish or distribute written matter which is threatening, abusive or insulting, in a case where, having regard to all the circumstances, hatred is likely to be stirred up against any racial group in Great Britain by the matter or words in question: Race Relations Act 1976, s. 70. This offence carries up to two years' imprisonment on indictment, or six months' summarily. Under the 1976 Act, it is not necessary that racial hatred should be *intended*; it is enough that hatred is likely to be stirred up—an objective test. The inference is that this offence could be committed negligently.

8. Public mischief. It is an offence, punishable summarily, to cause wasteful employment of the police by means of false reports: Criminal Law Act 1967, s. 5(2).

Generally, however, there is no duty to report offences at all; the offence applies only where reports are volunteered, which are in fact false, and where this is done knowingly: Criminal Law Act 1967, s. 5(2). For an important exception in cases of terrorism *see* 9.

9. Terrorism. The Prevention of Terrorism (Temporary Provisions) Act 1976, includes the following offences.

(*a*) Belonging to a proscribed organisation.

(*b*) Supporting a proscribed organisation.

(*c*) The commission, preparation or instigation of acts of terrorism.

(*d*) Remaining in the U.K. having become subject to an exclusion order made by the Home Secretary.

The Prevention of Terrorism (Temporary Provisions) Act 1976, is exceptional in that it made it an offence to simply fail to disclose information regarding terrorism which may be helpful to the police: s. 12(1) (*see* 8).

10. Criminal eviction and harassment. It is an offence:

(*a*) unlawfully to deprive the residential occupier of any premises in his occupation;

(*b*) to do acts calculated to interfere with the peace or comfort of the residential occupier, or persistently withdraw or withhold services (if done with intent to cause the residential occupier to give up occupation, or to refrain from exercising any rights thereto): Protection from Eviction Act 1977, s. 1(2), (3).

11. Conspiracy. Sometimes this is regarded as an offence against the state. Certainly this is true historically; for the modern law on conspiracy, however, *see* XXV, **13**.

12. Unlawfully entering or remaining on property. Like the modern law on conspiracy, this is now governed by the Criminal Law Act 1977. It is an offence under this Act to use or threaten violence for the purpose of securing entry into any premises (if done without lawful authority), provided that:

(*a*) there is someone present who is opposed to the entry and,

(*b*) the person threatening or using violence knows this: Criminal Law Act 1977, s. 6(1). The maximum penalty is six months' imprisonment.

It is also an offence if a person, who is on premises as a trespasser after having entered as such, fails to leave the premises on being required to do so: Criminal Law Act 1977, s. 7(6). This also carries a maximum penalty of six months' imprisonment.

13. Public nuisance and obstruction of the highway. This may also constitute a tort (*see* XV, **26**). Unlike the tort of private nuisance, public nuisance can take the form of an isolated event "if it is done under such circumstances that the public right to condemn it should be vindicated": *Mutters* (1864).

14. Criminal libel. Libel is also a tort (*see* XVIII). Criminal proceedings are rare. Whilst it was formerly an offence to spread false reports concerning a magnate (*Scandalum Magnatum* 1275), it is nowadays thought proper to bring a criminal action for libel only where the libel is a particularly serious one, and it is in the public interest to bring such an action. It is not, however, necessary (for a libel to be criminal), that it should tend to provoke a breach of the peace: *Goldsmith* v. *Pressdram Ltd.* (1977). Criminal libel differs from the tort of libel in that:

(*a*) justification (truth) is no defence (although it is a defence if the article is true, *and* it is in the public interest that it be published);

(*b*) fair comment is no defence;

(*c*) publication need not be to a third party: publication to the defamed person himself is enough since a breach of the peace may be thereby provoked;

(*d*) libelling a class of persons may be criminal (though not tortious).

15. Blasphemy. It is an offence at common law to publish blasphemous matter. Matter is blasphemous if it denies the truth of the Christian religion, or vilifies Christ. It is said that blasphemy is criminal because it tends to "shake the fabric of society generally": *per* Lord Sumner in *Bowman* v. *Secular Soc. Ltd.* (1917). In the very recent case of *Lemon* (1979) H.L., three of the law lords agreed that:

(*a*) it is not necessary that the publication should tend to provoke a breach of the peace; and

(*b*) it is not necessary that the accused should actually intend to blaspheme: it is enough that he intends publication.

This last point was the main area of dissent, though it was also suggested that in modern society, where many people subscribe to faiths other than Christianity, to protect the Christian faith specifically was wrong. The offence is currently under review by the Law Commission.

PROGRESS TEST 29

1. Define and distinguish between the various forms of treason. **(1)**

2. What is meant by: (*a*) perjury; (*b*) sedition; (*c*) public mischief. **(4, 5, 8)**

3. What are the rights enjoyed by a residential occupier with respect to: (*a*) a troublesome landlord; (*b*) a would-be squatter? **(10, 12)**

4. Define: (*a*) criminal libel; and (*b*) blasphemy. Outline the chief elements of these offences. **(14, 15)**

Cheques and Bills of Exchange
for Banking Students

BILLS OF EXCHANGE

1. Bills of Exchange. A bill of exchange is "an unconditional order in writing, addressed by one person to another, signed by the person giving it, requiring the person to whom it is addressed to pay on demand, or at a fixed or determinable future time, a sum certain in money, to, or to the order of, a specified person, or to bearer". Bills of Exchange Act 1882, s. 3(*i*).

A cheque is a bill of exchange: (*a*) drawn on a banker, and (*b*) payable on demand: B.E.A., s. 73.

There are three characteristics of *negotiability* common to every bill of exchange, cheque and promissory note.

(*a*) Valuable consideration is presumed and there is no need to state it.

(*b*) It can be transferred from A to B by
   (*i*) indorsement; or
   (*ii*) delivery

so that B can sue on it in his own name.

(*c*) B, provided he takes in good faith and for value, obtains a good title in spite of any defect in A's title.

2. Bills of Exchange Act 1882. This act codified the law relating to cheques and bills of exchange, which had been developed from the customs of merchants and bankers over preceding centuries.

The law relating to cheques is contained partly in the Bills of Exchange Act and partly in the Cheques Act 1957.

Most of the rules of law applied by the B.E.A. to bills generally apply also to cheques, except that, since cheques are bills payable on demand, the rules relating to presentation for acceptance are inapplicable.

3. Working of a bill. A bill can be issued by a businessman and drawn on his debtor (or by a customer on a bank), e.g. where A is owed £1,000 by B, A may draw a bill on B ordering him to pay the money (or part of it) to C or in accordance with C's instructions. C, the payee, may then sell ("negotiate") the bill to D for value, and D may then give it to E, etc., etc. The ultimate recipient of the bill will then be entitled to present it to B for payment, and if B has accepted liability he is contractually bound to pay the person who presents the bill to him.

Where bills are drawn between private persons (or companies) the drawee will generally be under no liability to a payee or later holder unless he first "accepts" the bill; until acceptance the drawee's contractual duties are to the drawer only.

There are therefore three necessary parties.

(*a*) X, who gives the order and signs it, is the *drawer*.

(*b*) Y, to whom the order is given, is the *drawee*.

(*c*) Z, to whom the money is to be paid, is the *payee*.

4. Order and bearer bills.

A bill may be drawn payable to bearer, or to the order of the drawer, payee, or, sometimes, the drawee.

(*a*) *Order bills*, i.e. payable to a named payee or some person designated by him. A bill is an order bill if:

(*i*) the bill itself so states; or

(*ii*) it is payable to a specific person without further words prohibiting transfer, e.g. "pay X or order", or simply "pay X". But a bill payable to "X only" is not an order bill.

(*b*) *Bearer bills* occur where:

(*i*) the bill itself so states, or

(*ii*) the last or only indorsement is in blank (*see* **17** (*f*)); or

(*iii*) the bill is payable to a fictitious or non-existent person.

A *non-existent* person is one who has never existed, or at least does not exist at present. A *fictitious* person is one who does exist but was not the person intended by the drawer to receive payment: *Bank of England* v. *Vagliano Bros.* (1891).

5. Inland and foreign bills.

(*a*) *An inland bill* is one which is or purports to be:

(*i*) both drawn and payable within the British Isles; or

(*ii*) drawn within the British Isles upon some person resident therein.

(*b*) *Other bills* are called "*foreign bills*", but unless the contrary appears on the face of the bill a holder may treat it as an inland bill.

6. Bills in a set. A set of bills means a bill executed in duplicate, triplicate, etc. The payment of one "part" of a bill in a set discharges the other parts.

But if the drawee mistakenly accepts two parts, or more, he will be liable on each part accepted as if it were a separate bill. Similarly, a holder who indorses several parts is liable on each.

It is common practice to draw foreign bills in a set to avoid delay or loss in transit.

7. Inchoate instruments. Where a person signs a blank piece of paper with intention that it may be converted into a bill, it operates as authority to fill it up as a complete bill for any amount using the signature already on it as that of drawer, acceptor, or indorser: s. 20.

NOTE: The paper must be delivered with this intention, not stolen: *Baxendale* v. *Bennett* (1878).

Similarly, if a person obtains a bill which is incomplete (inchoate) in any way he has implied authority to rectify the omission in any manner he thinks fit: s. 20(1). So, where A hands B a blank cheque (one with no sum mentioned), B or any later transferee may insert any value he thinks fit, and A will be liable on the cheque, even though it is completed fraudulently: *Lloyds Bank* v. *Cook* (1907).

8. Time of payment. A bill must be payable on demand or at a fixed or determinable future time: B.E.A. 1882, s. 3(*i*):

(*a*) *Payable on demand.* A bill is so payable if

(*i*) it is expressed to be payable "on demand" or "at sight" or "at presentation"; or

(*ii*) where no time for payment is expressed; or

(*iii*) where accepted or indorsed when overdue.

(*b*) *Determinable future time.* A bill is so payable when expressed to be payable

(*i*) at a fixed period "after sight or date", or

(*ii*) on or at a fixed period after the occurrence of some event which is certain to happen, though the time of happening may be uncertain, e.g. "the death of X", but not "the marriage of X", since X might never marry.

An instrument payable at a determinable future time is called a *time bill*; the period of time is called the *usance*.

(*c*) *Computation of time.* A bill may stipulate that it is to be paid at a fixed period after issue or after acceptance, e.g. "three months after acceptance". (In such cases month means calendar month.) Time then begins to run from the day after issue, or from the date of acceptance respectively. The period mentioned in the bill may be extended by addition of days of grace.

9. Acceptance of bills. The drawee is under no liability on the bill until he accepts it by signing the bill in such a way as to signify acceptance of liability to pay the money stated in the bill (s. 17), e.g. not by signing that he will give goods to the value of the bill instead of money.

Acceptance may be made before signature by the drawer, or (more usually) after. It may also be accepted when overdue or when previously dishonoured by non-acceptance or non-payment.

Acceptance may be either *general* (unqualified) or it may be *qualified*. Qualified acceptance may be:

(*i*) *conditional*, e.g. "accepted subject to deduction for expenses";

(*ii*) *partial*, e.g. for part only of the sum specified;

(*iii*) *local*, i.e. payable *only* at a particular place. (Merely naming a place for payment is generally acceptance, unless it is to be made *only* at the place named.);

(*iv*) *qualified as to time*, e.g. "accepted payable in six months" where the bill specified three months.

(*v*) *qualified as to drawee*, i.e. accepted by some of the drawees but not by all.

NOTE: The holder is entitled to demand general acceptance, and may treat the bill as dishonoured if qualified acceptance only is offered: s. 44.

10. Presentment for acceptance: s. 39. This is only necessary where:

(*a*) the bill is payable some time "after sight" or "after demand" (since presentation will enable calculation of the period after which the bill shall be payable);

(*b*) there is an express stipulation for presentment; or

(*c*) the bill is payable elsewhere than at the residence or place of business of the drawee, e.g. at a bank. (The drawee for his convenience may nominate his bank or some other place as the place of payment; in which case the bill is said to be "*domiciled*". Domiciling a bill is not qualified acceptance unless it is done in such a way as to prohibit the holder from seeking payment anywhere else.)

Presentment is excused (and the bill may be treated as dishonoured) where:

  (*i*) the drawee is dead, bankrupt, lacks capacity or is a fictitious person; or

  (*ii*) presentment is impossible; or

  (*iii*) acceptance is refused.

Presentment must be at a reasonable hour on a business day. Joint drawees must all be approached. Where a drawee is dead, presentment should be to his personal representatives: s. 41.

11. Referee in case of need. The drawer or any indorser who fears that a bill may not be accepted on presentment may designate some person other than the drawee as "referee in case of need", to whom a holder may apply for payment if he wishes in the event of dishonour by the drawee: s. 15. This practice is less common in England than on the continent.

A referee in case of need (or any other person) who accepts a bill after it has been dishonoured in this way is giving "acceptance for honour" of the drawer or any indorser on whose behalf he intervenes.

12. Presentment for payment. A bill *not* payable on demand must, after it has been accepted, be presented for payment on the day it falls due: s. 45. A bill *payable on demand* must be presented within a *reasonable* time. A bill not presented within due time is not invalidated, but cannot be enforced against persons who drew or indorsed it (unless that indorsement was added within a reasonable time).

Presentment must be made at a reasonable hour on a business day. It may be dispensed with:

  (*a*) where after reasonable diligence it cannot be effected;

  (*b*) where the drawee is a fictitious person;

  (*c*) where presentment is waived: s. 46.

13. Notice of dishonour. When a bill is dishonoured by non-acceptance or non-payment, notice must be given to the drawer and any indorsers whom the holder may wish to make liable. An indorser who is sued himself may similarly notify the drawer and any previous indorser, so making them also liable. No special form of notice is required; it may be oral or written providing it clearly identifies the bill. Return of a dishonoured bill to the drawer is sufficient notice. Notice must be given within a reasonable time of dishonour.

Where a foreign bill is dishonoured, formal notice of dishonour must be given by the process of *noting and protesting*, i.e. a notary public is instructed to present the bill for payment and to note upon it the answer obtained. The notary then issues a formal certificate of dishonour called the protest. If a notary public cannot be found, any householder may serve instead (the latter being more commonly employed today).

14. Lost instruments. Where a bill is lost before it is overdue the holder may apply to the drawer for a replacement, and the drawer can be compelled to comply. But the drawer is entitled to demand security from the holder against the possibility of the lost bill being found, the drawer thus becoming liable on both bills.

15. Discharge of bills.

(a) *By payment in due course*, i.e. to a bona fide holder without notice that the title is defective.

(b) *By an acceptor becoming the holder* at or after maturity of the bill.

(c) *By renunciation by the holder* of all rights against the acceptor. (Renunciation must be in writing unless the bill is delivered up to the acceptor.)

(d) *By intentional cancellation* by the holder or his agent.

(e) *By material alteration* of the bill or the acceptance, without the consent of all parties liable upon it, e.g. by alteration of the date, sum payable, time of payment, or substituting a qualified for a general acceptance.

NOTE: If the alteration is not apparent on the face of the bill a holder in due course may enforce the bill as though it had not been altered, i.e. with the alteration deleted: *Scholfield* v. *Londesborough* (1896).

NEGOTIATION OF BILLS

16. Meaning of negotiation. A bill is negotiated when it is transferred in such a way as to constitute the transferee the holder of the bill, i.e. by mere delivery of a bearer bill, or by delivery + indorsement of an order bill.

Negotiation *may be prohibited* by clear words written on the face of the bill, e.g. "not negotiable". (In the case of an ordinary bill of exchange, the words "not negotiable" prohibit its transfer entirely; but in the case of a cheque (*see* 27) they merely mean that the bill ceases to be a negotiable instrument, and becomes an ordinary assignable chose in action, i.e. the transferee of such a cheque will get no better title than his transferor had: *Wilson & Meeson* v. *Pickering* (1946).)

17. Indorsements: s. 32.

(*a*) *Must be written on the bill* (usually on the back) and the signature of the indorser alone is sufficient, without further words indicating transfer.

(*b*) *Manner of indorsement* should correspond with the drawing, e.g. if the payee's name is misspelt, he should indorse in the misspelt version (adding the correct version if he wishes).

(*c*) *Partial indorsement is ineffective*. The indorsement must relate to the total value of the bill.

(*d*) *Where there are several payees*, all should indorse, unless one has authority to indorse on behalf of the others, e.g. a partner on behalf of his firm.

(*e*) *Indorsement by an agent*. He should sign in such a way as to show he accepts no personal liability and signs merely as agent; if he fails to do so, he is personally liable. The usual form of agent's signature is: "J. Smith *per pro* Brown & Co."

(*f*) *Blank and special indorsements*. If the indorser merely signs his own name, without specifying the name of the transferee (*blank indorsement*), the bill becomes payable to bearer. Any subsequent holder can convert it back into an order bill by indorsing himself and adding the name of the person to whom he transfers it (special indorsement): s. 34.

Where a named indorsee is a fictitious or non-existent person the bill is treated as payable to bearer.

18. Restrictive and conditional indorsements.

(*a*) *Restrictive indorsement:* one which *prohibits* further transfer or *limits* transferability, e.g. "Pay X only, signed: J. Smith", or similarly, an indorsement indicating that the transferee is to receive payment only as agent for the indorser: s. 35.

(*b*) *Conditional indorsement:* one which restricts the indorser's liability on the bill, e.g. *sans recours* (without recourse), indicating that the indorser disowns all liability; or an indorsement *sans frais* (without expenses), indicating that the indorser will accept liability for the value of the bill, but not for the expenses of enforcing it. An indorsee is entitled to refuse any such indorsement, but if he accepts it he is bound by its terms: s. 33.

(c) *Falculative indorsement:* one which restricts the holder's liability on the bill, e.g. "Notice of dishonour waived", indicating that the indorser will accept liability on the bill, even though the holder fails to notify him properly if dishonour occurs.

19. Position of holder. A payee, indorsee, or bearer of a bill is a holder, and his rights depend on whether he is a holder for value or a holder in due course. (A payee cannot be a holder in due course.)

(a) *Holder in due course:* a person who has taken a bill:

    (i) complete and regular on the face of it,

    (ii) before it was overdue, and without notice that it was dishonoured (if such was the case),

    (iii) in good faith and for value, and

    (iv) without notice of any defect in the transferor's title: s. 29.

A holder in due course is entitled:

    (i) to sue on the bill in his own name, and

    (ii) defeat any defences depending on defects of title or arising from the relations of the parties prior to his taking the bill.

(Every holder is presumed to be in due course until the contrary is proved, e.g. by showing positively that he took the bill with knowledge that it was obtained by fraud or for an illegal consideration.)

(b) *Holder for value:* a holder of a bill for which value has at some time been given (not necessarily by the holder himself), e.g. a person to whom the payee or holder in due course gives a bill as a present.

A holder for value is entitled to sue in his own name, but takes the bill subject to any defects in title arising through fraud, illegality, etc. He receives no better title therefore than the person who transferred the bill to him. Consequently, if he obtains a bill from a holder in due course he will normally have a perfect title.

NOTE: A holder of a bill for which value has not been given cannot generally enforce it at all. But by B.E.A., s. 30, value is presumed to have been given for any bill, and a person seeking to defeat the claim of any holder on this ground must prove positively that value was not given.

20. Liability of drawer. By drawing the bill he engages:

(*a*) that it will be duly paid on presentment, and

(*b*) that if dishonoured, he will compensate the holder or any indorser for any loss suffered thereby.

As against a holder in due course he is precluded from denying the existence and capacity of the payee.

21. Liability of drawee.

(*a*) *Before acceptance.* He is not liable to any holder (though he may be personally liable to the drawer if he dishonours a bill properly drawn upon him).

(*b*) *After acceptance.* He becomes the person primarily liable on the bill, and engages that he will pay the bill according to the terms (if any) of his acceptance.

As against a holder in due course he cannot deny:

(*i*) the existence, capacity, and signature of the drawer;

(*ii*) the existence and capacity of the payee of an order bill (though he may deny the validity or genuineness of the payee's indorsement).

NOTE: Once the bill has been accepted, the drawee (acceptor) becomes the person primarily liable upon the bill, and the drawer and the indorsers are merely guarantors for him, and therefore are only liable if the acceptor fails to pay.

22. Liability of indorsers. Any person who indorses a bill engages that it will be duly paid upon presentment, and that if dishonoured he will compensate the holder (or any person who indorses the bill subsequently to his own indorsement) who is compelled to pay it.

He is precluded from denying:

(*a*) to a holder in due course—the genuineness of the drawer's signature and of all indorsements prior to his own; and

(*b*) to a later indorser—the validity of the bill or of his own title when he indorsed it.

23. Indorsement by a stranger. Any person who signs a bill otherwise than as drawer or acceptor incurs the liability of an ordinary indorser towards a holder in due course, even though he himself may be a stranger to the bill (i.e. not a party to it, but signing merely at the request, for instance, of the drawer, to add his credit to the bill).

24. Forgeries. When a signature on a bill is forged (or placed thereon without authority of the person whose signature it purports to be), such signature is *wholly inoperative*. No rights whatsoever can be acquired in the bill through such a signature: B.E.A., s. 24.

But note that the drawee after accepting the bill cannot later deny the genuineness of the drawer's signature, even though it was in fact forged: B.E.A., s. 54. And an indorser who has once signed a bill is similarly estopped from raising the defence of forgery of the drawer's or any earlier indorser's signature: s. 55.

CHEQUES

25. Definition. A cheque is a bill of exchange drawn on a banker and payable on demand: B.E.A., s. 73.

It is not necessary that the words "on demand" should appear on the cheque, since all bills are treated as payable on demand where no time appears for payment: B.E.A., s. 10.

26. Crossed cheques. The object of crossing a cheque is to convey instructions that it is not to be paid otherwise than through a bank, or to make some other stipulation as to the manner of payment.

(a) *General crossing:* by drawing two transverse lines across the face of the cheque ||, with or without the addition of the words "& Co." between the lines. The *effect* of such a crossing is to make the cheque payable only through a collecting banker, *i.e.* precluding payment over the counter (*see* 27).

(b) *Special crossing:* by adding the name of a particular banker, with or without the addition of the two transverse lines of the general crossing.

27. Forms of general crossing. In addition to the ordinary general crossing indicating payment through a banker, the following additional instructions may be added.

(a) *Not negotiable.* This deprives the cheque of its negotiability and it becomes an ordinary chose in action, i.e. it can be assigned, but the assignee will get no better title than the assignor had. Thus, where a clerk took a blank cheque from his employer which was already crossed "not negotiable", and fraudulently made it payable to P, it was HELD that the employer could recover the amount of the cheque from P, since the clerk had no title to the cheque and P could get no better title than the clerk had: *Wilson & Meeson* v. *Pickering* (1946).

(b) *Account payee only.* This is not a statutory crossing, but is recognised and obeyed by bankers' custom. A bank which fails to obey such instruction, by *collecting* money for a person other than the payee, may therefore be liable for negligence. (A *paying* bank is not generally affected by such a crossing.)

28. Duty of bankers as to crossed cheques. The banker is liable to the true owner for any loss occasioned where:

(a) *he pays a cheque crossed specially to more than one banker* (unless the additional special crossing merely indicates that one of the bankers named is to collect as agent for the other); or

(b) *he pays a cheque crossed generally otherwise than to a bank;* or

(c) *he pays a cheque crossed specially otherwise than to the banker named* in the crossing, or his agent.

29. Alteration of a cheque. Generally a *visibly altered* bill is void against all parties who have not assented to the alteration (*see* 15).

But a banker who pays a cheque which has been altered, where the alteration is not apparent, is protected against liability to his customer by reason of such payment, if the alteration or forgery was facilitated by the negligence of his customer: *London Joint Stock Bank* v. *Macmillan* (1918). Where a customer signs a series of blank cheques which are obtained by a rogue and used to obtain money from the bank, the bank is not liable for the customer's loss: *Welch* v. *Bank of England* (1955).

30. Protection of paying banker. The drawee bank is protected by statute against liability if it pays in the following circumstances:

(a) *Cheques with forged indorsements:* provided they are paid
  (i) in good faith; and
  (ii) in the ordinary course of business;
  (iii) without negligence: B.E.A., s. 60.

NOTE: The section applies to forged indorsements, and gives no protection where it is the drawer's signature which is forged.

(b) *No indorsement or irregular indorsement:* provided the cheque,
  (i) is drawn on the banker; and
  (ii) is paid in good faith and in the ordinary course of business: Cheques Act 1957, s. 1.

(c) *Crossed cheques:* provided the bank pays a cheque drawn upon it:

   (i) in good faith and without negligence;

   (ii) if crossed generally, to a banker, and if crossed specially, to the banker to whom it is crossed: B.E.A., s. 80.

31. Protection of collecting banker. A collecting banker is protected from liability where he receives payment for a customer who has no title or defective title where he does so in good faith and without negligence (whether or not the cheque is crossed): Cheques Act 1957, s. 4.

> NOTE: The section applies only to *customers.* A person becomes a customer as soon as he opens an account, i.e. where the bank obliges someone, not having an account, by cashing his cheques from time to time, this does not make that person a customer: *Commissioners of Taxation* v. *English, Scottish & Australian Bank Ltd.* (1920).

A collecting bank loses protection if it is negligent: e.g.:

(a) if it opens an account for someone without making reasonable enquiries: *Hampstead Guardians* v. *Barclays Bank* (1924);

(b) if it collects payment of a cheque made out to the customer's employer, without making enquiries as to the circumstances: *Underwood Ltd.* v. *Martins Bank* (1924);

(c) if it pays into a customer's private account a cheque payable to him only in his official capacity: *Ross* v. *London County Bank* (1919);

(d) if it receives payment for a customer of cheques clearly indicating they are payable to the customer only as agent for someone else: *Bute (Marquess)* v. *Barclays Bank* (1955).

32. Relation of bank and customer. The relationship is basically that of debtor and creditor (as long as the account is in credit). The bank is under a duty to cash all cheques properly drawn on the customer's account, providing such cheques do not exceed the amount of the customer's credit. If a bank wrongfully dishonours a cheque it is liable:

(a) *for nominal damages,* for the mere fact of dishonour; and

(b) *for any special damage* which the customer can prove that the dishonour caused him, e.g. by injury to his reputation in business. (Special damage is presumed in favour of a trader or businessman whose business cheque is dishonoured.)

The customer must exercise reasonable care in drawing his cheques, and must compensate the bank for any loss caused by his negligence, e.g. if this facilitates fraud: *London Joint Stock Bank* v. *Macmillan* (1918). But in the absence of negligence there is no duty on the customer to take precautions against forgery: *Kepitigalla Rubber Estates Ltd.* v. *National Bank of India* (1909).

A banker can raise the Limitation Act 1939 against a customer who tries to draw a cheque on an account six years after the last demand for payment: *Joachimson* v. *Swiss Bank Corpn.* (1921).

33. Termination of banker's authority. A banker's authority to pay a cheque drawn by his customer is terminated by:

(*a*) *countermand of payment*, oral or written;

(*b*) *notice of the customer's death*;

(*c*) *notice* of the presentation of a *bankruptcy petition* against the customer;

(*d*) *The making of a receiving order* in bankruptcy against the customer.

PROGRESS TEST
NEGOTIABLE INSTRUMENTS

1. What is a bill of exchange? How does it differ from a cheque? **(1)**

2. Distinguish between order and bearer bills. What is, and what is the effect of, an inchoate instrument? **(4, 7)**

3. Explain briefly the following: (*a*) an inland bill; (*b*) bills in a set; (*c*) qualified acceptance. **(5, 6, 9)**

4. When is presentment of a bill for acceptance necessary, and when is it excused? When is presentment for payment necessary? **(10, 12)**

5. How may a bill of exchange be discharged? **(15)**

6. Explain briefly the following: (*a*) referee in case of need; (*b*) notice of dishonour; (*c*) special indorsement; (*d*) holder for value. **(11, 13, 17, 19)**

7. How may an indorser of a bill: (*a*) prohibit transfer; (*b*) restrict his own liability; (*c*) increase his own liability? **(18)**

8. Explain the liability of: (*a*) the drawer; and (*b*) the drawee of a bill. **(20, 21)**

9. How far is it true to say that a person who signs a bill otherwise than as drawer or drawee accepts liability as a guarantor of the bill? **(22, 23)**

10. What is the effect of (*a*) forgery; (*b*) material alteration; (*c*) loss of a bill of exchange?   (**14, 15, 24**)

11. What is a holder in due course of a bill of exchange, and what are his rights?   (**19**)

A pays a gambling debt to B by cheque, payable to B or order. B indorses the cheque to C for value, without telling him how it was obtained. Can C enforce the cheque against A?

12. What is the effect of crossing a cheque, and what kinds of crossing are there?   (**26–28**)

13. State the provisions of the Bills of Exchange Act, and of any other statute, protecting: (*a*) a paying banker; and (*b*) a collecting banker.   (**30, 31**)

14. What is the relationship of a banker to his customer? When does a person become a customer of a bank, and how does the banker's authority on behalf of his customer terminate?   (**31–33**)

15. The X Bank frequently cashes cheques to oblige Y, a commercial traveller, employed by Z. X Bank cashes a cheque made out to "Y, agent for Z". It is now discovered that Y was defrauding his employer. Explain the position of the X Bank.   (**32, 33**)

Examination Technique

The first point concerning examination technique, perhaps, is that it is something which, so far as is possible, should be learnt *before* taking any examinations in law. The tutorial system, particularly, is designed to assist to that end, but there are some things a student can do alone to ensure that he uses his material to the best advantage.

A revision programme could well include the following.

(*a*) It is useful to go through your notes and essential source-materials making précis notes of these.

One good way of doing this is to attempt to summarise each topic according to the legal principle involved, adding only such information as is vital to your understanding of that principle, possibly in a different colour ink.

(*b*) Having reduced your materials to the essentials, read through your notes noting how much you understand. If neces-sary, compress the notes further so that all the material can be reduced into clear well understood statements of principles.

(*c*) Then, tackle some specimen questions, such as those given in Appendix III. Try to do this without the use of notes, referring to these only after you have attempted the question. It is helpful, also, to make a summary of those principles you feel are applic-able to the question, as well as the main cases you wish to cite, before embarking upon your answer.

There are several kinds of examination question; each requires a slightly different technique.

There are, however, several general rules applicable to all of these.

(*i*) Plan your answer before commencing.

(*ii*) Keep to the point of the question, and state the principles you use clearly.

(*iii*) Make sure you explain yourself—do not assume the examiner knows what it is you are getting at.

(*iv*) Make sure you time your answers so as to be certain of completing the examination.

384

(v) Above, all always cite authorities, in the form of relevant judicial decisions and statutes, to support each main point you make.

The kinds of examination questions you can expect to meet are as follows.

(a) *Problems.* These are very common in law examinations, though some subjects do not lend themselves to problem questions as much as others (e.g. the English legal system).

An example of a problem question might be: "A, a minor, obtains a radio on hire purchase from B. Being unable to afford the payments A sells the radio for cash to C. Advise B."

Such a problem involves several distinct issues, and your job is firstly to identify these. Thus, you should firstly make a note of the issues raised, which in fact are

(i) capacity of minors to contract;

(ii) liability to pay for purchase of necessaries;

(iii) conversion (Torts (Interference with Goods) Act 1977);

(iv) *nemo dat quod non habet.*

You should then state the legal principles applicable to these issues (for example: "(i) capacity—a minor is generally *not* liable in contract"), listing the main cases and statutes, thus building up a complete answer.

(b) *Straightforward "text-book" questions.* For example: "How far is English law Judge-made?" These are designed to test your memory, and your ability to organise your information.

Whilst it is obvious that this question is testing your knowledge of judicial law-making (and in particular the doctrine of precedent) you should be careful to present a balanced answer—thus, for example, judges might "make" law by interpreting statutes; on the other hand, the limitations upon the judges' ability to make law (implicit in the doctrine of Parliamentary sovereignty) should be mentioned, too.

(c) *"Quotation" questions.* For example: "The categories of negligence are never closed": *per* Lord Macmillan in *Donoghue* v. *Stephenson* (1932). Discuss. Whilst these are often similar to "text-book" questions, they call for a slightly different approach. They are often a little more difficult in so far as it is necessary, first and foremost, to decide what the quotation is saying—what does it mean? You may disagree with what the person quoted is saying, in which case you should present authorities supporting your opposing point of view.

Specimen Test Papers

Do not attempt these papers until you have thoroughly mastered the relevant parts of the book, and the progress tests attached thereto. Do each paper under strict exam conditions, bearing in mind the hints on exam technique in Appendix II. When you have completed a test, check your answer with the aid of text-references.

Allow THREE HOURS for each paper; all questions carry equal marks. Answer six questions.

TEST PAPER 1
ENGLISH LEGAL SYSTEM AND CONTRACT

1. What do you consider to be the main advantages and disadvantages of the English system of precedent? How far is a judge bound to follow the decisions of his predecessors on points of law?

2. Write brief explanatory notes on THREE of the following.

(a) The writ system.

(b) A corporation sole.

(c) The Crown Proceedings Act 1947.

(d) The Tribunals and Inquiries Act 1971.

(e) Undue influence.

3. Explain the relationship between statute law and common law. What rules govern the judicial interpretation of statutes?

4. Distinguish between nationality and domicile. How may British nationality be acquired, and how may domicile be changed?

5. State what you understand by contracts in restraint of trade. How are they classified?

A, a solicitor, sold his practice to B, and in the conveyance covenanted that he would not open another office as a solicitor within five miles of any of the three branch offices already operated by B, nor within fifty miles of the office which he sold to B. How far is this covenant enforceable?

6. How far do the courts assess damages for a breach of contract?

A ordered machinery from B, with which to completely re-equip his factory. A removed all the old machinery from his factory in readiness for delivery of the new machinery on 1st April, the date agreed with B. B failed to deliver on that date and as a result: (a) A's factory was closed for three weeks, until B finally delivered, and (b) A lost a very valuable contract. For how much of this damage can A claim compensation from B?

7. Distinguish between conditions and warranties in a contract. A sells a car to B, representing that the car has a new engine. This is untrue. What remedies has B when he discovers the truth?

8. How far is a minor liable on contracts made during his minority?

TEST PAPER 2
CONTRACT AND TORTS

1. Comment on the statement that there cannot be a contract to make a contract.

A orally agreed to sell his house to B, and confirmed the arrangement in a letter headed "subject to contract". B paid a deposit on the house, and then took possession. A later received a better offer from C, and told B that the contract was off, as he intended to sell to C. What rights, if any, has B?

2. How far is malice important in the law of torts?

Under an assumed name someone writes a letter to A's newspaper, which A publishes. Unknown to A, the letter contains an innuendo defamatory of B, who sues the newspaper for libel. B also sues C, a newsagent, who distributed the newspaper throughout the country. What defences have A and C?

3. When and how can the benefit of a contract be assigned? How does assignability differ from negotiability?

4. "The doctrine of consideration is the cornerstone of the English law of contracts." Explain the doctrine and state how far you agree with the statement.

5. "The ideas of duty and negligence are strictly correlative." Explain this statement.

While felling trees on his land, A notices an adult and child walking near by. He makes no attempt to warn either person, and both are injured by a falling tree. X, the adult, and Y, the child, were both trespassers. How far, if at all, is A liable in tort?

Would it make any difference to your answer if X was crossing the land in pursuance of a right of way?

6. How far is an employer liable for the torts of: (a) his servants, and (b) independent contractors?

B is employed by A as a bus conductor. When the driver of the bus is taken ill B takes over the driving. Never having driven a bus before, he cannot properly control it and collides with a car driven negligently by C. C is injured and sues A for damages in tort. Consider.

7. How far is a man liable for (a) contracts made, and (b) torts committed by his wife?

A is engaged by P as agent for the purchase of a house at not more than £3,000. A is unable to get a suitable house at this price and eventually buys one from X for £4,000, not telling X that he is acting as agent for P. P refuses to provide the money for the purchase and X wishes to sue for breach of contract. What remedies has he against A and/or P? Would it make any difference to your answer if P had purported to ratify A's contract with X?

8. What is the significance of the maxim "*In pari delicto porior est conditio defendentis*"?

The Government of India has laid an embargo on the import of certain goods from South Africa. A, in England, contracts with B to arrange to smuggle embargoed goods from South Africa to India, and receives from B a payment of £1,000 in advance. A now refuses to carry out his contract. What remedies are available to B?

9. There is a small natural lake on A's land which he has extended and made into a reservoir, for the benefit of himself and of his neighbour B. In unusually heavy rain the reservoir over-flows and water floods the houses of B and C. What are the liabilities of A?

TEST PAPER 3
EQUITY AND THE LAW OF PROPERTY

1. What kind of tenancies can exist in English land law, how are they created, and how are they terminated? What is the effect of a covenant in a lease that the tenant shall not assign the lease without the consent of the landlord?

2. Distinguish between easements and restrictive covenants. On the sale of land subjected to a restrictive covenant, will the purchaser be bound by the covenant?

3. (a) Explain concisely what is meant by dying testate and dying intestate.

(b) In what circumstances is a will revoked?

(c) A dies intestate leaving a house, £7,000 in shares, some personal jewellery, a car, and three racehorses. His widow, B, claims that the furniture in A's house was purchased with money lent to him by her. As well as a widow, A leaves a crippled son, aged twenty-six, and a widowed daughter aged twenty-three. How will his estate be distributed?

4. Distinguish between a trust for sale and a strict settlement. How may they be created?

Shortly before his death A purchased Blackacre and Whiteacre. He had Blackacre conveyed into the name of his son, B, and Whiteacre to his illegitimate son, C. After his death his executor, X, discovers that A was insolvent and tries to recover Blackacre and Whiteacre. Will X succeed in his claim?

5. How can land be mortgaged today: (a) in law, and (b) in equity? Explain the manner in which money could be borrowed on the security of the following items of property:

(a) shares in a limited company;
(b) jewellery;
(c) a life and endowment insurance policy;
(d) a mortgage of a farm.

6. Explain briefly the meaning of the following:

(a) secret trust;
(b) charity;
(c) profit a prendre;
(d) possessory lien.

7. What were the chief ways in which equity supplemented the common law? In your answer describe briefly the principal equitable remedies and explain how they can be awarded as alternatives to the remedy of damages in an action for breach of contract.

8. State briefly the rules governing testamentary capacity. Under the will of T, A and B are appointed trustees of the residue of T's estate, to hold the residue on trust for T's son X. X has predeceased T, and has left two children, Y and Z, who are minors. A and B are both killed in a plane crash two days after the death of T. Explain what will happen to the trust.

9. How far is it true to say: (a) that a trustee must not delegate from his trust, and (b) that a trustee must not profit from his trust? How, and by whom, can new trustees be appointed and existing trustees be removed?

Index